# American English File

**4**

## Third Edition

Christina Latham-Koenig
Clive Oxenden
Kate Chomacki

Paul Seligson and Clive Oxenden
are the original co-authors of
*English File 1* and *English File* 2

**OXFORD**
UNIVERSITY PRESS

# Contents

# Course overview

## American English File
Third Edition

Welcome to **American English File Third Edition**. This is how to use the Student Book, Online Practice, and the Workbook in and out of class.

IN CLASS

## Student Book

All the language and skills you need to improve your English, with Grammar, Vocabulary, Pronunciation, and skills work in every File.

**Use your Student Book in class with your teacher.**

AT HOME

## Workbook

Grammar, Vocabulary, and Pronunciation practice for every lesson.

**Use your Workbook for homework or for self-study to practice language and to check your progress.**

Go to
americanenglishfileonline.com
and use your Access Code
to log into the
Online Practice.

ACTIVITIES  AUDIO  VIDEO  RESOURCES

ONLINE

## LOOK AGAIN

- Review the language from every lesson.
- Watch the video and listen to all the class audio as many times as you like.

## PRACTICE

- Improve your skills with extra Reading, Writing, Listening, and Speaking practice.
- Use the interactive video to practice Colloquial English.

## CHECK YOUR PROGRESS

- Test yourself on the language from the File and get instant feedback.
- Try a Challenge activity.

## SOUND BANK

- Use the Sound Bank video to practice and improve your pronunciation of English sounds.

## Online Practice

*Look again* at Student Book language you want to review or that you missed in class, do extra *Practice* activities, and *Check your progress* on what you learned so far.

**Use the Online Practice to learn outside the classroom and get instant feedback on your progress.**

americanenglishfileonline.com

> Questions are never indiscreet; answers sometimes are.
> *Oscar Wilde, Irish author*

## 1 READING & SPEAKING

**a** Look at the photos of Simone Biles and Dan Stevens and read their biographical info. Have you watched any of her competitions, or seen any of his TV shows or movies? What did you think of them?

**b** Now read the interviews and complete the questions.

**c** Read the interviews again and focus on their answers. Write **S** (Simone) or **D** (Dan). Which question(s) helped you answer **S** or **D**?

**Who do you think...?**

1 ▢ doesn't eat any animal products
2 ▢ doesn't have a partner right now
3 ▢ is currently living in California
4 ▢ doesn't like insects
5 ▢ is romantic
6 ▢ is very family-oriented
7 ▢ becomes emotional when they're tired
8 ▢ likes to make the last point in a discussion

**d** Which of the questions in the interviews do you think are...?

- the most interesting
- the least interesting
- too personal to ask a person if you don't know them well

**e** Choose six questions from *Q&A* to ask your partner.

🔍 **Politely refusing to answer a question**

If you are asked a question you think is inappropriate, or simply don't want to answer, you can say, *I'd prefer not to answer that* or *I'd rather not answer that if you don't mind.*

**Glossary**
**decorated (adj.)** given a medal as a sign of respect
**podium (noun)** a small platform that a person stands on to give a speech or receive a medal

---

**Q&A**

Every week the newspaper *The Guardian* chooses people who have been in the news recently, and publishes a short interview with them called **Q&A**.

**S**imone Biles is a gymnast who was born in the state of Ohio in 1997. Biles has competed at the World Championships since 2013, and is now the most decorated gymnast in World Championship history. She has also won gold in the Olympic Games, and written an autobiography called *Courage to Soar*.

**1** _____'s your most treasured possession?
My Olympic medals.

**2** **What _____ you want to be when you were growing up?**
A nurse.

**3** **What _____ you like about yourself?**
I like to have the last word.

**4** **What _____ your most embarrassing moment?**
I was on the podium at the 2014 World Championships in China when a bee appeared out of nowhere and took a liking to my flowers.

**5** **What or _____ is the greatest love of your life?**
Food.

**6** **What _____ your superpower be?**
To be a witch. A good witch, of course. It would be cool to control things with my mind and do spells.

**7** _____ **did you last cry, and why?**
Just a few days ago. I was overtired.

**8** _____ **would you like to be remembered?**
As a confident, inspirational, and very bubbly person.

**9** _____ **word or phrase do you most overuse?**
"Oh my gosh."

*Adapted from The Guardian*

**D** **an Stevens**, the actor, was born in England in 1982. He played Matthew Crawley on the TV show *Downton Abbey*, until his character died suddenly in a special Christmas episode. He has since starred in many successful TV shows and movies, including *Beauty and the Beast*, *Legion*, and *The Call of the Wild*.

1 _____ were you happiest?
My wedding day, eight years ago.

2 What _____ you owe your parents?
A lot – and probably quite a lot of money.

3 _____'s your wallpaper?
A photo of my kids, Willow, Aubrey, and Eden, who are eight, five, and one.

4 _____ keeps you awake at night?
My three kids.

5 _____ would you most like to say sorry to?
To *Downton Abbey* fans, for ruining their Christmas one year.

6 What single thing _____ improve the quality of your life?
One of those robot vacuum cleaners.

7 _____ do you relax?
I go for walks in Griffith Park, in LA.

8 What _____ love feel like?
As if somebody's painted the world a different color.

9 _____ you have a "guilty pleasure"?
Yes, vegan cheesecake.

## 2 GRAMMAR question formation

a 🔊 **1.2** Listen to some journalists interviewing a famous actress who has just arrived in Toronto. Write down the four questions they ask.

b Answer the questions below with a partner.
Which question is an example of…?
- a question that ends with a preposition
- a subject question, where there is no auxiliary verb
- a question that uses a negative auxiliary verb
- an indirect question

c 🅖 p.132 Grammar Bank 1A

d 🅒 **Communication** Indirect questions **A** p.106 **B** p.110 Ask and answer indirect questions.

## 3 PRONUNCIATION intonation: showing interest

a 🔊 **1.5** Listen to some people asking questions 1–5. Who sounds more interested each time, **a** or **b**?
1 Do you have a big family?
2 What don't you like about the place where you live?
3 What sports or games are you good at?
4 Do you think you have a healthy diet?
5 What makes you feel happy?

b 🔊 **1.6** Listen and repeat the questions with interested intonation.

> 🔎 **Reacting to what someone says**
>
> When you ask someone a question and they answer, it is normal to show interest or sympathy. You can use:
> - expressions such as *Oh, really? I'm sorry. What a shame!*
> - exclamations such as *Wow! Me too! How interesting!*
> - follow-up questions such as *Why (not)? Why is that? Why do you say that?*

c 🔊 **1.7** Now listen to five conversations using the questions in **a**. Complete the expressions or questions that the people use to react to the answers.
1 *Wow*! That's a huge family.
2 _____? What's wrong with them?
3 _____ We could play a game one day.
4 _____ How long have you been a vegan?
5 _____? I can't think of anything worse!

d 🔊 **1.8** Listen and repeat the responses. Copy the intonation.

e Ask and answer the questions in **a** with a partner. Use interested intonation, and react to your partner's answers.

## 4 READING & VOCABULARY figuring out meaning from context

**a** Look at the cartoon. How do you think the candidate is feeling? How would you react if it happened to you?

**b** Read the title of the article and the first paragraph. Then look at interview questions A–G. With a partner, say how you would answer them. Which question would you least like to be asked?

A What do you usually do after a bad day at work?
B What's your biggest weakness?
C How would your enemy describe you?
D You have 50 red and 50 blue balls. How could you divide these between two containers to give the maximum probability of picking one of the colors?
E What's the most selfish thing you've ever done?
F Are you a nice person?
G What on your résumé is the closest thing to a lie?

# Would YOU get the job?

Interviews are a source of anxiety for most job-seekers. Job website Glassdoor has created a list of some of the toughest interview questions from the elite companies where they were asked, and offers an expert opinion on the best possible answers.

**1** _____ (The Phoenix Partnership)

**How to answer:** If you answer "nothing," then you may look too defensive, as if you are hiding something, even if you are innocent. The best tactic would be to reply that everyone presents the best side of themselves on a résumé – that is the point of the document – but that you think lying, and even exaggeration, is wrong.

**2** _____ (Condé Nast)

**How to answer:** You could just tell the interviewer that you are not the sort of person to make enemies, but that sometimes you've enjoyed a good-natured rivalry with someone, for example, in a sport. This will show your competitive side and your drive to succeed.

**3** _____ (Page Group)

**How to answer:** This is an occasion when you could give a light-hearted response. Something like, "I don't consider myself to be selfish, but I always make sure I have some time during the week for myself, so I can practice art / tennis / soccer / singing."

**4** _____ (Palantir Technologies)

**How to answer:** Everyone should be prepared to answer this question, whatever job you're interviewing for. There's no foolproof answer – it's a good idea to have thought about a list of areas that are not your biggest strengths, but that wouldn't affect the role that you are interviewing for.

Applying for a job at IKEA

Make a chair and take a seat

CANARY PETE

**5** _____ (Clearwater Analytics)

**How to answer:** If you are a serious math geek, then you might have a decent chance of answering this one. One answer would be to put a single red ball in one container and all of the other balls in the other container.

**6** _____ (Switch Consulting)

**How to answer:** Don't be afraid to talk about what you do to relax, and show how you have a healthy work–life balance. It's also a chance to say something about your personal life, which could be very helpful for making a good impression. For example, you could mention how you go to the gym to relax.

**7** _____ (Badoo)

**How to answer:** Don't just answer "yes" or "no." Think about your personality type and the culture of the company where you are interviewing. What is your gut feeling about the type of people that do well at the company? This should help you to give an appropriate answer.

*Adapted from* Mail Online

**c** Read the article once and complete it with questions A–G. Would you now feel more confident about answering the questions?

**d** Read the article again. With a partner, try to figure out what the highlighted words and phrases mean, and how you think they are pronounced. What helped you to figure them out?

**e** Now match the highlighted words and phrases to 1–8.

1 _____ (*noun*) a reaction based on feelings and emotions rather than thought and reason
2 _____ (*adj.*) designed so that it cannot fail
3 _____ (*phrase*) an answer that is intended to be amusing rather than serious
4 _____ (*noun, informal*) a person who is very interested in and who knows a lot about a particular subject
5 _____ (*phrase*) the number of hours per week you spend working compared with the number of hours you spend with your family, relaxing, etc.
6 _____ (*phrase*) the main reason for something
7 _____ (*phrase*) friendly competition
8 _____ (*noun*) people who are looking for a job

**f** Look at some more genuine interview questions. What do you think they would tell you about the candidate? Why? Do you think these kinds of questions really help interviewers to choose the best person for the job?

- What would you do if you were the one survivor of a plane crash? (Airbnb)
- Who do you think would win in a fight between Spider-Man and Batman? (Stanford University)
- What did you have for breakfast? (Banana Republic)
- Describe the color yellow to somebody who's blind. (Spirit Airlines)
- How many people flew out of Chicago last year? (Redbox software)
- What am I thinking right now? (TES Global)
- Who is your hero, and why? (General Electrics)
- Tell me something about your childhood. (Next)

**g** Choose two questions in **f** to ask a partner.

## 5 LISTENING

**a** Have you ever had an interview for a job or acceptance into a school? What kinds of questions did they ask you? Did you get the job or the acceptance?

**b** 🔊 1.9 Listen to four people talking about a strange question they were asked in an interview. Complete questions 1–4.

| What strange question were they asked? | How did they answer? | What happened in the end? |
|---|---|---|
| 1 If you could _____ _____ with _____ _____ from the past, who would you choose and why? | | |
| 2 Do you _____ a _____? Are you planning to _____ _____? | | |
| 3 Do you still _____ _____? | | |
| 4 _____ _____ would you like to be reincarnated as? | | |

**c** Listen again and make notes in the rest of the chart.

**d** Which of the questions do you think were acceptable to ask at an interview?

## 6 SPEAKING

**a** 🔵 **Communication** Tough questions **A p.106 B p.110** Ask your partner some difficult interview questions.

**b** Invent a tough interview question of your own, which you think might tell you something interesting about another person.

**c** Ask your question to as many other students as possible and answer theirs.

**d** Which questions did you think were the most interesting? Why?

When you have eliminated the impossible, whatever remains, however improbable, must be the truth.
*Sherlock Holmes in* The Sign of Four *by Arthur Conan Doyle*

**G** auxiliary verbs, *the…*, *the…* + comparatives | **V** compound adjectives, modifiers | **P** intonation and sentence rhythm

## 1 READING & LISTENING

**a** Look at the names below. Do you know what they have in common? Do you know anything about them?

the *MARY CELESTE*   the *USS CYCLOPS*   Amelia Earhart

**b** 🔊 1.10 Listen and find out. Do you think we will ever know what happened?

**c** 🔊 1.11 Read and listen to *The mystery of the lighthouse keepers*. Then cover the text and answer the questions with a partner.

**The facts**
1 What was the mystery and who discovered it?
2 What was strange about…?
- the lighthouse door
- a chair
- the rain jackets
- the clocks
- the logbook

**The theories**
3 What theories did people come up with?
4 Which of the theories do you think could be true? Why?
5 Which do you think are impossible? Why?

**d** Find words in the article that mean…

**Paragraph 1**
1 _____ (*noun*) something that is difficult to understand or explain (SYN *mystery*)
2 _____ (*verb*) to confuse somebody completely

**Paragraph 2**
3 _____ (*adj.*) far away from places where other people live

**Paragraph 3**
4 _____ (*adj.*) unexpected, surprising, or strange
5 _____ (*noun*) a mark, object, or sign that shows that somebody or something existed or was present (*He disappeared without a ~.*)

**Paragraph 4**
6 _____ (*verb*) to find the correct answer or explanation for something

# THE MYSTERY OF THE LIGHTHOUSE KEEPERS

The mystery of the Flannan Islands lighthouse keepers is one of the greatest puzzles in history, a case that has baffled real and amateur detectives for more than a century.

The Flannan Islands are seven uninhabited rocks that rise out of the sea. They form part of the Outer Hebrides, a chain of remote islands off the west coast of Scotland. For centuries, they were a danger for ships, so in 1899, a 75-foot lighthouse was built on the largest of the islands, and three lighthouse keepers were employed.

On December 26th, 1900, a steamship sailed to the island carrying three new lighthouse keepers to relieve the men who had spent three months alone in the Atlantic. But when they arrived at the lighthouse, they made an extraordinary discovery – there was nobody there! The lighthouse door was unlocked, and inside everything was neat, but one of the chairs was knocked over. One rain jacket was hanging on its hook, but the other two had disappeared.

The clocks had stopped. The last entry in the logbook was 9 a.m. on December 15th. But of the three keepers, Ducat, Marshall, and MacArthur, there was not a trace.

When the news of the keepers' disappearance reached the mainland, there was a huge amount of media speculation. Some suggested that the men had argued about a woman, and that one had murdered the other two before throwing himself into the sea. Others wondered whether perhaps they had been kidnapped by German agents who were planning an invasion of Britain, using submarines. Some thought they might have been carried away by a sea serpent, or a giant seabird, or even by a boat full of ghosts. An Edinburgh police officer, Robert Muirhead, was sent to the island to solve the mystery.

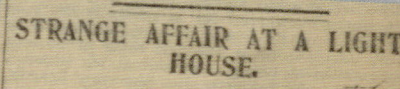

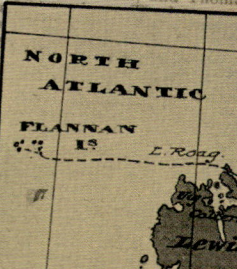

**STRANGE AFFAIR AT A LIGHTHOUSE.**

**Three Keepers Disappear.**

[P.A. TELEGRAM]

Intimation has been received at the Northern Lighthouse Board, Edinburgh, of the loss of the lighthouse staff at the Flannan Islands lighthouse.

The station was established in December last year, and was staffed by four men, three taking duty and the other having relief.

When the Board's steamer yesterday went to the islands to land the relieving keeper, it was found that the three men last on duty had disappeared, leaving no trace behind. They are the principal keeper (James Ducat) and Thomas Marshall and Don... an occasional keeper... member of the re...

It is surmised... during the storm... attempting to save... render assistance t... The relieving ke... been temporarily...

*Adapted from The Times*

**e** ◆ 1.12 Listen to the rest of the story. What was Muirhead's theory? What did people think of it at the time? What is the modern explanation?

> **Glossary**
> **Queen Elizabeth II** (known as the *QE2*) a famous transatlantic cruise ship
> **White Cliffs of Dover** very tall cliffs on the English coastline across from France

**f** Listen again. Why are the following mentioned?

1 a huge rock
2 *Queen Elizabeth II*
3 a paper in a scientific journal
4 1901
5 one man's rain jacket and the bodies of the men

## 2 GRAMMAR auxiliary verbs

**a** Talk in small groups.

**Have you (or has anybody you know)…?**
- seen or heard something that can't be explained, e.g., a ghost or a UFO
- had a strange coincidence, e.g., meeting someone in an unexpected place
- visited a fortune-teller, psychic, or faith healer

> 🔎 **Reacting to a story about something strange**
> When somebody talks about something strange or difficult to explain, we often react with these phrases.
>
> | How / That's | strange / bizarre / odd / weird / spooky. |
> | What a / an | weird story / amazing coincidence. |

**b** Look at the conversations and try to fill in the blanks with an auxiliary verb (*do*, *did*, *is*, *was*, etc.).

1 A I heard a weird noise in the middle of the night.
  B You ¹_____? What kind of noise?
2 A You don't believe in ghosts, ²_____ you?
  B No, I don't.
3 A I've never been to a fortune-teller.
  B Neither ³_____ I.
  C I ⁴_____. It was really interesting.
4 A I don't believe you really saw a UFO.
  B I ⁵_____ see one! It couldn't have been anything else.

**c** ◆ 1.13 Listen and check. Then in pairs, decide which highlighted phrase (1–5) is used…

A ☐ to add emphasis
B ☐ to say that you are different
C ☐ to check information
D ☐ to show surprise
E ☐ to say that you are the same

**d** ⒢ p.133 **Grammar Bank 1B**

## 3 PRONUNCIATION & SPEAKING
intonation and sentence rhythm

**a** ◆ 1.15 Listen to the conversations. Underline the highlighted auxiliary verbs (*did*, *don't*, *do*) that are stressed.

1 A I dreamed that I saw a ghost last night.
  B You did? So did I. How spooky!
2 A I don't believe in fortune-telling.
  B You don't? I do.
3 A You don't like horror movies, do you?
  B I do like them. It's just that sometimes they're too scary!

**b** Practice the conversations with a partner. Copy the rhythm and intonation.

**c** Complete sentences 1–8 so that they are true for you.

1 I'm not very good at _____. (activity)
2 I'm going to _____ tonight. (verb phrase)
3 I love _____. (a kind of music)
4 I don't like _____. (a kind of food)
5 've never read _____. (a famous book)
6 'd love to live in _____. (a town or country)
7 I was very _____ as a child. (adj. of personality)
8 I didn't _____ yesterday evening. (verb phrase)

**d** Work in pairs, **A** and **B**. **A** read your sentences to **B**. **B** respond with a reply question and then say whether you are the same or different. Then switch roles.

*I'm not very good at cooking.*
( *You aren't? Neither am I.*
*I'm going to watch Netflix tonight.*
( *You are? I'm not. I'm going to study.*

**e** ⒢ **Communication** You're psychic, aren't you? **A** p.106 **B** p.111 Make guesses about your partner.

## 4 LISTENING & SPEAKING

a   Look at the photo of a forest. How do you think you would feel if you were walking in it?

b   **◆)1.16** Now look at the photo and listen. Follow the instructions. Write your answers below.

**A walk in the forest**

1

2

3

4

5

6

c   Listen again and check what you have written. Make sure you have answered all parts of the questions.

d   **◆)1.17** Now listen to an explanation of what you have written. Make notes in the chart.

| A walk in the forest |
|---|
| 1   the person = |
| 2   the animal =<br>how you interact with it = |
| 3   the house =<br>no fence =<br>a fence = |
| 4   the table = |
| 5   the cup = |
| 6   the water =<br>how wet you get = |

e   Now use the notes to interpret what you wrote in **b**. Then compare with a partner and say what you agree with and what you disagree with.

*I put that the animal was a…, and it says that means…, but I don't think that's true.*

f   Do you believe in this kind of personality test? Do you believe that you can learn anything about someone's personality by…?

- analyzing their handwriting (graphology)
- looking at their hands (palmistry)
- analyzing the position of the sun, moon, and planets at the exact time of their birth (astrology)
- online personality quizzes, e.g., Buzzfeed

**g Grammar in context** *the…, the…*
**+ comparatives**

> *The bigger* the animal,
> *the more problems* you have.
> *The harder and more resistant* the cup is,
> *the stronger* your relationship is.
>
> Use *the* + comparative adjective or
> adverb, or *the more / less* (+ noun)
> to show that one thing depends on
> another, e.g.,
>
> - *The earlier we start, the sooner we'll
>   finish.* = If we start early, we'll finish
>   early.
> - *The more money you spend now, the
>   less you'll have for your vacation.* = If
>   you spend a lot of money now, you'll
>   have less for your vacation.

Rewrite the sentences using *the…,
the…* + comparative.

1 If you study a lot, you learn a lot.
   The _____,
   the _____.
2 If I drink a lot of coffee, I sleep badly.
   The _____,
   the _____.
3 If you have a lot of time, you do things
   slowly.
   The _____,
   the _____.
4 If you are in shape, you feel good.
   The _____,
   the _____.

🔊 **1.18 Now listen and check. Notice
the stress and intonation pattern in
the sentences.**

**h** Complete the sentences in your own
words. Then read your sentences to a
partner.

1 The more money I have,…
2 The earlier I get up,…
3 The faster American people speak,…
4 The less I eat,…
5 The harder I work,…
6 The more I exercise,…

**5 VOCABULARY** compound adjectives

**a** Look at some extracts from the listening in **4**. Can you
remember what words go in the blanks?

1 If there was no fence around the house, it means you are very
   open-_____, and welcome new ideas.
2 If you hardly got wet at all, it means that you depend less on
   your friends and are more self-_____.

**b** 🔊 **1.19** Listen and check. Do the compound adjectives in **a**
have a positive or negative meaning?

> 🔎 **Compound adjectives**
>
> Compound adjectives have two parts. The second part often
> ends in -ed or -ing, e.g., *good-natured, slow-moving*. The
> words are usually linked by hyphens.

**c** 🔊 **1.20** Listen to some more compound adjectives. Which
word has the main stress?

| | | | |
|---|---|---|---|
| absentminded | bad-tempered | big-headed | easygoing |
| good-tempered | laid-back | narrow-minded | open-minded |
| self-centered | strong-willed | tight-fisted | two-faced |
| well-balanced | well-behaved | | |

**d** With a partner, use the two parts of the words to try to
figure out their meaning. Which do you think are positive
and negative characteristics? Are there any that you think
can be either?

( *I think a* bad-tempered *person is somebody who gets angry easily…*

> 🔎 **Modifiers**
>
> We often use modifiers with adjectives of personality to
> make them stronger or less strong.
>
> **With positive characteristics**
>
> | My mom is | really / incredibly / extremely<br>very<br>pretty | good-tempered. |
> |---|---|---|
>
> **With negative characteristics**
>
> | My sister is | really / incredibly / extremely<br>very<br>rather / pretty<br>a little / kind of | bad-tempered. |
> |---|---|---|

**e** Tell your partner about people with the characteristics
below. Give examples of their behavior.

**Do you know somebody who is…?**
- very open-minded
- extremely absentminded
- a little tight-fisted
- pretty laid-back
- kind of two-faced
- very good-tempered
- incredibly strong-willed
- really self-centered

( *My cousin is pretty* laid-back. *She didn't even get
angry when her boyfriend crashed her car!*

🔵 **Go online** to review the lesson

## 1 ▶ THE INTERVIEW Part 1

**a** Read the biographical information about Jeff Neil. How do you think his previous experience helps him in his present job?

**Jeff Neil** is a career coach and the founder of a company called New Career Breakthrough in New York City. His job involves helping people to discover the right career options for them, and then to help them actually get a job, by advising them on their résumés and on interview techniques. His specialty is helping people who are making career transitions, e.g., from one industry to another. Before setting up his company, he worked for seven years as an HR (Human Resources) director.

**b** Watch Part 1 of an interview with him, where he talks about helping candidates when they are applying for a job. Check (✓) the three things he talks about.

1 ▢ Checking what there is about you on the Internet.
2 ▢ Choosing the right jobs to apply for.
3 ▢ Choosing what photos to send with your résumé.
4 ▢ Thinking about the skills and abilities a job needs.
5 ▢ Writing a good cover letter.
6 ▢ Writing a good résumé.

**c** Now listen again. Take notes about the advice he gives in the three areas you checked.

**Glossary**
**résumé** (BrE **curriculum vitae** or **CV**) a written record of your education and the jobs you have done that you send when you are applying for a job
**cover(ing) letter** a letter containing extra information that candidates send with their résumé

## ▶ Part 2

**a** Read five tips for the day of the interview. Now watch Part 2, where Jeff talks about the day of the interview. Are they **T** (true) or **F** (false)? Correct the F ones.

1 It's better to dress too formally than too casually.
2 You should try to find out beforehand what the company's dress style is.
3 You should arrive at the place where the interview is going to take place at least half an hour before the interview.
4 Don't take any electronic devices with you to the interview.
5 Be careful how you talk to other company employees before an interview.

**b** Watch again for more detail. Do you agree with all the tips?

**Glossary**
**LinkedIn** a social networking service for professional people

## ▶ Part 3

**a** Now watch Part 3 where Jeff talks about the interview itself. Complete the advice he gives.

1 If you want to ask about _____ and _____, either do this late in the interview, or wait for the employer to mention them.
2 _____ language and the _____ of your voice are just as important as what you actually say.
3 Be aware that the way you answer an "extreme" interview question can reveal things about your _____ .

**b** Listen again and answer the questions.

1 What's the biggest mistake job candidates make during an interview?
2 What's the most important thing for them to communicate in the interview?
3 Why does he mention people who were "slouched"?
4 What do you need to communicate with your tone of voice?
5 What "extreme" question did Jeff once ask?
6 What possible answers does he suggest? Why?

## 2 ▶ LOOKING AT LANGUAGE

> 🔍 **Make or do?**
> Jeff uses several expressions with *make* and *do*. These verbs are very common in expressions related to work, and are sometimes confused by learners of English because they just have one verb in their first language.

**a** Complete the extracts from the interview with the right form of *make* or *do*. Watch and check.

1 "...so some of the biggest mistakes that, that I've seen that people _____ on their résumé is they include everything."

2 "...as an employer, I don't care what you _____ 20 years ago or 30 years ago."

3 "You also want to _____ a Google search on your own name."

4 "...and to take an eight and a half sheet of paper and _____ three columns..."

5 "You want to _____ sure your cell phone is turned off."

6 "They're _____ a lot of eye contact directly with me."

**b** Now complete some more sentences related to the world of work.

1 They are going to _____ a decision about who gets the job by the end of the week.

2 Can I _____ a suggestion about how to re-organize the HR department?

3 We must _____ much more market research before we develop the new product.

4 All the new employees are going to _____ a training course next month.

5 Everyone in the company has _____ a big effort this year.

6 George is _____ a great job and I think he deserves to earn a higher salary.

7 I need to _____ a few phone calls before the meeting starts.

## 3 ▶ THE CONVERSATION

**a** Watch the conversation. How do they respond to the question? Write **D**, **S**, and **A** on the line in the appropriate place.

| Yes, definitely | It depends | Absolutely not |
|---|---|---|

**b** Watch it again. Match the sentence halves.

1 **Alice** Admitting you can't do something is OK if ☐
2 **Alice** If you say you can speak French on your CV and you can't, ☐
3 **Sarah** It's OK to exaggerate a bit about something if ☐
4 **Sarah** If speaking a language was essential for a job, ☐
5 **Debbie** If you lie and say you can do something, ☐
6 **Debbie** If you don't have many hobbies, ☐

A it's not very important for the job.
B you will have wasted the interviewer's time and given a bad impression of yourself.
C it's a good idea to exaggerate a bit.
D you say you are prepared to learn.
E it might be expensive for the company when they discover the truth.
F I wouldn't say I could do it.

**c** Do <u>you</u> think it's OK to slightly exaggerate on your résumé? Who do you agree with most, and why?

**d** Watch three extracts where the speakers are emphasizing something and complete the gaps.

1 I think it's a _____ _____ idea to even slightly exaggerate...

2 ...you might find yourself in a situation where you've wasted their time and you've just made yourself look _____ _____ silly.

3 I've _____ exaggerated on a CV.

**e** Now watch two more extracts. What does the speaker do with the missing word to make it more emphatic?

1 ...but I wouldn't do that if I knew the job was going to require me _____ that language...

2 ...you shouldn't outright lie because you _____ get caught out and a lot of the times it could cost a company a lot of money...

**f** Now have a conversation in groups of three.

1 Do you think that to get a job today, who you know is still more important than what you know?

2 Do you think résumés and interviews are a reliable way of selecting people for a job?

🔄 **Go online** to watch the video, review the lesson, and check your progress

**G** present perfect simple and continuous    **V** illnesses and injuries    **P** /ʃ/, /dʒ/, /tʃ/, and /k/

## 1 VOCABULARY illnesses and injuries

a Take the first-aid quiz with a partner. As you read the options, try to figure out the meaning of the highlighted words and phrases.

b **C Communication** Medical myths or first-aid facts? **A** p.106 **B** p.111 Check your answers to the quiz and explain the reasons to your partner.

c **V p.152 Vocabulary Bank** Illnesses and injuries

d What illnesses or injuries might you get if you are…?

eating out   hiking in the mountains
playing sports   visiting a tropical country

# MEDICAL MYTHS OR FIRST-AID FACTS?

First aid can help treat a minor injury, or even save a life in a medical emergency. However, it's important to know what **NOT** to do. Sometimes, incorrect first aid can actually be more harmful than helpful. So how useful is the advice you've heard? Take our quiz to find out.

For each question, decide which answers are myths (**M**) and which are facts (**F**).

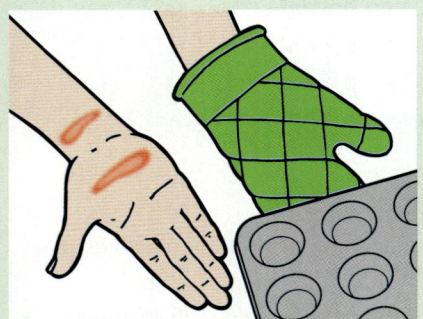

**1** What's the first thing you should put on a burn?
a    butter
b    cool running water
c    an ice pack

**2** How should you treat a sprained ankle?
a    put a hot, damp cloth on the ankle
b    put an ice pack on the ankle
c    put the leg up, e.g., on a chair

**3** What's the best thing to do for someone with hypothermia?
a    rub their arms and legs to warm them up
b    give them hot coffee
c    cover them in something warm, e.g., a coat or a blanket

**4** What's the first thing to do if someone is choking?
a    stand behind them and press their stomach inwards
b    make them continue to cough hard
c    hit them hard on the back

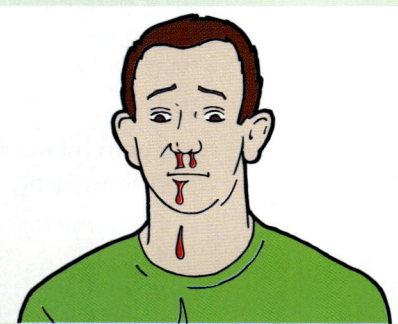

**5** What's the best way to stop a nosebleed?
a    tip your head forwards
b    pinch the soft part of your nose
c    tip your head backwards

**6** After you have cleaned a bad cut, what should you do…?
a    put on a bandage
b    put on antibiotic ointment
c    leave it open to the air

## 2 PRONUNCIATION /ʃ/, /dʒ/, /tʃ/, and /k/

| 1 ʃ | 2 dʒ | 3 tʃ | 4 k |
|---|---|---|---|
|  |  |  |  |

**a** How do you pronounce sounds 1–4 in the chart? Write the words from the box in the correct column.

ache  allergic  bandage  choking
emergency  infection  injury  pressure  rash
sick  stomach  temperature  unconscious

**b** 🔊2.5 Listen and check. Practice saying the words.

**c** Use the words in **a** to answer questions 1–3 about the sound-spelling rules.

1 What ways can you spell the /ʃ/ sound? Which do you think is the most common?
2 How do you often pronounce g before i and e?
3 Which two ways can ch be pronounced? Which do you think is the more common?

**d** 🅿 **p.166–7 Sound Bank** Look at the typical spellings for /ʃ/, /dʒ/, /tʃ/, and /k/, and more examples. Practice saying the words.

**e** 🔊2.6 Look at some more medical words. Are they the same in your language? Which sounds in **a** do they contain? Listen and check.

cholesterol  indigestion  injection
operation  scratch  surgeon  syringe

## 3 LISTENING & SPEAKING

**a** Talk in pairs. What would you do and why?

If you were on the street and saw someone who had a medical problem, what would your immediate reaction be?
a I wouldn't do anything myself, but I would wait to see if someone else was able to help.
b I'd call an ambulance and stay with the person until it came.
c I'd go up to the person and see if I could do any first aid.

**b** 🔊2.7 You are going to listen to Bettina, Umesh, and Alison talking about a time when someone needed first aid. First, listen to some extracts and complete the expressions.

**Bettina**
1 …he didn't have a _____, so I thought he was probably _____ _____ _____ _____ .
2 …he took her to one side to _____ _____ _____…
3 I kept going until the _____ _____ _____…
4 …because obviously she was _____ _____ .

**Umesh**
5 …an old lady stepped off the sidewalk in front of me and she _____ _____ _____ onto the street.
6 She'd fallen pretty hard, but she _____ _____ _____…
7 It was obviously an effort for her to sit up, it was _____ _____…

**Alison**
8 Then all of a sudden, he stopped walking and _____ _____…
9 Some teenagers in line _____ _____ _____…
10 …then they put him on a stretcher and _____ _____ _____ .

**c** 🔊2.8 Now listen to their stories. When the incident happened, did they help? Why (not)?

**d** Listen again and answer the questions for each story.
1 What was he / she doing when it happened?
2 Who needed first aid? Why?
3 What did he / she do?
4 What happened in the end?
5 How did he / she feel a) during the event, b) after the event?

**e** Talk in small groups.

Have you ever been in a situation where you had to give first aid? Who to? Where were you? What happened? How did you feel?

Has anyone ever had to give you first aid? Why? Where were you? What happened?

Have you ever received any first-aid training? If no, would you like to? In which jobs should people be given mandatory first-aid training?

What could you do if someone…?
• had a severe allergic reaction
• had a high temperature
• got very bad sunburn
• felt faint and dizzy
• got a big blister on their foot
• got food poisoning
• had an epileptic seizure

## 4 GRAMMAR present perfect simple and continuous

I have… and… and…

Not again…

**a** ◑ 2.9 Listen to a conversation between a doctor and a patient and answer the questions.

1 What symptoms does the patient have?
2 What does he think might be wrong with him?
3 What does he think he needs?
4 What does the doctor suggest?

**b** ◑ 2.10 Listen to what the doctor and receptionist say after Mr. Payne has left. What do they think of him? Do you know the name for someone like this?

**c** ◑ 2.11 Now listen to some extracts from the conversation in **a** and circle the correct form, present perfect simple or continuous. Are there any where you think both options would also be possible?

1 *I haven't been feeling / I haven't felt* well for a few days.
2 *I've been coughing / I've coughed* a lot and I keep getting headaches.
3 What *have you been taking / have you taken* for the headaches?
4 How many tablets *have you been taking / have you taken* today?
5 And *have you taken / have you been taking* your temperature this morning?
6 Yes. *I've been taking it / I've taken it* five or six times already.
7 I think I need a blood test. I *haven't had / haven't been having* one for two months.

**d** ⑥ p.134 Grammar Bank 2A

**e** In pairs, use the prompts to ask and answer the questions. The first question should be simple present and the second should be present perfect simple or continuous.

1 / often *get* colds?   How many colds / *have* in the last three months?
2 / *take* any vitamins or supplements?   How long / *take* them?
3 / *drink* much water?   How many glasses / *drink* today?
4 / *exercise*? What?   How long / *do* it?
5 / *eat* a lot of fruit and vegetables?   How many servings / *have* today?
6 / *walk* to school (or work or college)?   How far / *walk* today?
7 How many hours / *sleep* a night?   / *sleep* well recently?
8 / *be* allergic to anything?   / ever *have* a serious allergic reaction?

## 5 READING & SPEAKING

**a** Look at the title of the article on p.19 and read the first paragraph. With a partner, try to complete the definition of a *cyberchondriac*. Do you think the tone of the article is humorous or serious?

---

**cyberchondriac** /ˌsaɪbərˈkɒndriæk/ (*noun*) a person who compulsively searches the internet for information about _____

---

**b** Now read the whole article. Complete the summary of each paragraph with phrases a–e.

1 When the writer found out that she had a fast heart rate, she ▮
2 At the hospital, she discovered that she ▮
3 Since she returned from the hospital, she ▮
4 It's difficult to know from online information whether a condition ▮
5 A lot of online medical information ▮

a has been obsessively checking her symptoms online.
b googled the possible causes.
c isn't very reliable or up to date.
d was suffering from a chest infection and cyberchondria.
e is rare or very common.

**c** The highlighted phrases in the article are related to medicine. Match them to definitions 1–7.

1 _____ the medical treatment of a heart problem that involves an operation
2 _____ successful treatments for an illness that was thought to be impossible to cure
3 _____ **IDM** not feeling very well
4 _____ exaggerated reports in the news that make people worry
5 _____ the most terrible situations that could happen
6 _____ the speed at which your heart beats
7 _____ an illness that could kill you

# Confessions of a *cyberchondriac*

> I'm sure that's what I've got...

**1**   **A few weeks ago,** I was feeling <mark>under the weather</mark>. After days of intensive internet diagnosis, I finally went to see my doctor. After examining me, she told me that my <mark>heart rate</mark> was a little fast and sent me off to the hospital for some tests. Did I go straight there? Of course not. First I took out my phone, logged on to Google, and found out that the technical term for a fast heart rate is *supraventricular tachycardia*. Then I typed these two words into Google. Sadly, the problem with Dr. Google is that he isn't exactly a comfort in times of crisis. One website immediately scared me with a list of 407 possible causes.

**2**   I raced to the hospital, convinced that I probably needed <mark>open-heart surgery</mark>. Four hours later, I got a diagnosis. I had a chest infection…and a bad case of *cyberchondria*. The only consolation for the latter condition is that I'm in good company. A Microsoft survey of one million internet users last year found that 2% of all searches – a not-insignificant number – were health-related.

**3**   Unfortunately, once you have it, cyberchondria can be hard to cure. Since my trip to the hospital, I have been obsessively checking my pulse, swapping symptoms in chat rooms, and reading all about <mark>worst-case scenarios</mark>. What if the doctors got it wrong? What if the EKG machine was faulty? It's exhausting trying to convince yourself that you might have a <mark>life-threatening illness</mark>.

**4**   The Microsoft study also revealed another serious problem – that online information often doesn't discriminate between common and very rare conditions. One in four of all articles thrown up by an internet search for *headache* suggested a brain tumor as a possible cause. Although it is true that this <u>may</u> be the cause, in fact, brain tumors develop in fewer than one in 50,000 people. People also assume that the first answers that come up in searches refer to the most common causes, so if you type in *mouth ulcer* and see that *mouth cancer* has several mentions near the top, you think that it must be very common. However, this is not the case at all.

**5**   Another problem for cyberchondriacs is that online medical information may be from an unreliable source, or out of date. A recent American study showed that 75% of the people who use the internet to look up information about their health do not check where that information came from, or the date it was created. "Once something has been put up on the internet, even if it's wrong, it's difficult to remove," says Sarah Jarvis, a doctor. "This is a problem, especially with <mark>scare stories</mark>, and also with some alternative remedies that claim to be <mark>miracle cures</mark>, but which may actually do you harm." Check the information? Sorry, I don't have time – I'm off to buy a heart-rate monitor!

*Adapted from The Sunday Times*

Please **Do Not** Confuse Your **Google Search** With My Medical Degree

**d**   Now read each paragraph again carefully and choose a, b, or c.

1   The problem with Dr. Google is that the information is _____.
   a   insufficient    b   worrying    c   false

2   Microsoft's survey discovered that _____ searches are about health.
   a   very few
   b   a lot of
   c   the majority of

3   The information the writer has found since coming back from the hospital has _____.
   a   made her cyberchondria worse
   b   made no difference to her cyberchondria
   c   cured her cyberchondria

4   One of the problems with internet searches is that they _____.
   a   don't rank answers in order of probability
   b   only focus on common illnesses
   c   don't always give an answer

5   Most people are unlikely to check _____ health information was posted.
   a   why and by who
   b   how and when
   c   when and by who

**e**   In small groups, answer the questions. Ask for and give as much information as possible.

1   Do you know anyone who you think is a hypochondriac or a cyberchondriac? What kinds of things do they do?

2   Do you think people in your country worry a lot about their…?

| | |
|---|---|
| blood pressure | cholesterol level |
| digestive system | liver |

Give examples if you can. Are there other things related to health that they worry about?

## 6   WRITING

**W** p.115 Writing An informal email
Write an email to a friend explaining that you haven't been well, and saying what you've been doing recently.

**Glossary**
**EKG machine** electrocardiogram machine, used to test people's heart rate

Go online to review the lesson

**G** using adjectives as nouns, adjective order    **V** clothes and fashion    **P** vowel sounds

> Is someone different at age 18 or 60? I believe one stays the same.
> *Hayao Miyazaki, Japanese movie director*

## 1 READING & SPEAKING

**a** Think of an older person you know who seems much younger than they actually are. Circle any of the adjectives below that you would use to describe them.

active   brave   energetic   funny   glamorous   impulsive
independent   lively   open-minded   sociable

**b** Describe the person to a partner, and say what they do that makes them seem younger than their age.

**c** Look at the photo of Dilys and Sian. Approximately how old do you think they are?

# The joy of the age-gap friendship

**Modern life makes it hard for the old and the young to meet, and even harder to become best friends. What's the secret?**

## Dilys on Sian

I met Sian at an event where we were both speakers, and we just clicked. I could see she was just a great person, and smarter than most. She was a glamorous, lively woman, who talked about being an entrepreneur and her love for her father.

She started inviting me to different places. I went to the races with her – not the sort of thing I usually do. She brought fun back into my life when I was working hard to run a charity. The new experiences we share help to keep me alive. When I was sick last Christmas, she really rescued me. She came in like a hurricane, with decorations, firewood… I was feeling sad and afraid, and she told me that wasn't allowed.

▲ Dilys and Sian

### "She brought fun back into my life."

Sian's full of energy and warmth. I feel I understand her because she represents my younger self. Mine wasn't a typical path; I always wanted to be a little different. I was a dancer and taught the art of movement. I got married within six weeks, but divorced when my only son was seven. I've got the life I wanted, but it isn't always easy. I try to offer that perspective to Sian.

## Sian on Dilys

I met Dilys in Cardiff, where we both live, at an event called Superwoman. We were both invited to speak and were at the same table. Dilys did a lot of charity work with disabled people, as well as being the world's oldest female solo skydiver. I was there to talk about my media marketing company. We hit it off; I thought she was amazing and the way I want to be as I grow older.

We love to sit with take-out food and listen to Mozart. We like movies and the theater. She has a huge amount of energy and can dance for longer than me. She even persuaded me to do a skydive, despite my fear of heights. When we're in a cab, taxi drivers ask how we met, but we never think of our age gap. She advises me on my love life, work, and how to be a better person.

### "She's the way I want to be as I grow older."

I often walk into Dilys's house when I'm stressed and within seconds I'm more relaxed. She calms me down when I'm angry, and teaches me to see things from other people's point of view. Now, she's the first person I call when anything good or bad happens. My family says how much good she does me.

> **Glossary**
> **the races** a series of horse races that happen at one place on a particular day

*Adapted from* The Guardian

**d** Now read the article, where each woman talks about how they met and about their relationship. Who are the following sentences true for? Write **S** (Sian), **D** (Dilys), or **B** (both of them).

1 ☐ She admires the other person.
2 ☐ She cheered the other person up on one specific occasion.
3 ☐ She got along immediately with the other person.
4 ☐ She has done an extreme sport.
5 ☐ She has helped the other person to be more open-minded.
6 ☐ She has introduced the other to things she hadn't tried before.
7 ☐ She likes cultural activities.
8 ☐ She manages an organization that helps people.
9 ☐ She runs a company.
10 ☐ She's good at giving advice.
11 ☐ She's very energetic.
12 ☐ She doesn't like being in high places.

**e** Look at your answers to **d**. What do you think is the secret of Dilys and Sian's friendship?

**f** Now look at the photo of Dave and John. What do you think the age difference is between them?

▲ Dave and John

**g** ⓒ **Communication** The joy of the age-gap friendship
**A** p.107 **B** p.111 Read about Dave and John and compare what they say about each other.

**h** Complete some phrases from the four texts. Compare with a partner and explain what they mean in your own words.

1 **Dilys** We just cl_____.
2 **Sian** We h_____ it off.
3 **Sian** We never think of our age g_____.
4 **Sian** She…teaches me to see things from other people's p_____ of v_____.
5 **Dave** I've learned never to t_____ sides.
6 **John** (He loves cars;) I couldn't c_____ less.
7 **John** I l_____ up to him.

**i** Talk to a partner.
- Are you good friends with anyone who is a lot older or younger than you?
- If yes, how did you meet? Why do you get along well? What kind of things do you do together?
- If no, what advantages do you think there are to having a friend of a different generation?
- Is there a family member from a different generation who you are close to? What do you like about them?

## 2 GRAMMAR using adjectives as nouns, adjective order

**a** Look at the sentences in 1 and 2 below and decide if you think they are right (✓) or wrong (✗). Compare with a partner and say why you think the ✗ ones are wrong.

1 a ☐ In general, it's difficult for the old and the young to be good friends.
  b ☐ In general, it's difficult for the old people and the young people to be good friends.
  c ☐ In general, it's difficult for old people and young people to be good friends.

2 a ☐ Sian is a lively, dark-haired, Welsh woman.
  b ☐ Sian is a Welsh, lively, dark-haired woman.
  c ☐ Sian is a dark-haired, Welsh, lively woman.

**b** ⓖ p.135 Grammar Bank 2B

**c** Discuss the statements below in small groups. Do you agree? Why (not)?
- Young people don't respect the old as much as they used to.
- Politicians should be at least 40 years old – the young don't have enough experience for such a responsible job.
- Rich people are often less generous than poor people.
- The unemployed should take any job they can. Any job is better than no job.
- The homeless should be allowed to live rent-free in empty second homes.

## 3 VOCABULARY clothes and fashion

a Look at the title of an article about fashion. What's your answer to the question?

b Look at the photo of the Hoppen family and read the article. Complete the highlighted phrases with the clothes in the box.

> dress   jacket   jeans   sandals
> sweater   top   sneakers

# Can the same clothes work for all ages?

It's odd to imagine wearing the same clothes as your 55-year-old mother or even your 80-year-old grandmother, but fashion, it seems, has finally crossed the age divide. "It's not about what you 'should' wear when you're young or old," says designer Emilia Wikstead. "It's about finding the things that really suit you, regardless of your age."

The Hoppen family:
Plum Hoppen (21),
her mother Jenny (60),
her sister Daisy (31)
[= from left to right]

When three women of the same clothing and shoe size live under the same roof, clothes are bound to go missing. "I remember seeing this girl in the park and thinking, 'That's a nice dress; it looks like one of mine,'", says Jenny Hoppen. "And I realized it was Daisy, going to a wedding, wearing my dress and shoes." But even if they borrow from each other, the same piece looks different on them all.

In the photo, they are all wearing the same [1] cropped _____. Plum wears hers with [2] a leather _____ and [3] patterned _____, but they look just as good on Jenny with [4] a silk V-neck _____ and [5] red velvet _____, or on Daisy with [6] a see-through black _____ worn over [7] a black turtle-neck _____. "The principle we learned from our mother," says Daisy, "is to have our own sense of style and be adventurous."

c Whose "look" do you prefer? Do you ever borrow clothes or accessories from people in your family, or friends?

d **V** p.153 **Vocabulary Bank** Clothes and fashion

## 4 PRONUNCIATION vowel sounds

a 🔊 2.21 Look at the pairs of sound pictures below. Put two words from the box in each column. Listen and check.

> awful  cotton  dotted  hooded  jeans
> leather  linen  long  loose  patterned
> sandals  sleeveless  slippers  suit  vest  wool

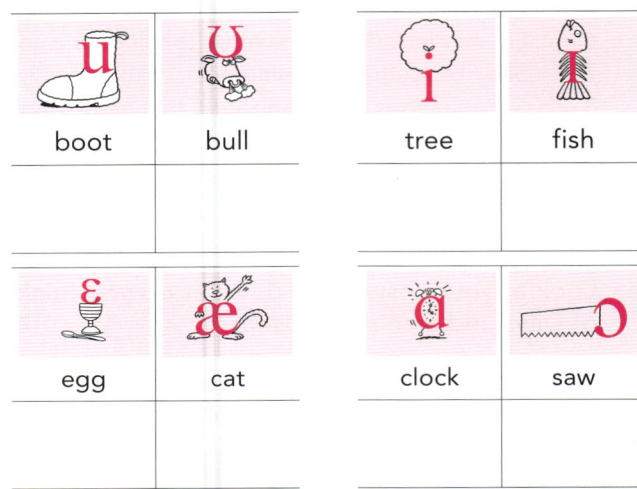

| boot | bull | tree | fish |
|------|------|------|------|
| | | | |

| egg | cat | clock | saw |
|-----|-----|-------|-----|
| | | | |

b **P** Sound Bank p.166 Look at the typical spellings for these sounds.

c 🔊 2.22 Listen to some phrases describing clothes. Is anyone in the class wearing them, or something similar?

d Talk in pairs. What would or wouldn't you wear…?

> to a formal interview   on the beach
> to work or school / college
> to a wedding   sightseeing in a city

## 5 LISTENING & SPEAKING

a Look at the clothes in the photos. What age group do you associate them with?

1 a cardigan and fur slippers

2 a leather miniskirt

3 very short shorts

4 tight jeans and a T-shirt with a slogan

5 a blazer and chinos

**b**  **2.23** Listen to a radio discussion about dressing your age. Match the clothes 1–5 in **a** to what the journalists say about them, A–F. There is one comment you don't need.

A ▢ "They never suit an older person."
B ▢ "They make younger men look older than they are."
C ▢ "A woman in her 70s looked great in one."
D ▢ "Middle-aged men tend to wear them a lot."
E ▢ "Older people should never wear clothes made of this material."
F ▢ "Your grandma probably won't like them as a present."

**c** Listen again and mark the opinions **T** (true) or **F** (false). Correct the **F** ones.

**Liza thinks that...**
1 90% of women dress younger than their age.
2 teenage girls would never dress older than their age.
3 it's fine for older women to wear trendy clothes.

**Adrian thinks that...**
4 very few men admit to dressing younger than their age.
5 Mick Jagger looks awful in many of the clothes he wears.
6 men usually wear a suit and tie to work.

**d** In pairs, think about what the journalists said, and try to complete their fashion rules.

| Liza | Wear whatever you think _____ and makes you _____. |
| Adrian | Dress for the age _____, not for the age _____. |

**e**  **2.24** Listen to the end of the discussion and check. Who do you agree with more, Liza or Adrian?

**f** Work in groups of three, and discuss three of the topics below. Take turns being the host. The host chooses the topic and manages the discussion. Try to use the language from the box.

- People should stop buying new clothes and buy more second-hand and vintage clothes.
- Men are just as interested in shopping for clothes as women.
- These days, nobody is prepared to suffer in order to look good. The most important thing is comfort.
- You can tell a lot about someone's personality from the clothes they wear.
- Cheap fashion means exploiting people in less developed countries.

---

🔍 **Managing discussions**
*Let's start with you, (Liza).*
*(Adrian,) what about...?*
*Let's go back to...*

*So, to sum up...*
*Can you let (Liza) finish?*
*Sorry. Go ahead.*

**Politely disagreeing**
*Sorry, but I don't agree.*
*True, but...*

*I'm not sure about that.*
*I agree up to a point, but...*

---

## 6 WRITING

**a** Imagine you have decided to sell two items of clothing on eBay. Write detailed descriptions, using the example below as a model. Set a starting price.

Blue and white striped cotton shirt – Size M
Condition: New without tags
"Never worn! Would look great with jeans. Perfect for the summer."
$12.99

**b** Now read some other students' ads. What would you like to bid for?

## 7 ▶ VIDEO LISTENING

**a** Watch an interview about the Hiut jeans company. What do you think is the unique selling point (USP) of their jeans?

**b** Watch the interview again. Then make notes under the following categories.

| Description of jeans |
| --- |
| 1 Material: *denim* |
| 2 Style: |
| 3 Celebrity wearer: |
| **History of company** |
| 4 When David and Clare started it and why: |
| 5 Who they employ: |
| 6 How many pairs of jeans they produce per week: |
| 7 How they try to make their jeans environmentally friendly: |

**c** Would you like to have a pair of Hiut jeans? Would you be prepared to join the no-wash club? Why (not)?

## GRAMMAR

**a** Complete the sentences with one word.

1 What were you and Sarah talking _____?
2 You didn't like her latest novel, _____ you?
3 My father loves opera and so _____ my mother.
4 **A** I've been to India twice.
  **B** You _____? I'd love to go.
5 What have you _____ doing since last week?

**b** Circle a, b, or c.

1 Could you tell me what time ____?
  a the bus leaves   b leaves the bus
  c does the bus leave
2 How many people ____ this computer?
  a do use   b use   c does use
3 You're not eating much. ____ like the food?
  a You don't   b Don't you   c Aren't you
4 **A** Why didn't you call me?
  **B** I ____, but your phone was off.
  a do call   b did called   c did call
5 The slower you work, ____ you'll finish.
  a later   b the later   c the later than
6 ____ three cups of coffee already this morning.
  a I've been having   b I've had   c I have
7 That was probably the worst movie ____!
  a I've ever seen   b I've never seen
  c I've ever been seeing
8 I met ____ in my language class today.
  a a Japanese
  b the Japanese
  c a Japanese woman
9 Some people think that ____ don't pay enough tax.
  a the rich   b the rich people   c rich
10 I got a ____ bag for my birthday.
  a beautiful leather Italian
  b Italian leather beautiful
  c beautiful Italian leather

## VOCABULARY

**a** Complete the compound adjectives.

1 My boss is very bad-_____. When things go wrong, he starts shouting at everyone.
2 I'm very _____minded. I tend to forget things.
3 I think Paul is very tight-_____. He never spends money unless he absolutely has to.
4 Sylvia won't have any problems at the interview – she's very self-_____.
5 That sweater is very old-_____. It looks like the kind of thing my grandpa would wear.

**b** Write words for the definitions.

1 bl_____ (verb) to lose blood from an injury
2 sw_____ (adj.) bigger than normal, especially because of an injury or infection
3 b_____ (noun) a piece of cloth used to tie around a part of the body that has been hurt
4 t_____ (noun) a pain in one of your teeth
5 r_____ (noun) an area of red spots caused by an illness or allergy

**c** Circle the correct verb or verb phrase.

1 I *have / feel* a little dizzy. I need to sit down.
2 She *burned / sprained* her ankle when she was jogging.
3 It was so hot in the room that I nearly *fainted / choked*.
4 This skirt doesn't *fit / suit* me. It's too big.
5 Can I go in jeans? I don't feel like getting *dressed / changed*.

**d** Circle the word that is different.

1 striped   dotted   plain   patterned
2 silk   cotton   fur   plaid
3 collar   sleeveless   hooded   long-sleeved
4 Lycra   scarf   vest   cardigan
5 fashionable   scruffy   stylish   trendy

**e** Complete with one word.

1 My mother had a very bad case of the flu last week, but she's beginning to get _____ it now.
2 Please lie _____ on the couch over there.
3 I'm feeling sick. I think I'm going to _____ up.
4 Do we really need to dress _____ for the party tonight?
5 Please _____ up your clothes in the closet.

## PRONUNCIATION

**a** Circle the word with a different sound.

| | | |
|---|---|---|
| 1 | ʧ | a**ch**e   **ch**oke   **ch**ange   ma**tch**es |
| 2 | ʃ | uncon**sci**ous   ra**sh**   fa**sh**ion   **s**uede |
| 3 | ɪ | **i**njury   str**i**ped   s**i**lk   bl**i**ster |
| 4 | ɛ | j**ea**ns   l**ea**ther   v**e**lvet   d**e**nim |
| 5 | u | c**ou**gh   fl**u**   s**ui**t   l**oo**se |

**b** Underline the main stressed syllable.

1 in|cre|di|bly
2 big-|hea|ded
3 an|ti|bi|o|tics
4 swim|suit
5 fa|shio|na|ble

## CAN YOU understand this text?

**a** Read the article once. Do the scientists who have studied Scott Kelly agree about the effect of space travel on the human body?

**b** Read the article again and choose a, b, or c.

1 Scientists expected that, after spending a year in space, Scott Kelly would be…
   a more intelligent.
   b taller and lighter.
   c younger.
2 Telomeres prevent…
   a aging.
   b radiation.
   c damage to our chromosomes.
3 Scientists are afraid that astronauts…
   a will not want to do long space flights.
   b will have a lot of long-term health problems.
   c won't be able to travel further than Mars.
4 In space, astronauts…
   a must use the gym twice a week.
   b exercise more than when they are in training.
   c are not allowed to eat whatever they like.

## ▶ CAN YOU understand these people?

🔊 **2.25** Watch or listen and choose a, b, or c.

| 1 | 2 | 3 | 4 |
| Sean | Harry | Maria | Mark |

1 One of the questions Sean was asked at a job interview was _____.
   a whether he liked working in restaurants
   b what his favorite basketball team was
   c who his favorite superhero was
2 In the house where Harry grew up, there is a ghost that _____.
   a all of her family has seen
   b all of her family has heard
   c all of her family is afraid of
3 Maria gave her little brother first aid when _____.
   a her mother was not at home
   b his older brother had hit him on the head
   c he fell off the sofa and cut himself
4 Mark meets younger friends _____.
   a through classes he teaches
   b at the theater
   c when he exercises

# Astronaut returns from space younger than his twin

**American astronaut Scott Kelly**, and his identical twin **Mark**, also a retired astronaut, may be the most studied siblings in the history of science. Each time one of them went into space while the other remained on Earth, both men would carry out dozens of experiments, including cognitive exercises, genetic sequencing, and testing for bacteria on their bodies. When Scott landed in Kazakhstan last year, after 340 days in space, he came back two inches taller, fifteen pounds lighter, and with a strong desire to jump into a swimming pool. Changes like these were predictable and temporary. Now, however, scientists have found the first signs of a change that no one expected – during his year on board the International Space Station, Scott's body had become younger.

One of the genetic indicators of human aging is the length of our telomeres. Telomeres are the caps at the end of each strand of DNA that protect our chromosomes, like the plastic tips at the end of shoelaces. Usually, telomeres get shorter as we age; they are about 11,000 molecules long when we are born and only about 4,000 long in old age, and this means that our DNA is increasingly vulnerable to damage as we get older. However, an analysis of Scott Kelly's cells, led by Susan Bailey, professor of radiation cancer biology at Colorado State University, showed that the 52-year-old astronaut's telomeres got longer while he was in space, before shrinking back again after returning to Earth.

In theory, expanding telomeres indicate the reversal of part of the aging process. However, they are also strongly linked to cancer. NASA is aiming to send humans to Mars and beyond, but many scientists worry that long-haul trips into space could cause astronauts to suffer from chronic and severe health problems. So this is definitely not good news, and it could have serious implications for the future of space travel.

Christopher Mason, assistant professor of physiology and biophysics at Cornell Weill Medicine in New York, takes a different view. Professor Mason's team also found changes in Scott Kelly's genes while he was in space. But he thinks this may be less a result of simply being in space, and more due to the intense NASA fitness regime. "On Earth, you might go to the gym on Tuesday and then decide you can't be bothered on Thursday and go out for a big dinner, but on the space station, the astronauts exercise extremely regularly, and all food and exercise is very controlled."

*Adapted from The Times*

🔄 **Go online** to watch the video, review Files 1 & 2, and check your progress

Airplane travel is nature's way of making you look like your passport photo.
*Al Gore, US politician and environmentalist*

**G** narrative tenses, past perfect continuous, *so / such…that*   **V** air travel   **P** irregular past forms, sentence rhythm

## 1 LISTENING & VOCABULARY air travel

**a** 🔊 **3.1** Listen to some announcements. Would you hear them when traveling by train or by plane? Write **T** or **P**.

A ☐ B ☐ C ☐ D ☐ E ☐ F ☐ G ☐ H ☐ I ☐ J ☐

**b** 🔊 **3.2** Listen again to the ones you would hear when traveling by train (or subway). What do you need to know if you want to travel on…?

1 the 9:04 train to Waterbury
2 the Hudson Line service to Grand Central Terminal
3 the 10:25 to Chicago, in the dining car
4 the J, M, and Z trains

**c** 🔊 **3.3** Listen again to the ones you would hear when traveling by plane. Answer the questions for each one.

- Would you hear it in the airport terminal or on the plane?
- What is it asking people to do?

**d** 🔊 **3.4** Listen to some extracts from the announcements 1–6 in **c**. What do these formal words and phrases mean?

1 approximately     4 place, personal electronic devices
2 locate            5 requiring
3 proceed to        6 disembark, rear

**e** 🅥 **p.154 Vocabulary Bank** Air travel

## 2 READING

**a** When you travel by plane, bus, or train, do you usually prefer to sit in the front, in the middle, or in the back? Do you prefer a window seat or an aisle seat? Why?

**b** Look at the seating diagram of a plane and the seats marked with an X. Then read the article about where to sit on a plane and match the seat numbers to the correct paragraphs.

# How to get the best seat

Every time you fly and have to choose a seat, you ask yourself, "Which is the best seat to choose?" The answer is that it depends entirely on your priorities as a passenger. *Telegraph Travel* has sifted through the research to reveal the top spots.

### If you want a speedy exit ☐
You're on a three-day weekend trip to Chicago, and you're traveling light with just a small carry-on bag in the ¹_____. You want to maximize the amount of time you spend at your destination and minimize the time spent on the plane. Verdict? You need to grab an aisle seat towards the front of the plane on the left, which is where the main exit is located and where passengers leave the aircraft from.

### If you want to sleep ☐
Sleep is hard to come by at an ²_____ of 35,000 feet. There are so many things conspiring against you that it's hard to nod off: the hum of the engines, the passenger next to you needing to get out, the lack of neck support in your seat. Some places, however, are better than others, for example, some areas of the ³_____ are less noisy. Window seats give you control of the window blind and a place to rest your head; they also mean you don't need to be woken up every time the passenger next to you needs to go to the bathroom. The verdict? A window seat at the front of the plane, where it is also quieter.

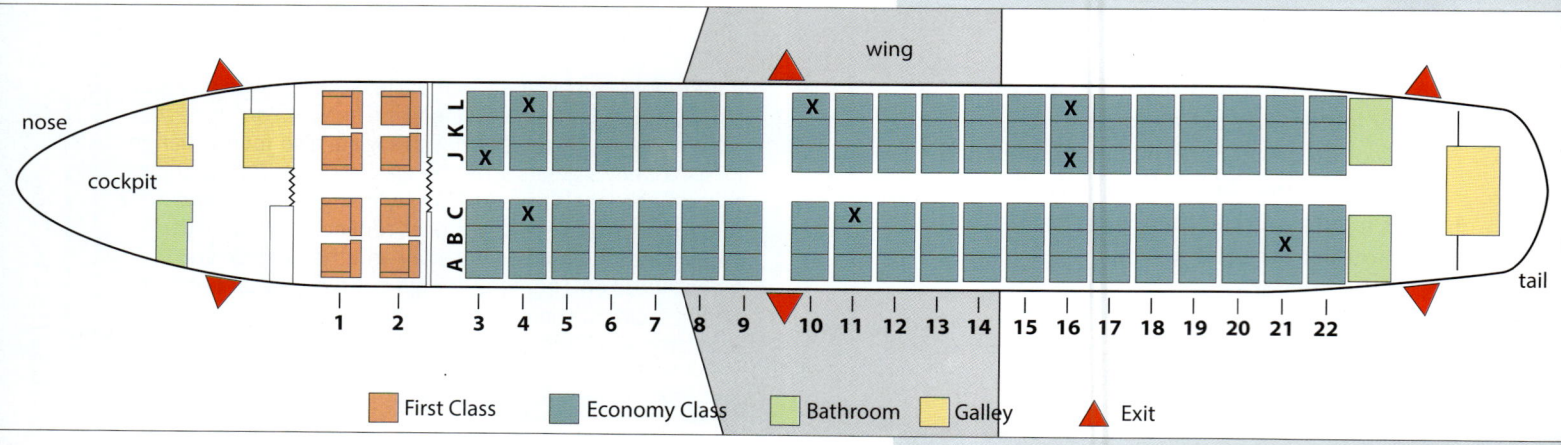

First Class     Economy Class     Bathroom     Galley     Exit

*Adapted from The Telegraph*

### If you don't like turbulence

Turbulence does, of course, shake the entire aircraft, but experts claim there are some seats on a plane where bumps will feel less intense. The verdict? Sit in the middle of the plane, above the wings, which help keep the plane steady when the going gets tough.

### If you need more legroom

Seats in exit rows have more legroom than most. These seats are, however, in such high demand that some airlines, especially ⁴_____ ones, charge more for them. They also come with restrictions: passengers in exit rows, for instance, must be willing to assist in the ⁵_____ of the aircraft during an emergency, so they are not available for children or people needing ⁶_____. The verdict? If you're traveling without children, if you're in shape, and you can afford it, choose a seat in an exit row.

### If you want a better dining experience

According to Professor Charles Spence – author of *Gastrophysics: The New Science of Eating* – plane food tastes better at the front of the aircraft, where it is quieter and the air is more humid. "Dry cabin air and the loud ⁷_____ noise all contribute to our inability to taste and smell food and drink," he told *Telegraph Travel*. Verdict? Sit as close to the cockpit as possible if you want to make plane food taste better. More often than not, you'll also get served first.

### If you're safety-conscious

Airlines and plane manufacturers will tell you that all seats are equal when it comes to matters of safety. However, some seats are more equal than others. A 2007 study by the magazine *Popular Mechanics* found that passengers sitting near the ⁸_____ of a plane were 40 percent more likely to survive a crash than those sitting in the first few rows. Verdict? Sit as far back as possible.

### If you want to have an empty seat next to you

If you are flying with a companion, try booking both the aisle and the window seat. You will often find that the middle seat – because it is the least favored by passengers traveling solo – has been left empty. Relax and enjoy it.

---

**c**  Now read the article again and complete it with a word or phrase from the box.

altitude   cabin   engine   evacuation
low-cost   overhead compartment
special assistance   tail

**d**  According to the information in the article, which do you now think would be the best seat for you?

---

**e**  **Grammar in context** *so / such...that...*

> There are so many things conspiring against you that it's hard to nod off...
>
> These seats are, however, in such high demand that some airlines, especially low-cost ones, charge more for them.

We often use *so / such...that* to express a consequence.

- Use *so* + adjective or adverb, e.g., *The taxi driver drove so quickly (that) we got to the airport on time.*
- Use *so much* + uncountable noun and *so many* + plural countable noun, e.g., *There was so much traffic / There were so many buses on the road (that) we nearly missed our flight.*
- Use *such a* + adjective + single countable noun, e.g., *It was such a great hotel (that) we want to go back there.*
- Use *such* + adjective + uncountable or plural noun, e.g., *We had such terrible weather / such small rooms (that) we didn't enjoy the vacation.*

**Complete with** *so, so much / many, such,* **or** *such a.*

1 The flight was _____ long that I got really bored.
2 I had _____ noisy child behind me that I couldn't sleep.
3 I slept _____ badly on the flight from New York that the jet lag was worse than usual.
4 There were _____ people at check-in that we had to stand in line for nearly 45 minutes.
5 We had _____ luggage that we had to get two carts.
6 We met _____ nice people in the hotel that we were never bored.

---

## 3  SPEAKING

In pairs, ask and answer the questions.

### If you have flown several times

1 How often do you fly? What kinds of airlines do you usually use?
2 When was the last flight you took? Where did you go? What for? Where did you sit?
3 Have you ever flown long-haul? Where did you go? How long was the flight? Did you get jet lag?
4 How do you feel about flying? Have you ever had a very bad experience on a flight?

### If you have never / hardly ever flown

1 When was the last time you went on a trip? Where did you go? What for?
2 How do you usually travel a) short distances, b) longer distances? Why do you choose to travel this way?
3 What's the farthest you've ever traveled? Why did you go there?
4 What's your favorite way of traveling? Why?

### Have you ever...

- been very delayed when traveling? How long for?
- missed a flight, train, or bus? Why? What did you do?
- had to sit near a screaming baby (or a child that kept kicking your seat) on a plane, train, or bus? What did you do?
- had to catch a connecting flight, train, or bus with very little time to spare? Did you catch it?

## 4 LISTENING

**a** You are going to listen to an airline pilot talking on a radio program. Before you listen, discuss questions 1–6 with a partner and imagine what the answers will be.

1 What weather conditions are the most dangerous when you are flying a plane?
2 Is turbulence really dangerous?
3 Which is more dangerous, take-off or landing?
4 Why do passengers have to turn off electronic devices and put their tray tables up during take-off and landing?
5 Is it really worth listening to safety demonstrations?
6 Do you ever get scared?

**b** 🔴 **3.9** Listen to the program. How many of the pilot's answers did you predict correctly?

**c** Listen again and take notes. How does he explain his answers?

**d** What did the pilot say that might make you feel more relaxed the next time you fly?

## 5 GRAMMAR narrative tenses, past perfect continuous

**a** Read a newspaper story about a Spirit Airlines flight. What had made its way onto the plane? What happened during the flight?

**b** Read the story again and circle the correct form of the verbs 1–8.

**c** Now look at a sentence from the story. What was the flight like before the bat appeared? What tense do you think the highlighted verb is?

> The plane had been flying for nearly 30 minutes before the creature made its appearance in the passenger cabin. Up until that point, the flight had been routine.

**d** 🅖 p.136 Grammar Bank 3A

**e** In pairs or groups, try to complete the two sentences in four different ways, using the four narrative tenses.

1 The police stopped the driver because he…
2 I couldn't sleep last night because…

# Routine flight goes "batty"

Passengers on a Spirit Airlines flight from Charlotte, North Carolina to Newark, New Jersey on July 31, 2018, were surprised when a bat was spotted flying on board. The plane had been flying for nearly 30 minutes before the creature made its appearance in the passenger cabin. Up until that point, the flight had been routine. Most passengers [1] had sat / were sitting quietly in their seats, enjoying a drink and a snack. Once passengers [2] realized / had realized that a bat was on the plane, they began taking videos as it frantically swooped through the cabin. One video posted to social media shows a passenger running down the aisle as others [3] had screamed / were screaming.

Peter Scattini, one of the passengers on board, [4] tweeted / was tweeting a video of the bat with the following text, "Me, twice a year: 'I'll never fly Spirit again.' Me, this morning, after deciding I'd rather save 12 dollars." Another passenger, who [5] had filmed / was filming the bat, posted a video that showed people laughing as they watched the bat fly through the cabin.

A spokesperson for Spirit Airlines said, "The bat was eventually corralled into a lavatory and [6] removed / had removed once on the ground by animal control officers. The aircraft was disinfected and searched as a precaution." The spokesperson continued, "It is believed the bat started its journey in Charlotte, flying into an overhead bin while our crews [7] had done / were doing overnight maintenance. No one was hurt in this incident, including the bat."

Videos of the bat [8] went / were going viral on social media, prompting hundreds of people to make jokes about the airline, including Stephen Colbert, host of The Late Show, who tweeted, "I can't believe there was a bat on a Spirit Airlines flight. I've only ever seen raccoons."

*Adapted from The Independent*

## 6 PRONUNCIATION irregular past forms, sentence rhythm

a Write the simple past of the following verbs in the chart, according to the pronunciation of the vowel sound.

~~become~~   ~~catch~~   cut   drive   fall   fight   fly   hear
hide   hold   hurt   keep   leave   lie   read
ride   say   sleep   tell   think   throw   write

| 1  | 2 | 3 | 4 |
|---|---|---|---|
|  |  | caught |  |
| 5 | 6 | 7 | 8 |
|  |  |  | became |

b Look at the verbs in **a** again. Which ones have a past participle that is different from the simple past form? Write these past participles in the chart.

c 🔊 **3.12** Listen and check. Then listen and repeat.

d Read a short anecdote about a flight. With a partner, guess what the missing verbs might be.

This ¹_____ when my **wife** and I were on a **flight** to **New York**, and we'd been ²_____ for a **few hours**. I was ³_____, and my **wife** was ⁴_____ a **movie**, when **suddenly**, we ⁵_____ an **announcement** – "Is there a **doctor** on **board**?" It ⁶_____ **out** that a **woman** was ⁷_____ a **baby**! Luckily, two **doctors** ⁸_____ **forward**, and the **baby** was ⁹_____ **safely**.

e 🔊 **3.13** Listen and fill in the blanks. Practice reading the anecdote aloud with the correct rhythm, with light stress on the main verbs and other **bold** words.

## 7 SPEAKING

a 🟢 **Communication** Flight stories **A** p.107  **B** p.112
Read a newspaper story. Then tell your partner the story.

b You are going to tell an anecdote. The story can either be true or invented. If it's invented, you must try to tell it in such a convincing way that your partner thinks it's true. Choose <u>one</u> of the topics below and plan what you're going to say. Use the language in the **Telling an anecdote** box to help you, and ask your teacher for any other words you need.

**Talk about a time when you...**

were robbed or lost something important when you were traveling or on vacation.

got completely lost while traveling in another city or country.

arrived home from a trip and had a surprise.

> 🔍 **Telling an anecdote**
>
> **Setting the scene**
> *This happened (to me) when I was...*
> *I was...-ing when...*
> *I..., because I had / hadn't...*
>
> **The main events**
> *I decided to..., because...*
> *So then I...*
> *Suddenly / At that moment,...*
>
> **What happened in the end**
> *In the end / Eventually,...*
> *It turned out that...*
> *I felt...*

c In pairs, **A** tell **B** your story. **B** show interest and ask for more details. Decide whether you think the story is true or not. Then switch roles.

*This happened to me a few years ago, when I was on vacation in Florida. I was swimming in the ocean one day when I saw a shark.*

*Really? How big was it?*

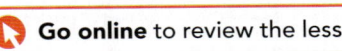

> A good story should make you laugh, and a moment later break your heart.
> *Chuck Palahniuk, US author*

**G** the position of adverbs and adverbial phrases | **V** adverbs and adverbial phrases | **P** word stress and intonation

## 1 GRAMMAR the position of adverbs and adverbial phrases

**a** Read four 50-word stories. With a partner, predict how you think each story ends.

# fiftywordstories.com

**fiftywordstories.com** is a website to which people from all over the world contribute 50-word stories in English.

### ① Sweet talking

"What are you reading there? It looks serious – you must be **incredibly** smart." He uses his usual pick-up lines on the train. Ask them a simple question. Then pay them a compliment. It **always** works. **Sadly** not this time. ▮

### ② Departed

"Is Mommy gone?"
"**Unfortunately** she is, sweetie."
"I miss Mommy."
"So do I, sweetie. Don't cry."
"Let's go and get Mommy, **right now!**"
"We can't do that, sweetie."
"Where is she?"
"She's in a **much** better place."
"WHERE?" ▮

### ③ Can't live without it

**Absolutely** alone. Silence imprisons her. Suffocating silence. She gets up and crosses the room. She presses the button.
Waits.
Three. Two. One.
**At once**, there is noise! Footsteps running down the stairs. Shouts and wonderful chaos **at last**! She smiles. Three voices shout in unison, ▮

### ④ Revenge is sweet

"You're sitting in my seat!" the woman said. She showed me her ticket and shouted **rudely**, "See? It's mine. Move."
I looked at the ticket **carefully**. Then I stood up **silently**.
As the train left the station, I whispered to her, ▮

**b** Read the four final sentences and match them to the stories. Which one do you think has the best ending?

A "She's gone to have a facial in a nice, *quiet* beauty salon."

B "Mom! The internet's not working!"

C "You have the right seat, but the wrong train."

D "My divorce papers," she replied <mark>angrily</mark>, and turned away.

**c** Look at the <mark>highlighted</mark> adverbs or adverbial phrases in the stories. Think about what they mean and write them in the correct place in the chart.

| Types of adverbs |
| --- |
| Time (when things happen, e.g., *immediately*) <br> *right now* _____  _____ |
| Manner (how you do something, e.g., *slowly*) <br> *rudely* _____  _____  _____ |
| Degree (describing / modifying an adjective, e.g., *very*) *incredibly* _____ <br> _____ |
| Comment (giving an opinion, e.g., *luckily*) <br> *sadly* _____ |
| Frequency (how often things happen, e.g., *rarely*) _____ |

**d** With a partner, decide where the **bold** adverbs should go in these sentences.

1 He speaks French and Spanish. **fluently**

2 I use public transportation. **hardly ever**

3 I thought I'd lost my phone, but it was in my bag. **fortunately**

4 It's important that you arrive on time. **extremely**

5 When I find out, I'll tell you. **immediately**

**e** 🔵 **p.137 Grammar Bank 3B**

**f** 🔴 **3.15** Listen to some sound effects and short conversations. Then use the **bold** adverb to complete the sentence.

1 When she got to the bus stop, the bus… **just**

2 They were having a party when… **suddenly**

3 He thought he had lost his boarding pass, but… **luckily**

4 The woman thought Andrea and Tom were friends, but in fact… **hardly**

5 The driver couldn't see where he was going because… **hard**

6 Salvatore couldn't understand the man because… **incredibly**

## 2 VOCABULARY adverbs and adverbial phrases

**a** Read another 50-word story. What do you think the missing word is?

### Hard rock

I <mark>nearly</mark> forget his birthday! I rush to the store. <mark>Lately</mark>, he enjoys listening to music, so I choose a Bluetooth speaker. I regret it now. His bedroom is <mark>near</mark> mine. The music is really loud! I open the door, and shout, "_____, it's <mark>late</mark>. Please turn the volume down!"

**b** Look at the <mark>highlighted</mark> adverbs. What's the difference between…?

a *near* and *nearly*    b *late* and *lately*

**c** 🟢 **p.155 Vocabulary Bank** Adverbs and adverbial phrases

## 3 PRONUNCIATION word stress and intonation

**a** 🔵 **3.18** Underline the stressed syllables in these adverbs. Listen and check.

| ab|so|lute|ly   ac|tu|a|lly   a|ppar|ent|ly   ba|si|ca|lly   de|fi|nite|ly |
| --- |
| e|spe|cia|lly   e|ven|tua|lly   fortu|nate|ly   gra|dua|lly   i|de|a|lly |
| in|cre|di|bly   luc|ki|lly   ob|vi|ous|ly   un|fortu|nate|ly |

**b** 🔵 **3.19** Listen and repeat the sentences, copying the stress and intonation of the adverbs.

1 There was a lot of traffic, and unfortunately, we arrived extremely late.

2 We definitely want to go abroad this summer, ideally somewhere hot.

3 It's incredibly easy – even a child could do it!

4 I thought Roberto was Portuguese, but actually he's Brazilian.

5 Apparently, Jack has been offered a promotion at work, but it will mean moving to New York.

6 I absolutely love Italian food, especially pasta.

## 4 WRITING

**a** You are going to write a 50-word story. It must be 50 words exactly (not including the title) and you must include at least two adverbs. Contracted forms (e.g., *I'd*) count as one word. First, in pairs, choose one of the titles below.

**A summer romance**   **A day to remember**
**The lie**   **Never again**

**b** Brainstorm ideas for the plot. Then together, write a first draft. Don't worry about the number of words.

**c** Now edit the story to make it exactly 50 words.

**d** Read two other pairs' stories. Which do you like best?

## 5 SPEAKING

**a** Look at the questions about reading habits and answer them with a partner.

### Reading habits

- **Which of the following do you read? How often?**

  PRINT
  comics or magazines
  fiction, e.g., classic or modern novels, short stories, graphic novels
  nonfiction, e.g., self-help books, history books, travel writing, guidebooks
  textbooks, manuals, or instructions

  ONLINE
  blogs    chat rooms / forums
  news reports and articles
  recipes    shopping websites
  social media    song lyrics
  study- or work-related articles

- **Why do you choose to read some things in print and some on-screen?**

- **What do you read, if anything, specifically to improve your English?**

**b** **© Communication** Reading habits p.108  Compare your reading habits.

## 6 READING & LISTENING

> **Reading for pleasure**
> When you read this story, you will understand it better and enjoy it more if you ask yourself questions from time to time. Think about…
>
> - the setting of the story: Where and when does it take place?
>
> - the characters: Who are they? What do they look like? What kinds of people are they? How do you feel about them?
>
> - the events of the story: What is happening at each stage? What might happen next?
>
> - the ending: What might have happened after the end of the story? What is the writer trying to say?

### Glossary
**franc** /fræŋk/ (*noun*) French currency, until the euro was introduced in 2002

# The Necklace
## BY GUY DE MAUPASSANT

### Part 1

**M**athilde Loisel was a pretty and charming girl, but born into a poor family. She was ambitious, and thought she deserved to be part of the highest level of French society. As she grew up, she was increasingly ashamed of her circumstances, but there was little she could do about it. Eventually, she married a clerk at the Ministry of Education.

They led a simple life, and Mathilde suffered. She felt that she deserved a life of luxury, and their poor house and ugly furniture, and just one young servant, made her miserable. She had no dresses, no jewelry, nothing. She never visited her one rich schoolfriend, Madame Forestier, because she could not bear to see the life that she herself would never have.

One evening, her husband came home, proudly holding in his hand a large envelope.

"Here," he said, "here's something for you."

She quickly opened it. It was an invitation from the Minister of Education to a party at the palace of the Ministry. But instead of being delighted, as her husband had hoped, she threw the invitation on the table.

"What do you want me to do with this?"

"My dear, I thought you would be pleased. You never go out, and this is a great occasion. I went to a lot of trouble to get the invitation. Everybody wants one and not many are given to the clerks. You will meet all kinds of important people there."

She looked at him impatiently and said, "What do you want me to wear to the party?"

He had not thought of that; he hesitated.

"The dress you wear to the theater—"

He stopped, as he saw that his wife was crying.

"What's the matter? What's the matter?"

Mathilde wiped her eyes and replied calmly, "Nothing. Only I have no dress, so I cannot go to this party. Give your invitation to some colleague whose wife has better clothes than I."

Her husband was heartbroken.

"Look here, Mathilde, how much would this cost, a proper dress?"

She thought for a few seconds, and answered, "I don't know exactly, but I think I could do it with four hundred francs."

He grew a little pale. He had saved exactly this amount for a short trip the following summer with his friends. But he said, "All right. I will give you four hundred francs. But make sure you get a pretty dress."

But as the day of the party drew near, Mathilde was still not happy. Although she now had her dress, she had no jewelry to go with it. When she told her husband, he suggested that she ask her friend Jeanne Forestier to lend her something.

Pleased with the idea, she went to her friend's house, and told her about her distress. Madame Forestier agreed to lend her something. She tried on several pieces, but nothing was right, until she suddenly saw a magnificent diamond necklace. To her joy, her friend let her borrow it.

**a** 🔊 **3.20** Read and listen to Part 1 of a short story. With a partner, continue sentences 1–8 **in your own words**.

1 Mathilde was unhappy because…
2 She never visited Madame Forestier because…
3 Her husband was proud when he came home one night because…
4 Mathilde threw the invitation on the table because…
5 Her husband was really upset because…
6 He was able to give her the money for a dress because…
7 Mathilde was still unhappy because….
8 She was delighted when she visited Madame Forestier because …

**When do you think the story takes place? What kinds of people are Mathilde and her husband? Who do you sympathize with more? Do you think Mathilde will enjoy the party?**

**b** 🔊 **3.21** Now listen to Part 2. Answer the questions with a partner.

1 Did Mathilde enjoy the party? Give examples.
2 How did they get home?
3 What did she discover when they got home?
4 What did her husband do?
5 What did they decide to do in the end?
6 How did they raise the money?
7 How did Madame Forestier react?

**How do you think their lives will change now?**

> **Glossary**
> **clasp** /klæsp/ (*noun*) a device that fastens something, such as a handbag, or the ends of a piece of jewelry
> **Palais Royal** /ˈpæleɪ rɔːˈjæl/ an expensive area of Paris

**c** 🔊 **3.22** Read and listen to Part 3. Answer the questions with a partner.

1 How did life change for Mathilde?
2 How did it change for her husband?
3 What had they achieved at the end of the ten years?
4 How had Mathilde changed over the ten years?

**Who do you think suffered the most, Mathilde or her husband? Why? What do you think would have happened if Mathilde hadn't lost the necklace? How do you think the story ends?**

**d** 🔊 **3.23** Listen to the end of the story. Did it end the way you expected?

**Do your feelings for Mathilde change during the story? What do you think might have happened after the final conversation? What do you think the message of the story is?**

> **Glossary**
> **Champs-Elysées** /ʃɑmz eiˈlizei/ the most famous and beautiful avenue in Paris, which goes from the Place de la Concorde to the Arc de Triomphe

## 7 WRITING

Ⓦ **p.116 Writing** A short story Write a short story of 140–190 words.

# Part 3

Mathilde now learned the terrible life of the really poor. Heroically, she made the best of it. The debt must be paid. She would pay it. They dismissed their servant; they left their house and rented a small attic under the roof.

She learned how to do housework, and how to cook. She washed the dishes, wearing out her pink nails on the greasy pots and the bottoms of the pans. She washed their dirty sheets and clothes. She took their rubbish down to the street every morning, and she carried up the water, pausing for breath on every floor. Wearing old, worn-out clothes, she went out to the greengrocer, the grocer, the butcher, with a basket on her arm, bargaining, insulted, fighting to save a sou here or there.

Every month, they had to pay back part of the money they had borrowed. Her husband worked in the evening, doing the accounts for a shopkeeper, and at night, often, he did copying at five sous the page.

This life lasted ten years. At the end of ten years, they had paid everything back, everything, with all the accumulation of interest.

With her badly combed hair, and her red hands, Mathilde now looked like an old woman. But sometimes, when her husband was at the office, she sat down by the window, and she thought of that evening long ago, of that party, where she had been so beautiful and so admired.

What would have happened if she had not lost that necklace? Who knows? Who knows?

> **Glossary**
> **sou** /suː/ (*noun*) an old French coin worth very little (100 sous = 1 franc)

🔘 **Go online** to review the lesson

## 1 ▶ THE INTERVIEW Part 1

**a** Read the biographical information about Marion Pomeranc. In what way are the two parts of her career connected?

**Marion Pomeranc** is the manager of literary programs at a non-profit organization in New York City called Learning Leaders. The programs involve encouraging children to read by providing books for children who don't have much access to them, and getting adults to come in and read to them, and discuss the books. She is also the author of three children's books, *The Hand-Me-Down Horse*, *The American Wei*, and *The Can Do Thanksgiving*. She believes in dealing with serious topics in her books such as hunger and immigration, but in a way that children can relate to.

**b** Watch Part 1 of an interview with her. Why does she mention these four books?

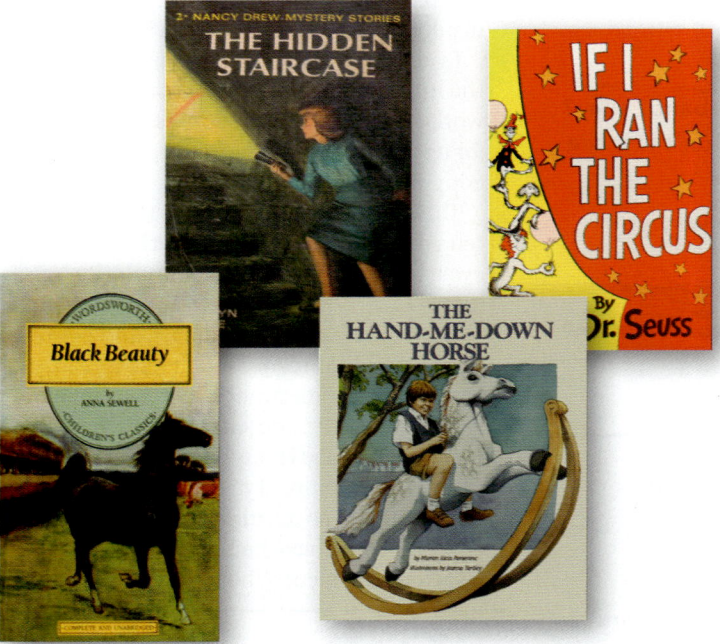

**c** Now watch again and mark the sentences **T** (true) or **F** (false). Say why the **F** sentences are false.

1 What Marion loved about *If I Ran the Circus* was the pictures.
2 She helped her parents to become readers.
3 She read to her son a few times a week.
4 Her son reads mainly fiction these days.
5 Marion doesn't like the fact that children's authors today write about real life.

**Glossary**
***Corduroy*** a children's book by Don Freeman about a teddy bear
**fiction** a type of literature that describes imaginary people and events

## ▶ Part 2

**a** Now watch Part 2. What does Marion say is important for getting a) teenagers to read more b) younger children to read.

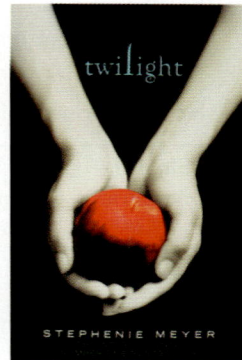

**b** Watch again. Check (✓) the things that she says are good for encouraging teenagers and children to read.

**Teenagers**
1 ☐ Not insisting on them finishing a book.
2 ☐ Getting them to buy e-books.
3 ☐ Suggesting that they read in bed at night.
4 ☐ Accepting that they don't just have to read books to become good readers.
5 ☐ Series of books where the same characters reoccur.

**Children**
1 ☐ Having a lot of books in the house.
2 ☐ Going to visit libraries or publishers.
3 ☐ Always buying them books as birthday presents.
4 ☐ Hearing authors talk about their books.
5 ☐ Books where children have a more active role than the adults.
6 ☐ Books with beautiful illustrations.

**Glossary**
**ads** abbreviation for advertisements
**goofy** silly or foolish

 **Part 3**

**a** Now watch Part 3. Is Marion positive or negative about new technology and the future of books?

**b** Watch again and answer the questions.

1 Why does she prefer to read on an e-reader these days?
2 Why does she think all children should have an e-reader ?
3 In what way does she think social media can be positive for kids?
4 How often does she read for pleasure? Where, when, and why?

## 2 ▶ LOOKING AT LANGUAGE

> 🔍 **Ways of giving yourself time to think**
> Marion often gives herself time to think when she is answering questions by repeating the question or stopping and starting again. She also uses filler sounds such as "um" and "uh," and certain words or phrases, e.g., *you know*, etc. that don't add meaning but that are used for this purpose.

🔊 **3.27** Watch some extracts from the interview and complete the missing words or phrases.

1 I What was it that you liked about Dr. Seuss?
   M _____ _____ _____ about Dr. Seuss is his use of language…
2 " _____ _____, the made-up words, the way the words flow together and sound."
3 "…or you can read the side of a cereal box. _____ _____, that's all reading."
4 "And I think if you'd look carefully at books that kids really like, it's the one where, where youth dominates. And _____ _____ rules the world a little bit."
5 I Do you think social media has decreased or increased people's literacy?
   M _____ _____ I think social media has had a positive effect on children.

## 3 ▶ THE CONVERSATION

**a** Watch the conversation. Who (E, D, or I)…?

☐ recommends one book
☐ recommends more than one book
☐ doesn't recommend a specific book

**b** Watch again. Answer the questions with **A** (Harry Potter), **B** (*The Diving Bell and the Butterfly*), or **C** (*Everything I Know About Love*).

Which book…?

1 ☐ did Emma tell lots of friends to read
2 ☐ has Ida never heard of
3 ☐ isn't very long
4 ☐ has David never read
5 ☐ does Ida think has influenced people from all over the world
6 ☐ is about the author's life and upbringing
7 ☐ was David both moved and uplifted by
8 ☐ does Emma think sounds good because you learn from other people's experiences
9 ☐ is set in the present day

**c** Have you read any of the books they mention? If no, did what they say make you want to read them? Is there a book you think everyone should read?

**d** Watch an extract and ⓒircle the vague language you hear. Are the other options also possible?

**Emma** I think, from, like, all of my friends that are my age, we all kind of read it when we were young and it just becomes, [1]*I mean / like*, everyone knows what you mean when you talk about your Hogwarts house, for example.

**Ida** Yeah.

**Emma** And you just [2]*kind of / sort of* lose yourself in this fantasy. The book that you read as a child, I still kind of re-read it every few years and a lot of people have said that it's helped them deal with, like, grief and…

**David** Wow!

**Emma** …[3]*stuff like that / things like that*. So, I think it's actually quite powerful.

**Ida** I think also because, like you were saying, you, you, [4]*kind of / sort of* grew up with it.

**e** Now have a conversation in groups of three.

1 Do you think people who read are normally more intelligent than people who don't?
2 Do you think that young people have problems reading long or difficult texts because of the kind of reading they do on social media? Is this a problem?

🔄 **Go online** to watch the video, review the lesson, and check your progress

# 4A Stormy weather

**G** future perfect and future continuous   **V** the environment, weather   **P** vowel sounds

> You cannot go through a single day without having an impact on the world around you.
> *Jane Goodall, UK anthropologist*

## 1 SPEAKING

**a** What do you understand by the expression *environmentally friendly*? Can you think of any synonyms? On a scale of 1–10, how environmentally friendly do you think a) your friends and family are, b) people in your town are?

**b** Complete the questionnaire and figure out your score. Then compare with a partner. Give examples to explain your answers.

**c** **C Communication** Your score p.108  Read about what your score means.

### Are you **really** as environmentally friendly as you think you are?

**A Your "values"**

Circle the statement (1–5) that best describes your habits. Write the number in the box.

1 I don't really do anything environmentally friendly.

2 I do one or two things that are environmentally friendly.

3 I do quite a few things that are environmentally friendly.

4 Most things I do are environmentally friendly.

5 Everything I do is environmentally friendly.

**Your value score =** ☐

**B Your "actions"**

How often do you do each of the following? Score each action from 1 (never) to 5 (always).

a ☐ turn off lights when you leave a room

b ☐ put on a sweater rather than turning up the heat

c ☐ avoid buying something with a lot of packaging

d ☐ take your own shopping bag

e ☐ use public transportation instead of driving

f ☐ walk or ride your bike

g ☐ buy recycled toilet paper

h ☐ avoid taking airline flights

i ☐ avoid leaving your TV on when you're not watching it

j ☐ turn the faucet off when brushing your teeth

**Your action score =** ☐

**Your overall score**

First, figure out your "actions" score. Take the average of section **B** (add up and divide by 10) and write the number in the box.

Subtract your "value" score **A** from your "action" score **B**.

## 2 GRAMMAR future perfect and future continuous

**a** Look at the title of the infographic. What predictions do you think it will make about the things in the box?

> energy   waste   transportation   food and water   the weather

**b** Now read the infographic. How many of your predictions were there? With a partner, say which ones…

1 you think are likely to happen in the next 20 years.
2 you think will definitely happen in the next 20 years.
3 you think probably won't ever happen.
4 you would most and least like to come true.

# How will we be living in 20 YEARS?

## ENERGY

Fossil fuels, like coal and gas, will be very expensive. Most people ¹ will have installed solar panels or wind turbines on their houses or apartment buildings to generate their electricity.

## WASTE

People ² will be recycling nearly 100% of their waste (and those who don't will have to pay a fine). All stores and cafés ³ will have stopped using plastic bags and single-use containers, like to-go coffee cups.

## TRANSPORTATION

Governments ⁴ will have invested a lot of money in public transportation. Everyone ⁵ will be riding their bikes, walking, or using the bus and train more. Low-cost airlines ⁶ will have disappeared and flights will be much more expensive.

## FOOD AND WATER

Farmers ⁷ will have stopped producing meat commercially and many kinds of fish ⁸ will have died out. Fresh water ⁹ will be running out in many parts of the world, and we ¹⁰ will be getting much of our water from the ocean (through desalination plants).

## THE WEATHER

We ¹¹ will be having more extreme weather, and heatwaves, hurricanes, floods, etc., will be frequent occurrences. Many ski resorts ¹² will have closed because of a lack of winter snow, and some low-lying beaches and vacation resorts ¹³ will have disappeared completely.

**c** Look at the highlighted verbs in the predictions. Which ones refer to…?

a an action or situation that will be finished in the future
b an action or situation that will be in progress in the future

**d** **G** p.138 **Grammar Bank 4A**

**e** Talk to a partner and say if you think the following predictions will happen. Explain why (not).

## In 20 years…

- everyone will be using their own reusable shopping bags, cups, and bottles.

- most people will have stopped eating any animal products and will be eating a vegan diet.

- all private swimming pools and golf courses will have been banned.

- people will be taking more vacations in their own country and fewer abroad.

- car companies will only be selling electric cars.

- most people in office jobs will be working from home.

 *definitely*, *probably*, and *likely / unlikely*
We often use verb + *definitely* or *probably*, and *be likely / unlikely* + infinitive when talking about the future, especially when we are making predictions.

> **I think…**
> it'll definitely happen.
> it's (very) likely to happen.
> it'll probably happen.
> it probably won't happen.
> it's (very) unlikely to happen.
> it definitely won't happen.

**f** Now make your own predictions about things in the box.

> fashion   health and medicine   housing
> politics   shopping   social media

## 3 VOCABULARY weather

**a** Look at the photos. What kinds of weather events can you see? When did you last see them where you live?

**b** **V** p.156 **Vocabulary Bank** Weather

## 4 PRONUNCIATION vowel sounds

**a** Look at the groups of words. What is the common sound in each group? Write the sound words for 1–10.

| | | |
|---|---|---|
| 1 | _owl_ | sh**ow**er  dr**ou**ght |
| 2 | _____ | bel**ow**  sn**ow** |
| 3 | _____ | c**oo**l  h**u**mid  mons**oo**n  typh**oo**n |
| 4 | _____ | fl**oo**d  th**u**nder |
| 5 | _____ | h**ea**vy  w**ea**ther |
| 6 | _____ | h**ea**t wave  br**ee**ze  fr**ee**zing |
| 7 | _____ | p**ou**ring  st**or**m  sc**or**ching  w**ar**m |
| 8 | _____ | dr**i**zzling  ch**i**lly |
| 9 | _____ | br**igh**t  **i**cy  l**igh**tning  m**i**ld |
| 10 | _____ | cl**ea**r  z**e**ro |

**b** **4.6** Listen and check. Practice saying the groups of words.

## 5 READING

**a** Read the introduction to the website of the Climate Stories Project. What is the project about?

**b** Now look at the photos and read what six people from different continents have to say about climate change. Then with a partner, try to label the photos with the countries where they are from.

**c** Read the stories again. Then look at the things in the list. For each one, say who mentions them and why they are significant.

1 one month's rainfall
2 September 21st
3 Los Angeles and Manhattan
4 the river
5 _przedwiośnie_
6 beautiful properties and parks

**d** Which person mentions things that are also happening where you live?

# Climate Stories Project

Today, more and more of us are feeling the effects of climate change on a personal and community level. The Climate Stories Project allows people from around the world to share their stories about climate change and explain the impact that it is having on our lives.

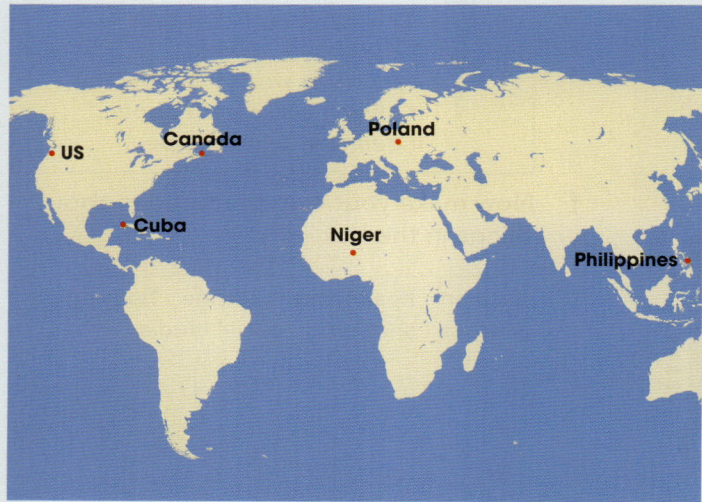

### Diana Maciaga
**from _____**

We don't have major hurricanes or wildfires, but you can see that the weather patterns have been changing. For example, the winters are much milder than they used to be 20 years ago, and in the summers, we often have a huge heat wave. We used to have a special name for a period that is between winter and spring: we call it _przedwiośnie_, and now it doesn't really happen. So for me, this is one of the most significant examples of the changes in climate.

### Umberto Crespo Palmarito
**from _____**

Here, the rainy season used to start in March and the rain stopped in November. Now, the heavy rain only starts in June. Years ago, it would be pouring rain every day. And now there can be a week, 15 days, without any rain. My grandfather and my father lived their life according to the weather because it was like a clock: it was never wrong. We used to say that September 21st was the day the weather changed. And now people don't say it. It's completely different from before.

## 6 LISTENING

**a** You're going to listen to Matt Wallace, a meteorologist, talking about his job. First, in pairs, read the questions and guess what he's going to answer.

1 What's the difference between a meteorologist and a TV weatherman?
2 How far ahead can you accurately predict the weather?
3 Are long-term forecasts ever accurate?
4 What's your favorite kind of weather?
5 In what ways have you noticed that the weather has changed in the last ten years?
6 Are you optimistic or pessimistic about climate change?

**b** ◀)) 4.7 Listen to the interview once. Did you guess correctly in **a**?

**c** Listen again. What examples does he give for the following?

1 an occasion when it's difficult to predict the weather
2 how weather in one part of the world affects another part
3 why thunderstorms are exciting to watch at night
4 some unusual weather this year in the US
5 the effects of climate change on the US weather

**d** Do you think Matt enjoys his job? Why?

## 7 SPEAKING

Talk to a partner.

### Let's talk about the weather
- What's your favorite kind of weather? And your least favorite?
- How does the weather affect your mood?
- Do people in your country complain much about the weather? What kind of weather in particular?
- In what ways has climate change affected the weather in your country?
- Are you optimistic or pessimistic about climate change?

**Have you, or has anyone you know, ever been somewhere when...?**
- it poured rain for days and days
- there was a flood
- there was a hurricane or it was incredibly windy
- it was absolutely freezing
- it was very foggy, or there was bad smog
- there was a terrible heat wave
- you were caught outside in a thunderstorm

🔍 **Modifiers with strong adjectives**
When you are talking about extreme situations, e.g., very bad weather, you can use:

1 normal adjectives with a modifier (*very, really, extremely, incredibly, unbelievably*), e.g., *It was incredibly cold / extremely hot / unbelievably windy*, etc.
2 strong adjectives, e.g., *It's boiling here – 100 degrees. It's freezing today*, etc.
3 Strong adjectives with *absolutely*, e.g., *It was absolutely freezing. The midday heat was absolutely scorching.*

**Nadine Lefort**
from _____

For many years, we had less snow in the winter, and then this past year we had an extreme winter – freezing, with terrible blizzards – so weather patterns are changing and it's less predictable. Another thing I notice is that the coasts seem to be eroding much more quickly than they were in the past. It's sad, because so many beautiful properties and parks are right on the coast and it will be a shame to see them gone. People are saying that they'd never buy or build in those places because they'll be gone in the future.

**Harou Abass Hadiza**
from _____

When I was in elementary school, my friends and I used to go to the river. It was green, and the air was cool and fresh. Some of us were afraid to go far from the riverbank when we were swimming, because the river was deep and had a strong current. However, in the last few years, we've been experiencing increasingly hot weather – extreme heat. Now the river isn't so deep, and it's dusty and dirty. Air quality in my city has also declined. There is more dust, due to desertification.

**Efleda Bautista**
from _____

I come from Tacloban City, the city that was hit by Typhoon Haiyan, and this is really a prime example of what climate change can do to destroy a community. We had a long drought, and then rainfall equivalent to one month's rainfall falling in one or two days in the city, and everywhere was flooded. That never happened before, and it's closely connected with climate change.

**Jordan Hamada**
from _____

There hasn't been a big snowstorm here for over ten years. This area is known for its rain, and there hasn't been much for the past few months, and I'm pretty surprised, because it's been so dry this winter. It's definitely not something I think about all the time, but I've seen some articles recently talking about how Los Angeles and Manhattan will eventually be under water, possibly in our lifetime, or the next generation's lifetime, and that makes it seem very real – that's definitely a scary thought.

🔁 **Go online** to review the lesson

**G** zero and first conditionals, future time clauses  **V** expressions with *take*  **P** linked phrases

## 1 LISTENING

**a** Look at the things on the list. How risky do you personally think they are? Why? Score them 1–5 (1 = not risky at all, 5 = very risky). Then compare in small groups. How similar are you in your attitude to risk?

- having cosmetic surgery
- riding a bike in your city
- smoking
- eating street food when you're traveling
- buying a used car
- hiking in the mountains
- online dating
- telling a lie on your résumé

**b** 🔊 **4.8** Listen to four people answering the question *Are you a risk-taker?* Write ✓, ✗, or ✓/✗ in the box. Which of the topics in the box does the risk they talk about relate to?

| | a job | a sport | a relationship | money |
|---|---|---|---|---|
| 1 Holly | | | | |
| 2 Natalie | | | | |
| 3 Tom | | | | |
| 4 Jeanie | | | | |

**c** Listen again and write **H** (Holly), **N** (Natalie), **T** (Tom), or **J** (Jeanie).

Who...?

1 ___ thinks his / her attitude about risk hasn't changed at all throughout his / her life
2 ___ thinks that the risk varies depending on the price
3 ___ had to make a life-changing decision
4 ___ is surprised about how positive he / she felt after doing a risky activity
5 ___ thinks most people take this kind of risk these days
6 ___ decided not to go right into working in an office
7 ___ wonders whether things might have been different if he / she hadn't taken the risk
8 ___ thinks the risk was worth taking because he / she learned some useful things for the future

**d** Which speaker do you think took the biggest risk? Why?

## 2 SPEAKING

**a** Work with a partner. **A** interview **B** with the questions in the green circles. After each question, write *R* if you think that **B** is prepared to take risks in that area. Then **B** interview **A** in the same way with the blue circles.

**b** Now compare your answers in each area. Decide which of you is the bigger risk-taker.

### Appearance

Have you ever done something dramatically different to your hair, e.g., had a very different hairstyle or hair color? How did you feel immediately afterwards?

Would you ever get a tattoo or a piercing?

### On the road

Do you drive a car or ride a motorcycle? Do you ever go really fast and break the speed limit?

Do you walk by yourself late at night, or take late-night taxis?

Where do you usually cross the street – at a traffic light or crosswalk, or just anywhere?

### Shopping and money

Do you have different PINs and passwords, or do you always use the same one?

Do you use internet or mobile banking? Do you think it's safe? Have you ever lost any money from computer fraud?

Have you ever bought something expensive on eBay or a similar site? Would you?

## 3 GRAMMAR zero and first conditionals, future time clauses

**a** Match the sentence halves.

1 If my dad finds out I've been hitchhiking,
2 When you're crossing the street in the US,
3 As soon as I've passed my driver's test,
4 If it's still snowing tomorrow,
5 When we've booked the flights,
6 Unless you lend her that money,
7 If his temperature hasn't gone down,
8 If it doesn't rain by the end of the week,

A all the plants in the garden will have died.
B he'll be furious.
C I'm going to buy a car.
D make sure you look left and right.
E she won't be able to buy a train ticket.
F we need to start looking for hotels.
G we won't be driving anywhere.
H he isn't going to school tomorrow.

### Food

If you were offered very unusual food that you'd never had before, would you try it? Why (not)?

If food is past its sell-by date, would you still eat it? Have you ever had food poisoning from eating something that wasn't fresh?

### Travel

Have you ever gone on vacation with someone you didn't know very well?

Have you ever taken selfies on vacation in a dangerous place, e.g., on the edge of a cliff?

Do you usually take out insurance when you travel?

If you're traveling somewhere, do you usually get to the station or airport with plenty of time, or do you always arrive at the last minute?

### Work and study

Would you accept a job abroad in a country where you didn't speak the language?

Have you ever put off studying for an exam to the last minute? Did you pass?

**b** Look at the highlighted verbs. In first conditional sentences and future time clauses, what forms or tenses can you use…?

1 after *if*, *when*, etc. (1–8)
2 in the main clause (A–H)

**c** Now look at two more conditional sentences. Do the **bold** clauses refer to a) something that is a possible consequence of the *if*-clause, or b) something that is always a consequence of the *if*-clause?

1 If you don't take out travel insurance, **you run the risk of paying expensive medical fees**.
2 If you use online banking, **it's essential to never share your password**.

**d** Ⓖ p.139 Grammar Bank 4B

**e** In pairs, complete each sentence in your own words.

1 Don't buy a used car unless…
2 You shouldn't think about getting a tattoo if…
3 Keep a first-aid kit in your house in case…
4 Children shouldn't use social media until…
5 Always take out travel insurance in case…
6 As soon as you've received your new credit card,…
7 Don't go hiking in the mountains on your own unless…
8 If you are taking a new job abroad,…

## 4 PRONUNCIATION linked phrases

**a** 🔊 4.12 Listen and complete the sentence below with three words. Can you explain why a) the first and second words are linked together, b) the second and third words are linked together?

I'll call you _____ the mail's been delivered.

**b** 🔊 4.13 Listen and complete the sentences with more linked phrases.

1 Don't call me _____ emergency.
2 As _____ concerned, you have to be crazy to want to do an extreme sport.
3 Be careful with your wallet, _____, don't use your phone on the street.
4 It was _____ experience that I've never forgotten it.
5 I dyed my hair blue a _____, and I hated it!
6 I was scared at first, but it was _____ the end.
7 _____, let's try to find a cheap hotel.
8 _____ world, everyone would earn a salary.

**c** In pairs, practice saying the highlighted phrases quickly, trying to link the words together. Then make personal sentences with as many of the phrases as you can.

*I never go to the doctor unless it's an emergency.*

## 5  READING

1
2
3
4

**a** Look at the photos and label them with a sport from the box. What other extreme sports do you know?

| bungee jumping   paragliding   skydiving   wingsuit flying |

**b** Now look at the title of an article about extreme sports, and read the article. Check (✓) the three reasons it gives.

1 ☐ More and more celebrities are taking them up.
2 ☐ Once some people have tried it, they can't stop.
3 ☐ People find traditional sports, like soccer, not challenging enough.
4 ☐ People want to have new experiences.
5 ☐ They are better known because you can watch other people doing them live online.
6 ☐ It's cheaper to do extreme sports than ever before.

**c** Look at 1–7 below and think about what information is missing: a name or a number. Then read the article again and fill in the blanks.

1 _____: the typical speed of a wingsuit flyer
2 _____: the age that Zanon was when he died
3 _____ and _____: the two men killed wingsuit flying in the US a few years ago
4 _____: the number of people who parachuted for the first time last year
5 _____: the percentage of female climbers now
6 _____: the woman who paraglided off a mountain in Turkey
7 _____: one of world's best female wingsuit flyers

**d** Read the last paragraph again. What do you think the writer means when he says *Maybe the future of extreme sports is about learning to be less extreme*? Do you agree?

**e** Talk to a partner.

Have you ever done an extreme sport?
Did you enjoy it? Why (not)?
Which extreme sport that you have never done would you most / least like to try?

**Glossary**
**Taft Point** a very high granite rock in Yosemite /yuˈsɛmɪti/ National Park, California
**GoPro** a compact action camera capable of taking photos and videos in extreme conditions

# WHY ARE DEADLY EXTREME SPORTS MORE POPULAR THAN EVER?

Two men leap from the top of the mountain and spread their wings to fly down one of the most dangerous routes in one of the world's most dangerous sports. Dario Zanon and Graham Dickinson are experts at wingsuit flying. Using pieces of cloth that join their arms and legs, they fly past cliff edges and between trees at over 110 mph. Then they release their parachutes and drift down to land. This video has been watched over ten million times on social media.

A few months later, Zanon returned to Chamonix and climbed the Aiguille du Midi on the other side of the valley, for a solo flight. On that Sunday, his body was found on the glaciers 5,000 feet below. He was 33. Most likely no one will ever know exactly which small thing went wrong. Small things become big quickly at 110 mph. It does happen to the best. Mark Sutton, the man who parachuted into the London Olympics stadium dressed as James Bond, was killed wingsuit flying in the Swiss Alps, while filming for EpicTV. Dean Potter, a famous US wingsuit flyer, died with his friend Graham Hunt. They had jumped from Taft Point in California.

Today extreme sports are booming. Skydiving is a good example – in 2006, the British Parachute Association recorded 39,100 first jumps, but last year there were 59,679. The number of people climbing Everest has rocketed since the 1990s, and the proportion of women climbers is increasing, up from about 16% in 2002 to 36% now.

"You just get into it and then progressively build up," says Jess Cox, 27, an instructor at her father's paragliding business. "Better flights involve going higher, further, doing acrobatic stuff." She shows me a video on her phone, of when she and a friend jumped off a mountain in Turkey. "Woo-hoo!" she squeals, watching. "I'd say that was one of the best days of my life. It's completely addictive. Some people become completely obsessed, quit their jobs, and just travel around the world, leaping off things." Science teacher Becky, on the other hand, didn't get addicted. "I did a skydive once and I've also done bungee jumping. The skydive was good, yes. I've no particular need to do it again. But," she says, "life would be a bit boring if people didn't try new things."

Extreme sports constantly push people to test the ultimate limits of their own safety. They are jumping blindfolded, or with their dog, or skydiving without a parachute into a giant net – and you'll find all these online, thanks to action cameras. One hundred hours of GoPro video are uploaded onto YouTube every minute, and sales of these cameras are growing at 50% a year. Watching other people do these things is attracting many more new participants.

A good soccer player or tennis player always wants to be tested against better opponents, but their opponents are human. In extreme sports, the opponent is danger. So how can you get better without killing yourself? Steph Davis, one of the world's best-known climbers and wingsuit flyers, wrote, "Perhaps getting better means becoming more elegant." Maybe the future of extreme sports is about learning to be less extreme.

## 6 VOCABULARY expressions with *take*

**a** 🔊 **4.14** Listen to Sophie Rees, who works in the ski industry, answering six questions about extreme sports. Match her answers 1–6 to questions A–F.

A ☐ Are you ever afraid that you might get injured or killed?

B ☐ Do you think extreme sports are more popular with men than with women?

C ☐ What other extreme sports have you done?

D ☐ What's the first extreme sport you did? When was it?

E ☐ Why do you enjoy extreme sports?

F ☐ Why do you think extreme sports are becoming more popular?

**b** Listen again. How does she answer each question?

**c** Look at three extracts from the interview with Sophie. Can you remember what the missing words are?

1 I take _____ my dad – we're both sports-crazy.

2 I think it's because I love taking _____; I love the adrenaline rush.

3 I think more and more people are taking _____ in extreme sports…

**d** Look at some more expressions and phrasal verbs with *take*. With a partner, try to figure out their meaning from the context.

**Expressions with *take***

1 My neighbor takes care of my son while I'm at work.

2 You should take advantage of that job offer. It's a great opportunity.

3 The concert will take place on March 6th.

4 You don't need to hurry. Take your time.

5 Regarding evaluation, coursework is taken into account, as well as exam results.

6 Lina took part in a charity walk and raised $500 for a local animal shelter.

7 The dog looked so hungry that I took pity on it, and gave it some of my food.

**Phrasal verbs with *take***

8 Take your jacket off – it's hot in here.
The flight will take off in about 20 minutes.

9 I'd love to take up snowboarding – it sounds really exciting.

10 My boyfriend's little sister has really taken to me – she always wants to play with me.

11 Our company is growing quickly. We're planning to take on three new employees in the marketing department.

12 Elias is taking me out for dinner tonight to a great new restaurant.
Please take the trash out. It's beginning to smell.

**e** 🄲 **Communication** I'll take a question **A p.108  B p.114**
Ask and answer questions with *take*.

## 7 WRITING

Ⓦ **p.117 Writing** For and against  Write a blog post.

## 8 ▶ VIDEO LISTENING

**a** Watch a documentary about Grace Doyle. How did surfing help her through a difficult time in her life?

> **Glossary**
> **surfboard** a long narrow piece of hard material that you stand on to surf (also **body~**, a short, light board that you ride lying on your front)
> **wipe out** to fall, especially when doing a sport such as surfing or skiing

**b** Watch the documentary again and complete the information with one or two words.

1 Grace is from a small town in _____.

2 She originally trained to be a _____.

3 She got interested in surfing when she was young because of her _____.

4 Grace has surfed abroad in places such as Central America, _____, and _____.

5 The global surfing business is worth about a _____ billion _____.

6 Grace thinks that media coverage is one reason why surfing has become _____.

7 According to Grace, people are attracted to surfing because it's _____ and _____.

8 If you fall off a big wave, you need to hold your _____ and _____.

9 Grace enjoys the balance between the danger of injury and the chance she might get the _____ _____ of her life.

10 In highly competitive surfing, there's a real risk that you could get _____ or even _____.

**c** Do you think doing something that gives you an "adrenaline rush" is always more enjoyable? What things do you do that are "both healthy and fun?"

Ⓝ **Go online** to watch the video and review the lesson

## GRAMMAR

**a** (Circle) a, b, or c.

1  When we got to Terminal 2, the flight from Seoul ____.
   a  had already landed   b  had already been landing
   c  already landed

2  When we arrived at the airport, we ____ that our flight was delayed.
   a  had discovered   b  were discovering
   c  discovered

3  We ____ for about an hour when suddenly the plane began to lose altitude.
   a  had been flying   b  were flying   c  flew

4  Nico's father ____.
   a  speaks English fluently   b  speaks English fluent
   c  speaks fluently English

5  ____. I just need another five minutes.
   a  I'm finished almost   b  Almost I'm finished
   c  I'm almost finished

6  The driver ____ in the accident.
   a  seriously was injured   b  was injured seriously
   c  was seriously injured

7  The car ____ 50,000 miles – we'll need to get it serviced.
   a  will soon have reached   b  will soon reach
   c  will soon be reaching

8  You can watch TV as soon as ____ your homework.
   a  you'll finish   b  you're finishing   c  you've finished

9  If the tickets cost more than $100, ____.
   a  I don't go   b  I'm not going to go
   c  I won't have gone

10  She won't get accepted into a good college ____ she works really hard next year.
   a  until   b  unless   c  in case

**b** Complete the sentences with the correct form of the verb in **bold**.

1  Imagine! This time tomorrow we _____ on the beach. **lie**

2  The game starts at 7:00. By the time I get home, it _____ already. **start**

3  You can't use your cell phone until the plane _____. **land**

4  Many people have problems sleeping if they _____ coffee after midday. **drink**

5  I want to spend a year traveling when I _____ from college. **graduate**

## VOCABULARY

**a** Write words for the definitions.

1  g_____ the place where you wait to board your flight

2  b_____ c_____ the place where you pick up your luggage after you've arrived

3  a_____ the passage between the rows of seats inside a plane

4  t_____ a series of sudden and violent changes in wind direction that affects flights

5  j_____ l_____ the feeling of being tired and confused after a long-haul flight

**b** (Circle) the correct word.

1  **A** How was your *trip / travel*?   **B** Great, thanks.

2  Gina and I haven't seen each other much *late / lately*.

3  Our hotel has a great view! We can *even / ever* see the Eiffel Tower!

4  I've been working too *hard / hardly* lately.

5  I love all pasta, but *especially / specially* lasagna.

**c** Complete with the verb in the past tense.

1  The wind bl_____ so hard that two trees fell down.

2  The taxi dr_____ me off outside the terminal.

3  It p_____ rain last night and I got really wet coming home from work.

4  She g_____ on the bus, but there was nowhere to sit.

5  We t_____ advantage of the good weather and spent the day at the beach.

**d** (Circle) the word that is different.

1  breeze   wind   hurricane   blizzard
2  chilly   boiling   hot   scorching
3  fog   damp   mist   smog
4  cold   freezing   bright   icy
5  hail   thunder   lightning   drought

**e** Complete with one word.

1  We checked _____ as soon as we got to the airport.

2  The most dangerous moments during a flight are when the plane is taking _____ or landing.

3  I've decided to take _____ running. I need to lose some weight.

4  Who do you take _____ most in your family?

5  The final will take _____ in Vancouver next Saturday.

## PRONUNCIATION

**a** Circle the word with a different sound.

| | | | | | |
|---|---|---|---|---|---|
| 1 | | pouring | storm | hardly | warm |
| 2 | | weather | heavy | changeable | pleasant |
| 3 | | lounge | snow | cold | closed |
| 4 | | luggage | flood | thunder | humid |
| 5 | | rain | aisle | lately | delayed |

**b** Underline the main stressed syllable.

1 e|ven|tua|lly     3 e|specia|lly     5 hurr|i|cane
2 gra|dua|lly       4 pa|ssen|ger

## CAN YOU understand this text?

**a** Read the article once. Which volcano is the most challenging to climb?

**b** Read the article again. Answer the questions with Misti (**M**), Ngauruhoe (**N**), or Teide (**T**).

1 It's famous because it was in a movie.
2 It's no longer an active volcano.
3 It can be freezing there, even in the summer.
4 It's the highest of the three volcanoes.
5 You don't have to have a guide.
6 You can see volcanic activity during the hike.

## ▶ CAN YOU understand these people?

🔊 4.15 Watch or listen and choose a, b, or c.

| 1 | 2 | 3 | 4 |
|---|---|---|---|
| Claudia | Rafael | Diarmuid | Julia |

1 When Claudia flew to Shanghai, ____.
   a the flight started in London
   b she was able to eat on the plane
   c the flight took off in the morning
2 Rafael ____.
   a often reads novels
   b doesn't read very fast
   c never reads online
3 When Diarmuid was living in Japan, and there were typhoons, ____.
   a he wasn't allowed to leave the house
   b a lot of people panicked
   c his building was destroyed
4 Julia enjoyed waterskiing ____ the dangers.
   a because she was addicted to
   b despite knowing about
   c because she was ignorant of

# INCREDIBLE VOLCANOES TO CLIMB

**Mount Misti** is Peru's most famous volcano. It is also its most active, so climbers must be aware of any eruption threats before attempting the exhilarating two-day hike to the summit. Due to the challenging environmental conditions, few people reach the top of the volcano. Ice picks and crampons are often a necessity, making this a difficult hike for a climbing novice, but a welcome challenge for anyone wanting to test their limits. You will need a guide, who will provide you with safe overnight accommodations. Along the way, look for hot gases hissing through volcanic cracks. From the summit, at 19,101 feet, you can look down at the city of Arequipa and see neighboring volcanoes Chachani and Pikchu Pikchu.

**Mount Ngauruhoe** has become one of New Zealand's most popular climbing locations since its star turn as Mount Doom in Peter Jackson's *The Lord of the Rings* trilogy. After its last eruption in 1975, Mount Ngauruhoe's Volcanic Alert Level has dramatically reduced, although it is still listed as an active volcano. Ngauruhoe is 7,515 feet high, and a 90-minute walk takes you to the foot of the volcano. The hike takes about eight hours altogether. The first 45 minutes are suitable for children and the elderly, but the climb then becomes more dramatic, with a steep slope and few opportunities to rest. It's a challenging hike across loose rock surfaces, ice caps and at times sub-zero temperatures, even in summer. This is one for adrenaline seekers. You will also need a guide.

**Mount Teide** is Europe's highest volcano. It lies 12,198 feet above sea level on Tenerife, the largest island in the Canaries. Last erupting in 1909, it is now a dormant volcano that attracts eager climbers each year. Hikers can attempt to reach Teide's summit throughout the year, but due to the scorching summer heat, it is best to climb it during the spring (April–May) and fall (September–October) when the weather is mildest. The terrain is not too treacherous, and the low altitude trails are accessible to climbers of all abilities. The five- to seven-hour trek to the summit is a challenging expedition, but when you reach the top and gaze down at Tenerife and its neighboring islands, all your efforts will be worthwhile.

🔍 **Go online** to watch the video, review Files 3 & 4, and check your progress

# 5A | I'm a survivor

> Survival can be summed up in three words – never give up. That's the heart of it, really. Just keep trying.
> *Bear Grylls, adventurer, writer, and TV host*

**G** unreal conditionals    **V** feelings    **P** word stress in three- or four-syllable adjectives

## 1 SPEAKING

**a** Read survival questions 1–6. How do you think you would you feel in each situation: calm, nervous, scared, or terrified?

1 **What would you do if you woke up in the middle of the night and thought that you could hear an intruder?**
  a I'd confront the intruder.
  b I'd keep still and quiet and hope that the intruder would go away.
  c I'd lock myself in a room and call the police.

2 **What would you do if you were driving and your brakes stopped working?**
  a I'd put the car in neutral gear.
  b I'd put the car in a lower gear.
  c I'd put the emergency brake on.

3 **What would you do if you were caught out in the countryside in a thunderstorm?**
  a I'd go down on my knees and make myself into a ball.
  b I'd lie flat on the ground.
  c I'd shelter under a tree.

4 **What would you do if you fell through ice into a lake?**
  a I'd take off my clothes and shoes and try to keep afloat.
  b I'd try to climb onto the ice from the place where I'd fallen in.
  c I'd keep as still as possible and shout for help.

5 **What would you do if you were hiking alone in the mountains and you got completely lost (and there was no cell phone signal)?**
  a I'd stay where I was and wait to be rescued.
  b I'd keep walking and try to find my way to my destination.
  c I'd try to find my way back to where I'd started from.

6 **What would you do if you were skiing out of bounds and were buried in an avalanche?**
  a I'd push my ski poles up through the snow to attract attention.
  b I'd curl into a ball and cover my head and wait to be rescued.
  c I'd use swimming movements to try to get to the surface.

**b** Now answer the questions, choosing a, b, or c. Compare answers in groups of three and give reasons.

**c** **Ⓒ Communication** It's an emergency! **A** p.108 **B** p.112 **C** p.114 Work in the same groups of three. Read the answers to the situations, then explain what you should and shouldn't do.

**d** Did you choose the correct answers to the questions in **b**?

## 2 READING & LISTENING

**a** Read the description of a reality TV show. Do you have any similar programs in your country?

> ***The Island with Bear Grylls*** is a reality TV program narrated by Bear Grylls, a well-known adventurer. It features two groups of participants who are placed on a remote, uninhabited Pacific island for five weeks, to test their survival skills. They are left alone, with only the clothes they are wearing and some basic tools and training. In season five, the groups were divided according to whether they were high or low earners.

**b** Read the first part of an interview with Ali Brookes on p.47. Would you like to learn any of these survival techniques? What do you think you would miss if you were on the island?

**c** Read the interview again. Choose the best words to complete the gaps.

1 challenge   program   aim
2 because   since   so
3 actually   anyway   apparently
4 complicated   difficult   easy
5 across   over   through
6 hurt   injured   sick
7 if   unless   until
8 Although   As   However
9 as well   even   though
10 definitely   ideally   obviously

**d** 🔊 5.1 Listen and check your answers. With all things considered, do you think she was positive or negative about the whole experience?

# ALI BROOKES,

**A 29-YEAR-OLD DOCTOR, WAS A PARTICIPANT IN SEASON FIVE, IN THE "HIGH EARNERS" GROUP.**

### Why did you decide to apply?

I'd always really enjoyed watching *The Island with Bear Grylls*. And I think it's really the ultimate [1]_____, being stranded on a desert island, having to survive there with no help at all. I love being outdoors and going on adventures, [2]_____ that side of it really appealed to me as well. So I sent off my application form, and the next thing I knew, I had a couple of interviews, and then I got a phone call saying they wanted me to go on *The Island*! Never in a million years, when I applied, did I think I'd [3]_____ get to go. So I was absolutely stunned when they told me they wanted me to go on the program, but at the same time, I was thrilled! And two weeks later, we were off on a plane to the island.

### What survival techniques did you learn?

So we learned a whole range of survival techniques. We learned how to make fire, which was actually quite complicated. You had to get the right wood from a particular type of tree on the beach, and then use pieces of that wood, and a shoelace to make fire. In our training, they made it look very [4]_____, they had the fire lit within a few minutes. But in reality, it took us a couple of days before we made fire, but we did get it, which was amazing. Once we had fire, we could then boil water for drinking. The water we found was brown and green and had stuff floating in it, so we would filter it [5]_____ a pair of pants or a shirt to get rid of the big clumps of dirt, and then we would boil it to kill off any bacteria or parasites. Amazingly, nobody got [6]_____ from drinking the water during our whole five weeks on the island. They also taught us how to build shelters to protect ourselves from the bad weather. In practice, the shelters were not that waterproof and we had a lot of very wet, cold nights. They taught us how to navigate by the sun and how to build up a map of the island as we explored it. It didn't stop us from getting lost though.

### Who or what did you miss most?

Before I went on the show, I said I'd miss my husband the most. But in fact, the thing I missed the most was most definitely food. It was all I could think about, and [7]_____ I couldn't sleep, I would go through a list of different pizza toppings in my head to try and get to sleep. I really missed having a good nights' sleep. [8]_____ we did build shelters off the ground to stop us getting bitten by the insects and other creepy crawlies, it was really uncomfortable. Having clean clothes, I missed that [9]_____. Putting on dirty, wet socks every morning is one of the worst feelings. Of course, I missed my friends and family too, but actually what I realized was that I didn't miss many things. I [10]_____ didn't miss having a phone, or a computer, or the internet. Though as I said, I did miss clean, dry socks.

---

**e** You're going to listen to Ali talk about her best and worst experiences on the island. First, read some things she mentions. Do you think they were things she enjoyed (✓), or things she found difficult (✗)?

- [ ] most of what we ate was yucca, which is like a potato
- [ ] the water we had to wash in was the ocean
- [ ] when it rained
- [ ] we were meeting all these new people we'd never met before
- [ ] (He) threw us out of the boat and told us to swim to the island
- [ ] we had a sports day and we had a talent show
- [ ] leaving the island

**f** 🔊 **5.2** Now listen to the second part of the interview with Ali and check your ideas in **e**.

**g** Listen again. What does she say about...?

1. a few coconuts
2. a wild boar
3. tension and arguments
4. a communal shelter
5. 35 days

**h** How many of the 16 people survived the whole five weeks? What general lesson did the participants learn as a result of their time on the island? Do you think you could survive on the island?

## 3 VOCABULARY & PRONUNCIATION
feelings; word stress

**a** 🔊 **5.3** Listen to two extracts from the interview. How did Ali feel? Fill in the blanks with adjectives.

> So, I was absolutely [1]_____ when they told me they wanted me to go on the program, but at the same time, I was [2]_____.

> ...seeing Bear pull up on his boat to come and collect us was just an amazing feeling. I felt both really [3]_____ and super [4]_____.

**b** **V** p.157 **Vocabulary Bank** Feelings

**c** 🔊 **5.7** Listen to some conversations and look at the extracts. <u>Underline</u> the stressed syllable in the **bold** adjectives.

1. Please come quickly. I'm **des|pe|rate**.
2. You weren't **o|ffen|ded** by what I said, were you?
3. To be honest, I was a little **dis|a|ppoin|ted**.
4. I'm completely **be|wil|dered** by so much information.
5. I was **a|sto|nished** – I really wasn't expecting it.
6. Yes, we'd be **de|ligh|ted** to. Thank you so much.
7. They were **de|va|sta|ted**. It was such a shock.
8. I was absolutely **horr|i|fied**. It was an awful accident.
9. I'm completely **o|ver|whelmed** – I don't know what to say.

**d** Practice saying the extracts, copying the intonation and stressing the correct syllable in the adjectives.

**e** Choose three adjectives from **c** and tell your partner about a time or a situation when you felt like that.

## 4 READING & LISTENING

**a** How much do you know about the Amazon rainforest? In small groups, complete the missing words.

1 The Amazon rainforest is in the continent of South America. It is roughly the size of **A**_____.
2 It covers a total of nine countries, including **Br**_____, Bolivia, **P**_____, Ecuador, **C**_____, Venezuela, Guyana, Suriname, and French Guiana.
3 The Amazon River, which flows through the northern part of the forest, is the **s**_____-**l**_____ river in the world.
4 The tree canopy is so thick that the forest floor is always **d**_____. Some trees grow up to 200 feet high.
5 There are about 50 indigenous **tr**_____ living in the forest that have never had any **c**_____ with the outside world.
6 Some of the most dangerous animals in the world live in the forest; these include poisonous **sn**_____, **fr**_____, and **sp**_____, as well as jaguars and piranhas.

**b** Read the beginning of a true survival story and then answer the questions below.

1 What was the three friends' original plan? How did this change?
2 What caused tensions between…?
  a the three men and the guide  b Kevin and Marcus
3 Why did they finally separate into two pairs? How did they decide to travel?

**Which pair would you have chosen to go with? Why? How would you have felt if you had been in Marcus's situation?**

**c** You are going to listen to part of a documentary and find out what happened to the four men. After each part, answer the questions with a partner.

🔊 5.8

1 What happened to Kevin and Yossi on the raft?
2 What piece of luck did Yossi have?

**Whose situation would you rather have been in, Kevin's or Yossi's? Why?**

🔊 5.9

3 How were Kevin and Yossi feeling?
4 What happened to Yossi on his first night alone in the jungle?

**What would you have done if you had been in Yossi's situation?**

# LOST IN THE JUNGLE

**FOUR YOUNG MEN WENT INTO THE AMAZON JUNGLE ON THE ADVENTURE OF A LIFETIME. ONLY TWO OF THEM WOULD COME OUT ALIVE…**

**In 1981,** three friends went backpacking in the Amazon rainforest in a remote area of Bolivia: Yossi Ghinsberg, 22, and his two friends Kevin Gale, 29, and Marcus Stamm, 29. They hired an experienced guide, an Austrian named Karl Ruprechter, who promised that he could take them deep into the rainforest to an undiscovered Indian village. Then they would raft nearly 125 miles back downriver. Karl said that the journey to the village would take them about seven days. Before they entered the jungle, the three friends made a promise that they would "go in together and come out together."

**The four men set off** from the town of Apolo and soon they had left civilization far behind. But after walking for more than a week, there was no sign of the village, and tensions began to appear in the group. The three friends started to suspect that Karl, the guide, didn't really know where the Indian village was. Yossi and Kevin began to get fed up with their friend Marcus because he was complaining about everything, especially his feet, which had become infected and were hurting.

**Eventually,** they decided to abandon the search for the village and just hike (instead of rafting) back to Apolo, the way they had come. But Kevin was furious because he thought that it was Marcus's fault that they had had to cut short their adventure. So, he decided that he would raft down the river, and he persuaded Yossi to join him, but he didn't want Marcus to come with them. Marcus and Karl decided to go back to Apolo on foot. The three friends agreed to meet in a hotel in the capital La Paz in a week.

**Early the next morning,** the two pairs of travelers said goodbye and set off on their different journeys…

**◑ 5.10**

5 Why did Yossi's spirits change from desperate to optimistic, and then to desperate again?

**How would you have felt at this point? What do you think had happened to Kevin?**

**◑ 5.11**

6 What had Kevin been doing all this time?
7 What did Kevin decide to do?
8 Why was he incredibly lucky?

**If you had been Kevin, what would you have done now?**

**◑ 5.12**

9 How did Kevin first try to get help?
10 Why was it unsuccessful?
11 What was his last attempt to find his friend?

**◑ 5.13**

12 How long had Yossi been on his own in the jungle? How was he?
13 What did he think the buzzing noise was? What was it?

**What do you think might have happened to Marcus and Karl?**

d Do you think you would have survived if you had been in Yossi's situation? Would you have done anything differently? Who do you sympathize with most?

## 5 GRAMMAR unreal conditionals

a Fill in the blanks with the verbs in the correct tense.

1 What would you do if you _____ (hike) alone in the mountains and you _____ (get lost)?
2 If I thought that I could hear an intruder in my house, I _____ (call) the police and I _____ (not confront) the intruder.
3 What would you have done if you _____ (be) in Yossi's situation?
4 If Kevin hadn't looked for his friend, Yossi _____ (die).

b Look at sentences 1–4 again. Which two refer to a hypothetical situation in the past? Which two refer to a hypothetical situation in the present or future?

c **G p.140 Grammar Bank 5A**

d With a partner, write two conditional story chains, one with second conditionals, and one with third conditionals.

1 If I had one year off work, I'd _____
_____.
If _____.
If _____.
If _____.
If _____.
*If I had one year off work, I'd go to South Africa.*
*If I went to South Africa, I'd probably go on a safari…*

2 If I hadn't been feeling so terrible, _____
_____.
If _____.
If _____.
If _____.
If _____.

e Read your stories to another pair. Whose did you like best?

## 6 WRITING

**W p.118 Writing A blog post** Write a post about how to keep safe in different situations.

**Go online** to review the lesson

**G** *wish* for present / future, *wish* for past regrets · **V** expressing feelings with verbs or *-ed* / *-ing* adjectives · **P** sentence rhythm and intonation

## 1 GRAMMAR *wish* for the present / future

**a** Look at some posts on a Pinterest board. Do you ever wish for any of these things? Which ones?

I wish you knew how much I really love you.

#1574
I wish my friends' houses were connected to mine by secret tunnels.

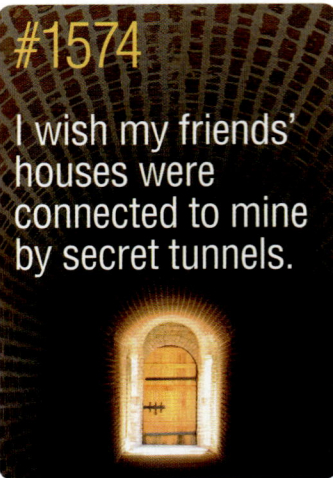

I wish I didn't have to go to work today.

I wish I could fly. Or speak Chinese. Both I think are equally impossible.

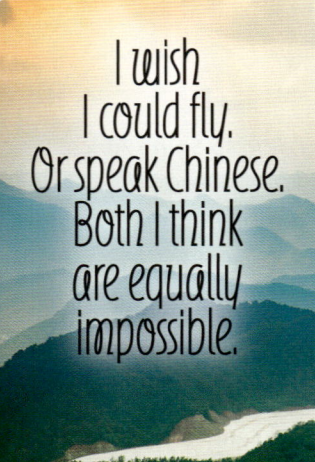

I wish I could eat as much as I wanted **WITHOUT** gaining weight.

I wish my family didn't live so far away.

I wish I could text my dog when I wasn't at home with her. Tell her I miss her. See what she's doing. Ask her to take a selfie for me.

**b** Now look at a WhatsApp group where friends have shared things that annoy them. Check (✓) the things that annoy you, too.

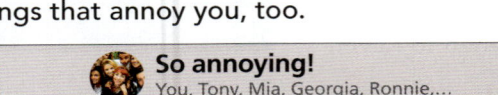

**So annoying!**
You, Tony, Mia, Georgia, Ronnie,…

I just got back from the movie theater – couldn't enjoy the movie. I wish they would ban people from eating in movie theaters. Some people just can't last for two hours without eating or drinking something. Grrr.  8:58 PM ✓✓

**Tony**
I wish soccer commentators would stop shouting "Goooal" in that ridiculous way. If we're watching, we can see that it's a goal, and if we're not watching, it's because we don't care.  8:58 PM

**Mia**
I wish people wouldn't put their bags on seats to try and stop people from sitting next to them.  9:17 PM

**Georgia**
I wish my boyfriend wouldn't fall asleep every time I want to talk to him.  10:03 PM

**Ronnie**
I wish my son would occasionally remember to fill up my car with gas after he borrows it.  10:11 PM

**Josie**
I wish people in call centers wouldn't use my first name like we were old friends.  10:47 PM

**Donna**
I wish my family would take their tissues out of their pockets before they put their clothes in the washing machine.  11:02 PM

**Ella**
I wish people wouldn't ask me "What are you doing?" when it's completely obvious what I'm doing.  11:35 PM

**Omar**
I wish people wouldn't leave supermarket shopping carts in the parking lot just because they're too lazy to take them back.  12:06 AM

**c** Compare the things you've checked with a partner. Which are your top three, and why?

🔍 **Expressing annoyance**

| | |
|---|---|
| It really annoys me when… | people eat potato chips at the movies. |
| It's so annoying when… | |
| It drives me crazy when… | |

**d** Compare the Pinterest posts in **a** and the messages in **b**. Then complete the rules with *would / wouldn't* + base form or simple past.

1 We use *wish* + person + _____ to talk about things you would like to be different in the present / future (but that are impossible or unlikely).

2 We use *wish* + person + _____ to talk about things we want to happen or stop happening because they annoy us.

**e** **G** p.141 **Grammar Bank 5B** *wish* for present / future

**f** Write two more things that annoy you and that you would like people to change, and two things that you would like to be different about yourself or your life. Use *I wish + would / wouldn't* and *I wish* + simple past.

**g** In pairs or small groups, compare what you've written. Did anyone come up with the same things?

## 2 VOCABULARY & SPEAKING expressing feelings with verbs or *-ed / -ing* adjectives

> **Ways of talking about how we feel**
>
> We can talk about how we feel in three different ways:
>
> 1 by using a **verb** (e.g., *annoy*)
> *People who eat in movie theaters really annoy me.*
>
> 2 by using an *-ing* **adjective** (e.g., *annoying*)
> *People who eat in movie theaters are really annoying.*
>
> 3 by using an *-ed* **adjective** (e.g., *annoyed*)
> *I get really annoyed when people eat in movie theaters.*

**a** Complete the sentences with the correct form of the word in **bold**.

1 It really _____ me when people drive close behind me. **infuriate**

2 I get very _____ when something goes wrong with my internet connection and I don't know how to fix it. **frustrate**

3 It's so _____ when I can't remember someone's name, but they can remember mine. **embarrass**

4 I used to love shopping at the mall, but now I find it _____. After an hour, I just want to go home. **exhaust**

5 I'm often _____ with my birthday presents. My expectations are obviously too high! **disappoint**

6 It _____ me that some people still don't do their banking online. **amaze**

7 I find speaking in public absolutely _____. I hate doing it. **terrify**

8 I've often been _____ by reading about how some successful people have overcome difficulties. **inspire**

9 I never find instructions for electronic devices helpful – in fact, usually they just _____ me. **confuse**

10 When I travel, I'm always _____ if I manage to communicate something in a foreign language. **thrill**

**b** ◉ **5.19** Listen and check. Then with a partner, say if the sentences are true for you or not. Give examples or reasons.

> **Feelings adjectives that have an *-ed* form but not an *-ing* form**
>
> A few *-ed* adjectives describing feelings don't have an *-ing* form, e.g., *impressed – impressive* **NOT** *impressing*

**c** Complete the sentences below with a form of the adjective in **bold**.

1 We are extremely **impressed** by your résumé. Your résumé is extremely *impressive*.

2 I get very **stressed** at work. My job is very _____.

3 I was really **scared** during the movie. The ending was especially _____.

4 I was **delighted** to meet Jane. She really is a _____ person.

5 I was really **offended** by what you said. What you said was really _____.

**d** In pairs, choose three squares and think about what you are going to say. Then talk to a partner.

| | |
|---|---|
| an embarrassing mistake you once made | something that makes you feel depressed |
| a movie or a book that you found really disappointing | something that really annoys you when you're shopping |
| something that you find frustrating about learning English | something that really stresses you in your daily life |
| someone who inspires you | some physical activity that you did that left you absolutely exhausted |

*I'm going to tell you about an embarrassing mistake I once made. I was emailing a colleague...*

## 3 READING & SPEAKING

**a** You are going to read an article about regrets. Which three areas of life do you think people tend to have the most regrets about? Choose from the box below.

career   education   family   health   love   money   travel

**b** Read the article once and check. How did the writer change someone's life?

# Regrets

Recently, I helped my son move into his freshman year dorm room at his college in Chicago and we discussed his hopes and plans for the next four years. That evening, I found myself thinking about how to help him make decisions he would never regret. I went to Twitter and typed, "What is your biggest regret?" The response was huge and devastatingly honest. I had asked a question that, surprisingly, a lot of people really wanted to answer.

I loved the light-hearted responses…

> "Not flying on Concorde to New York with Lionel Richie. He wanted to take me for dinner. I was working. #idiot"

But very few of them were like that. What emerged is that real regrets are not about bad things happening to you. They are about bad choices – a deep sorrow, or anger at yourself for something you did, or something you failed to do.

Most of the replies divided into different categories. Education was high up the list – there were many more regrets to do with school and college than I had expected.

> "Never going to university. Left me disadvantaged all my life. Never lived up to my potential."

> 1

> 2

Career-choice regrets made me realize a pattern was developing: regret seems most often to be about fear. Fear of doing the wrong thing, which then leads to an unfulfilled life.

> "Not following my dream to work in radio."

> 3

> 4

And then, perhaps less surprising, there was love: a few tweets from people regretting that they had declared their love and ended up having their heart broken, but many, many more regretting not being brave – regretting having been afraid. There's definitely a lesson in there: while there's always the possibility of rejection, it's better than the regret of not having tried.

> "Not telling someone I loved them. 20 years too late now."

> 5

It was encouraging that right alongside the people who regretted a life lived in fear were others who had made a change who were now regretting the time it had taken to find their solution.

> "Worrying too much about what other people thought of me."

> 6

Intriguingly, of all the replies, only two people mentioned money – one regretting an apartment they hadn't bought, one regretting a sale.

## ❤ Regret seems most often to be about fear. ❤

My favorite of all the replies was from @dorey1414. She tweeted me this:

> "I'm 54, no friends, or family, only 18 Twitter followers, but I have everything I need. Biggest regret – not listening in school."

At last, here was one tiny area where I could be useful! I retweeted her words and asked Twitter if they could help. Ten minutes later, her follower count had gone up to 24. By the morning, it was 360. She now has more than 900 and is massively excited about it, starting enthusiastic conversations with dozens of her new followers. Having left school before graduating and worked for 38 years in a job she doesn't enjoy, she now has a chance to change her life.

Before I flew home from Chicago, I texted my son with this advice: "Take risks – they may go wrong but it's better than regretting not having tried. And call your mother."

*Adapted from an article by Emma Freud in The Guardian*

**c** Read the article again. Complete 1–6 with tweets A–F. What kinds of words are left out in some of the tweets?

| A | "Being scared all the time. Moved to France – still scary but food and life is good!" |
|---|---|
| B | "Listening to my dad when he said my voice was too weak to be a singer." |
| C | "Marrying the first person who asked, because I thought no one would ever ask me." |
| D | "My regret: listening to teachers who said I was stupid because I can't spell. After two degrees was told I'm dyslexic. Am currently on fourth degree." |
| E | "Not getting a better education and working full-time from the age of 16." |
| F | "Not taking the job in Tokyo." |

**d** Look at the highlighted words in the article. Which are nouns and which are adjectives? If it's a noun, write the adjective, and vice versa.

**e** If you had read Emma Freud's tweet *What is your biggest regret?*, what would you have written?

> I would have written "Not starting to learn English when I was younger."

## 4 GRAMMAR *wish* for past regrets

**a** ▶ 5.20 Listen to three people talking about regrets. What thing does each person regret?

**b** Listen again and complete the sentences with *wish*. What tense do we use after *wish* to talk about a regret?

**Speaker 1**
I wish I _____.

**Speaker 2**
I wish I _____.
I wish she _____.

**Speaker 3**
I wish I _____.

**c** **G** p.141 **Grammar Bank 5B** *wish* for past regrets

**d** Write a regret with *I wish* for each of the categories below.

family   health   money   travel

## 5 PRONUNCIATION & SPEAKING
sentence rhythm and intonation

**a** ▶ 5.22 Listen and write down six more regrets with *wish*.

**b** Match regrets 1–6 from **a** with the sentences below.

- ☐ A Do you want me to call and make an excuse?
- ☐ B Yes, watching it on TV is never as exciting.
- ☐ C Well, it isn't too late. You're only 22.
- ☐ D Yes, you should have had more self-control!
- ☐ E Why don't you go back to the store and see if they still have them?
- ☐ F Yes, that wasn't a good move on your part. I hope she's not too upset.

**c** ▶ 5.23 Listen and check. In pairs, practice the conversations. Copy the rhythm and intonation.

**d** Work in small groups. Tell the other students about…

- a famous person from the past that you wish you'd met.
- a live event you wish you'd been to.
- something you wish you'd learned as a child.
- something you wish you hadn't bought.
- something you wish you'd spent more time on.
- a vacation or trip you wish you hadn't gone on.

## 6 LISTENING & WRITING

**a** ▶ 5.24 Listen to a poem about regret from a poetry website. What's the first line of each verse?

**b** Listen again, and for each verse, write down as many words as you can.

**c** Work with a partner. Compare the words you've written, and together, try to reconstruct the poem.

**d** Listen one more time and check your version.

**e** Together, write your own poem of at least three verses. Start each verse with *I wish I had / hadn't…*

**f** Read your poems aloud. Take a class vote for the best one.

## 1 ▶ THE INTERVIEW Part 1

**a** Read the biographical information about Candida Brady. Have you heard of any of the documentary films or people mentioned?

**Candida Brady** is a British journalist and filmmaker. She founded her film company, Blenheim Films, in 1996 and has produced and directed several films and documentaries on a variety of topics, including youth culture, music, and ballet.

In 2012, Candida completed her first full-length documentary feature film, *Trashed*, which follows the actor Jeremy Irons around the world as he discovers the growing environmental and health problems caused by waste – the billions of tons of garbage that we generate every day – and the way we deal with it. The soundtrack for the film was composed by the Greek composer Vangelis, who wrote the award-winning soundtrack to *Chariots of Fire*, and the film won several awards at film festivals. Her latest film, *Urban and the Shed Crew*, based on the memoir of writer Bernard Hare, is about a young boy's struggle to survive on the streets of Leeds in the 1990s.

**b** Watch Part 1 of an interview with her. Mark the sentences **T** (true) or **F** (false).

1 Candida made the film *Trashed* because she wanted people to know more about the problem of waste.
2 Jeremy Irons is a person who loves buying new things.
3 Candida was surprised that Jeremy Irons immediately loved the film proposal.
4 Vangelis is a good friend of Candida's.
5 Vangelis had previous experience working on projects related to the environment.
6 She didn't need to do much research before making the film because she was already an expert on the subject.

### Glossary

**rough cut** /rʌf kʌt/ the first version of a film after the different scenes have been put together
**Jacques Cousteau** a well-known French conservationist and filmmaker who studied the ocean and all forms of life in water

**c** Now watch again and say why the **F** sentences are false.

**d** Have you seen any documentaries about the environment? What did you learn from them?

## ▶ Part 2

**a** Now watch Part 2. Answer the questions.

1 Which was the bigger problem for Candida: making the film visually attractive, or trying not to make it too depressing?
2 What kind of pollution does she think is the most worrying: air, land, or water?

**b** Watch again. Complete the sentences with one word.

1 Candida had a _____ DOP (Director of Photography).
2 She wanted to film in beautiful places that had been _____ by man-made garbage.
3 She would have preferred to make a more _____ documentary.
4 They were very much aware that they wanted to offer _____ at the end of the film.
5 She says you have to dig down over a foot deep on a beach to find sand that doesn't have any _____ in it.
6 She says the pieces of plastic in the water become so fragmented that they're the same size as the zooplankton, which is in the _____ chain.

### Glossary

**Saida (or Sidon)** a port in Lebanon, its third largest city
**zooplankton** microscopic organisms that live in water

**c** Which kind of pollution, air, land, or water, is the biggest problem where you live?

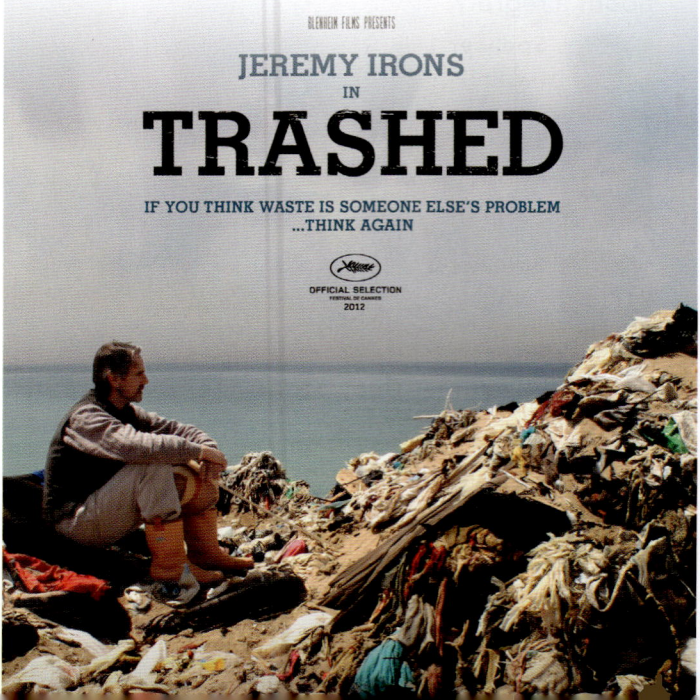

## ▶ Part 3

**a** Now watch Part 3. Answer the questions.

1 Who does she blame for the problem of waste?
2 Why does San Francisco offer a positive note at the end of the film?
3 Has the film changed her own habits?

**b** Watch again. What does she say about…?

1 hotels in San Francisco
2 her grandparents
3 her bicycle

---

**Glossary**

**zero waste** the recycling and re-using of all products
**bins** containers where people throw their garbage

---

**c** How much recycling do you do personally? Are you optimistic or pessimistic about the future of the environment?

## 2 ▶ LOOKING AT LANGUAGE

🔍 **Comment adverbs**
Candida uses a lot of comment adverbs (e.g., *unfortunately*) to clarify how she feels about what she is saying.

Watch some extracts from the interview and write in the missing adverbs.

1 "We ended up _____ filming in 11 countries…"
2 "…but the stories that I've chosen are universal and, _____, I spoke to, to people in communities, um, in more countries, um, than we actually filmed in…"
3 "…and so I sent him the treatment and _____ he, um, he loved it."
4 "…but _____, again, he was very shocked, um, by the film and really wanted to get involved."
5 "…yes and no, um, _____ enough. Obviously I had a wonderful DOP, Director of Photography, so, um, he can pretty much make anything look beautiful…"
6 "I did a lot of research and so, _____, these things were repeatable and, and in every country around the world…"
7 "_____, what's happened with the way that soft plastic degrades in water is that, um, the pieces become so fragmented…"

## 3 ▶ THE CONVERSATION

Simon     Joanne     Syinat

**a** Watch the conversation. Circle the correct phrase to sum up their conclusion.

They think being plastic-free is *definitely possible / possible but difficult / impossible*.

**b** Watch again. Answer with **S** (Simon), **J** (Joanne), or **Sy** (Syinat).

Who…?
1 ▢ gives an example of plastic straws
2 ▢ thinks that consumers need to lead the way
3 ▢ brings up the problem of plastic packaging in supermarkets
4 ▢ mentions that China no longer accepts other countries' recycling
5 ▢ suggests that it might be possible to be plastic free in 20 years' time
6 ▢ says that there is more plastic than fish in the sea
7 ▢ compares the use of plastic today to in the past
8 ▢ tells the others about bacteria that can eat plastic
9 ▢ talks about plastic bottles that you can use and then eat the plastic

**c** Do you agree with the participants about the possibility of being plastic free? Why (not)?

**d** Watch some extracts and match some of the different ways that the participants respond to what another person had said.

1 The deepest place on the planet… and they found plastic. ▢▢
2 …there's more plastic in the sea by weight than there are fish… ▢▢
3 …plastic bottles that actually you can then eat the plastic. ▢▢▢

A Yes, isn't that awful?
B Oh wow!
C It's depressing.
D Yes, it's very scary!
E I mean that's just so depressing, isn't it?
F I think that's just so amazing.
G That sounds pretty cool.

**e** With a partner, say what the function of each response is: responding to something positive or something negative.

**f** Now have a conversation in groups of three.

1 What kinds of things in everyday life do you think <u>really</u> make a difference to the environment?
2 What do you think the government could do to make people recycle more?

---

🌐 **Go online** to watch the video, review the lesson, and check your progress

# 6A Night night

**G** *used to, be used to, get used to*   **V** sleep   **P** /s/ and /z/

> Laugh and the world laughs with you; snore and you snore alone.
> *Anthony Burgess, UK author*

## 1 GRAMMAR *used to, be used to, get used to*

**a** Do you ever have problems sleeping? Why (not)? What kinds of things might make it difficult for people to sleep well?

**b** 🔊 6.1 Listen to three people, Carlos, Marc, and Steph, who all have problems sleeping at night. What are the main reasons they give? Have any of them solved the problem?

**c** 🔊 6.2 Listen to six extracts from the listening. Fill in the blanks with a few words.

**Carlos**
I can't get used to [1]_____ in a bedroom where there's light coming in from the streetlights outside.
I always used to [2]_____.

**Marc**
The main problem is that my body's used to [3]_____, not during the day.
It's really hard to get used to [4]_____ all night.
Before I became a police officer, I used to [5]_____ hours a night.

**Steph**
And just when I'm finally used to [6]_____, then it's time to fly back to the UK.

**d** Look the highlighted phrases. Answer the questions with a partner.
1 What do you think *used to* means after *be / get*?
   a tired of   b accustomed to   c good at
2 What's the difference between *be* + adjective, e.g., *be old, be used to*, and *get* + adjective, e.g., *get old, get used to*?
3 What form does the verb take after *used to* and *be / get used to*?

**e** 🅖 **p.142 Grammar Bank 6A**

**f** Talk to a partner. Ask for and give more information.
1 When you were a child, did you use to…?
   • share a room with a brother or sister
   • sleep with the light on
   • wake up very early in the morning
2 Do you ever have problems sleeping when you're staying somewhere new or different that you aren't used to (e.g., in a hotel)?
3 Do you think you would find it difficult to get used to…?
   • always going to bed after midnight
   • getting up at 5:30 a.m. every day
   • traveling long-haul a lot

## 2 PRONUNCIATION /s/ and /z/

**a** 🔊 6.5 Listen to sentences 1–3. In which one is *used to* pronounced differently? What's the difference?
1 I used to get up really late, but now I get up early.
2 It often takes time to get used to sleeping in a new bed.
3 Valerian is an herb that is used to help people to sleep better.

**b** 🔊 6.6 Listen and repeat some pairs of words where the only difference in pronunciation is the final *s* or *z*.

| | | | | |
|---|---|---|---|---|
| 1 | a | loose | b | lose |
| 2 | a | bus | b | buzz |
| 3 | a | niece | b | knees |
| 4 | a | ice | b | eyes |
| 5 | a | race | b | raise |
| 6 | a | peace | b | peas |
| 7 | a | price | b | prize |
| 8 | a | place | b | plays |

**c** 🔊 6.7 Listen to some sentences with words from **b**. Which word do you hear each time? In 1–4 the context will help you, but not in 5–8.

**d** Practice with a partner. Say one word from each pair in **b** to your partner. He / She says if it's a or b.

## 3 READING

**a** Look at the title of the article below and read the first paragraph. What exactly is *segmented sleep*?

# The way we used to sleep

### The forgotten benefits of segmented sleep

Sleeping for eight hours a night without waking up is not natural human behavior. For centuries, "segmented sleep" was standard. People used to go to bed early, sleep for a few hours, wake for an hour or two around midnight, and then sleep for about another three or four hours until sunrise.

This time when people were awake was called "the watch," and it was used for all sorts of activities. It was a chance to meditate and think about vivid dreams. More active people used the hour to visit sick family members, do housework, or even steal from the neighbors under the cover of darkness! It was an hour typically free from social demands. One 15th-century Italian woman wrote that it was a time when she was able to sew or write letters in privacy, when she was not "surrounded by men, performing jobs for men." Doctors also believed in the medical benefits that came from changing sleeping position, or taking medication during the watch. The practice of "first sleep" and "second sleep" is mentioned by many great authors, including Homer, Chaucer, Austen, Dickens, and Tolstoy.

Since we've gotten used to artificial light, however, segmented sleep has become both unfashionable and harder to achieve. We've now lost that hour between sleeps, a time when we can be awake and alone with our thoughts. Segmented sleep is arguably more natural than the sleep we experience nowadays. People who regularly wake in the night will no doubt be relieved to hear that there's nothing wrong with them.

*Adapted from the Quartz website*

**b** Now read the whole article and answer the questions.

1 What kinds of things would people do during "the watch"?
2 Was segmented sleep considered a good thing?
3 Why don't we sleep like this these days?

**c** Read about photographer Brennan Wenck-Reilly, who is usually awake during the night. Answer the questions.

1 How long is he usually awake for?
2 What does he do with the time?

## Things people do at night

**Brennan Wenck-Reilly, 36, San Francisco**

I spent two years living high up in the Andes, in Chacopampa in Bolivia. I was in the Peace Corps, a volunteer organization run through the US government. Chacopampa was a town that had no electricity 90% of the time. We [1] **u**_____ to follow the patterns of the sun, that is, I'd go to bed between 8:00 and 9:00 and get up at about 6:00 a.m. But at around midnight I'd wake up and then I'd be up till 3:00 a.m. or so. In those hours [2] **b**_____ midnight and 3:00, I would usually read, sometimes as much as 100 pages of a book.

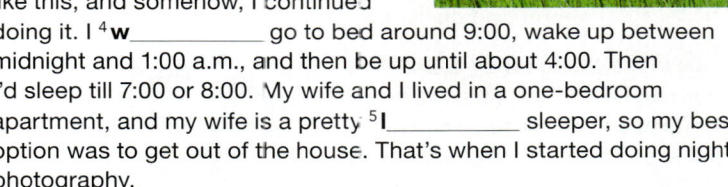

When I got back to San Francisco I'd [3] **g**_____ used to sleeping like this, and somehow, I continued doing it. I [4] **w**_____ go to bed around 9:00, wake up between midnight and 1:00 a.m., and then be up until about 4:00. Then I'd sleep till 7:00 or 8:00. My wife and I lived in a one-bedroom apartment, and my wife is a pretty [5] **l**_____ sleeper, so my best option was to get out of the house. That's when I started doing night photography.

San Francisco at that hour is quite magical. I often find [6] **m**_____ alone on the streets, or at the beach, in the woods. Part of the adventure is finding new locations, part is the solitude, and the reward is the image I get to take home. One of my favorites is this one of Angel Island. It was really [7] **w**_____, as you can see from the grass in the foreground.

If I don't [8] **l**_____ the house, I'll work on framing photos, or grading (I'm also a teacher), and sometimes I'll simply put on a movie. I also sometimes run – I used to have a running partner who lived a couple of blocks away. A couple of times a week we'd text each other around 1:00 or 2:00 a.m., and then meet at the street corner and run for about an hour. That lasted about a year, then we both [9] **e**_____ up moving away. Now I have young kids, but I long for them to be more independent so that I can once again go back to my sleep pattern.

*Brennan is now giving classes in night photography.*

**d** Read the text again and fill in the blanks.

**e** In pairs, explain why Brennan mentions these things.

> the sun   100 pages   one bedroom   the woods
> Angel Island   grading   the street corner   young kids

**f** If you woke up for an hour every night, what do you think you would do with the time?

## 4 VOCABULARY sleep

**a** Read some facts about sleep. Which did you find the most surprising? Were there any facts you already knew?

# FASCINATING FACTS ABOUT SLEEP

Studies have shown that male students **yawn** longer and more often than female students.

Many people take a **nap** after lunch. The so-called "post-lunch dip" is because we naturally feel **sleepy** at two times of day: 2:00 a.m. and 2:00 p.m.

People who **snore** can make a noise as loud as 100 decibels, equivalent to a jackhammer.

Covering yourself with heavy **blankets** can help you relax and get a better night's sleep. The pressure on the body produces serotonin, a chemical that helps with sleep, mood, and digestion.

People often change their **sheets**, but up to one third of the weight of a **pillow** can be made up of dead skin and bugs. And if you don't wash a **comforter** at least every six months, it can contain up to 20,000 live dust mites.

Scientists have produced flies that have **insomnia**. They lose their balance more often, are slower learners, and gain more fat – the same as humans who don't get enough sleep.

If you have taken **sleeping pills**, you aren't actually asleep, you're sedated. Some researchers think that this can cause memory problems.

**b** Look at the **bold** words in **a**. In pairs, figure out their meaning from the context.

**c** Now look at some words and phrases about sleeping habits. With a partner, say what you think they mean.

**be a light sleeper**   **fall asleep**

**be fast asleep**   **have nightmares**

**keep you awake**   **oversleep**

**set the alarm**   **sleep like a log**   **sleepwalk**

**d** Work in pairs. Do the *Vocabulary race.*

When your teacher says "go," write the correct word or phrase from **a–c** in the column on the right. As soon as you finish, raise your hand.

| | | |
|---|---|---|
| 1 | Most people start feeling ▮ at around 11:00 p.m. | *sleepy* |
| 2 | When people are tired, they often open their mouth and ▮. | _____ |
| 3 | When they get into bed, they put their head on the ▮. | _____ |
| 4 | In bed, many people sleep under a thick ▮ filled with feathers or synthetic material. | _____ |
| 5 | Other people prefer to sleep under ▮ and ▮. | _____ |
| 6 | Some people can't sleep because they suffer from ▮. | _____ |
| 7 | People sometimes have to take ▮ to help them go to sleep. | _____ |
| 8 | Some people who are asleep make a loud noise when they breathe, i.e., they ▮. | _____ |
| 9 | In hot countries, it's common to take a short ▮ in the afternoon. | _____ |
| 10 | A person who sleeps well "▮." | _____ |
| 11 | Someone who doesn't sleep very deeply is a ▮. | _____ |
| 12 | Some children ▮ if they watch scary movies before bedtime. | _____ |
| 13 | If you drink coffee in the evening, it may ▮. | _____ |
| 14 | In the middle of the night, most people are ▮. | _____ |
| 15 | As many as 15% of people ▮ during the night, getting out of bed and even getting dressed or eating. | _____ |
| 16 | When people need to get up early, they often ▮ (clock). | _____ |
| 17 | If you don't hear your alarm, you might ▮. | _____ |
| 18 | According to one study, 4.7% of Americans ▮ while driving. | _____ |

**e** 🔊 6.8 Listen and check. Did the pair who finished first also get the most correct answers?

## 5 LISTENING

**a** You're going to listen to a podcast by sleep expert Dr. Neil Stanley. First, with a partner, discuss how you think he might complete sentences 1–8 below about his bedtime routine.

1 I sleep in a different _____ from my partner.
2 I sleep under natural _____.
3 I'm obsessive about _____.
4 I sleep with the _____ open.
5 I don't have _____ late.
6 I drink _____ in the evenings.
7 I need _____ hours of sleep.
8 I _____ before going to sleep.

**b** 🔊 6.9 Now listen to the podcast and fill in the blanks with a word or number. Did you guess any of them correctly in **a**? Were you surprised by anything he does? What kind of person do you think he is?

**c** Listen again. Then with a partner, explain Dr. Stanley's reasons, using the prompts below.

1 Because then you don't…
2 Because you don't sleep well if…
3 Because it's really important to…
4 Because you need…
5 Because your body…
6 Because he isn't…
7 Because that's the amount…
8 Because it's his way of…

**d** Look again at the list in **a**. Do you usually do any of these things? Are there any that you would like to be able to do?

## 6 SPEAKING

In pairs, **A** ask the green questions, and **B** ask the red questions. Ask for and give as much information as possible, and react to what your partner says.

Do you usually sleep with your bedroom completely dark, or with the curtains or blinds open? Do you have problems sleeping if there's too much or not enough light for you? What temperature do you like the bedroom to be?

Have you ever worked at night? Did you have any problems sleeping the next day? Why (not)? Do you think you would be able to work at night and sleep during the day for a long period?

Do you take, or have you ever taken, sleeping pills? Do you have any tips for people who suffer from insomnia?

Do you watch TV in bed on a tablet or other device? Do you ever fall asleep while you're watching a TV show?

Did you use to have a bedtime routine when you were a child? Would someone read to you in bed? Did you have a favorite story?

Are you a light sleeper, or do you usually sleep like a log? Do you use something to help you wake up in the morning?

Do you often have nightmares or recurring dreams? Do you ever remember what your dreams were about? Do you ever try to interpret your dreams?

Do you snore? Have you ever had to share a room with someone who snores? Was this a problem?

Do you find it difficult to sleep when you're traveling, e.g., in buses or planes? What do you do if you can't get to sleep?

Have you ever flown long haul? Where to? Did you get jet lag? How long did it take you to get used to the different time zone?

Have you ever overslept and missed something important? What was it?

Have you ever stayed up all night to study for a test the next day? How well did you do on the test?

Do you ever take a nap after lunch or at any other time during the day? How long do you sleep for? How do you feel when you wake up?

Have you ever fallen asleep at an embarrassing moment, e.g., during a class or in a meeting?

🔄 **Go online** to review the lesson

> Music with dinner is an insult both to the cook and the violinist.
> *G.K. Chesterton, UK author*

**G** gerunds and infinitives | **V** music | **P** words from other languages

## 1 LISTENING & SPEAKING

**a** On a typical day, do you listen to music? When and where? How? Do you listen to different kinds of music at different times of the day? What makes you choose one kind of music over another?

**b** ◖6.10 Listen to Part 1 of a talk by John Sloboda, a music psychologist, about why we listen to music. Complete the reasons and examples 1–3 by writing key words or phrases.

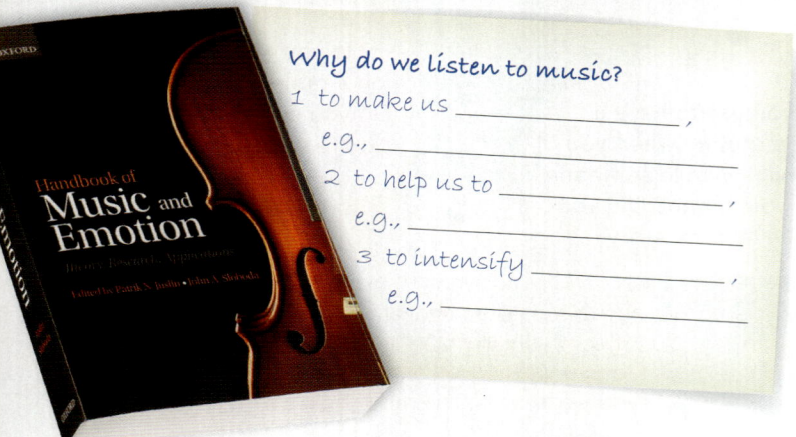

Why do we listen to music?
1 to make us _____ ,
   e.g., _____
2 to help us to _____ ,
   e.g., _____
3 to intensify _____ ,
   e.g., _____

**c** Compare your notes with a partner, and try to remember more about what John said. Then listen again and add to your notes.

**d** Can you think of times when you listen to music for one of these three reasons? What kinds of music do you listen to?

**e** ◖6.11 Now listen to extracts from four pieces of music that John is going to mention in Part 2 of his talk. How do they make you feel?

1 the first movement of Beethoven's *Seventh Symphony*
2 *Mars*, from *The Planets*, by Holst
3 Albinoni's *Adagio for Strings*
4 the music from the Hitchcock movie *Psycho*

**f** ◖6.12 Now listen to Part 2, where John explains why music can affect the way we feel. Complete the rest of the notes.

The human voice:
happy = people speak _____, the voice is _____
sad = people speak _____, the voice is _____
angry = people _____ their voices or _____
Music copies the human voice:
1 _____, _____-_____ music sounds happy.
2 _____ music with _____ pitches sounds sad.
3 _____ music with _____ rhythms sounds angry.
Emotions related to pieces of music:
1 _____ = the Beethoven
2 _____ = the Holst
3 _____ = the Albinoni
4 _____ = the movie music from *Psycho*

**g** Talk to a partner, and give reasons.

### What music would you play…?
- if you were preparing to go out and feeling happy and excited about it
- if you wanted to create a romantic atmosphere
- if you were feeling furious about something or somebody
- if you were feeling stressed or nervous
- if you were feeling depressed

*If I was feeling depressed, I'd play* Someone Like You *by Adele, because it makes me cry. It was my ex's favorite song…*

## 2 GRAMMAR gerunds and infinitives

**a** Look at some extracts from the listening in **1b**. Put the verbs in parentheses in the infinitive (with *to*), the base form (without *to*), or the gerund (*-ing* form).

1 Firstly, we listen to music to make us _____ important moments in the past. (**remember**)
2 When we hear a certain piece of music, we remember _____ it for the first time… (**hear**)
3 If we want _____ from one activity to another, we often use music to help us _____ the change. (**go, make**)

**b** ◖6.13 Listen and check.

## 3 VOCABULARY & PRONUNCIATION
music; words from other languages

a ◖ 6.16 Listen to some instruments and musicians and match them to a word in the lists.

**instruments**
- ☐ a bass gui<u>tar</u>
- ☐ a <u>ce</u>llo
- ☐ drums
- ☐ a flute
- ☐ a <u>key</u>board
- ☐ a <u>sax</u>ophone
- ☐ a vio<u>lin</u>

**musicians**
- ☐ a choir
- ☐ a con<u>ductor</u>
- ☐ an <u>or</u>chestra
- ☐ a so<u>prano</u>

c Look at sentences 1 and 2. Match the meaning of *remember* to A and B.

1 I **remember** meeting him for the first time.
2 Please **remember** to meet him at the train station.

A ☐ to not forget to do something; to do what you have to do
B ☐ to have or keep an image in your memory of something you did or that happened in the past

d **G** p.143 **Grammar Bank 6B**

e Tell your partner about…
- a piece of music you'll never forget hearing for the first time.
- something you sometimes forget to do before you leave the house in the morning.
- something you remember doing before you were five years old.
- something you have to remember to do today or this week.
- a job that needs doing in your house / apartment (e.g., the kitchen ceiling needs repainting).
- something you need to do this evening.
- a skill you tried to learn but couldn't.
- something you've tried doing when you can't sleep at night.

b ◖ 6.17 Listen and check. Practice saying the words. Then in pairs, try to add more words to the two groups. Can you play any of the instruments?

> 🔍 **Foreign words that are used in English**
> English has "borrowed" many words from other languages. In the field of music, many words come from Italian, Greek, and French. The English pronunciation is often similar to the pronunciation in the original language, e.g., *c* before *i* and *e* in words from Italian is /tʃ/, as in *cello* and *ciao*; and *ch* in words from Greek is /k/, as in *choir* and *orchestra*.

c In pairs, look at the "borrowed" words below and try to say them. <u>Underline</u> the stressed syllable.

| **Borrowed from…** | | |
|---|---|---|
| **Italian** | con**c**erto /kənˈtʃɛrtoʊ/ | me**zz**o-soprano /mɛtsoʊ səˈprænoʊ/ |
| **Greek** | **ch**orus /ˈkɔrəs/ | **rh**ythm /ˈrɪðəm/ sym**ph**ony /ˈsɪmfəni/ |
| **French** | ball**et** /bæˈleɪ/ | **en**core /ˈɑŋkɔr/ **g**enre /ˈʒɑnrə/ |

d ◖ 6.18 Listen and check. How are the pink letters pronounced?

e Which language do you think these words come from? With a partner, write **I** (Italian), **G** (Greek), or **F** (French). Do you know what they all mean?

architecture ☐   barista ☐   bouquet ☐   cappuccino ☐
chauffeur ☐   chef ☐   chic ☐   croissant ☐   fiancé ☐   graffiti ☐
hypochondriac ☐   macchiato ☐   microphone ☐   paparazzi ☐
philosophy ☐   psychic ☐   psychologist ☐   villa ☐

f ◖ 6.19 Listen and check. Practice saying the words.

g Does your mother tongue borrow words from other languages? Which languages in particular? In which fields (music, food, technology, etc.) are there a lot of "borrowed" words?

## 4 READING

a  Do you usually listen to music when you're working or studying? What kinds of music?

b  Quickly read an article about some research into music and work habits. Choose the best summary of the research findings.

1  Music helps you work better.
2  Choose the right music for the right task.
3  Classical music is best for creative thinking.

Adapted from The Telegraph

# Music while you work?

Some prefer to work in silence. Others find playing their favorite tunes loudly helps them to be productive. Up till now, it has been a matter of personal preference. But recently, scientific research has uncovered that listening to music while you work [1]_____ – although, it depends on [2]_____.

A study by Simone Ritter, at Radboud University in the Netherlands, and Sam Ferguson, at the University of Technology in Sydney, Australia, looked at how [3]_____, compared to working in silence. In their study, Ritter and Ferguson divided 155 volunteers into five groups, which were then given tasks to complete. Four of the groups did so while [4]_____, such as Holst's *Mars* and Vivaldi's *Spring*. The fifth group worked in silence.

Their study found that happy music improved "divergent thinking," which is all about creativity. However, they found that it had no impact on "convergent thinking," which is all about problem solving. So, if you need to be creative with your work, then you should [5]_____. But if you're trying to solve a problem, you're better off [6]_____.

c  Read the article again. Fill in the blanks with phrases A–F.

A  listening to classical music aimed at stimulating different moods
B  can actually be beneficial
C  put on some uplifting music to help get your brain working
D  listening to various types of music affected different types of thinking
E  opting for quiet solitude
F  what you're trying to achieve

d  Think about what you said in **a**. Would you now do anything different, based on the research?

e  You're going to read what four doctors say about playing music while they work. First, look at the photo and answer the questions with a partner.

1  Do you think that doing an operation is more of a creative task or more of a problem-solving task?
2  What do you think might be the advantages and disadvantages of having music in the operating room?

f  Now read what the doctors say. Did they mention any of the things you discussed in **e**? In a discussion between these four doctors, what would the general consensus be – music or no music while you work?

# What doctors listen to in the operating room

**RAMON TAHMASSEBI,** *orthopedic surgeon*

If I play cool music, it puts me in a better mood and I perform better. You want something that will get you in the right frame of mind, but what you pick depends on the length and the complexity of the operation – I try to have some crowd-pleasers, some easy listening, some singalong tracks. Last week, I started a big, three-hour operation at 4 p.m., and the team was supposed to finish work at 5 p.m. But I had a playlist, and afterwards everyone told me they were having fun, so they didn't mind staying late.

**SAFINA ALI,** *head and neck surgeon*

When you are operating, it is soothing and calming to have music. I listen to everything from hip-hop to classical. When I was training, I had to listen to Bruce Springsteen for ten hours at a time, because my boss loved him. My current boss likes to have classical music on, but we change it when he leaves. Most of the nurses are younger, so it's nice to have contemporary music like Taylor Swift, because you can talk about it. I prefer music to silence – it's too eerie; I feel like I am on my own.

**SAMER NASHEF,** *cardiac surgeon*

I never have music in the operating room. First, it's almost impossible to find a genre that fits the musical tastes of the 12 or so people it takes to do a heart operation. Second, music,

g  Read the article again. Write **RT, SA, SN,** or **GW.**

Who says that…?

1  ☐  it's very difficult to choose music that everyone likes
2  ☐  the choice of music depends on the type of operation
3  ☐  playing a variety of music tends to motivate the team
4  ☐  working in silence makes them feel alone
5  ☐  he / she sometimes switches off the music in the middle of an operation
6  ☐  his / her colleagues often choose the music
7  ☐  music gets in the way of doing the job well
8  ☐  he / she plays different music to suit different patients

h  With a partner, create a playlist of five songs that would help you to do a creative group task.

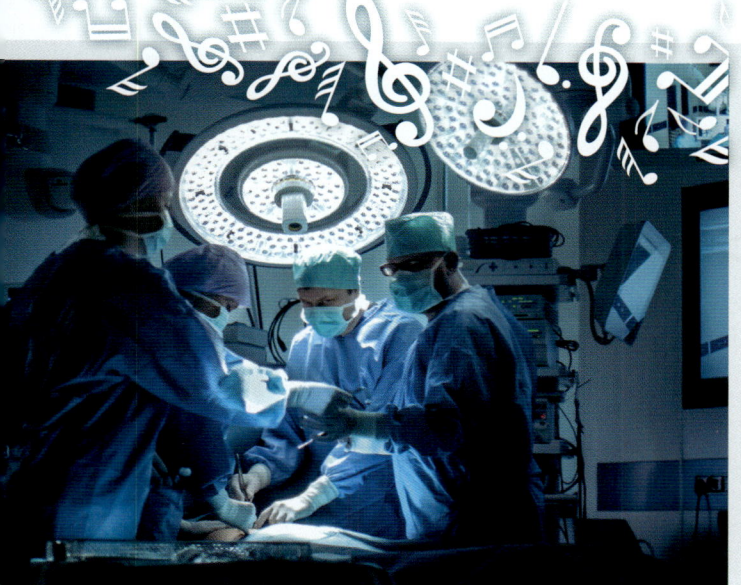

if it's emotionally engaging, is distracting, and if it's bland elevator music, it's irritating. The real reason, however, is communication. Those 12 people need to be able to talk to each other, to provide information, ask questions, hear the answers, and act – any extraneous noise interferes with that.

**GABRIEL WESTON,** *skin cancer surgeon*

I do surgery on people's faces using local anaesthetic, and they're awake during the operation. So I use music to get them to relax. Broadly, older people prefer classical and younger people prefer pop. I think it's sensible to let them know you care about their feelings. If there is a point when things get serious, you turn the music off. But in planned operations, there are long stretches when you're doing something you've done many times, but it still requires meticulousness, and music is good for this.

*Adapted from The Guardian*

## 5  SPEAKING

Work in small groups. Discuss the statements below. Do you agree? Why (not)?

The music that means the most to you is the music you listen to as a teenager.

When music is sung, the lyrics are as important as the music.

You always enjoy music more when you listen to it live.

The best decade for pop music was the 80s.

People who listen to classical music are generally more intelligent.

People who go to music festivals don't really go to listen to the music.

Most young people these days are not interested in opera and classical music.

All schoolchildren should be taught to play a musical instrument.

Anyone can learn to sing.

## 6 ▶ VIDEO LISTENING

a Watch an interview with pianist Isata Kanneh-Mason. What is unusual about her family? Why does the interviewer say that the future looks bright for the Kanneh-Mason children?

b Watch the interview again and answer the questions.

1  How did she first get interested in classical music?
2  What happened to her when she was 17?
3  What is her position in the family?
4  What instrument does her brother Sheku play, and how has he been successful?
5  What kind of relationship do the siblings have?
6  What sacrifices did Isata and her siblings make when they were growing up, and how did they feel about it?
7  What is Isata's main reason for choosing a piece of music, and why?
8  What does she mean when she says, "I'm just so lucky that my escape is what I do"?

c Do you know any very musical people or families, or a family where they are mostly interested in or good at the same thing?

Go online to watch the video and review the lesson

## GRAMMAR

**a** Complete the second sentence so that it means the same as the first.

1 They escaped from the jungle because they found the river.
They wouldn't have escaped from the jungle if they _____ _____ the river.

2 I can't go to dance classes because I work in the evening.
I would be able to go to dance classes if I _____ _____ in the evening.

3 We went to that restaurant because you recommended it.
We _____ _____ _____ to that restaurant if you hadn't recommended it.

4 Marta goes to bed late, so she's always tired in the morning.
If Marta didn't go to bed late, she _____ _____ so tired in the morning.

5 It's too bad I can't speak Spanish.
I wish _____ _____ _____ Spanish.

6 I regret not learning to play the piano when I was younger.
I wish _____ _____ _____ _____ the piano when I was younger.

7 I hate seeing your dirty clothes on the floor.
I wish _____ _____ _____ your dirty clothes on the floor.

8 After living in Hong Kong for a year I still find driving on the left difficult.
After living in Hong Kong for a year, I still can't get _____ _____ _____ on the left.

9 My hair was very long when I was a child.
When I was a child, I used _____ _____ very long hair.

10 I get up very early, but it's not a problem for me now.
I'm used _____ _____ _____ very early.

**b** Complete the sentences with the correct form of the **bold** verb.

1 I don't remember _____ you before. **meet**

2 The car needs _____. I'll take it to the car wash. **clean**

3 We managed _____ to the airport on time. **get**

4 Please try _____ late tomorrow. **not be**

5 My sister isn't used to _____ in such a big company. She was self-employed until recently. **work**

## VOCABULARY

**a** Complete the sentences with an adjective expressing a feeling.

1 Our son played incredibly well in the concert! We felt very pr_____.

2 I'm feeling a little h_____. I really miss my family.

3 Thanks for lending me the money. I'm very gr_____.

4 I shouldn't have bought that bag – it was so expensive. Now I feel really g_____.

5 When I heard that I'd won the prize I was completely st_____. I couldn't say anything!

**b** Complete the sentences with the correct form of the **bold** word.

1 That walk was _____. I need to rest now. **exhaust**

2 I was really _____ when I read Tim's email. **shock**

3 You really _____ me at the party last night! **embarrass**

4 It's very _____ when you think that you are going to miss your flight. **stress**

5 It _____ me when people who don't know me use my first name. **annoy**

6 Last night's concert was really _____. The orchestra didn't play well at all. **disappoint**

7 It always _____ me that people actually enjoy playing risky sports. **amaze**

8 We were _____ when we heard the news. **horrify**

9 What you said to Naomi was rather _____. I think you should apologize. **offend**

10 It was an incredibly _____ movie! **scare**

**c** Complete the missing words.

1 Could I have an extra p_____ for my bed, please?

2 My husband says I sn_____ really loudly at night.

3 I didn't sleep last night, so I'm going to take a n_____ now.

4 Last night I had a horrible n_____. I dreamed that I was lost in the jungle.

5 Don't forget to s_____ the alarm for tomorrow morning.

**d** Write the words for the definitions.

1 _____ the person who directs an orchestra

2 _____ a group of people who sing together

3 _____ a stringed instrument that you hold between your knees

4 _____ a woman who sings with a very high voice

5 _____ an electronic musical instrument, like a piano

## PRONUNCIATION

**a** Circle the word with a different sound.

| 1 | 🌳 | sleepy   delighted<br>relieved   keyboard |
|---|---|---|

| 4 | 🦓 | raise   miserable<br>lose   homesick |
|---|---|---|

| 2 | 🪚 | awake   yawn<br>exhausted   song |
|---|---|---|

| 5 | 🔑 | orchestra   chorus<br>psychology   chic |
|---|---|---|

| 3 | 🐍 | loose   place<br>eyes   course |
|---|---|---|

**b** Underline the main stressed syllable.

1 ab|so|lute|ly       3 in|fur|i|a|ting       5 sleep|walk
2 de|va|sta|ted       4 in|som|ni|a

## CAN YOU understand this text?

**a** Read the article once. According to Dr. Breus, what kinds of music should you listen to before going to sleep?

**b** Read the article again and choose the best words to fill the blanks.

1 a after  b while  c between
2 a effective  b affectionate  c harmful
3 a active  b relaxed  c alert
4 a adjust  b increase  c stop
5 a pride  b excitement  c boredom
6 a advise  b forbid  c order
7 a last  b first  c next
8 a possibly  b likely  c probably
9 a deeper  b comfortable  c uncomfortable
10 a as  b because  c if

## ▶ CAN YOU understand these people?

**◑ 6.20** Watch or listen and choose a, b, or c.

1 Christopher   2 Lemuel   3 Mary   4 Martina

1 If Christopher was left alone on a desert island, he thinks ____.
  a he would survive well because he was a boy scout
  b he wouldn't worry too much about being rescued
  c he would have an idea from movies about what to do
2 Lemuel finds it annoying when other people ____.
  a talk during lectures
  b don't walk fast enough on the street
  c bite their nails
3 Mary sometimes has problems sleeping when ____.
  a she's feeling depressed
  b her bedroom is too warm
  c she's been reading an exciting book
4 Martina likes listening to country music to help her to ____.
  a wake up
  b feel more energized
  c relax in the evening

---

# How you can use music to sleep better

## by Dr. Michael Breus

Music is a regular fixture in my daily life. I listen to music to keep motivated ¹_____ I exercise or work, to relax me when I travel, and to unwind before bed. It's especially ²_____ on nights when I'm feeling tense.

**Slow beats are best.** The body and brain are highly responsive to music, including its rhythm and tempo. Use up-tempo songs to get you moving in the morning, or to keep you ³_____ on a long drive. To move your body into sleep mode, use songs that have a rhythm of about 60–80 beats per minute – you can find lots of examples on YouTube. Your heart rate will ⁴_____ to match these slower beats, and your breathing will slow down, putting you closer to a sleeping state.

**Avoid emotional triggers.** Don't listen to music that makes you feel strong emotions, whether sadness or ⁵_____. These are not the songs you want to listen to at bedtime.

**Go lyric-free.** Lyrics can be mentally stimulating. I ⁶_____ my patients to choose music without words at bedtime. Give the cognitive centers of your brain a rest, rather than lighting them up.

**Be consistent.** Research suggests that the beneficial effects of music for sleep get stronger over time. If you're stressed out in the evenings, your new music routine might not make an immediate difference in the ⁷_____ few nights. Stick with it for a few weeks, and you'll find the soothing effects become stronger.

**Don't ignore the rest of your sleep environment.** If you're playing a Bach sonata in a room blazing with lights, or looking at a computer screen, you're not ⁸_____ to benefit from the sleep-inducing effects of the background music. Make sure your nightly routine and environment is soothing, calm, and dimly lit.

**Don't fall asleep with earphones.** If you want to listen to music as you fall asleep, that's fine. But don't use earphones, which can make sleep ⁹_____ and damage your ear canal.

**Pay attention to how you feel.** We all react differently to songs and find different meaning within them. Classical music is often used in studies, and is a popular choice for bedtime listening. But ¹⁰_____ it's not your thing, that's fine. Try jazz, or new age, or folk music. Whatever makes you feel calm and puts your body and mind in a restful mode is the right choice for you.

---

🔄 **Go online** to watch the video, review Files 5 & 6, and check your progress

# 7A Let's not argue

> Don't raise your voice, improve your argument.
> *Desmond Tutu, Nobel Peace Laureate*

## 1 GRAMMAR past modals: *must have*, etc.

*It wasn't me!*

**a** Look at the photo. With a partner, predict who the people are, where they are, and what they are arguing about. Use *could be*, *can't be*, and *must be*.

( *They can't be a family because… They must be…*

**b** 🔊 **7.1** Listen and check. Who is the "guilty" person in the photo?

**c** 🔊 **7.2** Listen to some extracts from the conversation again and complete them with *could have*, *might have*, *must have*, *can't have*, or *should have*.

1 You _____ _____ finished it.
2 One of you _____ _____ used it.
3 It _____ _____ been me.
4 _____ you _____ finished it last night…?
5 Someone _____ _____ given it to the cat.
6 …you _____ _____ put your name on it.

**d** Look at the blanks for phrases 1–6 in **c** and think about what they mean. Then with a partner, match them to meanings A–D. Write the number in the box before each phrase.

Which phrase (or phrases) means you think…?
A ☐☐ it's very probable (or almost certain) that something happened or somebody did something
B ☐☐ it's possible that something happened or somebody did something
C ☐ it's impossible that something happened or somebody did something
D ☐ somebody didn't do the right thing

**e** **G** p.144 **Grammar Bank 7A**

## 2 PRONUNCIATION weak form of *have*

> have | When he got home, he realized he must of left his bag at school, so he ran back, but when he

**a** Look at an extract from a child's homework above. Why do you think the child made that mistake?

> 🔍 **Weak form of *have***
> When *have* is an auxiliary verb, it is usually contracted in spoken English, e.g., *I've, you've*. If it's not contracted, it's pronounced /əv/, e.g., after a modal verb. The pronunciation is exactly the same as the weak form of *of*.

**b** 🔊 **7.5** Now listen to six sentences with past modals and repeat.

**c** 🔊 **7.6** Listen and write six sentences with either *have* or *of*.

**d** In pairs, read the conversations and complete **B**'s responses with your own ideas (for responses 5–8 you also need to use *must have, might have, should have*, or *couldn't have*). Then practice the conversations.

1 A It was my birthday yesterday!
  B You should have _told me_.
2 A I can't find my phone anywhere.
  B You must have _____.
3 A I definitely said we were meeting them at 7:00.
  B They may have _____.
4 A I'm so tired. I can't keep my eyes open.
  B You shouldn't have _____.
5 A I failed my math test.
  B _____.
6 A Why do you think Fiona and Brian broke up?
  B _____.
7 A Alberto didn't come to class yesterday.
  B _____.
8 A We're going to be late. There's so much traffic.
  B _____.

## 3 READING & SPEAKING

**a** Imagine four young people in their 20s are sharing an apartment. Which of the things in the box do you think causes the most arguments? Number them 1–5.

| food | housework | money |
|------|-----------|-------|
| noise | visitors | |

**b** Read an article for students about typical arguments in a shared house. What two categories are mentioned that are not in the box in **a**?

**c** Read the problems again. Then complete the article with solutions A–H.

A Don't pay your share either, and wait until the wi-fi gets cut off. Then suddenly, everyone will pay.

B Before you move in, get everyone to write their name on a piece of paper, and put them in a hat. The first person to be picked chooses first.

C Encourage everyone to try. Don't criticize other people's attempts. Try to help them improve.

D Get some ear plugs. Wax ones are the best.

E Have a chore schedule, including doing the dishes, cleaning, and taking out the trash.

F If you often need to get ready at similar times, take turns going first.

G Make sure everyone has their own refrigerator shelf space and kitchen cabinet space.

H Suggest that if they are going to come over often, then maybe they should contribute to rent / bills.

**d** Talk to a partner.

1 Look at the two solutions to each problem. Which one do you think is better? Can you suggest any other solutions?

2 Which problem would you find the most annoying? Have you ever had to deal with any of these problems yourself? What did you do?

### Glossary

**the direct debit "bounced"** a bill that was supposed to be paid automatically through the bank wasn't paid because there wasn't enough money in the account

# Classic student house arguments – and how to avoid them

Living in a shared student house can be one of college's greatest pleasures, but arguments will happen. What are the solutions?

**Who gets the biggest room when moving in?** There's always one housemate who is convinced they have the right to the biggest room.
Solutions:
• Adjust the rent so that the person with the biggest room pays more.
• 1

**The mess in the kitchen** You come home from a long day at school and can't get to the sink because of the enormous pile of pots and pans.
Solutions:
• Establish the 30-minute rule – nothing stays unwashed for over 30 minutes.
• 2

**The housemate whose boyfriend / girlfriend spends more time in your house than their own** They definitely do not live at your house, but you see them more than some of your housemates. And they use the electricity, the water, the wi-fi...
Solutions:
• Explain why it's annoying. It isn't personal, but with them there, there's less space for the rest of you.
• 3

**How to pay and split the bills** The joint account seemed like a good idea until some people's money stopped going in, and the direct debit "bounced" (incurring a charge), and the electricity bill, which was enormous, was forgotten about (another charge), and someone has gone to South America for three months.
Solutions:
• Get everyone to put in more money than will be needed in the account – then later pay the excess back (this is a good way of keeping a little extra cash in reserve, too).
• 4

**Taking too long in the bathroom** What are they doing in there?
Solutions:
• Have a kind word about the fact that there's only one bathroom.
• 5

**When they come in at 3 a.m.,** waking everybody up the night before a big test.
Solutions:
• Make sure your housemates know if you have to be up early for something. Likewise, let them know if you intend to be back late.
• 6

**Food stealing, "borrowing" clothes, etc.** "It was just there, so I took it."
Solutions:
• Label your stuff, so that it's obvious what's yours.
• 7

**Who can't cook, who won't cook?** Why is it always you who's left alone to make dinner in the evening? How come as soon as you've finished, everyone suddenly appears?
Solutions:
• Make a cooking schedule, so you know whose turn it is.
• 8

# 4 LISTENING & SPEAKING

**a** 🔵 Read the situation below. Then go to **Communication** Argument! **A** p.109 **B** p.113 Role-play an argument.

> You share an apartment with someone you didn't know before. At first, you got along really well, but recently there have been several things that have been annoying you, which you've both avoided talking about. Now you think the time has come to have a talk about them.

**b** 🔴 7.7 Listen to a psychologist giving some tips about how to argue better. Which two general points does she make?

1. ☐ Never avoid an argument by refusing to talk.
2. ☐ Try to avoid having an argument in the first place.
3. ☐ It isn't a bad thing to argue from time to time.
4. ☐ Always involve another person to mediate.

**c** Listen again. Check (✓) the ones you should say and put an (✗) for the ones you shouldn't. Why are they right or wrong?

1. ☐ "Look, you're not doing your share of the housework."
2. ☐ "I think we should take another look at how we divide up the housework."
3. ☐ "Sorry, it was my fault."
4. ☐ "You always forget our wedding anniversary."
5. ☐ "I didn't mean to shout. I'd rather not argue with you, but this is very important to me."
6. ☐ "And another thing: I was really disappointed with my birthday present."
7. ☐ "I'd rather talk about this tomorrow, when we've both calmed down."

**d** Look at the things in **c** that the psychologist recommends you <u>should</u> say in an argument. Then do the **Communication** activity in **a** again, with a new partner. Try to follow the psychologist's advice.

**e** **Grammar in context** *would rather*

1. *Listen, <mark>I'd rather talk</mark> about this tomorrow, when we've both calmed down.*
2. *<mark>I'd rather we didn't argue</mark>, but this is very important to me.*

1. We use *would rather* with the base form to talk about present / future preferences, as an alternative to *would prefer to*.

   *I'd rather go on vacation in July than August.*
   *Would you rather stay in or go out tonight?*
   *I'd rather not go out tonight. I'm really tired.*
   **NOT** ~~I'd not rather.~~

2. We can also use *would rather* + person + past tense to talk about what we would like another person to do, as an alternative to *I would prefer it if…*, e.g., *I'd rather you came on Saturday; I'm busy on Friday. I'd rather you didn't play your music so loudly, if you don't mind.*

Rewrite the <mark>highlighted</mark> phrases using *would rather*.

1. <mark>I'd prefer to go to the movies</mark> than to a club.
2. <mark>I'd prefer not to go to the party</mark> if my ex is going to be there.
3. <mark>Would you prefer to meet</mark> on Thursday morning or afternoon?
4. <mark>I'd prefer it if you didn't take photos.</mark>
5. <mark>I'd prefer it if your parents stayed</mark> in a hotel and not with us.

**f** Work in pairs. Look at the options and take turns asking and answering. Say why.

Would you rather…?
1. live on your own or share an apartment with friends
2. take an English class in London or New York
3. take a summer vacation or a winter vacation
4. stay up very late or get up very early
5. go to a concert or a sporting event

# 5 VOCABULARY verbs often confused

**a** 🔴 7.8 Listen to six short extracts. What's happening? Use a verb from the box.

| advise | argue | deny | discuss | refuse | warn |
|--------|-------|------|---------|--------|------|

1. *He's denying something.*

**b** 🟢 p.158 **Vocabulary Bank** Verbs often confused

**c** Complete the questions with the correct verb from each pair, in the right form. Then ask and answer with a partner.

1 Do you _____ if people are late when you have arranged to meet them, or do you think it doesn't _____? **matter / mind**

2 Can you usually _____ family birthdays, or do you need somebody to _____ you? **remember / remind**

3 Have you ever been _____ when you were on vacation? What was _____? **rob / steal**

4 What would you _____ people to do if they want to come to your country in the summer? What might you _____ them to be careful about? **advise / warn**

5 Do you think taking vitamin C helps to _____ colds? What other things can people do to _____ catching colds? **avoid / prevent**

6 Do you ever _____ clothes from friends or family? Have you ever _____ clothes to someone that they then ruined? **borrow / lend**

7 Have you ever _____ a trophy or medal for anything? Are there any games or sports where you absolutely hate being _____? **beat / win**

## 6 READING & WRITING

**a** Read the article once. Which of the tips do you think could also apply to a face-to-face argument? Which do you think are the most important?

**b** Look at some examples of posts on ChangeMyView. Which advice in the article could you use to improve the highlighted phrases? What could you change them to?

1 You must be crazy! Everybody knows that it will never be possible to completely eradicate plastic.

2 According to my mother, children who grow up bilingual find it easier to learn a third language.

3 You're completely wrong to say that all young people are addicted to technology.

**c** Work in groups of four. Each take one of the arguments below, and write a response arguing either for or against the statement.

1 Private schools and hospitals should be abolished.
2 The best way to save the planet is to become a vegan.
3 It's impossible to like the works of an artist or musician if you think they were bad people.
4 People should not be allowed to inherit money or property from their parents.

**d** Pass your paper to the next person in the group, and continue the thread. When you have all responded to each statement, read all the comments on each one. Who do you think argued most effectively, and why?

**Glossary**

**thread** a series of connected messages on a message board on the internet that have been sent by different people, e.g., a Twitter.

# How to win an online argument

When it comes to arguing face-to-face, many people use persuasive intonation or facial expressions to help win the argument. However, these are no use when you want to argue your case online. A recent study of comment threads on online forums has found that some words are more effective than others and that using numbers makes you more persuasive. Lillian Lee and her Ph.D. students at Cornell University analyzed almost two years of posts made on the forum site ChangeMyView, a website where users invite others to challenge their views and present alternative opinions.

## The best ways to win an argument

**Get your timing right** Typically, the first person to reply to the thread has a greater chance of changing the view of the original poster (OP) than someone who joins the debate later on.

**Use alternative terminology** Use words that are different from those used in the post. For example, if discussing climate change, describing it as *global warming* in a reply makes more of an impact than using the same terminology as the OP.

**Be polite** The study suggests that swearing or using aggressive terms instantly makes your argument less effective.

**Think about length** Longer replies in general tend to be seen as more persuasive.

**Use evidence** Using numbers, statistics, and examples to back up opinions makes people sound more convincing. The same is true of links to examples and outside sources.

**Show consideration for other's opinions** Phrases like "It could be the case that…" or "It may be true that…" show that you are open to other points of view. Although this sounds like it might signal a weaker argument, the researchers said it may make your argument easier to accept, by softening its tone.

**Check the language in the original post** Personal pronouns, such as *I*, suggest that a person is more open-minded to persuasion, whereas *we* and *us* suggest they are more stubborn. Stubborn people also use more emotive language and use decisive words such as *certain*, *nothing*, and *best*.

**Know when to give up** Finally, the researchers found that after four or five "back-and-forth" posts have been made, the chances of changing someone's opinion significantly drops.

Adapted from the Daily Mail

 Go online to review the lesson

**G** verbs of the senses   **V** the body   **P** silent consonants

> Botox should be banned for actors…Acting is all about expression; why would you want to iron out a frown?
> *Rachel Weisz, UK actress*

## 1 GRAMMAR verbs of the senses

**a** Look at the adjectives for feelings in the box. In pairs, take turns miming one of them for your partner to guess. You can only use your face and hands.

> astonished   embarrassed   disappointed
> shocked   miserable   scared stiff

**b** Look at the movie still of Keira Knightley. What kind of movie do you think it is? In pairs, focus on her expression and body language and choose a, b, or c to complete sentences 1–3 below.

1 She **looks like**…
  a the daughter of a rich family.
  b a servant who has dressed up in her mistress's clothes.
  c a singer who is about to perform.

2 She **looks**…
  a nervous.
  b embarrassed.
  c miserable.

3 She **looks as if**…
  a she's just broken off a relationship.
  b she's running away from someone she dislikes.
  c she's unsure about what to do.

**c** 🔊 **7.10** Now listen to a movie critic describing what's happening in the scene. Check your ideas in **b**.

**d** Look again at the sentences in **b**. What kinds of words or phrases do you use after *looks*, *looks like*, and *looks as if*?

**e** **G** p.145 **Grammar Bank 7B**

**f** Look at four more movie stills. With a partner, decide which of the movie types they belong to. Do you know anything about any of the movies?

> comedy   fantasy   historical drama
> horror

Keira Knightley, in *Atonement*

A   Meryl Streep

B   Eddie Redmayne

C   Frances McDormand

D   Daniel Kaluuya

**g** Now look carefully at their expressions and body language, and describe:

1 who you think the character is (using *look like* + noun).
2 how you think he / she is feeling (using *looks* + adjective).
3 what you think is happening (using *look as if* + clause).

**h** 🔊 **7.12** Listen to the movie critics and check your answers to **f** and **g**. Did you guess correctly?

**i** 🔊 **7.13** Listen to these sounds. What do you think is happening? Use *It sounds as if…* or *It sounds like…*

> *I think it sounds as if they've…*

**j** 🅒 **Communication** Guess what it is **A p.109 B p.113** Describe objects for your partner to identify using *looks, feels, smells,* or *tastes* + adjective, or *like* + noun.

## 2 READING & LISTENING

**a** Have you ever acted in a play or movie / video? Where and when? What was your role? Did you enjoy it?

**b** Read the first paragraph, the introduction to an article. What is the best way to do the exercises?

# How to improve your acting skills

Being an actor means having a lot of "waiting time," for example, when you're off set during a movie, not on stage in a play, or between jobs. One way to continue practicing and improving is to do some exercises and games that will develop your acting skills. Some of these can be done by yourself, but many are more fun in groups. Most of these techniques, acting games, and exercises were created by drama teachers, and are used in drama schools. They can also benefit you in everyday life, especially with communication skills.

**Exercise 1  Developing your imagination**

This exercise is aimed at developing your imagination, which is one of the most important components of an actor's success. In order for the audience to believe your acting, it's you who has to believe first that the life of your character is real. And to do that, you need to be able to build a small world of your character's life in your mind. Even just for one scene, you have to come up with answers for why you are doing what you are doing, why it is that way, etc.

The exercise is best done in a group. Look at an image of a person showing an emotion, e.g., smiling. Then between you, try to think of all the possible reasons why the person might be smiling, for example, he looks as if he might be remembering a funny movie, or he might have just booked a vacation abroad.

**c** Now read the instructions for the first exercise, **Developing your imagination**. Then do it in groups of 4–5, using the photograph below.

**d** 🔊 **7.14** Look at the names of three more exercises. Listen to a drama teacher explaining the exercises to his students. Which exercise helps with…?

- ☐ paying attention to details
- ☐ showing emotions
- ☐ using body language

**Exercise 2  Stroking an animal**

Think of [1]_____.
Then [2]_____.
Now [3]_____.

**Exercise 3  What were they wearing?**

One person [4]_____.
Sit [5]_____ and focus on [6]_____.
After three minutes, [7]_____ unless [8]_____.
Then the host [9]_____.

**Exercise 4  The "magic" image**

Choose [10]_____,
e.g., [11]_____,
and write down [12]_____.
Show [13]_____ to other people in the group. Choose no more than [14]_____.
When you have [15]_____, think of [16]_____.
Then create [17]_____ that combines [18]_____.

**e** Listen again and complete the instructions. Then compare with a partner and add anything you missed.

**f** Now, in your same groups, do the three exercises.

## 3 VOCABULARY & SPEAKING the body

a Look at the photos. Where do you think they were taken? What emotion do you think he is showing?

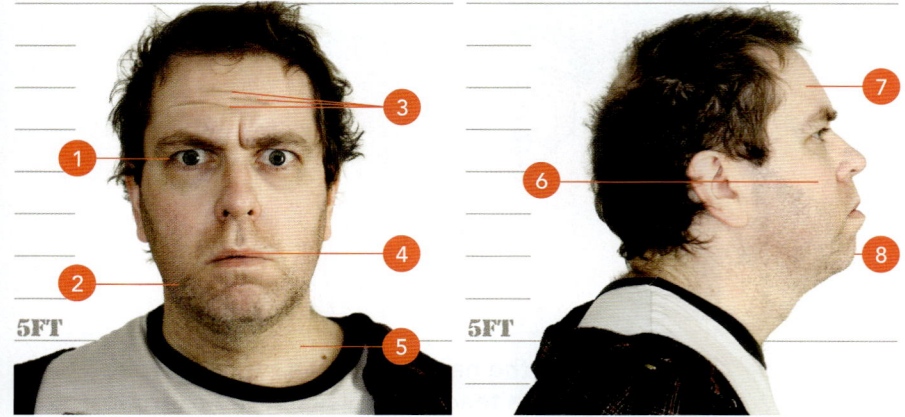

b Look at the photos and match the words in the box with 1–8.

| | cheek | 8 | chin | | eye | | forehead |
| | lips | | neck | | stubble | | wrinkles |

c Which word in **b** goes with these? Can you find them in the photo?

_____ brow    _____ lash    _____ lid

d 🔊7.15 Listen and check your answers to **b** and **c**.

e Ⓥ p.159 **Vocabulary Bank** The body

## 4 PRONUNCIATION silent consonants

a Cross out the "silent" consonant in these words.

calf   comb   kneel   palm   thumb   wrinkles   wrist

b 🔊7.19 Listen and check. What can you deduce about the pronunciation of…?

- *kn* and *wr* at the beginning of a word   • *mb* at the end of a word

c Look at the phonetics for some more words with silent consonants. In pairs, try to say them.

| 1 | /ˈɑnəst/ | 4 | /ˈwɪsl/ | 7 | /dɪˈzaɪn/ | 10 | /kɑm/ |
| 2 | /ˈfæsn/ | 5 | /aɪl/ | 8 | /hæf/ | 11 | /klaɪm/ |
| 3 | /ˈmʌsl/ | 6 | /daʊt/ | 9 | /hoʊl/ | 12 | /nɑk/ |

d 🔊7.20 Match words A–L to the phonetics in **c**. Then listen and check. What is the silent consonant in each one?

| A aisle | D design | G half | J muscle |
| B calm | E doubt | H honest | K whistle |
| C climb | F fasten | I knock | L whole |

e Practice saying the phrases below.

half an hour   I doubt it   calm down, dear   an aisle seat, please
designer clothes   anti-wrinkle cream   kneel down

## 5 READING & SPEAKING

a Look at the title of an article by Professor Thomas Ormerod about his research and read the first paragraph. What is the accepted "best way to spot a liar"? What was the purpose of Ormerod's experiment?

b Now read the rest of the article and match Ormerod's five key principles A–E to blanks 1–5.

A **Ask open questions**
B **Build rapport**
C **Look for changes in style**
D **Try to find contradictions**
E **Use surprise questions**

c Read the article again and mark the statements **T** (true) or **F** (false). Correct the **F** statements.

1 Body language as a way of identifying a liar can be helpful if you know someone well.
2 The "fake" passengers in Ormerod's experiment were given a false cover story.
3 All passengers passing through airport security during the experiment were interviewed by the trained security officers.
4 The more information passengers were asked for, the more difficult it was for them to lie successfully.
5 Officers were told to be suspicious of passengers who always gave short answers.
6 The experiment proved that verbal clues are as effective as body language in helping to identify a liar.

d In pairs, play *Truth or lie*. Switch roles for question 2, etc.

A Ask **B** question 1 below. Ask follow-up questions, using techniques from the article, and decide if **B** is telling the truth.
B **A** will ask you question 1 below. You must answer, *Yes, I have.* If you have had the experience, tell the truth. If you haven't, invent answers to **A**'s follow-up questions.

1 Have you ever walked out in the middle of a play, movie, or concert?
2 Have you ever sprained your wrist or ankle?
3 Have you ever been caught cheating on an exam?
4 Have you ever been stopped by the police?

e Did any of Thomas Ormerod's techniques help you to tell if your partner was telling the truth or not?

# The best way to spot a liar...or is it?

**How easy is it to know whether someone is telling the truth or lying?** Some people aren't very good at pretending, while others are far more expert. Most of us are familiar with the kind of body language that tends to indicate deception, such as avoiding eye contact, blushing, fidgeting, or laughing nervously; and identifying whether somebody is telling the truth can be fairly straightforward with people we know well, our children, family, or friends. However, research shows that relying only on body language to spot a liar is, in fact, very unreliable, especially when you are not familiar with how a person usually behaves. In fact, according to one study, just one in 400 people manage to make a correct judgement based on nonverbal indicators with more than 80% accuracy. Just because someone looks nervous does not mean they are guilty, and in more formal contexts, such as interviewing crime suspects or in security screening at airports, the consequences of getting it wrong can be very serious. So, my research team and I devised an experiment to develop a more reliable method of lie detection, which relies not on how people behave, but on what they say.

We tested out our method on passengers at airport security. First, we recruited a selection of "fake" passengers of different nationalities, such as American, German, Swiss, and Canadian, and offered them an extra fee if they passed through a security interview without being spotted. Each person prepared a convincing cover story about their life and work history and the purpose of their plane trip. They were all given valid tickets and passports, and were asked to dress appropriately and carry suitable luggage. A team of trained officers then made a random selection of passengers passing through security, and carried out specially constructed interviews in order to try to spot the "fakes."

**So, what kinds of things did the officers ask in these interviews?** These are the key principles we used to increase the chance of finding out if someone was lying:

1 _____ Officers were asked to give the impression that this was a fairly casual conversation, and to put passengers at ease with general, friendly questions such as "How are you today?" and "Did you have a good trip to the airport?"

2 _____ We told officers to use questions such as "Can you tell me about…?", "Can you explain to me who…?" and so on, that required passengers to give more information, rather than just answering "yes" or "no."

3 _____ Passengers were asked, for example, for extra information about a family member or about the company that they worked for; handling unexpected questions is more difficult for a liar than for a truthful person.

4 _____ Officers were encouraged to ask follow-up questions to test passengers' statements. For example, if the passenger claimed to work in Oxford, the officer might ask them about their trip to work, to check if they could report that accurately, and to try to spot any gaps in expected knowledge.

5 _____ Liars are often more confident when they feel in control of a conversation, but if they start to feel undermined or challenged, they begin to limit their responses. We told officers to watch out for people who started to reply with much shorter answers, or who showed a tendency to become evasive in their answers, not replying directly to the questions.

The aim was to put all passengers under gentle pressure, which would increase the chance that something a "fake" passenger might reveal during a conversation would give them away. The officers were also told not to pick up a lie immediately – rather, to encourage the liar to continue to talk, and then to challenge them when they were sure they were lying. And the results were striking. The security officers using our interview technique were over 20 times more likely to detect the lying passengers than officers using traditional behavior observation methods.

Professor Thomas Ormerod

---

## 6 WRITING

W p.119 Writing Describing a photo  Write a description of a picture, speculating about what the people are doing, feeling, etc.

Go online to review the lesson

## 1 ▶ THE INTERVIEW Part 1

**a** Read the biographical information about Simon Callow. Have you seen any of his movies?

**Simon Callow** is an English actor, writer, and theater director. He was born in London in 1949 and studied at Queen's University, Belfast, and the Drama Center in London.

As a young actor he made his name when he played the part of Mozart in Peter Shaffer's production of *Amadeus* at the Royal National Theater in London in 1979, and he later appeared in the movie version. As well as acting in the theater, he has also appeared in TV dramas and comedies and in many movies including *Four Weddings and a Funeral* and *Shakespeare in Love*. He has directed both plays and musicals and was awarded the Laurence Olivier award for Best Musical for *Carmen Jones* in 1992. He has written biographies of the Irish writer Oscar Wilde and Orson Welles, the American actor and movie director. He was awarded the CBE in 1999 for his services to drama.

**b** Watch Part 1 of an interview with him. Mark the sentences **T** (true) or **F** (false).

1 His first job was as an actor at The Old Vic theater.
2 When he watched rehearsals he was fascinated by how the actors and the directors worked together.
3 Acting attracted him because it involved problem solving.
4 Playing the part of Mozart in *Amadeus* was a challenge because he wasn't a fictional character.
5 Mozart was the most exciting role he has had because it was his first.

**c** Now watch again and say why the **F** sentences are false.

### Glossary

**The Old Vic** one of the oldest and most famous of the London theaters
***Amadeus*** is a play by Peter Shaffer about the life of the composer Wolfgang Amadeus Mozart. It was also made into a movie of the same name. In the play, Mozart is portrayed as having a very childish personality, which contrasts with the genius and sophistication of his music.
***The Marriage of Figaro*** one of Mozart's best-known operas
**box office** the place at a theater or movie theater where tickets are sold
**rehearsals** /rɪˈhɜːrslz/ time that is spent practicing a play or a piece of music
**auditorium** /ˌɔːdɪˈtɔːriəm/ the part of a theater where the audience sits

**d** Have you seen any movies or plays based on the lives of real people? Did you agree with the way they were portrayed?

## ▶ Part 2

**a** Now watch Part 2. Answer the questions.

1 Which does he prefer, acting in the theater or in movies?
2 Complete the two crucial differences he mentions about acting in the theater:
There's an _____.
Every single performance is utterly _____.
3 Who does he say are the most important people in the making of a movie, the director, the editor, or the actors? Why?
4 Does he think acting in movies is more natural and realistic than theater acting? Why (not)?

**b** Watch again. What is he referring to when he says…?

1 "It's important because you have to reach out to them, make sure that everybody can hear and see what you're doing."
2 "…I mean you never do, you never can."
3 "So, in that sense, the actor is rather powerless."
4 "…there are some, you know, little metal objects right in front of you, sort of, staring at you as you're doing your love scene…"

### Glossary

**(film) editor** the person whose job it is to decide what to include and what to cut in a movie
**editing suite** /ˈedətɪŋ swiːt/ a room containing electronic equipment for editing video material

**c** Do you ever go to the theater? Do you prefer it to the movies? Why (not)? What plays have you seen?

## ▶ Part 3

**a** Now watch Part 3. What does he say about…?

1 watching other actors acting
2 the first great actors he saw
3 Daniel Day-Lewis
4 wearing makeup
5 the first night of a play

Daniel Day-Lewis

Laurence Olivier

### Glossary

**John Gielgud** a famous stage and movie actor (1904–2000)
**Ralph Richardson** a famous stage and movie actor (1902–1983)
**Laurence Olivier** a famous stage and movie actor (1907–1989)
**Edith Evans** a famous stage and movie actor (1888–1976)
**Peggy Ashcroft** a famous stage and movie actor (1907–1991)
**Daniel Day-Lewis** a famous movie actor (1957– )
**stage fright** nervous feelings felt by actors before they appear in front of an audience

**b** Are there any actors you particularly enjoy watching? Why do you like them? Which of their characters do you like best?

## 2 ▶ LOOKING AT LANGUAGE

> 🔍 **Modifiers**
> Simon Callow uses a wide variety of modifiers (*really*, *incredibly*, etc.) to make his language more expressive.

Watch some extracts from the interview and complete the missing adjective or modifier.

1 "…I thought what a wonderful job, what a _____ **interesting** job…"
2 "My job was to reconcile that with the fact that he wrote *The Marriage of Figaro*, and that was **tremendously** _____."
3 "…its fame, almost from the moment it was announced, was **overwhelmingly** _____ than anything I had ever done…"
4 "They're _____ **different** media, they require different things from you as an actor…"
5 "…you bring _____ **different** things to them."
6 "The beauty of the theater is that every single performance is **utterly** _____ from every other one."
7 "As a young man, and a boy, I was _____ **lucky** to see that fabled generation of actors, of, of Gielgud and Richardson, Olivier,…"

## 3 ▶ THE CONVERSATION

Mark    John    Devika

**a** Watch the conversation. Check (✓) the correct option to sum up their conclusion.

They agree that…
1 ☐ a live performance is always better because of the atmosphere.
2 ☐ a recorded performance is usually better because there are no distractions.
3 ☐ it's impossible to generalize because it depends on the event.

**b** Watch again. What do Devika and Mark say about the following things? Are they positive or negative?

1 **Devika** a big flashy superhero film
2 **Devika** some Shakespeare or any modern plays
3 **Mark** factors that could sway your enjoyment
4 **Mark** a major rugby match recently
5 **Devika** a crowd of other people enjoying the music

**c** Do you agree with the participants about the live performances being better than recorded ones?

**d** Watch some extracts and complete the missing phrases.

1 That's a _____ _____ _____. I love going to the cinema.
2 I think _____ _____ _____ _____ it's better or worse…
3 But if you go to a live one though, then you participate, _____ _____, because you're part of it. .
4 If you're sitting, _____ _____, high up or with a slightly obstructed view…
5 I've been to plenty of live music events – concerts and festivals and things, _____ _____, around the country, and I love them.
6 That's intriguing _____ _____, the difference between the two.

**e** Which of the phrases in **d** do they use to…?

☐☐☐☐ give themselves time to think
☐☐ check the others agree

**f** Now have a conversation in groups of three.

1 Do you think it's essential these days for an actor to be good-looking?
2 Which is more important in a movie, the actors or the special effects?

🔵 **Go online** to watch the video, review the lesson, and check your progress

G the passive (all forms); *have something done; it is said that..., he is thought to..., etc.*   V crime and punishment   P the letter *u*

A society gets the criminals it deserves.
*Val McDermid, Scottish crime writer*

## 1 LISTENING

**a** Imagine you are alone on the street at night in an area that you don't know well. Would you feel nervous? What might you do to feel safer?

**b** Read the introduction to a page from a police crime prevention website and look at the pictures. With a partner, decide what advice you think is shown in each picture, and what the missing word in the headings might be.

**c** 🔊 8.1 Now listen to a Metropolitan Police podcast. Complete the headings. What advice did you predict correctly in **b**?

**d** Listen again and answer the questions.
1 What should you plan in advance?
2 Why is it important to look confident?
3 What three things shouldn't you do on the street on a cell phone?
4 What kinds of things should you keep out of sight?
5 Why should you walk facing oncoming traffic?
6 What three things make places safer to walk at night?
7 What should you do during an evening when you're out with friends?
8 Why shouldn't you get into a stranger's car at an airport?

**e** Was any of the advice about street crime new to you? Which tip do you think is the most useful? How safe / unsafe is your town, or the area where you live?

# Stay safe

Street crime is often unplanned, so making yourself less of a target, moving with purpose, and being aware of your surroundings will go a long way to keeping you safe when you're out and about. Here are eight important pieces of advice.

**1** Be _____

**2** Be _____

**3** Be _____

**4** _____ it

**5** Go _____ the flow

**6** Trust your _____

**7** Make a _____

**8** Look out for _____

*Adapted from the Metropolitan Police website*

## 2 VOCABULARY crime and punishment

**a** How much do you think you know about keeping your home safe? Can you "beat the burglar"? Take the quiz to find out.

### Beat the burglar

**1** What's the most common time of day to **be burglarized**?
  a between 10:00 a.m. and 12:00 p.m.
  b between 2:00 p.m. and 5:00 p.m.
  c between 10:00 p.m. and 12:00 a.m.

**2** How long do you think a **burglar** usually takes to search someone's house?
  a 10 minutes   b 20 minutes   c 30 minutes

**3** What two things influence a burglar to choose a house to **break into**?
  a it's in an expensive area
  b there's no one at home
  c there are trees and bushes around the house

**4** Which are the most common things that burglars **steal**, apart from money?
  a laptops and tablets
  b paintings and antiques
  c jewelry

**5** What is the best place in the house to hide your valuables?
  a the living room        d the kitchen
  b the master bedroom     e the study
  c a child's bedroom

**6** What is most likely to prevent a **burglary**?
  a a dog   b a burglar alarm

**b** **C Communication** Beat the burglar **A p.109 B p.113** Find out the answers, according to an ex-burglar.

**c** Now **A** tell **B** the answers to questions 1–3, and **B** tell **A** the answers to questions 4–6.

**d** Match the highlighted words in the quiz to definitions 1–5.

  1 _____ (*noun*) a person who breaks in and steals from a private house
  2 _____ (*verb, passive*) to have somebody enter your house and take things that belong to you
  3 _____ (*noun*) the crime of entering a house illegally and stealing things from it
  4 _____ (*phr. verb*) to enter a place by force
  5 _____ (*verb*) to take something without intending to return it or pay for it

**e** 🔊 8.2 Listen and check.

**f** **V p.160 Vocabulary Bank** Crime and punishment

## 3 PRONUNCIATION & SPEAKING
### the letter *u*

**a** Look at the words in the box. Which sound does the letter *u* make? Put them in the correct row.

| accuse drugs judge jury mugger punishment smuggling | |
|---|---|
| ∧ | |
| ʊʊ | |
| /yu/ | |

**b** Now look at the pink letters in some more words that include the letter *u*. Put them in the correct row, according to how the vowel sound is pronounced.

| burglar caught fraud guilty murderer stalk | |
|---|---|
| ɪ | |
| ər | |
| ɔ | |

**c** 🔊 8.5 Listen and check your answers to **a** and **b**. Then answer the questions.

  1 Is the vowel sound before a double consonant short or long?
  2 How do we pronounce *gu* before the letters *a*, *e*, and *i*, as in *guard*, *guess*, *guilty*?

**d** 🔊 8.6 Listen and write five sentences. Then practice saying them.

**e** Talk in small groups. Ask for more details.

What do you think are the most common crimes in your town or city?

Have you ever witnessed a crime? What was it? Where? What happened?

Do you know anyone…?
  • whose phone or bicycle has been stolen
  • whose car has been vandalized
  • who has been stopped by the police while driving
  • who has been mugged
  • who has been burglarized
  • who has been offered a bribe

## 4 GRAMMAR the passive (all forms); *have something done; it is said that…, he is thought to…*, etc.

a Read three true crime stories. In which story was someone…?

A caught because of what they stole
B caught because of what they wrote on
C caught because of what they said

### 1 The partial pay stub

A man from Illinois thought he had a clever plan to avoid ¹*catching / being caught* during a bank robbery. He entered the bank and passed a teller a note that read, "Be Quick Be Quiet. Give your cash or I'll shoot." The teller gave the robber $400. However, the man ²*failed / was failed* to notice that he had written the note on part of his pay stub. The other part of the pay stub, including the robber's name and home address, ³*found / was found* outside the bank by police officers!

### 2 The Apple iDiot

Last week in San Francisco, a woman had her iPhone stolen. A thief rode his bike up to her on the sidewalk, ⁴*snatched / was snatched* the iPhone out of her hands, and rode away. However, unknown to him, the woman worked for Apple and ⁵*was demonstrating / was being demonstrated* the iPhone's new GPS tracking device to some customers. The tracker worked, and the thief ⁶*caught / was caught* a few minutes later.

### 3 Parlez-vous français?

The victim was hysterical when the Calgary police arrived at her house. A window ⁷*had broken / had been broken* and her jewelry was gone. While the police were there, her French-speaking father ⁸*called / was called*. She explained to him, in French, that it was all a plan to get the insurance money. She didn't know that Officer Meharu speaks six languages, including French. She ⁹*has been charged / has charged* with fraud.

b Read the stories again. Circle the correct form of verbs 1–9, active or passive.

c Look at the extract from story 2.

A woman **had her iPhone stolen**.

Does it describe…?
1 something the person arranged for someone to do for her
2 something bad that happened to her

d 🔊 8.7 Now look at another headline and listen to the news story. In what way was the robber polite?

### The most-polite robber

e Listen again and complete extracts 1–4. How is the structure different between 1 and 4, and 2 and 3?

1 Police in Stockport are looking for a man who is said _____ _____ the most-polite armed robber.
2 It is believed _____ _____ _____ a tall man in his early 40s…
3 It is thought _____ _____ _____ _____ at least four stores in Stockport in recent weeks.
4 He is reported _____ _____ _____ to his victims…

f 🅖 p.146 Grammar Bank 8A

## 5 READING

a Work in pairs. Discuss the questions.

1 Do you post photos on social media sites like Facebook or Instagram? How often? What kinds of photos do you post?
2 Who do you allow to see your posted photos? Why?
3 How do you feel when other people post photos of you without your permission?

b You're going to read an article about Steve Bustin, who had problems with some photos he posted on Facebook. First, look at the four photos. Then read the article once and answer the questions.

1 Who are the people in photo A? Who did "Martin" say they were?
2 Why did photos B and C make Constance suspicious?
3 What had happened in photo D? How did the scammer use it?

c Read the article again. Choose a, b, or c.

1 When Steve received Constance's email he felt ____.
   a surprised  b happy  c sorry
2 Constance was attracted to Martin because ____.
   a she liked his profile photo
   b he paid her a lot of attention
   c he reminded her of her husband
3 Thanks to a website about dating scams, Constance was able to find out who ____.
   a "Martin" really was
   b the photo was really of
   c had originally posted the photo
4 In a typical dating scam, men like Martin start by ____.
   a being very nice to women
   b asking women for money
   c trying to get women's sympathy
5 As a result of the scam, Steve has decided to be more careful about ____ on social media.
   a posting vacation photos
   b who can see what he posts
   c contacting friends and family

d Look at the highlighted words in the article related to scams and try to figure out what they mean. Then match them to a synonym in the box.

| | | | |
|---|---|---|---|
| careful | chosen | fraud | give |
| make use of (in a dishonest way) | | | |
| said that (even though it wasn't true) | | | |
| thought that | trick (*verb*) | | |

# A case of identity theft

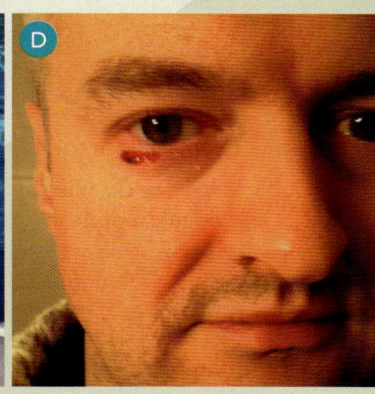

*Adapted from the Mirror website*

**I sighed when I glanced at the email on my phone.** It was from a woman named Constance, a complete stranger to me, who [1] was under the impression that we'd been in a relationship for several months. It has become an all-too-familiar story. Over the past two years, my photos have been used to [2] con 11 women on dating websites. These are just the ones I know about; the real number could be much higher.

I called Constance and listened as she explained she'd met a man named Martin Peterson on Elite Singles. He said he was Danish and a widower. Constance had joined the website hoping to find love after losing her husband three years earlier, and Martin had seemed kind and understanding. He was interested in everything about her, texting her every morning and calling her for cozy chats in the evening. But on his dating profile were several photos which were, in fact, of me! She forwarded me the pictures, and I shuddered when I saw one of me and my sister, who Martin had said was his dead wife.

Constance had begun to be suspicious of Martin when she noticed his hair color and style change within the space of a few hours. He [3] claimed he was on a business trip, and sent her a photo of me sitting in a hotel garden having breakfast, with my curly gray hair in need of a trim. Later in the day, he sent a second photo of me by a swimming pool, in which my hair was shorter and darker. In fact, these photos had been taken several years apart and had been "harvested" from my Facebook account. Constance began to look carefully at all the pictures he had sent. She researched dating [4] scams online, and found a way to find out where a picture had originated. By dragging a picture of Martin into a "reverse image search" on Google, she discovered that the pictures of the man she'd believed to be a Danish widower were actually of me, a public speaker from Brighton, UK.

People like "Martin" are known to [5] prey on older women. First, they gain their trust and bombard them with attention, and then they say they are traveling abroad for work, where they are involved in an accident. Finally, they ask the woman to transfer money for medical treatment or flights home. A few years ago, I scratched my face, and posted a photo online of me with blood on my face. This picture has now been used by the scammer several times – he sends it alongside a picture of a smashed-up car, and says he's been involved in a serious accident. Fortunately, Constance didn't [6] hand over any money. But other women have, including one woman who lost thousands of dollars.

These days, I'm a lot more conscious of what I post online. I always used to share pictures of everything: vacations by the pool, work speeches, me and my dog, fancy parties... Now I've changed my privacy settings on social media. I suppose my account was [7] targeted because I had a range of photos and the scammer could build a whole life from them. An expert told me that my pictures had probably been sold as a bundle on the black market. I now encourage all my friends and family to be [8] wary about what they post – once they're out there, there's nothing you can do about it. Unfortunately for me, my identity is no longer my own.

## 6 SPEAKING

a How common do you think identity theft is these days? What can people do to avoid it from happening?

b Look at the questions on the right. For each one...
- decide what you think.
- think of reasons for your opinions.
- decide how you think the "crime" should be punished.

c Now discuss the questions in groups.

### Do you think it should be illegal to...?
- post a photo or video of someone online without their permission
- post aggressive or threatening tweets or messages
- download music, books, and movies without paying for them
- own an aggressive breed of dog
- squat in an unoccupied house (live there without paying rent)
- paint graffiti on a wall or fence
- smoke outdoors, e.g., in parks or on the street
- kill another person in self-defense

**If yes, how do you think they should be punished? If no, say why not.**

## 7 WRITING

Ⓦ p.120 Writing Expressing your opinion  Write an article for an online forum, saying what you think about some aspects of crime.

🔵 **Go online** to review the lesson

> For most people no news is good news, but for journalists good news is not news.
> *Gloria Borger, US political commentator*

**G** reporting verbs  **V** the media  **P** word stress

## 1 LISTENING & SPEAKING

**a** Talk to a partner.

1 Where do you get your international, national, and local news from?
2 Look at the topics in the box below. What kinds of news are you usually interested in?

---
arts and culture   business   celebrity gossip
crime   the environment   food & drink   health
local / national news   politics   sports   technology
TV and entertainment   the weather   world news
---

3 What kinds of news headlines, e.g., a death, news about a celebrity, a sports score, might make you want to read the whole article?
4 What stories are in the news right now in your country?

**b** Look at the headlines and photos for two news stories that were reported in the same week. What do you think they are about?

**300 Years of Instant Ramen**

**Egyptian zoo denies their zebra is a donkey**

**c** 🔊 8.11 Listen to the stories and check. Were you correct?

**d** Listen again and complete the information.

1 The truck filled with instant ramen was stolen from…
2 The victim had permission to park from…
3 Lt. Allen Stevens says this is the first…
4 On average, one package of instant ramen noodles costs…
5 Mahmoud Sarhan was visiting the zoo when he saw…
6 He was sure it was a donkey because…
7 A vet who looked at the photo said that…
8 The zoo's owner wouldn't admit that…

**e** Look at two more headlines and photos from the same week's news. With a partner, guess what they are about.

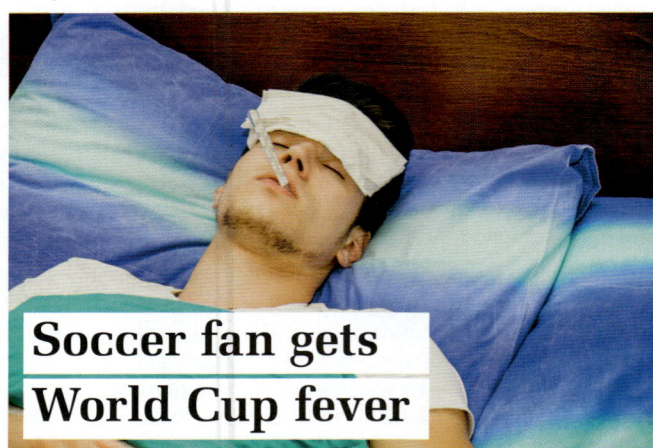

**Soccer fan gets World Cup fever**

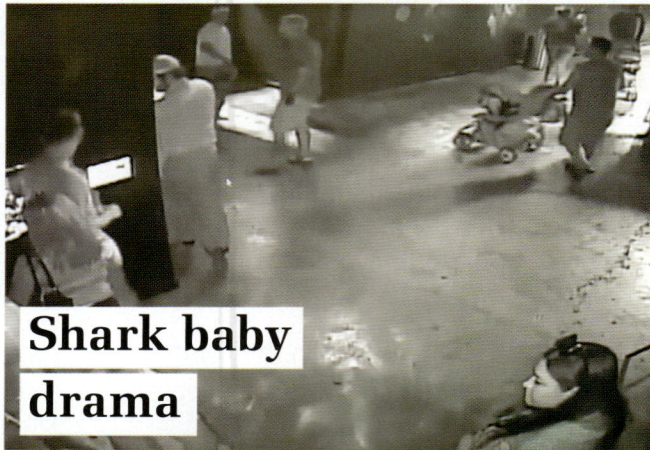

**Shark baby drama**

**f** 🌐 **Communication** Strange, but true **A** p.109 **B** p.113 Read the stories and check, then tell each other what happened.

**g** Three of the four stories are true and one is fake news. Which one do you think is the fake?

## 2 GRAMMAR reporting verbs

**a** Look at some extracts from the four news stories. Match them to the direct speech A–F.

1 The victim **persuaded the gas station's owner to give** him permission to park the tractor-trailer there.

2 While **most nutritionists probably would not recommend eating** instant ramen more than once or twice a month,...

3 A zoo in Egypt **has denied painting** a donkey with black stripes…

4 …a local vet…**agreed to examine** the photo.

5 He **advised me not to take** soccer so seriously.

6 He **threatened to steal** another shark if he felt it was necessary.

A ☐ "OK, I'll take a look at it."
B ☐ "It's not good to eat a lot of it."
C ☐ "I'll do it again if I have to."
D ☐ "Don't do it – it's not very important."
E ☐ "Please let me park here."
F ☐ "We definitely didn't do it."

**b** **G** p.147 Grammar Bank 8B

## 3 PRONUNCIATION word stress

**a** Look at the two-syllable reporting verbs in the box. All of them except four are stressed on the second syllable. Circle the four exceptions.

| | | | |
|---|---|---|---|
| a\|ccuse | ad\|mit | ad\|vise | a\|gree |
| con\|vince | de\|ny | in\|sist | in\|vite | o\|ffer |
| or\|der | per\|suade | pro\|mise | re\|fuse |
| re\|gret | re\|mind | sug\|gest | threa\|ten |

**b** 🔊 8.13 Listen and check.

> 🔎 **Spelling of two-syllable verbs**
> If a two-syllable verb ends in consonant–vowel–consonant and is stressed on the second syllable, the final consonant is doubled before an -ed ending, e.g., <u>re</u>gret > regretted, ad<u>mit</u> > admitted. However, when the stress is on the first syllable, the final consonant is not doubled, e.g., <u>offer</u> > offered, <u>threaten</u> > threatened.

**c** Complete the sentences below with the correct reporting verb in the past tense.

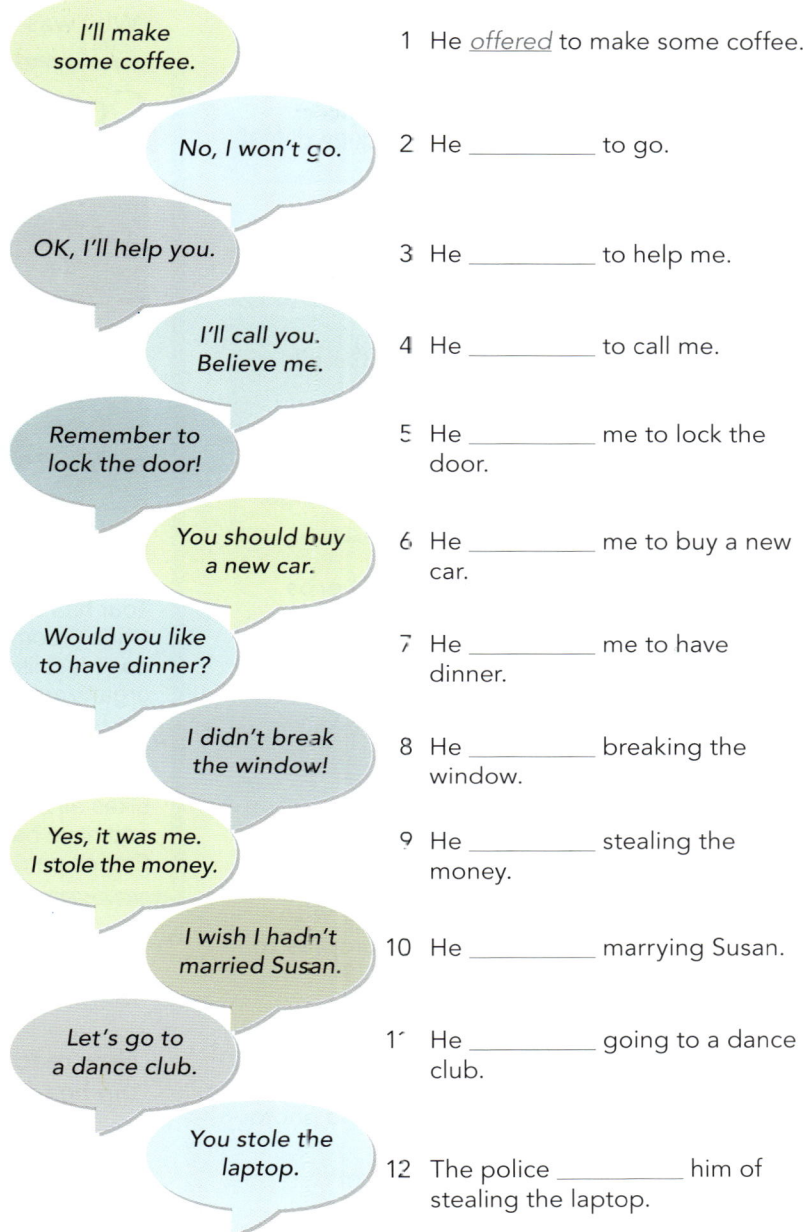

1 He <u>offered</u> to make some coffee.

2 He _____ to go.

3 He _____ to help me.

4 He _____ to call me.

5 He _____ me to lock the door.

6 He _____ me to buy a new car.

7 He _____ me to have dinner.

8 He _____ breaking the window.

9 He _____ stealing the money.

10 He _____ marrying Susan.

1′ He _____ going to a dance club.

12 The police _____ him of stealing the laptop.

**d** 🔊 8.14 Listen and check.

**e** Cover the right-hand column in **c**. Look at the direct speech and say the reported sentence, linking the verbs and *to* where appropriate.

> 🔎 **Linking**
> Remember that if a word ends in a /t/ or /d/ sound, e.g., regular past tense verbs, and the next word begins with a /d/ or /t/ sound, the two words are linked, e.g., offered ‿ to.

**f** 🔊 8.15 Listen to some more sentences in direct speech. Then report them using the verb you hear.

1 🔊 *I didn't steal the wallet!* **deny**  *He denied stealing the wallet.*

## 4 VOCABULARY & SPEAKING
the media

**a** Look at the four headlines. What four categories of news are they?

1. Team manager to **quit** after shocking defeat

2. 21-year-old **tabbed** to become party leader

3. Reality TV star **to wed** girlfriend after one-week engagement

4. Companies **split** after unsuccessful merger

**b** Guess the meaning of the **bold** verbs. Then match them to a word or phrase from the box.

| | |
|---|---|
| is going to marry | is predicted |
| leaves | separate |

**c** ⓥ p.161 **Vocabulary Bank** The media

**d** Look at the questions below. Decide if you personally agree or disagree with them. Think of reasons and examples to support your opinion.

**Is it ever OK...?**
- for journalists to access other people's phones or email accounts
- for the media to publish stories and photos about celebrities' private lives
- for the paparazzi to take photos of well-known people when they are at home or on vacation
- to censor the news
- to publish news articles that aren't completely true

*I think it's perfectly OK for / to...*

*I think it can be OK for / to..., depending on the circumstances.*

*I don't think it's ever OK for / to...because...*

**e** Work in small groups. Take turns asking one question. Give your opinion and explain why. Then discuss with the group. What is the majority opinion on each topic?

## 5 READING

**a** Read a news report about the Tour de France bicycle race. Why was Chris Froome said to be disappointed?

# Competitors' disappointment over Tour de France route

CYCLISTS have begun to complain that their enjoyment of the Tour has been spoiled by periods of intense uphill cycling. Cyclist Chris Froome said, "Even though it's called the Tour de France, I don't feel like I'm getting to experience the real France at all. The organizers have planned a route that goes right through some of the hilliest parts of the country, when there are much quicker flat roads we could use. I was hoping we could stop off at a vineyard, or have lunch at an authentic local brasserie, but we're just on our bikes all day. I spent six months taking night courses in French and have barely been able to speak a word, because I pass every French person I meet at 30 mph."

**b** Read the article again. At what point did you realize that this is not a serious piece of news? Are there any other features of the article that made you suspicious?

**c** Now read an article about how to spot fake news. Complete the headings with a word from the box.

addresses date fake images name sense spellings trust

**d** Read the article again and answer the questions about each section.

Introduction  Why do many online sites publish fake news?
1. Why don't you need to worry about a Category Six hurricane?
2. What was suspicious about the story in the *Denver Guardian*?
3. What was the problem with the URL *ABC.com.co*?
4. What was wrong with the photos of a news report about a terror attack in Brussels?
5. Why does a lot of spelling mistakes in a news article mean that it might be fake?
6. How would you know that the Twitter handle @WarrenBuffet was fake?
7. Why might an emotionally disturbing image with a news story be a telltale sign?
8. What should you do before making an important decision based on online information?

# 8 tips on how to spot fake news

Fake content has become a daily reality of life online, with hundreds of sites creating false or exaggerated stories for political or personal gain. In spite of the efforts of big tech companies to limit the spread of fake news, some stories fall through the cracks. The expert advice is that it's always useful to have a critical eye and to be on the lookout for misleading stories. There are several telltale signs to look for. Fake news experts Will Moy, director of fact-checking charity Full Fact, and Cambridge University researcher Sander van der Linden offer their tips.

### 1  Beware of stories that don't make _____

One of the key signs of fake news is that the stories are highly improbable. During last year's Hurricane Irma, a hugely popular viral story claimed that it was a Category Six hurricane that would "wipe cities off the map." Category Six hurricanes do not exist. Moy says, "Extraordinary claims need extraordinary evidence. If somebody says Elvis is alive, ask for a song before you believe it."

### 2  Check the _____ of the news site that published it

Unfamiliar sites built to sound like news organizations are behind many fake news stories, but the names of the sites are often a hint that stories may be fake. When the *Denver Guardian* made claims about Hillary Clinton's emails, there was one small problem – there is no such paper as the *Denver Guardian*. It sounds real, but it is completely fake. "Be careful of websites that you haven't heard of before," says Moy.

### 3  Beware faked website _____

Some sites may try to impersonate real news outlets with URLs that seem similar but have slight differences. For instance, one fake news site impersonated ABC news using a URL that read *ABC.com.co*, rather than *abcnews.go.com*.

### 4  Check the _____

False news stories often include timelines that make no sense, or contain the wrong dates. For instance, images purporting to be of a 2016 terror attack in Brussels were actually from a 2011 attack on Moscow's Domodedovo Airport.

### 5  Look for unusual _____ and mistakes

Often, the sign that news is fake is that it is of low quality, with spelling errors and an overuse of capital letters. Real news sources will employ editors to remove these errors and ensure accuracy.

### 6  Look out for _____ celebrity accounts

"Sometimes stories can spread online after being shared by a social media account designed to impersonate a real person," says Sander van der Linden. "Think about the fake tweets that were supposedly sent out by billionaire Warren Buffett. Someone was impersonating him, and millions of people did not notice that the Twitter handle read 'WarrenBuffet,' while his real name is Warren Buffett."

### 7  Google-search the _____

Fake news sites will often use unrelated or doctored photos. Google-search them to see where they came from and check how accurate they are against other legitimate news sites. Other hoaxers will use deliberately disturbing imagery in an attempt to hook in readers, van der Linden says. "Emotional content is more likely to go viral, for example, imagine the effect of a fake story containing disturbing images about the effects of a fake disease."

### 8  If you're unsure, double check with a source you _____

Fake news stories will often appear on just one site, so if you're unsure, check against a reliable news source. "When it matters, double check," says Moy, "particularly when it comes to health or other life decisions. Always use a trustworthy source."

Adapted from The Telegraph

---

**e** Can you remember these adjectives from the text for…?

1 something you shouldn't believe:
exa_____, mis_____, impr_____, doc_____

2 something you should believe:
leg_____, rel_____, tru_____

**f** Which news websites do you think are a) reputable, b) untrustworthy? Can you think of any examples of exaggerated or fake news?

## 6  ▶ VIDEO LISTENING

**a** Watch the documentary *The speed of news* once. Number the ways of delivering news in the order they are mentioned.

- [ ] cable TV
- [ ] Facebook
- [ ] live Twitter feeds
- [ ] radio and television
- [ ] The Boston News-Letter
- [ ] the telegraph line

**b** Watch the documentary again and answer the questions.

1 Where is the Newseum? How many different newspapers are there?
2 Who was Edward Teach? When was he killed?
3 How were early newspapers distributed? Why was this a problem?
4 How was news communicated during the American Civil War?
5 Why were Civil War news reports not very accurate?
6 Which inventions created the age of mass media?
7 What event appeared on Twitter seconds after it occurred?

**c** Are there any newspapers or magazines in your country that have existed for a long time? What reputation do they have these days? Do you ever read them?

---

🔍 **Go online** to watch the video and review the lesson

## GRAMMAR

**Complete the second sentence so that it means the same as the first.**

1 I'm almost sure you left your phone in the restaurant.
  You _____ _____ _____ your phone in the restaurant.

2 It was wrong of you not to tell me you'd borrowed my car.
  You _____ _____ _____ me you'd borrowed my car.

3 It's possible that the backpackers got lost.
  The backpackers _____ _____ _____ lost.

4 I'm sure it wasn't Jake's fault. He wasn't there last night.
  It _____ _____ _____ Jake's fault. He wasn't there last night.

5 I think somebody has tried to break in.
  It looks _____ _____ somebody has tried to break in.

6 This meat has a very similar taste to beef.
  This meat _____ _____ beef.

7 I don't like cooking fish because then there's an awful smell in the kitchen.
  I don't like cooking fish because then the kitchen _____ _____.

8 The accident happened when they were repairing the road.
  The accident happened when the road _____ _____ _____.

9 They'll probably never find the murderer.
  The murderer will probably _____ _____ _____.

10 People think the burglar is a teenager.
  The burglar is thought _____ _____ a teenager.

11 People say that crime doesn't pay.
  It _____ _____ that crime doesn't pay.

12 We want someone to fix the shower.
  We need to have _____ _____ _____.

13 "I think you should talk to a lawyer," I said to Keiko.
  I advised Keiko _____ _____ to a lawyer.

14 "I didn't kill my husband," Margaret said.
  Margaret denied _____ _____ _____.

15 "I'm sorry I'm late," James said.
  James _____ _____ _____ late.

## VOCABULARY

**a** Circle the correct verb.

1 Please *remind / remember* the children to do their homework.
2 A I'm so sorry.
  B Don't worry. It doesn't *mind / matter*.
3 The robbers *stole / robbed* $50,000 from the bank.
4 If you know the answer, *raise / rise* your hand. Don't shout.
5 Don't *discuss / argue* about it! You know that I'm right.
6 My brother *refuses / denies* to admit that he has a problem.

**b** Circle the word that is different.

1 palm    calf    wrist    thumb
2 kidney    lung    hip    liver
3 wink    wave    hold    touch
4 robber    vandal    burglar    pickpocket
5 fraud    smuggler    theft    terrorism
6 evidence    judge    jury    witness

**c** Write the verbs for the definitions.

1 _____ to bite food into small pieces in your mouth
2 _____ to rub your skin with your nails
3 _____ to look at something or somebody for a long time
4 _____ to make a serious, angry, or worried expression
5 _____ to find a way of entering somebody's computer
6 _____ to demand money from somebody by threatening to tell a secret about them
7 _____ to give somebody money so that they help you (especially if it's dishonest)
8 _____ to leave your job (especially in newspaper headlines)

**d** Complete the missing words.

1 The *Sunday Times* TV cr_____ wrote a very negative review of the show.
2 This paper always supports the government. It's very b_____.
3 The journalist's report was c_____ by the newspaper. They cut some of the things he had wanted to say because of government rules.
4 My favorite n_____ is the woman on the six o'clock news on channel 2.
5 The article in the newspaper wasn't very acc_____ – a lot of the facts were completely wrong.

## PRONUNCIATION

**a** Circle the word with a different sound.

| | | | | | |
|---|---|---|---|---|---|
| 1 | aʊ | elbow | frown | eyebrows | vow |
| 2 | h | honest | heart | hip | hack |
| 3 | ɔ | fraud | caught | yawn | journalist |
| 4 | ʌ | lungs | touch | shoulder | smuggle |
| 5 | /yu/ | argue | refuse | news | jury |

**b** Underline the main stressed syllable.

1 re|a|lize      3 van|da|lism      5 ob|jec|tive
2 black|mail     4 co|mmen|ta|tor

## CAN YOU understand this text?

**a** Read the article once. What is a *web sleuth*?

**b** Read the article again and complete it with phrases A–F.

A any information is obviously welcome
B are fascinated with crime and missing persons
C there's still a debate about whether amateur sleuthing is good or bad
D the police have come to the site for help
E these instances aren't very common
F he never looked back

## ► CAN YOU understand these people?

◐8.19 Watch or listen and choose a, b, or c.

1 Melanie      2 Erica      3 Victoria      4 Diarmuid

1 Melanie _____.
  a argues with her sister about housework
  b always wins arguments with her sister
  c hates arguing with her sister
2 When Erica acted in the play *A Woman's Worth* she _____.
  a felt nervous because her family was in the audience
  b played a woman who was afraid of marriage
  c played a woman who had problems with her boyfriend
3 Victoria witnessed a crime where the criminal _____.
  a escaped
  b was caught
  c was injured
4 Diarmuid _____.
  a is skeptical about what he reads in the news
  b gets his news mainly from newspaper apps
  c is only really interested in sports news

---

# Solving crimes from the bedroom

**It seems that people are starting to take the law into their own hands. Is it time for the police to take web sleuths seriously?**

Carl Koppelman, a former accountant from California, is part of a not-so-small community of citizen-detectives who [1]_____. They look through all the clues, police reports, and online tips to uncover what the police may have missed. Carl discovered the world of sleuthing after reading an article about Jaycee Lee Dugard. The man who held her captive for 18 years had just been arrested and Jaycee had been reunited with her family. He was eager to discuss it with other people, and after finding an online forum, [2]_____. Carl says that his interest has turned into an obsession. "I read through the stories…and thought it was just fascinating. You had average, everyday, normal people going on websites and solving crimes that the police have never been able to."

Tricia Arrington-Griffith owns the website WebSleuths. She can recall many times that [3]_____. "In 2014, a detective came to us with a piece of evidence, a particular T-shirt, from an unsolved murder. Within 36 hours, one of our members had found out exactly where the T-shirt was made, how much it cost, and where it was sold." Tricia says that the police

were incredibly grateful on this occasion, but she admits that [4]_____. She believes that the police mainly view citizen-detectives as troublemakers. "And we have had other problems," she admits. "WebSleuths was my first introduction to unpleasant behavior online."

So what do the police really think? Stewart Smith, an ex-Crime Prevention Officer, says, "I personally feel that the work many of these sleuths do is fantastic. Police resources are limited, so [5]_____." But sleuths must be "careful and considerate in their investigations, especially towards family members." Family members just like Karen Downes. Her daughter, Charlene, disappeared over 14 years ago in Blackpool, U.K., and there's been no trace of her since, but hundreds of people are still trying to solve the mystery online. Karen is delighted with the helpful and respectful amateur sleuths, but her husband Bob disagrees. Claims that he killed his own daughter were posted all over the internet by citizen-detectives; he was even physically attacked on the street, and this is not unusual behavior. So [6]_____. It's clearly a fascinating hobby, but all citizen-detectives need to make sure they are familiar with the law and behave appropriately.

---

► Go online to watch the video, review Files 7 & 8, and check your progress

Many a small thing has been made large by the right kind of advertising.
*Mark Twain, US author*

**G** clauses of contrast and purpose   **V** advertising, business   **P** changing stress on nouns and verbs

## 1 VOCABULARY & SPEAKING

**a** Look at the ad for Red Bull. Do you think it's a clever ad? Why do you think it might have gotten Red Bull into trouble?

### Advertising scandals that cost some brands millions

In advertising, there's a big difference between exaggerating the truth and making false **claims**.

Many companies have been caught using **misleading** claims like "scientifically proven" with "guaranteed results" in their **advertisements**. For such companies, it can cost millions, and lead to a damaged reputation.

Several examples of false advertising scandals have affected big **brands** – some are still ongoing, and not all companies have had to pay up, but each suffered a certain amount of negative **publicity**.

#### Red Bull

Energy drink company Red Bull **was sued** in 2014 for its **slogan** "Red Bull gives you wings." The slogan, which the company has used in **advertising campaigns** for nearly two decades, went alongside marketing claims that the caffeinated drink could improve a consumer's concentration and reaction speed.

Benjamin Careathers was one of several **consumers** who brought the case against the Austrian drink company. He said he had been a regular consumer of Red Bull for 10 years, but that he had not developed wings – or shown any signs of improved intellectual or physical abilities.

The company settled the case by agreeing to pay out a maximum of $13 million – including $10 to every US consumer who had bought the drink since 2002.

*Adapted from Business Insider*

**b** Read the article and check your answers to **a**. Why do you think Benjamin Careathers did what he did?

**c** Look at the highlighted words and phrases related to advertising. With a partner, try to figure out what they mean. Then match them to their meanings 1–9.

1 *advertisements* (also *ads*) notices, pictures, or videos telling people about a product
2 _____ (*noun*) statements that something is true, although it has not been proved and other people may not agree with or believe it
3 _____ (*noun*) types of product made by a particular company
4 _____ (*verb*) was taken to court to ask for money because of something they said or did that harmed you
5 _____ (*adj.*) giving the wrong idea or impression, making you believe something that is not true
6 _____ (*noun*) people who buy goods or use services
7 _____ (*noun*) series of advertising messages with the same theme
8 _____ (*noun*) the attention that is given to somebody / something by newspapers, television, etc.
9 _____ (*noun*) a word or phrase used in advertising that is easy to remember, to attract people's attention or to suggest an idea quickly

**d** Work in threes, **A**, **B**, and **C**. Look at three products whose ads cost their brands money. What problems do you think there were with the ads?

**e** **C Communication** Misleading ads **A** p.110 **B** p.112 **C** p.114
Read about the advertisements and tell each other what the problem was.

**f** Talk in groups of three. Give examples.

1 Have you bought something recently that wasn't as good as the advertisement made you think it would be? How was the ad misleading?
2 What are viral ads? Have you ever forwarded one to other people? Do you have a favorite one?
3 Is there a brand that you think has a really good logo or slogan? Does it make you want to buy the product?
4 Can you think of a recent ad that made you <u>not</u> want to ever buy the product? Why did the ad have this effect on you?
5 Do you find pop-up ads annoying when you are doing something online? Do you think they are necessary? Why is it that they often seem directed at you personally?
6 Do you think it's immoral for advertisers to try to persuade people without much money to buy products they can't afford?

## 2 LISTENING

**a** ◀) **9.1** Listen to a marketing expert talking about six marketing techniques used by advertisers. Complete the messages they use with two or three words.

1 "Get a _____ when you subscribe to our magazine for six months."
2 "There are _____ left! Buy now while supplies last!"
3 "_____ it."
4 "_____ can look like this."
5 "A recent _____ found that our toothpaste cleans your teeth better than any other brand."
6 "_____, I'm a doctor (or a celebrity)."

**b** Listen again. Answer the questions for each message in **a**.

1 Why does it attract us?
2 Why is it misleading?

**c** Which of the six techniques might influence you to buy the product? Are there any that would actively discourage you? Why do you think we keep falling for these techniques, even though we know what's going on?

OLAY DEFINITY

Because younger-looking eyes never go out of fashion

"Olay is my secret to brighter-looking eyes"

Olay Definity eye illuminator.
Reduces the look of wrinkles and dark circles for brighter, younger-looking eyes.

## 3 GRAMMAR clauses of contrast and purpose

**a** Look at some extracts from the listening in **2**, and complete them with phrases A–G.

1 In spite of _____, its price was really included in the magazine subscription.
2 Even though _____, and maybe don't even like them, we immediately want to be among the lucky few who have them.
3 So as to _____, they use expressions like, "It's a must-have"…
4 …and they combine this with a photograph of a large group of people, so that _____.
5 The photo has been airbrushed in order to _____, with perfect skin, and even more attractive than they are in real life.
6 It was probably produced for _____, and paid for by them, too.
7 Although _____, do you really think she colors her hair with it at home?

A the company itself
B the actress is holding the product in the photo
C we can't fail to get the message
D make us believe it
E we don't really need the products
F what the ad said
G make the model look even slimmer

**b** ◀) **9.2** Listen and check. Then look at the highlighted word(s) in 1–7 and the phrases A–G that follow them. Which ones express a purpose?

**c** **G** p.148 Grammar Bank 9A

**d** **Sentence race** Try to complete as many sentences as you can in two minutes.

1 I think the advertising of junk food should be banned, so that…
2 In spite of a huge marketing campaign,…
3 Although they have banned cigarette advertising,…
4 She applied for a job with a company in Seoul, so as to…
5 He decided to continue working, despite…
6 Even though the ad said I would notice the effects after a week,…
7 I took my laptop to the store to…
8 We went to our head office in New York for…

## 4 READING

**a** Look at the products in the photos. Can you think of anything they have in common?

A

B

C

D

**b** Read the first part of "Razors and Blades," an unadapted chapter from a book by economist Tim Harford. As you read, in order to quickly check any words or phrases that you don't know, first, try to guess meaning from context, then use the glossary, and finally, if necessary, use a dictionary. Check your answer to **a**.

**FIFTY THINGS THAT MADE THE MODERN ECONOMY**
'Every Tim Harford book is cause for celebration' MALCOLM GLADWELL
**Tim Harford**
AUTHOR OF THE UNDERCOVER ECONOMIST

**c** Read it again and mark the sentences **T** (true) or **F** (false). <u>Underline</u> the information in the text that tells you this.

1 King Camp Gillette's idea behind the United Company was that it would provide basic products cheaply.
2 This vision of the United Company had a great influence on the modern economy.
3 It is more expensive to produce a printer than to produce the ink.
4 Two-part pricing involves selling one thing cheaply, but making another essential component very expensive.
5 King Camp Gillette's first blades were relatively inexpensive.
6 Sony only makes a very small profit on each PlayStation 4 it sells.

# RAZORS & BLADES
## Part 1

In 1894, a book was written by a man who had a vision. The book argues that "our present system of competition" breeds "extravagance, poverty, and crime." It advocates a new system of "equality, virtue, and happiness," in which just one corporation – the United Company – will make all of life's necessities as cost-effectively as possible. These, by the way, are "food, clothing, and habitation." Industries which, "do not contribute" to life's necessities will be destroyed. The book's author had a vision that has ended up shaping the economy. But, as you may have guessed, it wasn't this particular vision. No, it was another idea, which he had a year later. His name was King Camp Gillette, and he invented the disposable razor blade.

If you've ever bought replacement cartridges for an inkjet printer, you are likely to have been annoyed to discover that they cost almost as much as you paid for the printer itself. That seems to make no sense. The printer's a reasonably large and complicated piece of technology. But how can it possibly cost almost as much to supply a bit of ink in tiny plastic pots? The answer, of course, is that it doesn't. But for a manufacturer, selling the printer cheaply and the ink expensively is a business model that makes sense, and is known as two-part pricing. It's also known as the razor-and-blades model, because that's where it first drew attention – suck people in with an attractively priced razor, then repeatedly fleece them for extortionately priced replacement blades.

King Camp Gillette invented the blades that made it possible. Before this, razors were bigger, and when the blade got dull, you'd sharpen it, not throw it away and buy another. He didn't immediately hit upon the two-part pricing model, though: initially, he made both parts expensive. The model of cheap razors and expensive blades evolved only later. Nowadays, two-part pricing is everywhere. Consider the PlayStation 4. Whenever Sony sells one, it loses money: the retail price is less than it costs to manufacture and distribute. But that's okay, because Sony coins it in whenever a PlayStation 4 owner buys a game. Or how about Nespresso? Nestle makes its money not from the machine, but the coffee pods.

### Glossary
**suck somebody in** (*phr. verb*) to involve somebody in an activity or a situation, especially one they do not want to be involved in
**fleece** (*verb, informal*) to take a lot of money from somebody by charging them too much
**hit upon** (*phr. verb*) think of a good idea suddenly or by chance
**coin it (in)** (*idiom*) make a lot of money

From Fifty Things that Made the Modern Economy

**d** Now read the rest of the chapter. Answer the questions with a partner.

1 How are companies that have been successful with two-part pricing products trying to stop other companies selling the disposable parts cheaper?

2 Why might customers stay with a more expensive original brand?

3 What does the author suggest that King Camp Gillette might have thought of the razor-and-blades sales model?

## Part 2

Obviously, for this model to work you need some way to ¹_____ customers from putting cheap, generic blades in your razor. One solution is legal: patent-protect your blades. But patents don't last forever. Patents on coffee pods have started expiring, so brands like Nespresso now face competitors selling ²_____, compatible alternatives. Some are looking for another kind of solution: technological. Just as other people's games don't work on the PlayStation, some coffee companies have put chip readers in their machines to stop you from trying to brew a generic cup of coffee.

Two-part pricing models work by imposing what economists call "switching costs." They're especially prevalent with digital goods. If you have a huge library of games for your PlayStation, or books for your Kindle, it's a big thing to switch to another platform. Switching costs don't have to be ³_____. They can come in the form of time, or hassle. Say I'm already familiar with Photoshop; I might prefer to pay for an expensive upgrade ⁴_____ buy a cheaper alternative, which I'd then have to learn how to use. Switching costs can be psychological, too – a result of brand loyalty. If the Gillette company's marketing department persuades me that generic blades give ⁵_____ shave, then I'll happily keep paying extra for Gillette-branded blades.

Economists have puzzled over why consumers ⁶_____ the two-part pricing model. The most plausible explanation is that they get confused by the two-part pricing. Either they don't realize that they'll be exploited later, or they do realize, but find it hard to pick the best deal out of a ⁷_____ menu of options. The irony is that the cynical razors-and-blades model – charging customers a premium for basics like ink and coffee – is about as far as you can get from King Camp Gillette's vision of a single United Company producing life's necessities as cheaply as possible.

### Glossary

**patent** (noun) an official right to be the only person to make, use, or sell a product or invention

**chip reader** (noun) a device to get information from a microchip

**switching costs** (noun phrase, idiom) how much it will cost you to change from one brand to another

**hassle** (noun, informal) a situation that is annoying because it involves doing something difficult or complicated that needs a lot of effort

**puzzle over** (phr. verb) to think hard about something in order to understand or explain it

**e** Read it again and choose the correct word or phrase for each blank.

1 a avoid  b encourage  c prevent
2 a cheaper  b pricier  c more expensive
3 a economical  b inevitable  c financial
4 a as well as  b rather than  c in order to
5 a an inferior  b a superior  c a similar
6 a tolerate  b reject  c like
7 a simple  b straightforward  c confusing

**f** Do you own any products that use a two-part pricing system? Do you buy generic ink, coffee, etc., or do you buy the branded ones? Why?

## 5 VOCABULARY business

**a** Look at two extracts from "Razors and Blades." Which two verbs mean "to make things in large quantities"? Which one is specifically "using machinery"?

> Consider the PlayStation 4. Whenever Sony sells one, it loses money: the retail price is less than it costs to manufacture and distribute.

> … King Camp Gillette's vision of a single United Company producing life's necessities as cheaply as possible.

**b** ⓥ p.162 **Vocabulary Bank** Business

## 6 PRONUNCIATION & SPEAKING changing stress on nouns and verbs

**a** ◉9.8 Listen and <u>underline</u> the stress on the **bold** words. Which syllable is stressed when the word is a) a verb, b) a noun?

1 We **ex|port** to customers all over the world.
2 One of our main **ex|ports** is cheese.
3 Sales have **in|creased** by 10% this month.
4 There has been a large **in|crease** in profits this year.
5 The new building is **pro|gre|ssing** well.
6 We're making good **pro|gress** with the report.
7 Most toys these days are **pro|duced** in China.
8 The demand for organic **pro|duce** has grown enormously.

**b** Look at some more words that can also be verbs and nouns, and have the same pronunciation rule. Practice saying them first all as verbs and then as nouns.

decrease   import   permit   record   refund   reject

**c** Say if the following are true of your country / region, or of you. Give examples.

We export more food than we import.
Not many stores sell organic produce.
Unemployment has decreased over the last five years.
Smoking is not permitted in public places.

◔ **Go online** to review the lesson

**G** uncountable and plural nouns  **V** word building: prefixes and suffixes  **P** word stress with prefixes and suffixes

# WHAT MAKES A CITY ATTRACTIVE?

Is there an "art to making attractive cities"? Alain de Botton, writer and founder of alternative education group *The School of Life*, seems to think so, and has made a video that he claims explains just how to do it. "It's not a mystery why we like some cities so much better than others," he says. "There are six fundamental things a city needs to get right."

### Order and variety
A love of order is one of the reasons people love Paris and New York, but we must avoid too much of it. The key is to create an "organized complexity." De Botton gives the example of the square in Telc, Czech Republic, where the individual houses are different in color and detail, but all the buildings are the same height and width.

### Visible life
Streets need to be full of people and activity in order to be beautiful instead of bleak. Sadly, modern cities often contain too many characterless office buildings and industrial zones where there is no street life.

### Compactness
Good cities are compact, not sprawling. Think Barcelona as opposed to a spread-out city like Phoenix, Arizona. De Botton says that attractive cities have beautiful squares that are ideal meeting places. The best designed are those that are not too large, so that people can recognize a face on the other side of the square.

### Orientation and mystery
The best cities offer a mixture of big and small streets. But too many cities prioritize vehicles over humans. A city should be easy to navigate for both humans and vehicles, with big boulevards for orientation and small streets to allow us to wander and create a sense of mystery and exploration.

### Scale
Our urban skylines have become dominated by tall buildings dedicated to banking and commerce. Instead, we should be building at an ideal height of five stories, resulting in dense and medium-rise cities, like Berlin and Amsterdam.

### Local color
The sameness of cities is a problem. Cities need to demonstrate their local culture and history. They should be built from locally sourced materials in a way that suits their individual climate and traditions.

*Adapted from The Guardian*

## 1 READING

**a** Look at the title of the article. How attractive do you think the city where you live (or your nearest city) is? What score would you give it out of 10?

**b** Read the article once. With a partner, explain what the six criteria mean. Do you agree with any of them? Does your city meet any of them?

**c** Can you think of any things that Alain de Botton hasn't mentioned? Make a note of them. Then talk in small groups, and make a group list.

*For me, one thing that's missing is water. I think the most beautiful cities always have a river running through them, or are near the ocean.*

## 2 LISTENING & SPEAKING

**a** ◑9.9 You're going to listen to five well-traveled people talking about the most beautiful city they've been to. Look at the countries. Which city do you think they're going to say? Listen to their first sentences and check.

1 _____, Italy        4 _____, Scotland
2 _____, Brazil       5 _____, Japan
3 _____, Canada

**b** ◑9.10 Listen and try to write the names of some places in these cities that they're going to mention. Compare in pairs and agree on the spelling.

the _____ Bridge        the _____ Museum
the _____ Canal         the _____ Steps
the _____ Opera         the River _____
   House                     the _____ Temple
the Bosque _____

**c** ◑9.11 Now look at photos 1–5 and listen to what the speakers say about each city. What is the place in the photo? Is it something to see or something to do? What information do they give about it?

**d** Listen again. What other thing(s) does each speaker recommend? Did they mention any of Alain de Botton's six criteria?

**e** Did they mention anything from your group's list in **1c**?

**f** Talk in small groups.

1 Have you been to any of the cities the speakers mention? Do you agree with what they say? Of those you haven't visited, which one would you most like to go to? Why?

2 What's the most beautiful city you've ever been to? What's one thing you would recommend to see and do there?

3 Are there any cities you haven't really liked? Why?

## 3 GRAMMAR uncountable and plural nouns

**a** Circle the correct form.

1 A good city guidebook will give you *advice / advices* about what to see.

2 You may have *some bad weather / a bad weather* if you go to London in March.

3 Walking around cities in the summer can be *hard work / a hard work*.

4 It's best not to take *too much luggage / too many luggages* if you take a quick vacation to a city.

5 The old town center is amazing, but *the outskirts is / the outskirts are* a little depressing.

6 I just heard *an interesting news / some interesting news*.

**b** **G** p.149 Grammar Bank 9B

**c** Play **Just a minute** in small groups.

## JUST A MINUTE

> **RULES**
>
> One person starts. He / She has to try to talk for a minute about the first subject below.
>
> If he or she hesitates for more than five seconds, he / she loses his / her turn and the next student continues.
>
> The person who is talking when one minute is up gets a point.

the most beautiful scenery I've seen

the traffic in my town / city

the police in my town / city

the weather I like most

good advice I've been given

what's in the news right now

clothes I love wearing

modern furniture

chocolate

## 4 READING & SPEAKING

**a** Look at this photo of Songdo, a new city in South Korea. What do you think might be the advantages or disadvantages of living there?

**b** Now read an article about Songdo. Answer the questions with a partner.

1 What are the three main advantages of living in Songdo?
2 Which two things that were promised haven't happened yet?
3 What other disadvantages are mentioned?

**c** Read the article again. For each of the highlighted words and phrases, choose the best meaning, a or b.

1 a advantages   b disadvantages
2 a break its promise   b keep its promise
3 a leaving home   b going home
4 a not enough   b too much
5 a very advanced   b very simple
6 a be different from   b be similar to
7 a overpopulated   b underpopulated
8 a close together   b spread out

**d** Talk to a partner.

1 If you went to live in Songdo, what would you like best and what would you miss the most?
2 What's the most modern city you've ever been to? Why did you go there? What did you think of it?
3 If you had to choose between an ultra-modern megacity and a classically beautiful old city, which would you prefer?
4 What is the approximate population of your city or nearest big city? Do you think it will grow? What effect might the change in population have on the city and its services?

# Is this the future

Three years ago, 35-year-old English teacher Lee Mi-Jung moved with her husband from the small coastal city of Pohang across the South Korean peninsula to Songdo. Described as the world's "smartest city," it was planned as a showpiece of 21st-century urban design, promising an efficient trash system, an abundance of parks, and a vibrant international community – all the [1] perks of megacity Seoul without the capital city's crowded sidewalks, choking traffic, and air pollution. The city claimed to do "nothing less than banish the problems created by modern urban life." And for foreign corporations looking for access to Asian economies, Songdo would be a glitzy business capital to rival Hong Kong and Shanghai. "I'd imagined this would be a well-designed city, that it would be new, modernized, and simple –unlike other cities," says Lee. "So my expectations were high."

As far as hi-tech conveniences go, Songdo does [2] deliver. Pneumatic tubes send trash straight from Lee's home to an underground waste facility, where it's sorted, recycled, or burned for energy generation. Everything, from the lights, to the temperature in her apartment, can be adjusted via a central control panel, or from her phone. During the winter, she can warm up the apartment before [3] heading home. But the one thing she hasn't been able to find is a vibrant community.

"When I first came here during the winter," Lee says, "I felt something cold." She wasn't just talking about the coldness of the weather, or the chilly modernism of the concrete high rises all over town. She felt [4] a lack of human warmth from neighborhood interaction. "There's an online forum where we share our complaints," she said, "But only on the internet – not face to face."

Songdo was built on reclaimed land from the Yellow Sea. The 1,500-acre development sits an hour outside of Seoul. It was planned as an eco-city. Its buildings and streets have sensors that monitor energy use and traffic flow. There's a [5] state-of-the-art water-recycling facility and plenty of green spaces, including a 100-acre oceanside park modeled on, and named after, New York City's Central Park.

# of cities?

For a place that is striving to become car-free, however, the roads of Songdo are crazily wide, with as many as ten lanes. These are partly intended to [6] echo the wide, tree-lined boulevards of Paris, and also wide enough for city planners to, say, put in a light rail or streetcar network, which may bring Songdo one step closer to fulfilling its car-free promise. But for now, cars are still common, and, for residents like 32-year-old Lindy Wenselaers from Belgium, they're an essential tool. Lindy ended up buying a car after only five months in Songdo – she could no longer face a 20-minute walk to the nearest supermarket in the wintry weather. She misses the lack of direct connections from one part of town to another; on the weekend, she often drives an hour to Seoul.

Songdo's biggest problem is that it only has a third of the people it was designed for. Parts of it feel more like a [7] sparsely populated American 1970s suburb. The wide roads and [8] sprawling scale means that human activities are located far apart from one another. Occasionally, you see small touches, like an artificial *hanok* village (a traditional village where houses with old-school architecture remain intact) to remind you that, yes, you are still in Korea. It's not exactly a ghost town, as some reports have claimed, but as you drive past cluster after cluster of identical concrete residential high-rises, it feels empty, and there's a curious urban silence. "There's a ton of people living here, but you don't really see them," says Wenselaers. "The city is alive, but it's invisible."

*Adapted from the CityLab website*

---

## 5 VOCABULARY word building: prefixes and suffixes

 **Prefixes and suffixes**

A **prefix** is something that you add to the beginning of a word, usually to change its meaning, e.g., *pre* = before (**pre**-*war*), or a negative prefix like *un*- or *dis*- (**un**healthy, **dis**honest). A **suffix** is something you add to the end of a word, usually to change its grammatical form, e.g., *-ment* and *-ness* are typical noun suffixes (*enjoy***ment**, *happi***ness**). However, some suffixes also add meaning to a word, e.g., *-ful* = full of (*stress***ful**, *beauti***ful**).

**a** Answer the questions. Check your answers in the article in **4**.

1 What prefix can you put before *city* to add the meaning a) *enormous*, b) *environmentally friendly*?
2 Add suffixes to the words in the box to make nouns.

abundant   cold   connect   convenient   develop
expect   modern   neighbor   pollute   silent

**b** ⓥ **p.163 Vocabulary Bank** Word building

## 6 PRONUNCIATION & SPEAKING word stress with prefixes and suffixes

 **Word stress on words with prefixes and suffixes**

Multi-syllable words always have a main stressed syllable. This usually remains the main stress even when we add a prefix or suffix – the exception is *-ation*. However, there is usually secondary stress on prefixes, e.g., *un-* in *unemployment*.

**a** <u>U</u>nderline the main stressed syllable in these words.

a|cco|mmo|da|tion   an|ti|so|cial   bi|ling|ual   en|ter|tain|ment
go|vern|ment   home|less   lone|li|ness   mul|ti|cul|tu|ral
neigh|bor|hood   o|ver|crow|ded   po|ver|ty   un|der|de|ve|loped
un|em|ploy|ment   van|da|li|sm

**b** 🔊 9.18 Listen and check. Practice saying the words.

**c** Talk in small groups. Give reasons and examples.
**Which city (or region) in your country or abroad do you think...?**

- is very multicultural
- offers great entertainment
- has low levels of poverty and unemployment
- has a bilingual or trilingual population
- is very eco-friendly

- s very overcrowded
- has very serious pollution problems
- has a lot of homeless people
- has some very dangerous neighborhoods
- suffers from vandalism and antisocial behavior

## 7 WRITING

ⓦ **p.121 Writing** A report  Write a report for a website about good places for eating out or entertainment in your city.

Go online to review the lesson

## 1 ▶ THE INTERVIEW Part 1

**a** Read the biographical information about George Tannenbaum. Have you seen any ads for the companies he has worked with?

**George Tannenbaum** was born in 1957 in Yonkers, New York and was educated at Columbia University in New York. He has worked on advertising campaigns for many well-known companies such as IBM, Mercedes-Benz, Gillette, Citibank, and FedEx.

Today, he is Executive Creative Director and Copy Chief at Ogilvy and Mather Advertising in New York.

**b** Watch Part 1 of an interview with him and answer the questions.
1 Which other members of his family have worked in advertising?
2 When did George start working in advertising?
3 What wasn't he allowed to do when the family was watching TV?
4 Why does he think jingles are so memorable?
5 What kind of ads were the H.O. Farina TV commercials?
6 What happens in the story of Wilhelmina and Willie?

### Glossary
**jingle** a short song or tune that is easy to remember and is used in advertising on radio or television

**H.O. Farina** a company that has been making cereals since the 1940s. They ran an advertising campaign in the 50s based on a cartoon character named Wilhelmina.

**c** Are there any jingles or slogans that you remember from your childhood? Why do you think they were so memorable? Are there any others that have gotten into your head since then?

## ▶ Part 2

Tommy Lee Jones in a BOSS advertising campaign

**a** Watch Part 2. Complete the notes with one or two words.
1 George says that a commercial is made up of three elements:
   1 _____
   2 _____
   3 _____
2 The acronym AIDA stands for:
   A _____
   I _____
   D _____
   A _____
3 According to George, using a celebrity in advertising is a way of _____, but he isn't a _____ of it.
4 George thinks that humor in advertising is _____.

### Glossary
**a depilatory** /ə dɪˈpɪlətɔri/ a product used for removing unwanted hair

**Tommy Lee Jones** a US actor born in 1946, winner of an Oscar for the 1993 movie *The Fugitive*

***Mad Men*** a well-known US TV series about advertising executives in the 1960s who worked in offices in Madison Avenue in New York

**b** How important do you think celebrities are in advertising? What about humor?

## ▶ Part 3

**a** Watch Part 3 and (circle) the correct phrase.

1 He thinks that billboard and TV advertising will *remain important / slowly decline*.

2 He tends to notice only *bad ads / well-made ads*.

3 He thinks Nike ads are very successful *because of their logo and slogan / because they make people feel good about themselves*.

4 He thinks Apple's approach to advertising was very *innovative / repetitive*.

5 Their advertising message was *honest and clear / modern and informative*.

> **Glossary**
> **billboard** /ˈbɪlbɔrd/ a large board on the outside of a building or on the side of the road, used for putting advertisements on

**b** Are there many billboards in your town or city? Do you think they make the streets uglier or more attractive?

## 2 ▶ LOOKING AT LANGUAGE

> 🔍 **Metaphors and idiomatic expressions**
> George Tannenbaum uses a lot of metaphors and idiomatic expressions to make his language more colorful, e.g., *took the baton* = continued the family tradition, (from relay races in track and field).

**a** Watch some extracts from the interview and complete the missing words.

1 "You know they, what do they call them, _____ **worms**?"

2 "They **get into your** _____ and you can't get them out sometimes…"

3 "And I bet you I'm getting this _____ **for word** if you could find it."

4 "…we do live in a celebrity culture and people, you know, **their ears** _____ **up** when they see a celebrity."

5 "Have billboards and TV commercials **had their** _____?"

6 "…because you've got a **captive** _____."

7 "they became kind of the gold standard and they rarely **hit a** _____ **note**."

**b** Look at the **bold** expressions in **a** with a partner. What do you think they mean?

## 3 ▶ THE CONVERSATION

Simon · Joanne · Syinat

**a** Watch the conversation. What do they all conclude by the end?

**b** Watch again. Mark the sentences **T** (true) or **F** (false).

1 Syinat thinks we recognize certain brands because we are surrounded by advertising.

2 Joanne says her children don't see advertising at home because they don't have a TV.

3 Simon sometimes buys things without realizing that he's been influenced by advertising.

4 Joanne says her children don't understand the power of advertising.

5 Simon thinks it's a good idea to restrict advertising to children, like in Sweden.

6 Syinat thinks advertising doesn't really affect children.

**c** Do you agree with the participants that everybody is influenced by advertising?

**d** Watch the extracts and complete the highlighted phrases. In which extracts does the speaker a) give themselves time to think, b) make something clearer?

1 …and you're being influenced, so, for example we, _____ _____ _____ certain brands just because they're everywhere around us.

2 You know, we barely, we _____ _____ watch TV and we have a TV, we just don't watch very much…

3 …but you see pictures in magazines and they're starting to be – my eleven-year-old, is _____ _____ _____ a little bit more cynical about what he sees…

4 Yeah, especially for children, I mean I, I, _____ _____, _____ _____ younger siblings and it's kind of like "Ooh, all of my friends have this toy, so I must have it as well"

5 So, I think, um, _____ _____ definitely I think that the answer to the question is yes…

**e** Now have a conversation in groups of three.

1 Are there any products you think shouldn't be advertised, or shouldn't be advertised to young children?

2 Do you think ads reinforce stereotypes?

## 1 SPEAKING & LISTENING

**a** Look at the cartoon. Do you think the father gives a good answer? Why (not)?

**b** Read the article. With a partner, try to explain the meaning of the highlighted science words. Use the context to help you.

**c** Now answer questions 1–8. Choose the correct option.

**d** 🔊 10.1 Listen to a scientist explaining each fact. Did you get the answers right?

**e** Listen again. What did the scientist say about…?
1 the reason we can see more blue light than violet light
2 the effect of the Sun's heat on ocean water
3 the number of daylight hours that the moon is visible
4 six hours per year
5 what happens in your brain when you blink
6 the function of the cornea
7 the effect of cooler air on water vapor
8 what happens when something with a high mass is compressed

**f** Which questions do you think you could now answer if you were asked them by a child?

# Daddy, why...?

**"Why is the sky blue?" "Why is the sea salty?"**
**Children are always asking difficult questions like these about the world around us, but in a recent survey, nearly 25% of parents said they didn't know the answers, and 21% admitted that they made the answers up!**

**Can you answer eight simple science questions that parents struggle to answer?**

**I** Why is the *sky blue*?

**A** Because the light from the Sun reflects off the blue water of the ocean.
**B** Because the Earth's atmosphere scatters more blue light than red light from the Sun.

**2** Why is the *sea salty*?

**A** Because salt dissolves into the water from seaweed and other plants.
**B** Because salt dissolves into the water from the land around it.

**3** Why can *we sometimes see* the *moon during the day*?

**A** Because as it rotates around the Earth, it reflects the Sun's rays during daytime as well as night time.
**B** Because sometimes during the day, the Sun doesn't shine as brightly.

**4** Why do *we have a leap year*?

**A** Because every four years, the Earth goes around the Sun slightly faster.
**B** Because the Earth takes slightly more than 365 days to go around the Sun.

Daddy, where does rain come from?

Well, rain is liquid water in the form of droplets that have condensed from atmospheric water vapor and they become heavy enough to fall under gravity.
The major cause of rain production is moisture moving along three-dimensional zones of temperature...

**5** Why do *we blink*?

**A** To keep our eyes moist and clean.
**B** To help us stay awake.

**6** Why does *cutting onions make us cry*?

**A** Because they produce a gas that irritates our eyes.
**B** Because they give off dry particles that irritate our eyes.

**7** What is a *cloud*?

**A** A mixture of warm gases rising from the Earth.
**B** A mixture of water vapor, ice, and dust floating in the sky.

**8** What is a *black hole*?

**A** A place in space where gravity pulls so hard that even light cannot get out.
**B** A "vacuum cleaner" in space that swallows up everything around it.

Adapted from The Telegraph

## 2 VOCABULARY & PRONUNCIATION science; stress in word families

**a** Look at the questions and complete the subject column in the chart.

What is the name for the study of....?
1  the natural and physical world
2  forces, heat, light, sound, and electricity
3  how solids, liquids, and gases react with each other
4  people, animals, and plants
5  the moon and the planets
6  how characteristics are passed through generations
7  plants and their structure
8  animals and their behavior

| subject | person | adjective |
|---|---|---|
| 1 *science* | *scientist* | *scientific* |
| 2 | | |
| 3 | | |
| 4 | | |
| 5 | | |
| 6 | | |
| 7 | | |
| 8 | | |

**b** ◆10.2 Listen and check. Then try to complete the other two columns.

> 🔍 **Stress in word families**
> In some word groups, the stressed syllable changes in the different parts of speech, e.g., *science*, *scientist*, *scientific*.

**c** ◆10.3 Listen and check. Underline the stressed syllables in the words. In which groups does the stress change on the adjective?

**d** Practice saying the word groups.

**e** ◆10.4 Listen and write six phrases using words from the chart in **a**.

**f** Complete the sentences with a word from the box.

---
clone   discovery   drugs   ~~experiments~~   guinea pigs
laboratory   research   side effects   tests   theory
---

1  Scientists **carry out** *experiments* in a _____.
2  Archimedes **made** an important _____ in his bathtub.
3  Isaac Newton's experiments **proved** his _____ that gravity existed.
4  Before a **pharmaceutical company** can sell new _____, they have to do _____ to make sure they are safe.
5  Scientists have to **do** a lot of _____ on the possible _____ of new drugs.
6  People can **volunteer** to be _____ in **clinical trials**.
7  In 1996, scientists were able to _____ a sheep for the first time, which they named Dolly.

**g** ◆10.5 Listen and check, and mark the stress on the multi-syllable words in **bold**. Practice saying the sentences.

## 3 SPEAKING

Work with a partner. **A** interview **B** with the questions in the green circles. Then **B** interview **A** with the blue circles.

Which scientific subjects do / did you study in school? What do / did you enjoy the most / the least?

Do you think it's more important to study science than arts in school / college?

Which scientist (living or dead) do you most admire? Why?

Which scientific subjects from school are / have been most useful to you?

Are you OK with eating genetically-modified food? Why (not)?

If you were sick, would you agree to be a guinea pig for a new kind of treatment?

Do you think it is acceptable for animals to be used for cosmetics testing? Is any animal testing acceptable?

Is it worth spending millions of dollars sending expeditions to distant planets, e.g., Mars? Why (not)?

Would you clone your pet? Do you think it will ever be acceptable to clone a person?

What would you most like scientists to discover in the near future?

## 4  READING

**a**  Talk to a partner. Have you seen any movies or TV shows, or read any books, where…?

- people discover aliens that look a little like humans on another planet
- spaceships travel faster than the speed of light
- people can teleport themselves long distances
- people can make themselves invisible
- machines look and behave like humans
- people can learn something very quickly by plugging themselves into a computer

**b**  Read an article about the sci-fi concepts in **a**. Score each one from 1–5, according to what the writer says about how likely it is to happen (1 = very unlikely, 5 = very likely). Then compare with a partner. Did you agree on the scores?

# The reality of sci-fi

**Just how plausible are the ideas we hear about in science fiction?** *LiveScience* **examines some popular concepts.**

### Aliens that look like us

Many fictional aliens have a human-type body. But how likely is it that intelligent alien life would develop a body shape similar to ours? It seems unlikely that organisms evolving for millions of years on another world would fit comfortably into our clothes. But the evolutionary circumstances on alien planets may have been similar to those that led humans to develop arms and legs, and fingers to manipulate tools. Some scientists say that our two-legged, symmetrical body shape could be the "optimal design for an intelligent being." Perhaps there is no other choice than for intelligent aliens to look like humans.

### Traveling faster than light

Einstein's general theory of relativity says that nothing can travel faster than light. However, this theory doesn't place limits on the speed at which space expands or contracts. Some physicists believe that faster-than-light travel is a real possibility. A type of energy bubble around a spaceship, for instance, could in theory make space-time contract in front of the ship and expand behind it. Gerald Cleaver, a physicist at Baylor University, says that the objects inside the bubble would move faster than the speed of light in relation to the space around.

*Adapted from the LiveScience website*

### Teleportation

Digital information can be transmitted via computers, and in a similar way, some physicists have transmitted another type of information (called quantum information) nearly 10 miles (16 kms). However, this is a long way from teleporting actual material, or indeed, a person. Scientifically speaking, teleportation faces extreme obstacles. There are ideas for how to do it, but these are only speculative right now.

### Invisibility cloaks

In the Star Trek universe, enemies hide, or "cloak," their spaceships. Scientists say that anti-detection technologies might be possible, but invisibility cloaks like those in science fiction and fantasy are quite a way off. "What you see in Harry Potter is far-fetched," says David Smith, professor of electrical and computer engineering at Duke University. "However, in the last few years, researchers have made a lot of progress on making objects invisible. Partial cloaks that work like sophisticated camouflage – rather like the alien in the 1987 movie *Predator* – might be achievable," says Smith.

### Intelligent machines

Robots and computers are already far better than humans at factory work or calculations. However, machines still cannot manage many basic activities, such as tying a shoelace while having a conversation. "From 50 to 60 years of Artificial Intelligence research, we know that teaching machines to do a specific task, for example, playing a game, is a lot easier than creating a machine that has the common sense of a three-year-old child," said Shlomo Zilberstein, a professor of computer science. Many scientists believe that highly intelligent machines will be available in the coming decades. But it is questionable whether computers will achieve the human-like ability to feel or understand free will – an idea at the heart of many sci-fi stories.

### Instant learning

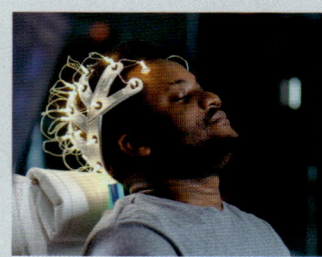

In the movie *The Matrix*, knowledge can be uploaded into the brain in seconds, via a computer plugged into the skull. Some emerging research suggests that the speed at which we learn a skill can be technologically boosted. For instance, scientists have managed to stimulate the brain to improve performance of visual tasks. Perhaps someday, the acquisition of knowledge and skills could happen at broadband-like speeds via surgically implanted and plug-in hardware. "The concept is not totally implausible," says neuroscientist Bruce McNaughton. "But it might take a couple of hundred years."

**c** With a partner, look at the <mark>highlighted</mark> words and phrases in the article on p.98. Check what ideas they refer to. Then decide whether they mean a) likely, b) not very likely, but possible, or c) extremely unlikely.

**d** Which thing in the article do you think…?
- might happen in the next 50 years
- you would really like to happen
- will never happen

> 🔍 **Talking about future possibilities**
> *I'm pretty sure…will*
> *I'd really like…to happen / exist / be invented*
> *I don't think…will ever…*

**e** In small groups, discuss the possibility of the following things happening, and whether or not they would be a good thing.

a colony on Mars
bringing extinct animals back to life
flying cars    space tourism
controlling the weather

**5 GRAMMAR** quantifiers: *all, every, both,* etc.

**a** With a partner, circle the correct word or phrase.

1 Some scientists think that *all / every* intelligent aliens would have a human-like body shape.
2 *All the / All* evidence suggests that scientists could invent a way to make things invisible.
3 Einstein's theory of relativity doesn't explain *all / everything* about the universe.
4 *No / None* machines can currently tie a shoelace and hold a conversation at the same time.
5 *Both / Both of* David Smith and Shlomo Zilberstein are computer scientists.
6 *Either / Neither* teleportation nor instant learning are going to be easy to achieve.

**b** 🅖 **p.150 Grammar Bank 10A**

**c** Take the Science quiz with a partner.

**d** 🔊 **10.9** Listen and check.

# Science Quiz

**1** In "direct current," the electrons…
a move in only one direction.
b move in both directions.
c don't move at all.

**2 Helium gas can be found…**
a only in liquid form.
b in neither liquid nor solid form.
c in both liquid and solid form.

**3 Adult giraffes remain standing…**
a some of the day.
b all day.
c most of the day.

**4 Of all the water on our planet,… is found underground.**
a hardly any of it
b about half of it
c most of it

**5 Snakes eat…**
a only other animals.
b either other animals or eggs.
c either other animals or fruit.

**6 A diamond can be destroyed…**
a by either intense heat or acid.
b by both intense heat and acid.
c only by intense heat.

**7 The human brain can continue to live without oxygen for…**
a nearly two minutes.
b nearly six minutes.
c a few hours.

**8 In our solar system,…**
a neither Pluto nor Neptune are now considered to be planets.
b both Pluto and Neptune are considered to be planets.
c Pluto is no longer considered to be a planet.

**9 When we breathe out,…**
a most of that air is oxygen.
b none of that air is oxygen.
c some of that air is oxygen.

**10 An individual blood cell makes a whole circuit of the body in…**
a nearly 60 seconds.
b nearly 45 seconds.
c a few minutes.

pluto

neptune

# 10B Free speech

> Tell the audience what you're going to say, say it, and then tell them what you've said.
> *Dale Carnegie, US writer and lecturer*

## 1 GRAMMAR articles

**a** Who was the first man to walk on the moon? In what year?

**b** 🔊 10.10 Listen to the original recording of the first words spoken from the moon. With a partner, try to complete the sentence and answer the questions.

> THAT'S ONE _____ STEP FOR _____, ONE GIANT LEAP FOR _____.

1 What do you think the difference is between *a step* and *a leap*?
2 What do you think *mankind* means?

**c** 🔊 10.11 Listen to an interview about the moon landing. What was the controversy about the words Armstrong actually said? What's the difference in meaning between *a man* and *man*? Did new technology prove him right or wrong?

**d** Listen again and answer the questions.

1 When did Armstrong write the words he was planning to say when he first stepped on the moon?
2 Does Armstrong say he wrote, "*That's one small step for man…*" or "*That's one small step for a man…*"?
3 Why doesn't the sentence everybody heard make sense?
4 What did Armstrong think he said?
5 Who is Peter Shann Ford? What did he discover?
6 How did Armstrong feel when he heard about this?

**e** Read some more facts about Armstrong. Are the highlighted phrases grammatically right or wrong? Correct the mistakes.

1 Neil Armstrong was born in the US.
2 He was a shy boy, who loved the books and the music.
3 He studied aeronautical engineering in the college.
4 He was the first man who set foot on moon.
5 His famous words were heard by people all over the world.
6 Before becoming a astronaut, he worked for the US Navy.
7 After 1994, he refused to give the autographs.
8 In 2005, he was involved in a lawsuit with an ex-barber, who tried to sell some of the Armstrong's hair.

**f** **G** p.151 Grammar Bank 10B

**g** **C** **Communication** True or false **A** p.110  **B** p.114 Complete quiz sentences with articles.

## 2 READING

**a** Read the introduction to the article. What do the highlighted words and phrases mean?

**b** Look at the eight people in the photos on p.101. What do you know about them? Match sound bites A–H to the people in the photos.

A "I have the heart and stomach of a king…"
B "Government of the people, by the people, for the people…"
C "…The laws that men have made."
D "We shall never surrender."
E "Ask not what your country can do for you; ask what you can do for your country."
F "I have a dream…"
G "…it is an ideal for which I am prepared to die."
H "Yes, we can."

**c** 🔊 10.15 Listen and check.

**d** Now read about the circumstances in which four of the speeches in **b** were made. Complete them with the person and the sound bite. Do you know in what context the other four people made their speeches?

**e** Read about the speeches again and answer the questions with **QE**, **AL**, **EP**, or **NM**.

Who…?

1 _____ conveyed his / her message without mentioning a key word
2 _____ gave part of his / her speech without notes
3 _____ gave the speech before a famous ocean battle
4 _____ summed up his / her message in ten words
5 _____ wanted to convince his / her critics at home that they were wrong
6 _____ was applauded for a long time after the speech
7 _____ was helped in the delivery of the speech by his / her former occupation
8 _____ did not live to see his / her cause made law

**f** Talk to a partner.

1 Whose speech would you most like to have heard in person? Why?
2 Do you know anyone today who you consider to be a great speaker?
3 Which past or present politicians or public figures in your country do you think are or were a) very good speakers, b) very poor speakers?

# The best speeches of all time

**Barack Obama**

**Emmeline Pankhurst**

**Nelson Mandela**

**Abraham Lincoln**

**Elizabeth I**

**Winston Churchill**

**John F. Kennedy**

**Martin Luther King, Jr.**

**Using [1]sound bites and having [2]the gift of the gab – the secrets of some of the world's greatest orators.**

The perfect speaker, says Cicero, the Roman statesman considered the greatest [3]orator of all time, must be well read in the history of his country and the politics of the day. He (it was always "he" in those days) must command the language with humor, [4]wit, and psychological insight. The main point, though, says Cicero, is that you need to know the main point. If you cannot describe your main point, you probably don't have one. By this standard, who is or was a great speaker? Who gave the finest speeches?

**1** _____ **to her troops before the invasion of the Spanish Armada Tilbury (port on the River Thames), August 9, 1588**

### THE SOUND BITE

**WHY IS IT SO GOOD?** This is a speech all about character, and it is a defiant speech about gender. With the Spanish Armada gathering in the North Sea, about to attack, Elizabeth knew the nation was in peril and that she faced her sternest test. She would have known, as she spoke at Tilbury, that at court, people were saying that a woman could not command the armed forces. A failure by a king would be attributed to one of many factors. A failure by a queen would be put down to her gender. Rather than ignore the question, Elizabeth chooses, brilliantly, to confront it.

**2** _____ **to soldiers during the American Civil War Gettysburg, Pennsylvania, November 19, 1863**

### THE SOUND BITE

**WHY IS IT SO GOOD?** Lincoln describes the ideal of democratic government in a single sentence. He gets so much into those ten words that it is surprising he needs all 272 for the whole speech. Lincoln is saying that the Civil War has to be waged for the principles of the founding fathers, who drafted the Declaration of Independence, particularly the principle of all people being equal, and at this moment, they are being betrayed. What he means, in a word he never actually uses, is slavery. Almost every American president since Lincoln has gone to Gettysburg to pay homage to Lincoln and to the American constitution. One who did not was John F. Kennedy, who, in 1963, had to ask ex-president Eisenhower to stand in for him. Kennedy had to go down to Dallas on urgent political business. He never came back.

**3** _____ **, campaigning for votes for women Portman Rooms, London, March 24, 1908**

### THE SOUND BITE

**WHY IS IT SO GOOD?** Some of the finest speakers in the history of rhetoric got into trouble because of their speeches. Pankhurst was in prison several times, and gave this speech after being released from one of them. The audience was not expecting her to appear, and the ovation when she did was prolonged. Over and above the injustice of women being excluded from the vote, she is making the practical case that the law would be improved and democracy would be enriched if it opened the door to women. Tragically, Pankhurst died three weeks before her case was accepted by the British government in 1928.

**4** _____ **at his trial Supreme Court of South Africa, Pretoria, April 20, 1964**

### THE SOUND BITE

**WHY IS IT SO GOOD?** The greatest speeches are the words said at the most momentous occasions, as here, where a political prisoner pleads for his life against an unjust apartheid state. Mandela speaks for more than three hours. Throughout, he is extremely reasonable, like the lawyer he once was, taking pains to reassure the white population he means them no harm. He had learned the last words by heart, and delivered them from memory, looking directly at Judge De Wet. When he finished, there was a 30-second pause – an eternity. In the gallery, a woman burst into tears.

Adapted from The Times

## 3 LISTENING & SPEAKING

**a** Have you ever had to make a speech or give a talk or presentation in front of a lot of people? When and where? How did you feel? Was it a success?

**b** Look at the cartoon. What point is it making about public speaking?

**c** 🔊 **10.16** Now listen to Part 1 of a radio program where expert Lynne Parker gives tips for public speaking. Complete her six tips using between one and four words. Were any of your ideas mentioned?

1 Be _____.
2 If you're using PowerPoint, don't just _____.
3 Maintain _____ with your audience.
4 _____, _____, _____.
5 Include a couple of good _____.
6 Listen to _____.

**d** Listen again and add more information about each tip.

|       | Dos | Don'ts |
|-------|-----|--------|
| Tip 1 |     |        |
| Tip 2 |     | –      |
| Tip 3 |     |        |
| Tip 4 |     | –      |
| Tip 5 |     |        |
| Tip 6 |     | –      |

**e** 🔊 **10.17** Now listen to Part 2, an interview with Anya Edwards from Chile, who was a finalist in an international public speaking competition. Does she agree with any of Lynne's points?

**f** Listen again. Choose a, b, or c.

1 Participants in the competition have to first compete ____.
   a in London   b in their own country   c in their own language
2 In the impromptu speech in the finals, you have to speak for ____ minutes.
   a three   b five   c fifteen
3 Anya thinks that being nervous is ____.
   a unavoidable   b an advantage   c a disadvantage
4 She thinks public speaking is more difficult than acting because ____.
   a you have to know your subject   b you have to be more convincing
   c you have less support
5 She thinks learning to speak in public ____.
   a was useful for her, but may not be useful for everybody
   b is useful for everybody   c wasn't a particularly useful experience
6 Her tip for creating the content of a speech is to start by ____.
   a recording ideas   b drawing a mind map
   c organizing your thoughts

**g** Which one tip did you think was the most useful? Were there any that you don't really agree with?

## 4 VOCABULARY collocation: word pairs

> 🔍 **Word pairs**
> *Try not to continually walk **up and down**...*
> Some pairs of words in English that go together always come in a certain order, for example, we always say *black and white*, not *white and black*. This order may sometimes be different in your language. Some word pairs are idioms, e.g., *dos and don'ts* means things you should or shouldn't do.

**a** How do you say *up and down* and *black and white* in your language? Are the words in the same order?

**b** Take one word from **box A** and match it to another from **box B**. Then decide which word comes first, and join them with *and*.

> **A** backwards, effect, forget, health, learn, lightning, pros, quiet, supply, sweet
>
> **B** cause, cons, demand, forgive, forwards, live, peace, safety, short, thunder

**c** Look at some common word pairs joined with *or*. What is the second word?

right or _____     sooner or _____     dead or _____
now or _____       all or _____          rain or _____
more or _____      once or _____

**d** 🔊 **10.18** Listen and check your answers to **b** and **c**.

**e** Match the word pair idioms to their meanings.

1 [ ] I'm <mark>sick and tired</mark> of listening to you complain.
2 [ ] I didn't buy much, just a few <mark>odds and ends</mark>.
3 [ ] I get headaches <mark>now and again</mark>.
4 **A** What's for lunch?  **B** [ ] <mark>Wait and see.</mark>
5 [ ] <mark>By and large</mark>, I enjoyed my time at school.
6 [ ] The National Guard was called in to restore <mark>law and order</mark>.
7 [ ] Despite the storm, we arrived <mark>safe and sound</mark>.
8 [ ] It was <mark>touch and go</mark> as to whether we'd get to the airport in time, but luckily we just made it.

| | |
|---|---|
| A in general | E sometimes |
| B a situation in which the law is obeyed | F uncertain, with the possibility that something may go wrong |
| C fed up | G small things |
| D without problem or injury | H wait patiently |

**f** Complete the sentences with a word pair from e.

1 I don't have much work to finish, just a few _____.
2 I don't see my uncle very often, just every _____.
3 Let's _____ if the weather warms up before we decide to go out or not.
4 After lots of adventures, she arrived home _____.
5 A few things went wrong on the first night of the play, but _____, it was a success.
6 After the riots, the government sent soldiers in to try to establish _____.
7 I'm _____ of my boss! I'm going to look for a new job.
8 The operation was successful, but for a few hours it was _____.

## 5 PRONUNCIATION & SPEAKING
pausing and sentence stress

**a** ◀)) 10.19 When people give a talk, they speak more slowly than usual, and they divide what they say into small chunks, with a brief pause between each. Listen to the beginning of a talk and mark the pauses.

> Good afternoon, everyone/and thank you for coming. I'm going to talk to you today about one of my hobbies, baking. I've loved baking since I was a child. My grandmother taught me to make simple cookies and cakes, and later, when I was a teenager, I watched a lot of TV shows and online videos to learn how to make more complicated ones. What I like about baking is that it's very creative and it makes other people happy…

**b** Now practice giving the beginning of the talk, pausing and trying to get the correct rhythm.

**c** You are going to give a three-minute presentation to other students. You can choose what to talk about, for example:
- a hobby you have or a sport you play
- an interesting person in your family
- a famous person you admire
- the good and bad side of your job or class

Decide what you are going to talk about and make a plan for what you want to say.

**d** In groups, take turns giving your presentation. Then have a short question and answer session.

## 6 ▶ VIDEO LISTENING

**a** Watch a short documentary called *Powerful speeches*. What was Sarah's first impression of Barack Obama? In her opinion, why is he such an effective public speaker?

**b** Watch it again and complete the sentences with two or three words.

1 In 2004, Barack Obama was a little known _____ from _____ .
2 American leaders have a _____ _____ of giving great speeches.
3 President Roosevelt famously said "the only thing we have to _____ is _____ _____ ."
4 Public speaking is still important in the age of the _____ and _____ _____ .
5 Many public speaking techniques come from the _____ _____ and _____ .
6 The first technique is to _____ a _____ .
7 A great way to reinforce a point is to _____ with your _____ .
8 To make an argument sound more complete, give _____ _____ .
9 Barack Obama uses anaphora when he repeats the words "_____ _____" .
10 Great words have the power to bring _____ _____ .

**c** What did you learn that might help you next time you have to speak in public?

Go online to review the lesson

## GRAMMAR

Choose a, b, or c.

1 He got a good job, _____ not having the right degree.
   a although   b despite   c in spite

2 My uncle still works, _____ he won the lottery last year.
   a in spite of   b despite   c even though

3 I called my sister to remind her _____ the flowers.
   a to buy   b for buy   c for buying

4 Jane opened the door quietly _____ her parents up.
   a to not wake   b so that she not wake
   c so as not to wake

5 Jin Lee bought _____ for her camera.
   a some new equipments
   b some new equipment
   c a new equipment

6 Let me give you _____ – don't marry him!
   a a piece of advice   b an advice   c some advices

7 I need to buy a new _____.
   a pant   b pants   c pair of pants

8 There's _____ milk. I'll have to get some from the store.
   a no   b any   c none

9 _____ in that store is incredibly expensive.
   a All   b All of them   c Everything

10 They shouldn't go sailing because _____ of them can swim.
   a both   b either   c neither

11 Let's take them _____ flowers or chocolates when we go for dinner.
   a both   b either   c neither

12 I was in _____ hospital for two weeks with a broken leg.
   a the   b –   c a

13 I now live next door to _____ school where I used to go.
   a the   b –   c a

14 _____ Lake Baikal is the deepest lake in the world.
   a The   b –   c A

15 _____ Getty Museum is in Los Angeles.
   a The   b –   c A

## VOCABULARY

a Complete with the correct form of the **bold** word.

1 A lot of research is being done into _____. **gene**

2 Many important _____ discoveries were made in the 19th century. **science**

3 We live in a very safe _____. **neighbor**

4 Many people in big cities suffer from _____. **lonely**

5 His _____ came as a terrible shock. **die**

b Add a prefix to the **bold** word.

1 New Delhi in India is a very **populated** city.

2 I asked for an aspirin, but the receptionist didn't understand me because I had **pronounced** it.

3 A **national** company is a large company that operates in several different countries.

4 Gandhi wrote most of his **biography** in 1929.

5 Anne is unhappy with her job because she's **paid**.

c Complete the missing words.

1 Will the company take a l_____ this year?

2 He borrowed $50,000 to s_____ _____ his own business.

3 Ikea is the market l_____ in cheap furniture.

4 The company is planning to l_____ its new product in the spring.

5 The bank has br_____ all over the country.

6 It's a bad idea to mix b_____ with pleasure.

7 In a real estate boom, house prices r_____.

8 The drug has some very unpleasant s_____ effects.

9 We need to c_____ out some more experiments.

10 Would you ever be a g_____ pig in a clinical trial?

d Complete the two-word phrases.

1 I'm going to the mountains for some peace and _____.

2 He arrived home from his adventure safe and _____.

3 Sooner or _____, we'll have to make a decision.

4 It's a very dangerous city. There's no law and _____.

5 It's our last chance to do this. It's now or _____.

## PRONUNCIATION

a Circle the word with a different sound.

| | | | | | |
|---|---|---|---|---|---|
| 1 | æ | populate | expand | antidote | gravity |
| 2 | ɑ | product | government | poverty | modernism |
| 3 | ɪr | volunteer | theory | research | sincere |
| 4 | ʃ | recession | expectation | decision | antisocial |
| 5 | θ | death | though | width | thought |

b Underline the main stressed syllable.

1 bi|o|lo|gi|cal   3 mul|ti|cul|tu|ral   5 man|u|fac|ture
2 phy|si|cist   4 in|crease (*verb*)

## CAN YOU understand this text?

**a**  Read the article once. Why did Stephen Hawking never change his computer voice?

**b**  Read the article again and choose a, b, or c.

1  Stephen Hawking used a computer voice synthesizer to communicate for over…
   a  30 years.
   b  40 years.
   c  55 years.

2  He started using the voice when…
   a  he was diagnosed with motor neuron disease.
   b  he lost the power of speech after an operation.
   c  pneumonia caused him to lose his voice.

3  His accent surprised people because…
   a  the synthesizer was made in Britain.
   b  they expected his voice to sound British.
   c  American accents were not popular in Britain.

4  Stephen Hawking…
   a  thought that his accent sounded very American.
   b  told the Queen that his accent wasn't American.
   c  said his accent sounded different to different people.

## ▶ CAN YOU understand these people?

🔊 **10.20  Watch or listen and choose a, b, or c.**

**1** Thomas  **2** Devika  **3** Sean  **4** Sophie

1  Thomas admires Nike because of its ____.
   a  slogan and customer service
   b  logo and marketing
   c  name and the quality of its product

2  Devika thinks that ____ cities will change a lot in the next 20 years.
   a  some European
   b  modern, wealthy cities
   c  developing industrial

3  Sean thinks that art ____.
   a  takes a lot of time to study
   b  isn't as important as science
   c  should focus on climate change

4  Sophie passed her exam although ____.
   a  she didn't do her PowerPoint presentation
   b  she didn't enjoy doing her PowerPoint presentation
   c  her PowerPoint presentation was a disaster

## THE VOICE OF REASON

### Why Stephen Hawking's voice computer spoke with an American accent

Stephen Hawking, the legendary English cosmologist, author of *A Brief History of Time*, was regarded as a brilliant theoretical physicist, and for the British people, a national treasure. However, his famous computer-generated voice left many people puzzled.

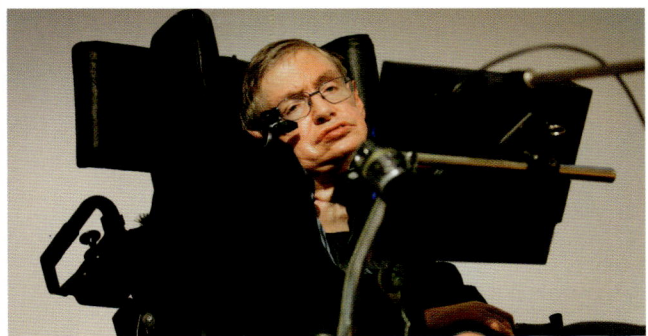

Hawking died in 2018 at the age of 76. In 1963, while studying at Oxford, he was diagnosed with amyotrophic lateral sclerosis (ALS), a rare form of motor neuron disease. Incredibly, despite a poor prognosis, he lived with the disease for 55 years until his death. After catching pneumonia in 1985, Hawking had to have a tracheotomy to allow him to breathe. This left him unable to speak. After that, the professor's primary means of communication was a computer voice synthesizer that he controlled first with a hand-held clicker, and later with a sensor attached to his cheek. This computer-generated voice, known by its US developers as "Perfect Paul," became Hawking's iconic voice, recognized around the world.

One thing that puzzled many people, however, was why his computer spoke with an apparent American accent, in spite of the fact that he was born in Oxford, in the UK. The Queen even quizzed him on the matter, asking him, "Have you still got that American voice?" when meeting him at an event at St. James' Palace. He joked back, "Yes, it is copyrighted actually."

Hawking had previously answered the question on his own website. Explaining how his speech worked, he wrote: "When I have built up a sentence, I can send it to my speech synthesizer. I use a separate hardware synthesizer, made by Speech Plus. It is the best I have heard, although it gives me an accent that has been described variously as Scandinavian, American, or Scottish."

He also explained that he would have been able to change the accent of his computer when the technology advanced, but had decided against it. Hawking added: "My old system worked well and I wrote five books with it, including *A Brief History of Time*. It has become my trademark and I wouldn't change it for a more natural voice with a British accent. I am told that children who need a computer voice want one like mine."

🔎 **Go online** to watch the video, review Files 9 & 10, and check your progress

# Communication

## 1A INDIRECT QUESTIONS
### Student A

**a** Make indirect questions starting with the phrase in parentheses and ask them to **B**.

1 What's the time? (Could you tell me…)
2 Where were the last Olympic Games held? (Can you remember…)
3 Is there a good pizza restaurant near here? (Do you know…)
4 How many players are there on a baseball team? (Do you have any idea…)
5 How old are you? (Would you mind telling me…)

**b** Answer **B**'s questions.

## 1A TOUGH QUESTIONS
### Student A

**a** You're going to interview **B** for a job as a manager in your company. Ask the tough questions below, and ask him / her to give reasons for his / her answers. Then say if you would give him / her the job and why (not).

1 Which one aspect of your personality would you change if you could, and why?
2 If you could have dinner with anyone from history, who would you choose?
3 If you were an animal, which animal would you be?
4 What kinds of things make you angry?
5 If you had to spend the rest of your life on a desert island (with plenty of food and water), what two things would you want to have with you?
6 Which TV or movie character would you most like to be?
7 What's the best (or worst) decision you've ever made?
8 If I came to your house for dinner, what would you cook for me?

**b** Now **B** is going to interview you. Answer the questions. Try to think quickly and make a good impression. Give good reasons for your answers.

## 1B YOU'RE PSYCHIC, AREN'T YOU? Student A

**a** Imagine you're a psychic. Use your psychic powers to complete the sentences below about **B**.

1 Your favorite color is _____.
2 You were born in _____ (a place).
3 You really like _____ (a sport or hobby).
4 You _____ (an activity) last weekend.
5 You haven't been to _____ (a city or country).
6 You would like to be able to _____.
7 You can't _____ very well.
8 You're very good at _____.

**b** Now check if your guesses are true. Say the sentences to **B** and check with a tag question. Try to use falling intonation.

*Your favorite color is pink, isn't it?*

**c** Now **B** will check his / her guesses about you. Respond with a short answer. If the guess is wrong, tell **B** the real answer.

**d** Count your correct guesses. Who was the better psychic?

## 2A MEDICAL MYTHS OR FIRST-AID FACTS?
### Student A

**a** Read the answers carefully to questions 1, 3, and 5. Then look back at the quiz on p.16 and make notes.

**b** Take turns. Tell your partner the correct facts, and explain why the myths can cause problems.

1 The correct answer is **b**. Run cool or lukewarm water on the burn for between 5 and 20 minutes. This will cool the skin and stop blisters from forming.
**a** and **c** are **myths**. Putting anything that is oily on a burn can increase the risk of infection, and ice or iced water will make the damage worse.

3 The correct answer is **c**. Remove any wet clothes, wrap the person in something warm and dry like a coat or a blanket, especially their head, and try to protect them from the wind.
**a** and **b** are **myths**. Rubbing causes a person to lose more heat, and although a hot drink can also help, it should be caffeine-free.

5 The correct answers are **a** and **b**. Pinch the soft part of your nose firmly and tip your head forwards.
**c** is a **myth**. Tipping your head backwards can be dangerous if the bleeding is severe.

## 2B  THE JOY OF THE AGE-GAP FRIENDSHIP Student A

a  Read what Dave says about John.

## Dave (53) on John (34)

I first met John when I gave him a lift to a music festival. It was the first festival I'd been to since I was a teenager. He jumped into my car with a friend of ours. My first impression was that he was a little ignorant because he didn't want to join in our conversation about cars, but he works as a journalist and so I thought he must be an interesting person, which, as I later found out, he is.

We go to the gym together and, mostly, we go out for dinner or a drink. Our friendship was a gradual process. I talked to him a lot and gave him advice when he was getting divorced. I also counseled his ex-wife, because I was also friendly with her – I've learned never to take sides, something I've tried to teach John. He's a pretty private person, so I think it's good to get him to open up more.

I love the fact that he doesn't take himself too seriously. We're just comfortable with each other and can laugh in any situation. We both like being the center of attention, and if one is getting more, the other won't like it. We complain about each other, but he's very loyal. I've never noticed the age difference. Hopefully, he'll be happy to push me around in a wheelchair in my old age.

b  With **B**, compare what they say about each other. Talk about…

- how they met.
- what their first impressions of each other were, and how they changed.
- what they do together.
- what they have in common, and how they are different.
- what they like about each other.

c  Do you think you would get along well with Dave or John?

## 3A  FLIGHT STORIES Student A

a  Read a news article about a flight. What would you have done if you had heard the announcement? How would you have felt?

# NIGHTMARE OVER THE ATLANTIC

**At 6:35 p.m. on January 13,** Brit sh Airways flight 206 took off from Miami to London. It had been flying for about three hours, and was over the Atlantic, when suddenly a voice came out of the loudspeakers. "This is a passenger announcement. We may shortly have to make an emergency landing on water."

Immediately, panic broke out and passengers were screaming and shouting. Most people thought that the plane was about to crash into the Atlantic. But about 30 seconds later, the cabin crew started to run up and down the aisle saying that the message had been played by accident, and that everything was OK. By this time, a lot of the passengers were crying, and trying to get their life jackets out from under their seats.

Afterwards, many passengers said that they had been traumatized, and that it had been the worst experience of their lives. They complained that the captain hadn't given them any explanation until just before landing, and even then, hadn't told them what had really happened. Later, a British Airways spokesperson apologized to passengers on the flight, and said that a pre-recorded emergency announcement had been activated in error.

b  Imagine that you were one of the passengers on the plane. You are going to tell **B** what happened. Look at the words and phrases in the box and plan what you are going to say.

---
**Setting the scene**
Jan. 13   Miami   London   three hours
passenger announcement   emergency landing   water
**The main events**
panic   scream   shout   crash into the Atlantic
30 seconds later   crew   aisle   by accident   cry   life jackets
**What happened in the end**
passengers   traumatized   complain   captain
just before landing   spokesperson apologized   error

---

c  Now tell **B** your story.

*This happened to me a few years ago, when I was flying from Miami to London…*

d  Listen to **B**'s story. Which situation do you think was more scary?

## 3B  READING HABITS  Students A+B

a  **B** close your book. **A** ask **B** the questions.

b  Switch roles. How similar are your reading habits?

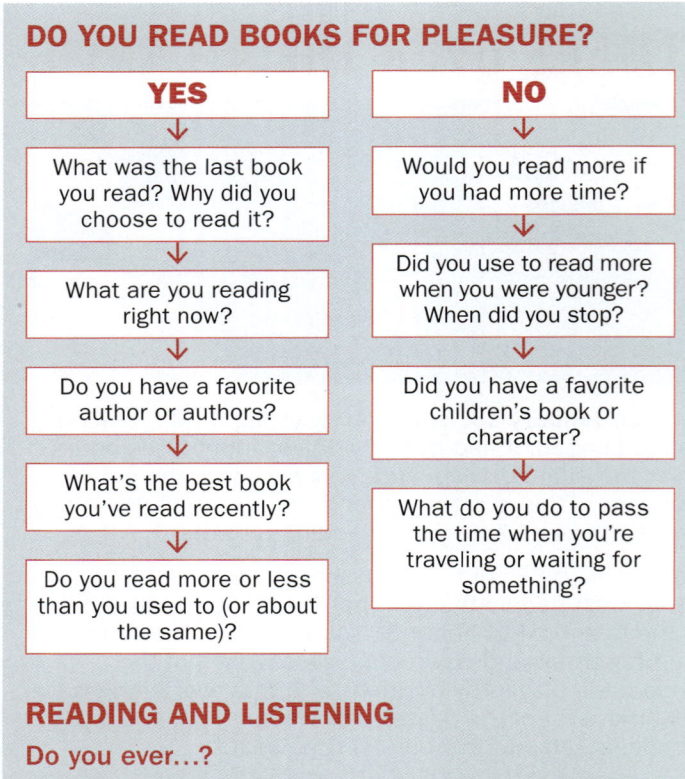

**DO YOU READ BOOKS FOR PLEASURE?**

| YES | NO |
|---|---|
| What was the last book you read? Why did you choose to read it? | Would you read more if you had more time? |
| What are you reading right now? | Did you use to read more when you were younger? When did you stop? |
| Do you have a favorite author or authors? | Did you have a favorite children's book or character? |
| What's the best book you've read recently? | What do you do to pass the time when you're traveling or waiting for something? |
| Do you read more or less than you used to (or about the same)? | |

### READING AND LISTENING

Do you ever…?

- listen to a song and read the lyrics at the same time
- watch movies or TV in English with English subtitles
- read books and listen to them on audio at the same time, e.g., Graded Readers

## 4A  YOUR SCORE  Students A+B

a  Read about what your score means.

b  Do you agree with it? Compare your results with a partner.

If the final number is zero or minus, you live up to your environmentally friendly intentions. The bigger the difference between the two numbers, the greater your failure to live up to your green values.

Most people are not very successful. When these questions were put to 100,000 people in a survey, it turned out that, although most of us do easy things (like turning off faucets and TVs), few of us make real sacrifices.

## 4B  I'LL TAKE A QUESTION  Student A

a  Complete the phrasal verbs or expressions.

1  Who do you take _____ more, your father or your mother?

2  Do you take _____ _____ yourself, or are you very laid-back about your health?

3  Have you ever <u>not</u> taken _____ _____ a good opportunity and then regretted it?

4  Has any big sporting event ever taken _____ in your (nearest big) city? Did you go to it?

5  Do you sometimes get annoyed by little things that people do, or do you take no _____? What kinds of things?

b  Ask **B** your questions.

c  Answer **B**'s questions. Give examples to explain your answers, and then return the question.

> **Giving examples**
> We often use *for example* or *for instance*, to give examples.
>
> *I usually get up quickly, but sometimes I take my time,* **for example / for instance**, *on the weekend.*

## 5A  IT'S AN EMERGENCY!  Student A

a  Read the answers to survival questions 1 and 2. Make notes under these headings:

**You should…**          **You shouldn't…**

1  However strong you are, it's usually a mistake to confront the intruder. They may have a weapon and react violently. Take your phone and lock yourself (and your family) in your bedroom or bathroom, and move a piece of furniture against the door. Then call the police.

2  Whether you're driving an automatic or a manual car, the first thing to do is to put your car in a lower gear. This will slow down the car and will hopefully allow you to put on the emergency brake. Putting the car into neutral won't slow the car down – it will just make the car more unstable and on a hill, it might even make the car go faster.

b  Now use your notes and tell **B** and **C** what you should and shouldn't do.

## 7A ARGUMENT! Student A

**a** Read the instructions carefully for the role-play and think about what you are going to say.

> You share an apartment with **B**. The problems are the following:
>
> - You found the apartment, and moved in first, so obviously, you chose the best room. Recently **B** has been making some sarcastic comments about this.
> - **B** has two friends who are always hanging out at the apartment. You don't have a problem with them, but they are often in the kitchen or living room and you don't have much privacy. They also spend a lot of time online and you think the wi-fi is slower when they're around.
> - You often eat at home in the evening; it's cheaper, and anyway you like cooking, especially spicy dishes like curries. You sometimes offer food to **B** if you've just made something, which he / she frequently accepts. However, **B** never ever cooks. You think that at the very least, **B** should pay for some takeout from time to time, for you to share.
>
> This is your chance to tell **B** how you feel, but try not to lose your temper. Try to find a good solution to each problem.

**b** Have the argument with **B**. Try to agree on a course of action.

> You start the conversation: *OK, I think now is a good time to talk about a few problems that have come up recently…*

## 7B GUESS WHAT IT IS Student A

**a** Look at the pictures below. You are going to describe them to **B**. Say what kind of thing each one is, and then use *looks*, *smells*, *feels*, or *tastes*.

 cabbage  mango  rose  popsicle  fur coat

**b** Describe your first thing to **B** in as much detail as possible. **B** can then ask you questions to identify what the thing is.

> *It's a kind of vegetable. It looks like a green ball. It tastes strong, and I think it smells awful when it's being cooked. You can use it to make…*

**c** Now listen to **B** describe his / her first thing. Don't interrupt until he / she has finished describing. You can ask **B** questions to identify what the thing is.

**d** Continue taking turns to describe all your things. Who guessed the most right?

## 8A BEAT THE BURGLAR Student A

Read the answers to questions 1–3.

> 1 **a** Most burglaries take place between 10 a.m. and lunchtime. The average burglar will wait for adults to go to work and children to go to school, to be sure the house is empty.
>
> 2 **b** An experienced burglar would spend a maximum of 20 minutes in a house.
>
> 3 **a and c** A burglar will usually go for a house that looks expensive, in a good area. They'll often choose a house where there are trees or bushes outside that are good places to hide before or after. That way, there's less chance of neighbors seeing them. Most burglars wait for a house to be empty before they break in, but there are others who prefer it if the owners are at home in bed, so they know where they are and won't get surprised by them suddenly coming home.

## 8B STRANGE, BUT TRUE Student A

**a** Read the article once. Then write down ten key words on a piece of paper to help you remember the story.

### Soccer fan gets World Cup fever

*A man who thought he had "World Cup fever" had actually gotten malaria, doctors have confirmed.*

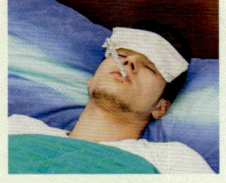

Tom Booker, from Swindon, UK, had been telling friends that he was so excited about the start of the World Cup that he had started to feel very sick. "I was shaking all the time," he told our reporter. "When I started feeling awful, I thought it must be the soccer. It seemed obvious that the prospect of non-stop soccer on TV featuring the best players in the world was making me hallucinate."

Booker, who had just returned from a vacation in Goa, continued to suffer from headaches and stomach pains, and eventually fainted during the semi-finals. He was rushed to the hospital, where he was diagnosed with malaria. "My doctor advised me not to take soccer so seriously." Booker is now recovering well. "I do feel a little stupid," he admitted. "But soccer is my life."

> **Glossary**
> **hallucinate** (*verb*) see or hear things that aren't really there (e.g., because of a high temperature)

**b** Tell **B** your story in your own words, using your key words to help you.

> *There was this man named Tom Booker, and just before the World Cup, he started to feel sick…*

**c** Now listen to **B**'s story, and ask **B** to clarify or rephrase if there's anything you don't understand.

## 9A MISLEADING ADS Student A

**a** Read about the **Volkswagen** ad. Find out...

1 what the advertising campaign claimed.
2 why it was misleading.
3 what happened in the end.

**b** Take turns telling each other the information about your ad.

**c** Which of the three ads do you think was the most seriously misleading? Why?

> **Volkswagen**
>
> On March 29, 2016, the Federal Trade Commission (FTC) filed a lawsuit against Volkswagen about the advertising campaign it used to promote its supposedly "Clean Diesel" vehicles.
>
> The FTC alleged that "Volkswagen deceived consumers by selling or leasing more than 550,000 diesel cars based on false claims that the cars were low-emission, and environmentally friendly." In 2015, it had also been discovered that VW had been cheating in emissions tests on its diesel cars in the US for the past seven years.
>
> In the end, the company agreed to pay a fine of over $4 billion for false advertising, and may have to pay much more for violating the Clean Air Act.

## 10B TRUE OR FALSE Student A

**a** Fill in the blanks in your sentences with *the* where necessary.

1 ____ Andes is ____ longest mountain range in ____ world. (**T**)
2 ____ Loch Ness is ____ largest lake in Scotland. (**F** – It's the second largest. Loch Lomond is the largest.)
3 ____ capital of ____ United States is ____ New York City. (**F** – It's Washington, D.C.)
4 ____ Tahiti is an island in ____ Pacific Ocean. (**T**)
5 ____ Uffizi gallery is ____ most famous art museum in ____ Rome. (**F** – It's in Florence.)
6 ____ South America is larger than ____ North America. (**F**)
7 ____ Mount Vesuvius is a volcano in ____ north-west Italy. (**F** – It's in south-west Italy.)
8 ____ Brooklyn Bridge connects ____ Brooklyn and ____ Manhattan. (**T**)

**b** Now read your sentence 1 to **B**. He / She says if the information is true or false. Correct his / her answer if necessary.

**c** Now listen to **B**'s sentence 1 and say if you think it's true or false. If you think it's false, say what you think the right answer is.

**d** Continue taking turns to say your sentences. Who got the most right answers?

## 1A INDIRECT QUESTIONS Student B

**a** Make indirect questions starting with the phrase in parentheses and ask them to **A**.

1 Where did you buy your bag? (Could you tell me...)
2 What year were the Rio Olympics? (Can you remember...)
3 How long does this class last? (Do you know...)
4 When did Germany last win the World Cup? (Do you have any idea...)
5 Do you have any allergies? (Would you mind telling me...)

**b** Answer **A**'s questions.

## 1A TOUGH QUESTIONS Student B

**a** **A** is going to interview you for a job as a manager in his / her company. Answer the questions. Try to think quickly and make a good impression. Give good reasons for your answers.

**b** Now interview **A** for a similar job in your company. Ask the tough questions below, and ask him / her to give reasons for his / her answers. Then say if you would give him / her the job and why (not).

> 1 Which three adjectives describe you best?
> 2 If you were a car, what type of car would you be?
> 3 How do you usually treat animals?
> 4 Who do you admire most, and why?
> 5 If you could be a superhero, what would your superpowers be?
> 6 Tell me about something in your life that you're really proud of.
> 7 If Hollywood made a movie about your life, who would you like to see play the lead role as you?
> 8 If you could have six months with no obligations or financial limitations, what would you do with the time?

## 1B  YOU'RE PSYCHIC, AREN'T YOU?  Student B

**a** Imagine you're a psychic. Use your psychic powers to complete the sentences below about **A**.

1  You were born in _____ (a month).
2  You don't like _____ (a kind of music).
3  You're going to _____ (an activity) tonight.
4  You've seen _____ (a movie).
5  Your favorite season is _____ .
6  You didn't like _____ (a kind of food) when you were a child.
7  You can play _____ (a musical instrument).
8  You wouldn't like to live in _____ (a place).

**b**  **A** is going to make some guesses about you. Respond with a short answer. If the guess is wrong, tell **A** the real answer.

**c**  Now check if your guesses are true. Say the sentences to **A** and check with a tag question. Try to use falling intonation.

*You were born in July, weren't you?*

**d**  Count your guesses. Who was the better psychic?

---

## 2A  MEDICAL MYTHS OR FIRST-AID FACTS?  Student B

**a**  Read the answers carefully to questions 2, 4, and 6. Then look back at the quiz on p.16 and make notes.

**b**  Take turns. Tell your partner the correct facts, and explain why the myths can cause problems.

2  The correct answers are **b** and **c**. Get the person to sit down and raise their leg by putting it on a chair. Then put an ice pack on the ankle. These two things will help to reduce the swelling.
**a** is a **myth**. Applying heat to an area increases blood flow, which can increase swelling, so the injury will take longer to get better.

4  The correct answers are **b** and **c**. First check the mouth and encourage them to keep coughing. If this doesn't work, hit the person's back hard five times.
**a** is not the <u>first</u> thing you should try. Abdominal thrusts (also known as the Heimlich maneuver) won't work if the choking is due to an allergic reaction or throat injury. It should only be used if the person can't talk, cough, or breathe. In this case, stand behind the person and push up with your fists against their stomach suddenly, up to five times.

6  The correct answers are **a** and **b**. After cleaning the cut with soap and water, or just water, put on antibiotic ointment and a bandage to stop the wound from getting infected.
**c** is a **myth**. An uncovered wound is unprotected, which makes it less likely that it will heal.

---

## 2B  THE JOY OF THE AGE-GAP FRIENDSHIP  Student B

**a**  Read what John says about Dave.

### John (34) on Dave (53)

A group of us had tickets to a music festival and my friend said that a guy named Dave, who was a little older, would give us a lift. He arrived in his BMW. He didn't look his age, but he talked about cars for five hours and I thought he was really boring. However, the next day, he barbecued some great food for us, and I thought, maybe he's not so bad after all.

We live around the corner from each other, so we started meeting at a local restaurant, or watching local bands play. We still go to festivals. The funny thing is, we don't have much in common. He loves cars, I couldn't care less. I love sports, he doesn't understand soccer. But we both like talking to people. We're competitive in our friendship, so for example, we're always trying to be funnier than each other. We argue a lot, mostly about politics, (I'm more left-wing and he's more right-wing), but then we're best friends again.

Being around someone like Dave, who is so full of life, is refreshing. Our friendship is fun, but it goes a lot deeper. I look up to him in some ways. My dad died when I was 19 and Dave is someone I can talk to about that. Maybe he sees me as some sort of weird son. He's not just fun – he's a really kind person. If I were in trouble and could only make one call, it would be to Dave.

**b**  With **A**, compare what they say about each other. Talk about...

- how they met.
- what their first impressions of each other were, and how they changed.
- what they do together.
- what they have in common, and how they are different.
- what they like about each other.

**c**  Do you think you would get along well with Dave or John?

## 3A FLIGHT STORIES Student B

**a** Read a news article about a flight. What would you have thought if you had heard the bang? How would you have felt?

## EXPLODING ENGINE CAUSES EMERGENCY LANDING

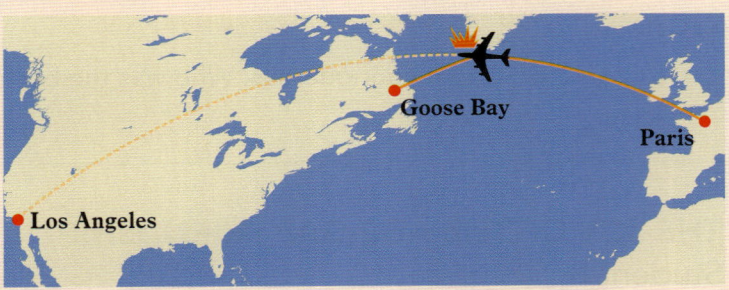

Passengers traveling on an Air France flight from Paris to Los Angeles had been relaxing and enjoying movies and food when, five hours after take-off, just after they had crossed the southern tip of Greenland, they suddenly heard a loud bang.

The cabin started vibrating, some passengers screamed, and everybody knew something was wrong. Passengers nervously joked to each other as they tried to figure out what had happened. Some thought the plane had hit a bird. But passengers sitting in window seats said they had seen one of the engines exploding. The cabin crew walked through the aisles reassuring passengers, and then the captain confirmed that there had been an explosion in one of the engines.

The atmosphere was tense, but about two hours later, the plane landed at a military airfield in Goose Bay on the far northeast edge of Canada, which is used as an emergency landing spot for transatlantic flights. There were no injuries among the 520 passengers. Passengers completed their journeys to Los Angeles on two planes sent by Air France to Goose Bay.

**b** Imagine that you were one of the passengers on the plane. You are going to tell **A** what happened. Look at the words and phrases in the box and plan what you are going to say.

---
**Setting the scene**
Air France   Paris   Los Angeles   relax   movies and food
five hours   Greenland   bang

**The main events**
cabin   vibrate   scream   joke   bird   window seats   engine
explode   cabin crew   aisles   captain   confirm   explosion

**What happened in the end**
land   Goose Bay, Canada   no injuries   complete journey
two planes
---

**c** Now listen to **A**'s story. Then tell **A** your story.

> *This happened to me a few years ago, when I was flying from Paris to Los Angeles…*

**d** Which situation do you think was more scary?

## 5A IT'S AN EMERGENCY! Student B

**a** Read the answers to survival questions 3 and 4. Make notes under these headings:

You should…          You shouldn't…

**3** Look for an area of low ground and make yourself as small a target as possible. Go down on your knees with your feet together and head on the ground. This makes it less likely that lightning will strike you. Lying flat will expose more of your body to the lightning, and sheltering under a tree is very dangerous, because if it gets hit by lightning, a branch may fall and injure you.

**4** First, keep your clothes on. They can trap air, which will keep you warm and help you to float. Turn towards the direction where you fell – the ice was strong enough to hold you once – and kick your feet to get your body horizontal. Use your elbows to pull yourself out and then roll off the ice. Don't try to stand and run, as this might cause the ice to break again.

**b** Now use your notes and tell **A** and **C** what you should and shouldn't do.

## 9A MISLEADING ADS Student B

**a** Read about the **Dannon** ad. Find out…
  1 what the advertising campaign claimed.
  2 why it was misleading.
  3 what happened in the end.

**b** Take turns telling each other the information about your ad.

**c** Which of the three ads do you think was the most seriously misleading? Why?

---
**Dannon**

Ads for Dannon's popular Activia brand yogurt landed the company with a bill of $45 million in 2010. The yogurts were marketed as being "clinically" and "scientifically" proven to boost your immune system and able to help to regulate digestion.

The Activia ad campaign, endorsed by actress Jamie Lee Curtis, claimed that the yogurt had special bacterial ingredients. As a result, the yogurt was sold at 30% higher prices than other similar products.

The lawsuit against Dannon began in 2008, when US consumer Trish Wiener made a complaint. The judge overseeing the case said that the claims were not proven. As well as being given a fine of $45 million, Dannon was ordered to remove the words "clinically" and "scientifically proven" from its labels.
---

## 7A ARGUMENT! Student B

**a** Read the instructions carefully for the role-play and think about what you are going to say.

> You share an apartment with **A**. The problems are the following:
>
> - When you started sharing the apartment with **A**, he / she was already living in the house and he / she had taken the best and biggest room. Your room is much smaller and there's only really enough room in it for your bed! But you're both paying the same rent. This isn't fair!
> - You have two good friends who often come to hang out with you at the apartment. Recently, **A** has been unfriendly to your friends, sometimes not even saying hello when they come in. And **A** has also started complaining that the wi-fi is slow because your friends are using it. How ridiculous! That can't be true.
> - **A** seems to spend all his / her time in the kitchen cooking. He / She makes a lot of spicy food, which means that the whole apartment smells like curry. You don't dislike curry, and have even occasionally accepted some of **A**'s cooking, just to be polite, but you hate the smell in the apartment. You can't see the point of cooking and prefer getting your own takeout or ready-made meals.
>
> This is your chance to tell **A** how you feel, but try not to lose your temper. Try to find a good solution to each problem.

**b** Have the argument with **A**. Try to agree on a course of action. **A** will start.

## 7B GUESS WHAT IT IS Student B

**a** Look at the pictures below. You are going to describe them to **A**. Say what kinds of thing each one is, and then use *looks*, *smells*, *feels*, or *tastes*.

camembert   jasmine   kitten   vinegar   chili pepper

**b** Now listen to **A** describe his / her first thing. Don't interrupt until he / she has finished describing. You can ask **A** questions.

**c** Now describe your first thing in as much detail as possible. **A** can then ask you questions to identify what the thing is.

> *It's a kind of French cheese. It's round and usually comes in a wooden box…*

**d** Continue taking turns to describe all your things. Who guessed the most right?

## 8A BEAT THE BURGLAR Student B

Read the answers to questions 4–6.

> **4 a** These days burglars are usually looking for things like laptops and tablets, which are easy to sell, and not so easy for the owner to identify if the burglar later gets caught.
>
> **5 c** There's a typical order burglars use when they search a house for valuables. They start with the master bedroom, and then the living room. After that, the dining room, the study, and then the kitchen. The last place would be a child's bedroom. You wouldn't usually expect to find anything worth taking there.
>
> **6 a** Burglars don't like dogs, especially noisy ones, because they're unpredictable.

## 8B STRANGE, BUT TRUE Student B

**a** Read the article once. Then write down ten key words on a piece of paper to help you remember the story.

> ### Shark baby drama
>
> *A man who was accused of stealing a shark from a Texas aquarium has said he did so in an attempt to rescue it.*
>
> On a visit to the San Antonio Aquarium, 38-year-old Anthony Shannon was caught on security cameras trying to steal a shark. He lifted the 16-inch-long shark, named Miss Helen, from a tank, wrapped her in a blanket, and took her away in a stroller. Shannon has now been charged with stealing the fish and taking her to his home. Miss Helen was reported to be one of around 25 sharks being kept at Mr. Shannon's home, along with an unknown number of crabs.
>
> Shannon claimed he was afraid that Miss Helen's life was in danger. In an interview with local news, Shannon said that he was sorry for the theft, but that he could justify his behavior because it was an "emergency." He threatened to steal another shark if he felt it was necessary. Miss Helen was returned to the aquarium. Staff members denied keeping the animals in bad conditions and said the water was tested every day.
>
> **Glossary**
> **stroller** (*noun*) a small folding seat on wheels in which a small child sits and is pushed along

**b** Listen to **A**'s story, and ask **A** to clarify or rephrase if there's anything you don't understand.

**c** Tell **A** your story in your own words, using your key words to help you.

> *There was this man named Anthony Shannon, and when he visited the San Antonio Aquarium in Texas, he…*

## 4B  I'LL TAKE A QUESTION  Student B

**a** Complete the phrasal verbs or expressions.

1 Do you get up very quickly in the morning or do you take _____ _____ ?
2 Have you taken _____ a new sport or hobby recently, or is there one you would like to take _____ ?
3 If you were thinking of buying a new phone, what factors would you take _____ _____ ?
4 Have you ever taken _____ _____ a charity walk or some other kind of fundraiser that benefited your community?
5 Who takes the trash _____ in your house, you or someone else?

**b** Answer **A**'s questions. Give examples to explain your answers, and then return the question.

**c** Ask **A** your questions.

> 🔎 **Giving examples**
> We often use *for example* or *for instance* to give examples.
> *I take after my mother,* **for example** / **for instance** *we both have the same sense of humor.*

## 10B  TRUE OR FALSE  Student B

**a** Fill in the blanks in your sentences with *the* where necessary.

1 ____ capital of ____ Netherlands is ____ Amsterdam. (**F** – It's The Hague.)
2 ____ Amazon is ____ longest river in ____ world. (**F** – It's the Nile.)
3 ____ Panama Canal connects ____ Atlantic Ocean to ____ Pacific Ocean. (**T**)
4 ____ Atacama desert is in ____ northern part of ____ Chile. (**T**)
5 ____ Black Sea is in ____ southwest Europe. (**F** – It's in southeast Europe.)
6 ____ biggest lake in ____ world is ____ Lake Victoria in ____ Africa. (**F** – It's Lake Superior in Canada / the US.)
7 ____ Mount McKinley is ____ highest mountain in ____ Alaska Range. (**T**)
8 ____ Greenwich Village is in ____ downtown New York City. (**T**)

**b** Now listen to **A**'s sentence 1 and say if you think it's true or false. If you think it's false, say what you think the right answer is.

**c** Now read your sentence 1 to **A**. Correct his / her answer if necessary.

**d** Continue taking turns to say your sentences. Who got the most right answers?

## 5A  IT'S AN EMERGENCY!  Student C

**a** Read the answers to survival questions 5 and 6. Make notes under these headings:

**You should…**          **You shouldn't…**

5 The number one tip is to stay where you are, or find a sheltered space nearby if it's night time, and wait to be rescued (especially if you have told someone where you were going to walk). But make sure you stay in the open during the day, so that you can be seen by a helicopter. Make a fire, or tie a piece of bright clothing to a stick, to attract attention. Never keep walking, as you will only get further lost and make it more difficult for searchers to find you.

6 Abandon any equipment, as it could pull you further down, and use swimming movements to try to get to the surface. Don't try to dig yourself out, as this is almost impossible. If you're covered and can't get to the surface, try to thrust part of your body through the snow, so rescuers can see you. But the best thing to do if you are skiing off the trail is to always carry avalanche safety equipment with you, including a two-way radio.

**b** Now use your notes and tell **A** and **B** what you should and shouldn't do.

## 9A  MISLEADING ADS  Student C

**a** Read about the **Olay** ad. Find out…
1 what the advertising campaign claimed.
2 why it was misleading.
3 what happened in the end.

**b** Take turns telling each other the information about your ad.

**c** Which of the three ads do you think was the most seriously misleading? Why?

**Olay**

In 2009, an Olay ad for its Definity eye cream showed former model Twiggy looking wrinkle-free – and a whole lot younger than her then 60 years. It turned out that the ads were retouched.

The British Advertising Regulator (ASA) banned the ad, after more than 700 complaints were made against it. It was concluded that the digitally-altered ads gave a "misleading impression of the effect the product could achieve."

Olay's parent company Procter & Gamble responded that it was "routine practice to use post-production techniques to correct for lighting and other minor photographic deficiencies before publishing the final shots as part of an advertising campaign."

# Writing

## 1 AN INFORMAL EMAIL

**From:** Anna
**To:** johnstons586@gmail.com
**Subject:** News!

Hi Olivia,

Sorry that I havent been in touch for a while, but I've been sick. I got the flu last week and I had a temprature of 102°F, so I've been in bed since four days. I'm feeling a little better today, so I've been catching up on my emails. Luckly my college classes don't start until next week.

How are you? What have you been doing? Anything exciting. Here everyone are fine (apart from me and my flu!). My brother Mike started his new job with a software-company – I think I told you about it when I wrote last time – anyway, so far, he's really been enjoying it. How is your family? I hope their well.

I have some good news – I'm going to a conference in your town in may, from the 16th to the 20th. Could you recomend a hotel where I could stay near the downtown area? It needs to be somewhere not too expensive because my college is paying. I'll have a free half-day for siteseeing. Do you think you'll be able show me around? That would be great.

Well, that's all for now. Please give my regards to your family.

Hope to hear from you soon.

Take care,

Anna

PS Please reply to this email address. I've stopped using the old Yahoo one.

🔍 **Beginning an informal email**
When you are writing an informal email, it is more usual to start with *Hi* than with *Dear*.

**a** Read the email from Anna. It has 12 highlighted mistakes – four grammar or vocabulary, four punctuation, and four spelling. With a partner, decide what kind of mistake each one is and correct it.

**b** Read Anna's email again and find phrases that mean...
emailed, messaged, or called
reading and replying to
Have you been doing anything fun?
I don't have anymore news.
send my best wishes to

**c** You're going to answer Anna's email. Look at the **Useful language** expressions and try to complete them.

🔍 **Useful language: an informal email**
**Opening expressions**
Thanks [1]_____ your email / letter.
It was great [2]_____ hear from you.
Sorry that I haven't been in touch for a while. / Sorry for [3]_____ writing earlier.
I [4]_____ you and your family are well.

**Responding to news**
Glad to [5]_____ that you're all well.
Sorry [6]_____ hear about your final grades.
Good [7]_____ with the new job.
Hope you [8]_____ better soon.

**Closing expressions**
Anyway, / Well, that's all [9]_____ now.
[10]_____ my regards (love) to…
Hope to hear from you soon. / Looking [11]_____ to hearing from you soon.
Take [12]_____ / (Lots of) love
[13]_____ wishes / Regards

**Something you forgot and want to add**
[14]_____ Don't forget to send me the photos you promised.

**d** **Plan** the content of your email.
1 Underline the questions in the email that Anna wants you to answer.
2 Underline other places in the email where you think you need to respond, e.g., *I've been sick.*
3 Think about how to respond to each of the things you've underlined.

**e** **Write** 140–190 words, in two or three paragraphs. Use informal language (contractions, etc.), and expressions from **Useful language**.

**f** **Check** your email for mistakes (grammar, punctuation, and spelling).

🔵 p.19

## 2 A SHORT STORY

**I**t was only a small mistake, but it changed my life forever. I had been working at J.B. Simpson's for ten years. It was a small ¹ _family-run_ company that exported outdoor furniture. I was ² _____ happy with my job. I got along ³ _____ with the owner, Arthur Simpson, but not with his wife, Linda. She was a loud, ⁴ _____ woman, who ⁵ _____ used to turn up at the office and start criticizing us for no reason. Everyone disliked her.

One afternoon, Mrs. Simpson came in while I was finishing writing a report. She looked at me and said, "If I were you, I wouldn't wear that color. It doesn't suit you at all." I was wearing a ⁶ _____ pink shirt that I was very ⁷ _____ of, and her comment really annoyed me. I typed a ⁸ _____ message to Alan Simmonds in sales. "Watch out! The old witch is here!" and pressed send. A couple of minutes later, I was surprised to receive a message from Mr. Simpson, asking me to come to his office ⁹ _____. When I opened the door, I saw his wife glaring at the computer screen. I realized, to my horror, what I had done. I had clicked on Simpson instead of Simmonds. ¹⁰ _____, I was packing my things. I had been fired!

**a** Read the story. What was the "small mistake"? What happened in the end?

**b** Using adverbs and adjectives helps to make a story come alive and makes it more enjoyable to read. Complete the story with an adjective or adverb from the box.

| aggressive | an hour later | ~~family-run~~ | fond |
| frequently | immediately | new | quick | very | well |

**c** You may want to write some dialogue as part of your story. Rewrite the following with the correct punctuation. Use the dialogue in the story to help you.

> i want to talk to you about an email you sent
> Mr. Simpson said coldly

**d** Look at the highlighted time expressions in **Useful language** and complete them.

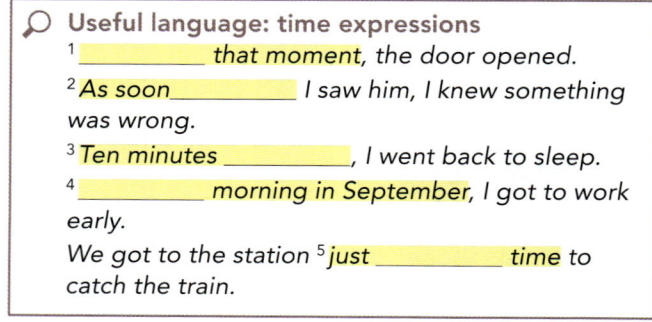

🔍 **Useful language: time expressions**
¹ _____ that moment, the door opened.
² As soon_____ I saw him, I knew something was wrong.
³ Ten minutes _____, I went back to sleep.
⁴ _____ morning in September, I got to work early.
We got to the station ⁵ just _____ time to catch the train.

**e** You are going to write a story beginning with one of the sentences below. With a partner, choose which story to write, and discuss what the plot could be.

| 1 | It was eleven o'clock at night when my phone rang. |
| 2 | As soon as I saw my mother's face, I knew something was wrong. |
| 3 | We had been driving for four hours when we saw the sign for a small hotel and decided to stop. |

**f** **Plan** the content.
1 Write a quick outline of what happens in the story (50–60 words).
2 Think about what tenses you need for each part of the story, e.g., how to set the scene, what significant events had happened before the story starts.
3 Think about how you could improve your story by adding extra details, and using more adjectives and adverbs. Think also about where you might want to include some dialogue.

**g** **Write** 140–190 words, organized in two or three paragraphs. Set the scene and then tell the story. Use the time expressions in **Useful language** to make the sequence of events clear.

**h** **Check** your short story for mistakes (grammar, punctuation, and spelling).

🔴 p.33

## 3 FOR AND AGAINST

**a** Read a post about adventure sports on a blog site called *For and against*? Do you think there are more advantages or more disadvantages?

**b** Read the blog post again and complete it with the linking expressions from the box (two of them are interchangeable).

> although   another advantage   because of
> for example (x2)   furthermore   in addition
> on the other hand   ~~the main advantage~~
> to sum up

**c** Put the linking expressions from **b** in the **Useful language** chart below.

> 🔍 **Useful language: linking expressions**
>
> **To list advantages / disadvantages**
> *the main advantage*
>
> _____
>
> **To add more points to the same topic**
>
> _____
>
> _____
>
> **To introduce an example**
> *For instance,…*
>
> _____
>
> **To make contrasting points**
> *However,…*
> *In spite of (the fact that)…*
>
> _____
>
> _____
>
> **To give a reason**
> *Because (+ clause)…*
> _____ *(+ noun)…*
>
> **To introduce the conclusion**
> *In conclusion,…*
>
> _____

**d** You are going to write a post for the site. Choose one of the titles below.

### Going to work abroad: an exciting opportunity or a scary one?

### Being a celebrity: a dream or a nightmare?

---

| Home | About | Blog | Subscribe |
| --- | --- | --- | --- |

Everything has two sides to it, a positive one and a negative one. Post your opinions on our blog…

# Adventure sports – fun or too risky?

**Every year, more and more people are tempted by the idea of going on an adventure sports vacation, especially during the summer months.**

Spending your vacation being active and enjoying the outdoors has a lot of advantages. [1]*The main advantage* is that adventure sports, like many other physical activities, offer health benefits and help keep your mood positive, [2]_____, when you practice extreme sports your brain releases endorphins because of the adrenalin rush and that makes you feel happy. [3]_____ is the self-confidence that you gain from doing these activities. [4]_____, the lessons learned from facing the difficulties and the risks of these extreme sports may be very valuable in everyday life.

[5]_____, there are also some important disadvantages. [6]_____ they make you feel good, risky sports can be extremely dangerous. The possibility of getting seriously injured while performing these activities is very high, and some adventure sports, [7]_____ skydiving or cliff jumping, can even have fatal consequences. [8]_____ these risks, you need to be in very good shape to practice these sports during a vacation, which means that they are not for everyone. [9]_____, they are likely to be expensive because they require a lot of equipment, safety measures, and well-trained and qualified instructors.

[10]_____, adventure sports vacations have both advantages and disadvantages. Whether they suit you or not depends on your level of fitness, your personality, and how much you can afford.

Like | Share | Comment

---

**e** **Plan** the content.

1 Decide what kinds of things you could say to start the post for the topic you chose, for example, why young people choose to go abroad or why people today are so interested in famous people. This will give you material for the introduction.

2 List two or three advantages and disadvantages, and number them in order of importance.

3 Decide if you think there are more advantages than disadvantages.

**f** **Write** 140–190 words, organized in four paragraphs: introduction, advantages, disadvantages (or disadvantages then advantages), and conclusion. Use a formal style (no contractions or colloquial expressions). Use the linking expressions in **Useful language**.

**g** **Check** for mistakes (grammar, punctuation, and spelling).

 **p.43**

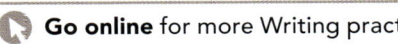

# How to keep children safe in your home

You probably think that your home is a very safe place. But this may not be true if you have children coming to visit. Here are some tips to prevent accidents. / First, look at the bedroom where the children are going to sleep. Make sure the beds are not under a window, in case a child tries to climb out. If a very small child is going to sleep in the bed, you could put some pillows on the floor next to the bed, in case the child falls out. The next place to check is the bathroom. Many people keep medicines in a drawer or on a shelf above the sink. But this can be dangerous, because children may find them and think they are candy. You should keep them in a locked cabinet. Finally, take a look at the kitchen, which is the most dangerous room in the house for children. Knives should be kept in drawers that children can't reach, and make sure that all cleaning liquids are in high or locked cabinets. If you follow this simple advice, children who come to stay will never be at risk in your home.

16:03 Thursday 2nd May

a  Look at the three pictures. What do you think should and shouldn't have been done? Read the advice from a health and safety blog and check.

b  This blog post was originally written in five short sections. Mark / where each new section should begin.

c  You are going to write a health and safety blog post. With a partner, choose one of the titles below.

**How to keep safe if you go hiking in the mountains**

**How to keep safe on a day at the beach**

**How to keep safe on a long drive**

d  **Plan** the content.
1  Think of at least three useful tips.
2  Think of a good introductory sentence (or sentences).

e  **Write** 140–190 words, organized in paragraphs. Use expressions from **Useful language** below, and write in a neutral or informal style.

> 🔍 **Useful language: giving advice**
> *Don't forget to… / Remember to…*
> *Make sure you…*
> *You should…*
> *Never…*
>
> **Reasons**
> *…in case*
> *…so (that)*
> *…because it might…*

f  **Check** your blog post for mistakes (grammar, punctuation, and spelling).

↩ p.49

## 5 DESCRIBING A PHOTO

**a** Look at photo 1 and read the description. Do you agree with what the writer says about the people?

**b** Complete the description with a word or phrase from the box.

across from    behind    in front of
in the background    in the center
~~in the foreground~~    on the left
outside

**c** You are going to write a description of photo 2. **Plan** the content. With a partner, look at the photo carefully and decide what you think the people are thinking or feeling. Decide how to organize what you want to say into paragraphs.

**d** **Write** 140–190 words. Use the phrases in **Useful language** to help you.

> 🔍 **Useful language: describing a photo or picture**
> *In the foreground / center / background of the photo…*
> *The (man) looks as if / looks as though…*
> *It looks as if / as though…*
> *The (woman) may / might be… / Maybe the woman is…*
> *The photo reminds me of…*

**e** **Check** your description for mistakes (grammar, punctuation, and spelling).

← p.73

I think this is a photo of a family in their house. However, they are not posing. None of the people are looking at the camera.

¹ *In the foreground*, we can see the inside of a room with glass doors leading to a yard. ² _____ of the photo, there is a girl sitting at the table, resting her head on one hand, with an open book ³ _____ her. There are two other empty chairs around the table. The girl is smiling; she looks as if she's daydreaming, maybe about something she's read in the book. ⁴ _____ of the photo, there is a woman, who looks older than the girl, maybe her mother. She's standing with her arms folded, looking out of the glass doors into the yard. She seems to be watching what's happening ⁵ _____, and she looks a little worried.

⁶ _____, we can see a patio, and ⁷ _____ that, a beautiful yard. Outside the glass doors on the right, we can see a boy and a man, who may be father and son. The boy is standing, facing the man, who is crouching down ⁸ _____ him. It looks as though they're having a serious conversation. Maybe the boy has been misbehaving, because it seems as if he's looking at the ground.

This photo reminds me of a David Hockney or Edward Hopper painting – it makes you speculate about who the people are and what they are thinking.

## 6 EXPRESSING YOUR OPINION

**a** Read the title of the magazine article. Do you agree or disagree? Then quickly read the article and see if the writer's opinion is the same as yours.

**b** Complete the article with a word or phrase from the box below.

---
finally   first   for instance   in addition   in conclusion
in most cases   ~~nowadays~~   second   so   whereas
---

**c** You are going to write an article for a magazine. With a partner, choose one of the titles below.

> **Downloading music or movies without paying is as much of a crime as stealing from a store.**

> **Squatters who live in an unoccupied property should not be forced to leave it.**

**d** **Plan** the content. The article should have four or five paragraphs.

1 **The introduction:** Think about what the current situation is and what your opinion is.

2 **The main paragraphs:** Try to think of at least two or three clear reasons to support your opinion. You could also include examples to back up your reasons.

3 **The conclusion:** Think of how to express your conclusion (a summary of your opinion).

**e** **Write** 140–190 words, organized in four or five paragraphs (introduction, reasons, and conclusion). Use a formal style (no contractions or colloquial expressions). Use the phrases in **b** and in **Useful language**.

---
🔍 **Useful language: ways of giving your opinion**
*(Personally) I think… / I believe…*
*In my opinion,…*
*In addition,… / Also,…*
*In conclusion,… / To sum up,…*

**Ways of giving examples**
*There are several things we can do,*
*for example / for instance / such as…*
*Another thing we can do is…*
*We can also…*

**Sequencing words**
*Firstly, / Secondly, / Thirdly, / Finally,…*
---

**f** **Check** your article for mistakes (grammar, punctuation, and spelling).

 p.79

---

# Community service is a bad punishment for sports stars who commit crimes

[1]*Nowadays* in the US when a star athlete commits a crime, he or she is usually sentenced to community service instead of serving time in a jail or prison.

[2]_____, for these high-profile people, I believe that community service is a very bad option.

[3]_____, the community service that star athletes are asked to complete is often very different from the community service that non-celebrities must complete. [4]_____, star athletes might fulfill their community service by coaching kids at sports camps [5]_____ non-celebrities often perform court-ordered community service by picking up garbage on roadsides or digging ditches.

[6]_____, kids often view sports stars as role models. So when a sports star never goes on trial for committing a crime, kids assume that if you're famous you can get away with breaking the law.

[7]_____, in some cases, once celebrities complete their community service, the crime doesn't go on their records. This sends kids the wrong message: if you're famous the laws don't apply to you in the same way as they do for non-famous people.

[8]_____, I think that when sports stars are sentenced to community service for their crimes, they should also be fined. They usually have a lot of money [9]_____ they can afford to pay larger fines than non-celebrity criminals.

[10]_____, I believe that star athletes who commit crimes should be sentenced to more than community service. They should also be fined or serve time in prison for more serious crimes.

## 7 A REPORT

**a** Read the report on restaurants. With a partner, think of suitable headings for paragraphs 1, 3, and 4.

**b** You have been asked to write a report on either **good places for eating out** or **entertainment in your town** for an English language magazine. With a partner, **plan** the content

1 Decide which report you are going to write.
2 Decide what headings you can use to divide up your report.
3 Decide what information to include under each heading.

**c** **Write** 140–190 words, organized in three or four paragraphs with a heading. Use a neutral / formal style, and use expressions from **Useful language** for generalizing.

> 🔍 **Useful language: talking in general**
> Most / The majority of (movie theaters in my town…)
> (Movie theaters) are usually / tend to be (pretty expensive)
> In general… / Generally speaking…
> almost always… / nearly always…

**d** **Check** your report for mistakes (grammar, punctuation, and spelling).

⟵ p.93

---

# Eating out in New York City

This report describes various options for students who want to eat out while staying in New York City.

**1** _____

**Fast food** – The majority of fast-food restaurants are cheap and the service is fast, but they are often noisy and crowded, and of course the food is the same all over the world.

**World food** – New York City has restaurants offering food from many parts of the world, for example India and Thailand. These are often relatively inexpensive and have good-quality food and a nice atmosphere.

**2** _Value for money_

**Gastropubs** – These are pubs that serve high-quality food but tend to be slightly cheaper than the majority of mid-range restaurants. Generally speaking, the food is well-cooked and some have very imaginative menus.

**Diners** – You can usually get a good sandwich, hamburger, or bowl of soup in a diner without spending too much. Some diners are open 24 hours, so if you're hungry late at night, a diner might be your best option.

**3** _____

There are many options if you want to try somewhere special, but be aware that this almost always means spending a lot of money. French restaurants, for example, are often expensive, and also restaurants run by celebrity chefs.

**4** _____

- Don't make your meal cost more by ordering expensive drinks.
- If you have a special restaurant in mind, don't forget to book in advance because the best restaurants are usually full, especially on the weekend.
- All New York City restaurants get inspection grades based on cleanliness and food safety standards. The grades are displayed near the front door of restaurants. Check before you go inside.
- Even if you have a limited budget, take advantage of the different restaurants that New York City has to offer.

# Listening

🔊 **1.2**

**All four journalists** Excuse me…, Excuse me…, Cindy…, Cindy…

**Journalist 1** Just a few questions…

**Actress** OK, OK, but you have just one minute.

**Journalist 1** What brings you to Toronto?

**Actress** I'm here to accept an award and do some interviews.

**Journalist 2** How long are you going to be in Toronto for?

**Actress** Just 48 hours, then I'm flying back to the States.

**Journalist 3** That's a very short stay. Don't you like Toronto?

**Actress** I love Toronto, but unfortunately my new movie starts shooting on Monday.

**Journalist 4** There've been rumors that you and your husband are having relationship problems. Can you tell us if there's any truth in that?

**Actress** No, no, no, no. No comment. No more questions.

🔊 **1.9**

**1 Dominic**

**Interviewer** Have you ever been asked a strange question in an interview?

**Dominic** Yes, it was my first interview when I was applying to Sarah Lawrence University in New York – where I'm studying now.

**Interviewer** What was the question?

**Dominic** The question was, if you could have dinner with three people from the past, who would you choose and why?

**Interviewer** And what did you answer?

**Dominic** It was one of the first questions I was asked, and I said, "I can't answer this right now. Can I answer this at the end?" because I couldn't think of anyone. So they said, "OK," and then they asked me the question again later, and I said something ridiculous like John Lennon, um, Picasso, and, uh, I can't even remember who the third person was, it was another sort of artist or musician I think.

**Interviewer** Do you think it was a good question?

**Dominic** Yes, because it made me think, I mean, it wasn't something I was expecting at all, and all the other ones were more yes / no, direct questions, so this one made me think a little more.

**Interviewer** And you got in?

**Dominic** Yes, I did.

**2 Heidi**

**Interviewer** Have you ever been asked a strange question in an interview?

**Heidi** Yes, I have, that was many years ago, it was one of my first job interviews, in London, actually, after I moved to London from Germany. It was for a financial department, and the manager who interviewed me, I can't remember, but I believe he was German, he asked me, "Do you have a boyfriend?", and "Are you planning to get pregnant?"

**Interviewer** That's illegal now, isn't it?

**Heidi** Yes, I know, and I believe that was illegal then.

**Interviewer** And what did you answer?

**Heidi** I said no, I didn't have a boyfriend, and I had no plans to get pregnant any time soon, but at that point, it was clear to me that I didn't want to work for that company.

**3 Sean**

**Interviewer** Have you ever been asked a strange question in an interview?

**Sean** Yes. I was being interviewed for a job with an advertising agency and the interviewer kept checking information on my résumé and then asking me about it, and he saw that I'd studied philosophy in college, and he said, "Oh, I see that you studied philosophy in college. Do you still practice philosophy?"

**Interviewer** What did you answer?

**Sean** I said the first thing that came into my head, I said, "Well, I still think a lot."

**Interviewer** Was the interviewer impressed?

**Sean** Well, he obviously liked the answer because I got the job.

**4 Alice**

**Interviewer** Have you ever been asked a strange question in an interview?

**Alice** There's one I can think of, which was when I was being interviewed for a job with a company in Canada.

**Interviewer** What was it?

**Alice** Well, the interviewer asked me, "What animal would you like to be reincarnated as?"

**Interviewer** Weird question!

**Alice** Totally.

**Interviewer** What did you say?

**Alice** So I said a cat, because it was the first thing I thought of and because cats have a good life – well, at least in the US they do. And then the interviewer immediately looked embarrassed and said that he'd been told to ask me that question to see how I would react, but that he thought it was a stupid question.

**Interviewer** What happened in the end?

**Alice** I didn't get the job, so maybe the interviewer wasn't very fond of cats!

🔊 **1.10**

On December 4th, 1872, a ship called the *Mary Celeste* was found floating in the Atlantic. There was no one on board. The ship wasn't damaged, and everything was in order, although the lifeboat was missing. None of the crew or passengers were ever seen again.

On March 4th, 1918, a huge ship called the *USS Cyclops* left Barbados with 300 people on board, and sailed into what we now call the Bermuda Triangle. Then it disappeared without a trace. No distress call was made and no bad weather was reported in the region. A huge search for the *Cyclops* was launched – boats and planes scoured the area for wreckage or survivors – but nothing of the enormous ship was ever seen again.

On July 2nd, 1937, Amelia Earhart, the famous American aviator, took off with her navigator from New Guinea, in a small plane, on the last stage of their around-the-world flight. It was the last time they were seen alive. $4 million dollars were spent on the search, but no trace of Amelia or the navigator was ever found.

🔊 **1.12**

An Edinburgh police officer, Robert Muirhead, was sent to the island to solve the mystery. Muirhead was a hard-working, practical investigator, and not at all superstitious. Among other clues, he found equipment lying all over the island, and also a huge rock, much too heavy for any men to carry, lying on the steps leading up to the lighthouse. In the end, the only explanation he could think of was that the men had been carried off by an enormous wave.

Muirhead's explanation was immediately rejected. But more than 100 years later, in 1995, the ship *Queen Elizabeth II* was hit by a 100-foot wave that according to her captain, "came out of the darkness" and "looked like the White Cliffs of Dover."

Then a paper published in a scientific journal recently proved that the "monster wave," which for centuries had been considered a sailors' myth, is a mathematical reality: many smaller waves can suddenly combine in mid-ocean and create a huge wave of devastating force. Most marine scientists now agree that it is a naturally occurring (though rare) event.

So finally, the only explanation that fits the facts is that the three lighthouse men had rushed out to attend to some emergency and had then been swept away by an enormous wave. Inspector Muirhead, it now appears, was almost certainly right. He solved the case back in 1901, but he had to wait another century for the proof.

However, science still cannot answer all the questions surrounding the Flannan Islands mystery. Why did one man leave his rain jacket behind? Why were the bodies of the men never found? Maybe these are things we will never know.

🔊 **1.16**

**A walk in the forest**

I'm going to describe a situation and ask you some questions. Answer quickly without thinking about it too much, the first thing that comes into your head. Are you ready?

Imagine that you're walking through a beautiful forest. The sun is out, there's a light breeze. It's a really beautiful day. You're walking with one other person.

**Question 1** Who are you walking with?

As you walk through the forest, you come across an animal.

**Question 2** What kind of animal is it? A big animal or a small one? How do you interact with the animal?

Now you're walking deeper into the forest, and you come to a clearing, where there are no trees. There's a house in the middle of the clearing.

**Question 3** How big is the house? Does it have a fence around it or not?

You walk up to the door of the house and it's open. You go in, and you see a table.

**Question 4** What is there on the table? Are there any people sitting around it?

You finish looking around the house and you leave out of the back door. There's a huge yard behind the house. You go into the yard, and in the middle you find a cup.

**Question 5** What is the cup made of? Is it a ceramic cup? Metal? Plastic? Paper?

As you walk to the end of the yard, you come to some water. You must cross this water in order to get home.

**Question 6** What kind of water is it? A lake? A river? A small pond? How do you cross it? How wet do you get?

What you have just done is a psychological test that analyzes how you interact with other people. Now I'm going to tell you what your answers mean.

The person you were walking with is an important person in your life.

The animal represents problems in your life. The bigger the animal, the more problems you have. How you interact with the animal represents how you deal with your problems. If you were aggressive or decisive, that means you confront your problems, try to solve them. If the interaction was peaceful, then you're a more passive person and often wait for problems to go away.

The house represents your ambitions. The bigger the house, the more ambitious you are. If there was no fence around the house, it means you're very open-minded, and welcome new ideas. If it had a fence, then you're more convinced that you're right, and tend to surround yourself by people who agree with you.

The table represents how you're feeling right now. If there was food or there were flowers on the table, and people sitting around it, this suggests that you're feeling happy in your relationships. No food, flowers, or people suggests that someone in your family or a friend is making you unhappy.

The cup represents how strong your relationship is with the person you're walking with, and how long the relationship will last. The harder and more resistant the material of the cup is, the stronger your relationship is.

The water represents your friends. If you saw a large river or lake, you have a big social circle and like to be surrounded by people. If you got very wet when you crossed it, your friends are very important for you. If you hardly got wet at all, it means that you depend less on your friends and are more self-sufficient.

🔊 2.8

**Bettina** So, my husband and I were out shopping in our local town, and I saw a man lying on the ground. He was just a stranger, not someone I knew, and his wife was there, standing by him. And I used to be a nurse in the ER, so I went straight up to him to see if I could help. He was a little blue, I felt his pulse and he didn't have a pulse, so I thought he was probably having a heart attack. I felt calm because I knew what to do – um, I started doing cardiac massage, you know, putting your hand on the chest and pressing down fast and at regular intervals, and my husband talked to the man's wife, he took her to one side to calm her down, because obviously she was in shock. I kept going until the ambulance turned up and the man was still alive then, and they took him to the hospital. I was really happy that I could do something.

**Umesh** So, I was riding my bike to work one morning, and just as I was coming around the corner, an old lady stepped off the sidewalk in front of me and she tripped and fell onto the street. I just managed not to ride my bike into her, and I dropped my bike and I went over to see if she was OK, and it was busy on the street because the stores were just opening and lots of people were around. She'd fallen pretty hard, but she was still conscious and she told us she was sure she'd broken her arm. Somebody stopped the traffic, and I helped move her to the sidewalk, somebody else went and got a chair from one of the stores, and someone else called an ambulance, and we stayed with her until it came. It was obviously an effort for her to sit up, it was very painful, so I let her lean against me. I remember I was kind of worried because I'd left my backpack on the bike with all my things in it and I was worried someone was going to steal it, but I couldn't move because I was holding the woman up.

Later, I went to visit her in the hospital and she'd actually broken her shoulder in two places and had to have an operation. I think though, if I'd just been walking past, I wouldn't necessarily have gone to help, but because it had happened right in front of me, I felt I had to do something, and now I'm, I'm glad I was able to do something – I felt pretty good about it afterwards.

**Alison** So, I was waiting for the bus at the end of my street to go into work. A very big man, very tall man walked past the bus stop and I noticed him particularly because he was wearing very dirty clothes and he was walking in kind of a strange way, and to be honest, I thought he might be dangerous. Then all of a sudden, he stopped walking and fell backwards, and hit the back of his head on the sidewalk. He fell so hard on the back of his head that it made a really loud noise. And then he just lay still. Some teenagers in line called an ambulance and I stood by the man. I felt completely helpless. He was breathing, but I didn't really know what to do. The ambulance arrived pretty quickly, and the paramedic took the man's hand and talked to him, and then they put him on a stretcher and took him away. Afterwards, I thought I should've done more, I should've maybe turned him on his side, or put a coat under his head – at least, I should have held his hand to show someone was there. I felt kind of ashamed because I think the reason why I didn't help him more was because he was dirty and scruffy, and I was scared of him.

🔊 2.9

**Doctor** Hello again, Mr. Payne. What's the problem this time?

**Mr. Payne** Doctor, I haven't been feeling well for a few days. I've been coughing a lot, and I keep getting headaches. I have a temperature today.

**Doctor** What have you been taking for the headaches?

**Mr. Payne** Acetaminophen. But I read on the internet that headaches can be the first symptom of a brain tumor.

**Doctor** How many tablets have you taken today?

**Mr. Payne** I took two before breakfast.

**Doctor** And have you taken your temperature this morning?

**Mr. Payne** Yes. I've taken it five or six times already. It's high.

**Doctor** Let me see. Mmm…well, your temperature seems to be perfectly normal now.

**Mr. Payne** I think I need a blood test. I haven't had one for two months.

**Doctor** Well Mr. Payne, you know, I think we should wait for a few days and see how your symptoms…um…develop. Take two more acetaminophen and go to bed early tonight.

**Mr. Payne** But…

**Doctor** Goodbye, Mr. Payne. Goodbye.

🔊 2.10

**Receptionist** Your next patient is Mrs. Morris – here is her file…

**Doctor** How many times has Mr. Payne been to the Health Center this month?

**Receptionist** Uh, six times, I think…

**Doctor** That Mr. Payne! He's a complete pain in the neck…

🔊 2.23

**Host** Welcome to today's program. The topic is age and fashion, and the question is, do people these days dress their age, and should they? Our guests are both fashion journalists with well-known magazines. Hello, Liza and Adrian.

**Liza, Adrian** Hello. Hi!

**Host** Hi. Let's start with you, Liza.

**Liza** Well, the first thing I'd like to say to all the young people out there is, next time you give your grandma a warm cardigan and some fur slippers for her birthday, don't be surprised if she asks for the receipt, because she'll probably want to go out and change them for something more exciting.

**Host** So you think these days older women dress much younger than they used to?

**Liza** Oh, absolutely. Think of women like Meryl Streep, Catherine Deneuve, Helen Mirren, Jane Fonda… When Jane Fonda was in her seventies, she appeared on a talk show wearing a leather miniskirt – she looked fabulous! But, of course…

**Adrian** I have to say, I saw that show and I thought Jane Fonda looked awful…

**Host** Adrian, can you let Liza finish?

**Adrian** Sorry. Sorry, go ahead.

**Liza** Well, what I was going to say was that it isn't just famous women who are dressing younger; some recent research says that nine out of ten women say that they try to dress younger than their years.

**Adrian** What about younger women?

**Liza** Well, yes, of course it depends on your age. A lot of teenage girls try to dress older than they are, maybe to get into clubs. But I would still say that from 30 onwards, most women try to dress younger than they are.

**Host** And do you think there's anything wrong with that?

**Liza** Nothing at all, it's a question of wearing what suits you. And that could be anything, from current trends to classics. I mean, OK, there are a very few things that can look a bit ridiculous on an older woman, like, let's see, very short shorts…but not many.

**Adrian** I think very short shorts look ridiculous at any age, well, on anyone over 15 or so.

**Host** Adrian, what about men? Do you think they also try to look younger than their age?

**Adrian** Well, interestingly, in the research Liza mentioned, only 12% of the men who were questioned said that they had ever thought about dressing to look younger. But actually, I think a lot of them weren't telling the truth. Look at all those middle-aged men you see wearing jeans which are too tight and T-shirts with slogans. I think they look terrible, as if they're trying to pretend they're still in their twenties.

**Liza** Sorry, but I don't agree. I think Mick Jagger looks great in tight jeans and T-shirts. They suit him!

**Adrian** True, but Mick Jagger is one in a million. Most men of his age can't carry it off. Personally, I do think that men should take their age into account when they're buying clothes.

**Host** Let's go back to the idea of dressing older than your age. Do you think that men do that too?

**Adrian** Yes, definitely, some do. Some men in their twenties look as if they were 20 years older by wearing blazers and chinos, or wearing a suit and a tie to work when these days most men don't dress like that.

**Liza** Maybe they've just started work and they want their bosses to take them more seriously?

**Adrian** Well, maybe.

**Host** I think we're running out of time. So, to sum up, Liza, Adrian, what would your fashion rules be?…

**) 2.24**

**Host** So, to sum up, Liza, Adrian, what would your fashion rules be? Liza?

**Liza** Wear whatever you think suits you and makes you feel good.

**Host** And Adrian?

**Adrian** Dress for the age you are, not for the age you wish you were.

**Host** Liza, Adrian, thank you very much.

**) 3.1**

A Good afternoon. This is your captain speaking. I'd like to welcome you all aboard JetBlue Flight 23 to Los Angeles. We are currently cruising at an altitude of 33,000 feet at an airspeed of 400 miles per hour. The weather along the way looks good and we are expecting to land in Los Angeles approximately 15 minutes ahead of schedule. So, sit back, relax, and enjoy the rest of the flight.

B Attention passengers. This is a track change. The 9:04 New Haven Line train from Grand Central Terminal with service to Waterbury will now depart from track 103. Passengers traveling on the 9:04 New Haven Line train to Waterbury, please go to track 103. The train is boarding.

C Attention please. Hudson Line service from Croton-Harmon to Grand Central Terminal may experience delays of 10 to 15 minutes because of track work. We apologize for any inconvenience.

D Ladies and gentlemen, we ask for your attention for the following safety instructions. Please review the safety information card located in the seat pocket in front of you. There are six emergency exits on this aircraft, all marked with exit signs. Take a minute to locate the exit closest to you. Note that the nearest exit may be behind you.

E This is the final boarding call for passengers Alice and Christopher Carter for Delta Flight 2116 to Las Vegas. Please proceed to Gate three immediately. I repeat. This is the final boarding call for Alice and Christopher Carter. Thank you.

F Ladies and gentlemen, welcome aboard United Flight 78 to San Francisco. We are currently third in line for take-off and are expected to be in the air in approximately seven minutes time. We ask that you please fasten your seatbelts at this time and place all carry-on luggage securely underneath the seat in front of you or in the overhead compartments. We also ask that you make sure your seat backs and tray tables are in their full upright and locked positions for take-off. Please turn off all personal electronic devices at this time.

G The next train arriving on track 3 will be the 10:25 AmTrak Texas Eagle with service to Chicago, making stops at Lincoln, Bloomington-Normal, Pontiac, and Joliet. Please board using all doors. Full meal service is offered in the dining car, which is located at the back of the train.

H This is a Brooklyn-bound F train. The next stop is Delancey Street. Change here for the J, M, and Z trains.

I This is the pre-boarding announcement for AeroMexico Flight 5279 to Mexico City. We're now inviting those passengers with small children, and any passengers requiring special assistance, to begin boarding at this time. Please have your boarding pass and identification ready. Regular boarding will begin in approximately ten minutes time. Thank you.

J We have now landed in London Gatwick. Please disembark by either the front or rear exits. Make sure you have all your personal belongings with you.

**) 3.9**

**Interviewer** With me in the studio today I have Richard, who's a pilot, and he's going to answer some of the most frequently asked questions about flying and air travel. Hello, Richard.

**Richard** Hello.

**Interviewer** So, Richard, the first question is, what weather conditions are the most dangerous when flying a plane?

**Richard** Probably the most dangerous weather conditions are when the wind changes direction very suddenly. Uh… this tends to happen during thunderstorms and tropical storms and it's especially dangerous during take-off and landing. But it's very unusual – I've been flying for 25 years now and I've only experienced this three or four times.

**Interviewer** What about turbulence? Is that dangerous?

**Richard** It can be very bumpy and very uncomfortable but it isn't dangerous. Even strong turbulence won't damage the plane. Pilots always try to avoid turbulence, but it can sometimes occur without any warning, which is why we always advise passengers to wear their seat belt all the time during the flight.

**Interviewer** Which is more dangerous, take-off or landing?

**Richard** Both take-off and landing can be dangerous. They are the most dangerous moments of a flight. Pilots talk about the "critical eight minutes" – the three minutes after take-off and the five minutes before landing. Most accidents happen in this period. But I would say that take-off is probably slightly more dangerous than landing. There is a critical moment just before take-off when the plane is accelerating, but it hasn't yet reached the speed to be able to fly. If the pilot has a problem with the plane at this point, he has very little time – maybe only a second – to abort the take-off.

**Interviewer** Why are passengers asked to turn off their electronic devices during take-off and landing?

**Richard** It's mainly because they don't want passengers to be distracted, in case there's an emergency. It has nothing to do with the devices interfering with aircraft controls, I mean, aircraft control systems are so sophisticated now, that they wouldn't cause any interference. Incidentally, that's also the reason why people have to put their tray tables up. If we had to abort take-off or have an emergency evacuation a tray table could cause a passenger injury or prevent other passengers from getting out easily.

**Interviewer** Is it really worth listening to safety demonstrations?

**Richard** Definitely. I can tell you for a fact that when pilots are passengers during a flight they always identify the nearest emergency exit and count how many rows in front or behind it is.

**Interviewer** Do you ever get scared?

**Richard** I've been asked this many times and the answer is no – honest to goodness. I've been flying since I was 16 and there's never been a single occasion where I've felt scared in the air. Bear in mind you've been asking me about dangerous situations, but these are incredibly rare.

**Interviewer** Thank you very much, Richard.

**) 3.21**

**Part 2**

The day of the party arrived. Mathilde was a success. She was the prettiest of them all, elegant, smiling, and mad with joy. All the men stared at her, asked her name, and asked to be introduced. She danced all night in a cloud of happiness.

They left at about four in the morning. It was a cold night, and her husband could not find a cab.

They walked towards the Seine, shivering and finally found one. When they got home, Mathilde took off her cloak, but as she glanced at the mirror to see herself one last time, she suddenly gave a cry. Her husband, half undressed already, asked –

"What is the matter with you?"

She turned to him, in terror.

"The necklace. I have lost Madame Forestier's diamond necklace!"

He jumped up, frightened –

"What? How? It is not possible!"

They searched everywhere, but they did not find it. They had no way of contacting the cab driver. Her husband rushed out, and retraced their steps from the Ministry to where they had caught the cab. He came back at about seven o'clock in the morning. He had found nothing. He went to the police, to the newspapers, and to the cab companies to offer a reward, hoping against hope that it would be found.

"You must write to your friend," he said, "that you have broken the clasp of her necklace and that you are having it repaired. That will give us time to decide what to do."

By the end of the week they had lost all hope. The next day they went from jeweler's to jeweler's, looking for a necklace like the one Mathilde had borrowed.

In a shop in the Palais Royal, they found a diamond necklace that seemed to them absolutely identical. The price was thirty-six thousand francs.

Monsieur Loisel had eighteen thousand francs which he had inherited from his father. He borrowed the rest, asking a thousand francs from one friend, five hundred from another, doing business with money lenders, and signing promises to pay which he was not sure he would be able to keep. Finally, he was able to raise the eighteen thousand more that they needed.

When Mathilde took the necklace back to Madame Forestier, she said, coldly,

"You should have brought it back sooner. I might have needed it."

**) 4.7**

**Host** And moving on to our next guest… We all know that one of our favorite topics of conversation here in the US is the weather, especially after this summer's scorching temperatures in the Southwest, along with the unusual below-average temperatures in the Northeast. Now, we have with us in the studio meteorologist Matt Wallace, and earlier in the show we asked listeners to tweet us any questions they had about the weather, and now Matt's going to answer some of them for us. Welcome to the show, Matt.

**Matt** Thanks, Jennie.

**Host** So, the first question for you from our listeners is: What's the difference between a meteorologist and a TV weatherman?

**Matt** Well basically, a meteorologist collects all the data, whereas a TV weatherman, well, is given the information and presents it on the radio or on TV or wherever. Keep in mind, a few TV weathermen are also trained meteorologists, but not many.

**Host** How far ahead can you accurately predict the weather?

**Matt** I think typically, we can forecast about five to seven days ahead on average. But some weather is more predictable than others. If there's high pressure, with not much changing, we could forecast, maybe, seven to ten days ahead. On other occasions, it can be very uncertain, we don't know even over just a few hours, so for example, if there's a lot of low cloud at airports, it will be very difficult for us to know when the cloud is going to clear enough for aircraft to take off or land.

**Host** Are long-term forecasts ever accurate?

**Matt** In terms of forecasting as far ahead as next summer or winter, there's a very new system where we can see how what's happening in one part of the world might affect another weather system somewhere else, so, like, weather in the Arctic, the Gulf of Mexico, the Caribbean, and even the Pacific Ocean all make a difference to the weather in the US. So we can't get real detail that far ahead, but we can get a general trend.

**Host** What's your favorite kind of weather?

**Matt** Thunderstorms, especially at night, because they're very exciting. You can see things like the lightning moving around inside the clouds, especially when the lightning really highlights the shape of the clouds. You never quite know what weather might come out of a thunderstorm, it's a kind of "weather factory" really. It can generate large amounts of rain of tremendous intensity, it can bring very strong winds, large hail, snow sometimes… there's just incredible power and majesty in thunderstorms.

**Host** In what ways have you noticed that the weather has changed in the last ten years?

**Matt** Well, in fact, over the last ten years, I don't think the weather has changed an awful lot. This year we've had an intense heatwave in Texas with over 30 days of 100-degree temperatures, while in Alaska—typically one of the wettest places in the US—there's been a drought, it's unusual, yes, these are quite extreme for the US, I guess, but it's not unprecedented, both have happened before, and both will happen again. There's evidence to show that maybe extreme weather is happening a little bit more frequently; certainly globally, looking at the science, it tends to have gotten more extreme than it has been in the past, and it's obviously becoming a little warmer as well, so yeah, but I haven't necessarily noticed it myself day to day.

**Host** Are you optimistic or pessimistic about climate change?

**Matt** I'm pretty pessimistic about it. I think in the US, it will probably lead to more frequent, more extreme heat waves in the South and in Southern California, potentially colder and longer winters in the Northeast, and some more extreme weather as well, more intense rainfall, and a greater risk of extreme flooding in the Midwest and in the Pacific Northwest.

**Host** Matt, thank you very much for coming and answering our questions…

### 4.8

**1 Holly**

**Interviewer** Are you a risk-taker?

**Holly** Generally definitely not, and I think that started early in life when I was little. I hated getting hurt, so I thought, if I don't take any risks, I won't get hurt, and so I think even to this day I'm not really a risk-taker.

**Interviewer** Can you give me an example of a risk you have taken?

**Holly** Well, as I said I don't usually take risks, for example, I hate flying. I only fly if there's no alternative, and I drive safely, carefully, because I don't want to put myself or my family in any danger. But once, someone persuaded me to try scuba-diving. I was very worried in the beginning, until I knew what I was doing. My mom was absolutely horrified that I was going to try it, so maybe it's a personality thing. In my family, my children are the same way, but anyway, in the end I was pretty happy I tried scuba-diving, it's one of the best things I've ever done! That's so interesting, isn't it, so even for me, I can see that sometimes taking a risk has a positive outcome.

**2 Natalie**

**Interviewer** Are you a risk-taker?

**Natalie** I'd say that, on the whole, that I am, yes.

**Interviewer** Can you give me an example of a risk you've taken?

**Natalie** Well, something I do a lot is buy things on eBay. And there, you're buying something you, you've never seen, you're relying on what the seller says about it, but you're going to calculate the risk based on their description, and how much you're paying, so if it only costs $10.00, it's not a great risk, however, if it's an expensive item, you might lose some money. But I guess that's something that most people take a risk on now.

**3 Tom**

**Interviewer** Are you a risk-taker?

**Tom** I am in some ways, I mean I've done some things that were physically dangerous – but when it comes to things like money, then I think I'm much more conservative.

**Interviewer** Can you give me an example of a risk you've taken?

**Tom** Well, when I finished college, my mom and dad just wanted me to apply for a normal kind of job, like, working for a company, but I decided that I wanted a little more fun while I was that age, so I decided to spend some time working as a restaurant manager, and I worked at lots of different food and drink festivals all over the world. I knew it would affect my résumé, because employers are always asking you questions about why you chose to do that, how was that useful to you, and just saying it seemed like a fun idea isn't a very good answer. After two or three years, I realized that it was going to be pretty hard for me to keep on doing the job past the age of about 30. But now I'm glad I did it, and actually maybe it gave me what they call soft skills, like being flexible and dealing with people, which are really useful in my job now – I work in sales in a computer software company – so yeah, I think the risk was worth it in the end.

**4 Jeanie**

**Interviewer** Are you a risk-taker?

**Jeanie** Um, not really, no, I don't think I am. Though once I took a really big risk.

**Interviewer** What was it?

**Jeanie** When I graduated from college I went right into a really well-paid job straightaway, um, and after about two years I was doing really well and enjoying it a lot. And then, through some friends, I met this guy, Marco, and we fell in love immediately, I know people think love at first sight doesn't really happen, but it did. Anyway, um, he was – is – a scientist, a marine biologist, um, and after we'd been going out for maybe two months or so he was offered a job working in Australia and he said, "Come with me." I did think about it for a little bit, but not much, and I left my well-paid job to follow a man I'd known less than three months to the other side of the world. My parents were horrified. I was horrified myself, actually. But I married him and we're still together. So it was definitely worth it, but on the other hand, um, I haven't really had a career as such, and if I hadn't gone with him then, maybe I would've had a different kind of life. Who knows?

### 4.14

1 Skiing was the first extreme sport that I did. I started when I was six and I haven't really stopped since. I take after my dad – we're both sports-crazy. He got me into skiing so he could take me on winter vacations.

2 I've done a lot of extreme sports in the mountains, such as mountain biking, and rock climbing, and ice-walking across glaciers. I've also done white-water rafting recently. It's very hard work, but really worth the energy.

3 I think it's because I love taking risks, I love the adrenaline rush.

4 I don't really think about getting injured or killed. I've never had a bad accident, but I've had some scary moments, where I knew if I made a mistake, I could get seriously hurt. But I've never really thought there was a chance I could die.

5 I think more and more people are taking part in extreme sports because they're becoming more accessible, and there's much more exposure than before on TV and on social media. Like I said before, it's the adrenaline rush that people really enjoy – you can't always get that in your everyday life.

6 A few years ago, I would have said men were much more associated with extreme sports. However, I think it's becoming a little more equal between men and women. Extreme sportswomen are really appreciated, because they're going against the gender stereotype, but, men do still seem to dominate, maybe because they were more involved when the sports were first recognized.

### 5.2

**Interviewer** What was the most difficult or challenging part of your experience?

**Ali** Well, because you're, um, put on the island with just the clothes on your back and a few basic tools, it means that anything you eat you have to find, catch, and kill, if necessary. So for the first week, we didn't eat anything at all except a few coconuts. Um, so I lost four kilos in just a week. Um, after that most of what we ate was yucca, which is like a potato, grows in the ground. But you have to walk a lot to find it, um, and even then it would only be the equivalent of having a small potato each, um, every day. So we were still hungry. We were able to catch some fish, um, and then we did manage to kill a wild boar. And also because of the lack of food we became really weak, so it was hard you, hard even to go out for a stroll along the beach. That became really difficult. It was also difficult being dirty all the time, because the water we had to wash in, uh, was the ocean. So you're obviously salty and covered in sand and you never really feel clean. Um, when it rained, which was all the time, the ground would become really muddy and everything would just get absolutely filthy. We had a couple of weeks where the weather was really bad, so we were completely soaked, really freezing cold, wet, miserable, and hungry. Um, and the other thing that was really difficult was the tension between the groups and also within our group, because everyone was very stressed and hungry and tired, it didn't take much for arguments to occur. And there's nowhere to escape from on the desert island.

**Interviewer** What were the highlights?

**Ali** So at first, even just landing on the island was a highlight, um, because we were so excited and we were meeting all these new people, um, we'd never met before, and we were full of enthusiasm and energy. Um, and we just had lunch, so we weren't hungry. Um, so when Bear Grylls picked us up on his boat and drove us round the island, um, and then he stopped in the middle of the ocean and threw us out of the boat and told us to swim to the island, um, which was so exciting. Um, and the last week was also a real highlight for me because the two groups came together and we built a communal shelter in the middle of the beach so everyone – for everyone to sleep in and to enjoy, and we had a really good time. The weather at this point, um, had turned really good and so, we had a sports day and we had a talent show, and even a wedding! It was a really fun week. Um, but I think probably leaving the island was the real highlight – best day of my life, even. Um, it was so good to know that we'd survived for 35 days. And seeing Bear pull up on his boat, uh, to come and collect us was just an amazing feeling. I felt both really proud and super relieved.

**Interviewer** Out of the 16 people that landed on the island, 13, including Ali, managed to last the whole five weeks. Two participants decided to leave before the end, and unfortunately, one had to go to the hospital with an eye injury. By the last week, the participants had all realized that they were much more effective working together as one big team than trying to survive in separate groups. How much money they earned or what their background was turned out to be completely irrelevant. Both teams worked hard, kept their moral high, and survived.

🔊 5.8

Yossi and Kevin soon realized that going by river was a big mistake. The river got faster and faster, and soon they were in rapids.
The raft was swept down the river at an incredible speed until it hit a rock. Both men were thrown into the water. Kevin was a strong swimmer and he managed to swim to land, but Yossi was swept away by the rapids.
But Yossi didn't drown. He was carried several miles downriver by the rapids, but he eventually managed to swim to the river bank. He was totally exhausted. By an incredible piece of luck, he found his backpack floating in the river. The backpack contained a little food, insect repellent, a lighter, and most important of all…the map. But the two friends were now separated by a canyon and three or four miles of jungle.

🔊 5.9

Kevin was feeling desperate. He didn't know if Yossi was alive or dead, but he started walking downriver to look for him. He felt responsible for what had happened to his friend because he had persuaded him to go with him on the river.
Yossi, however, was feeling very optimistic. He was sure that Kevin would look for him, so he started walking upriver, calling his friend's name. But nobody answered.
At night Yossi tried to sleep, but he felt terrified. The jungle was full of noises. Suddenly, he woke up because he heard a branch breaking. He turned on his flashlight. There was a jaguar staring at him…
Yossi was trembling with fear. But then he remembered something that he had once seen in a movie. He used the cigarette lighter to set fire to the insect repellent spray and he managed to scare the jaguar away.

🔊 5.10

After five days alone, Yossi was exhausted and starving. Suddenly, as he was walking, he saw a footprint on the trail – it was a hiking boot. It had to be Kevin's footprint! He followed the trail until he discovered another footprint and then another. But suddenly he realized that the footprints weren't Kevin's footprints. They were his own. He had been walking around in a circle. At that moment Yossi realized that he would never find Kevin. In fact, he felt sure that Kevin must be dead. He felt totally depressed and at the point of giving up.

🔊 5.11

But Kevin wasn't dead. He was still looking for Yossi. But after nearly a week, he was also weak and exhausted from lack of food and lack of sleep. He decided that it was time to forget Yossi and try to save himself. He had just enough strength left to hold onto a log and let himself float down the river.
Kevin was incredibly lucky – he was rescued by two Bolivian hunters who were traveling downriver in a canoe. The men only hunted in that part of the rainforest once a year, so if they had passed by a short time earlier or later, they wouldn't have seen Kevin. They took him back to the town of San José, where he spent two days recovering.

🔊 5.12

As soon as Kevin felt well enough, he went to a Bolivian army base and asked them to look for Yossi. (*"My friend is lost in the jungle. You must look for him."*) The army officer he spoke to was sure that Yossi must be dead, but in the end Kevin persuaded them to take him up in a plane and fly over the part of the rainforest where Yossi might be. But the plane had to fly too high over the rainforest and the forest was too dense. They couldn't see anything at all. It was a hopeless search. Kevin felt terribly guilty. He was convinced that it was all his fault that Yossi was going to die in the jungle. Kevin's last hope was to pay a local man with a boat to take him up the river to look for his friend.

🔊 5.13

By now, Yossi had been on his own in the jungle for nearly three weeks. He hadn't eaten for days. He was starving, exhausted, and slowly losing his mind. It was evening. He lay down by the side of the river ready for another night alone in the jungle.
Suddenly he heard the sound of a bee buzzing in his ear. He thought a bee had got inside his mosquito net. But when he opened his eyes, he saw that the buzzing noise wasn't a bee…
It was a boat. Yossi was too weak to shout, but Kevin had already seen him. It was a one-in-a-million chance that Kevin would find his friend. But he did. Yossi was saved.
When Yossi had recovered, he and Kevin flew to the city of La Paz and they went directly to the hotel where they had agreed to meet Marcus and Karl.
But Marcus and Karl were not at the hotel. The two men had never arrived back in the town of Apolo. The Bolivian army organized a search of the rainforest, but Marcus and Karl were never seen again.

🔊 5.20

1  One thing I really regret is not being brave enough to ask out a girl who I met at a party last summer. I really liked her but I was just too scared to invite her on a date in case she said no. I wish I'd tried. I'm absolutely sure we would have gotten along. Now it's too late – she's engaged to another guy!

2  Um, I wish I'd had more time with my grandmother. She died when I was 12, and since then I've discovered that she must have been a really fascinating person, and there are so many things I'd love to have been able to talk to her about. She was Polish, but she was in Russia, in St. Petersburg, during the Russian Revolution and she knew all sorts of interesting people at the time: painters, writers, people like that. I was only a kid, so I never asked her much about her own life. Now, I'm discovering all about her through reading her old letters and papers, but I wish she'd lived longer so that I could have talked to her about those times face-to-face.

3  When I was in college, I had the chance to earn two degrees at the same time—a four-year degree in aeronautical engineering and a Master's degree in mechanical engineering. My parents were eager for me to study for both degrees because they thought I'd probably get better job offers when I graduated. But I was totally against the idea because my engineering classes were hard, and I spent a lot of my time studying. Plus, I wanted to hang out with my friends every now and then and have some fun. So, I ended up graduating with one degree, and I have a good job. But now I wish I'd listened to my parents because if I want to advance my career at my current job, I have to go back to school and get my Master's degree in … mechanical engineering.

🔊 6.1

1  **Carlos**

**Interviewer** Why do you have problems sleeping?

**Rafa** Well, I'm Mexican, but I moved to New York a few years ago when I married an American woman. I've been living here for three years now. I have a lot of problems falling asleep at night because our bedroom just isn't dark enough. I can't get used to sleeping in a bedroom where there's light coming in from the streetlights outside. In Mexico, I always used to sleep in complete darkness because my bedroom window had blinds and when I went to bed, I used to close the blinds completely. But here in New York, our bedroom window just has curtains and curtains don't block out the light enough. It takes me a long time to fall asleep at night and I always wake up more often than I used to do in Mexico.

**Interviewer** So why don't you just get thicker curtains?

**Carlos** Because my wife doesn't like sleeping in a completely dark room. She says that she feels claustrophobic if the room is too dark.

**Interviewer** Ah, yes, some people do feel like that.

2  **Marc**

**Interviewer** Why do you have problems sleeping?

**Marc** Well, I'm a police officer, so I have to do shift work, which means I work at night every other week, so I start work at 10:00 at night and finish at 6:00 in the morning the following day. The main problem is that my body's used to sleeping at night, not during the day. So it's really hard to get used to being awake all night and trying to work and concentrate when your body is just telling you to go to bed.

**Interviewer** But isn't it something you eventually get used to?

**Marc** Actually no, because I work during the day for one week and then the next week I work at night, which means that just when my body has gotten used to being awake at night and I go back to working in the day, and then of course I can't get to sleep at night because my body thinks it's going to have to work all night.
The other problem is that when I get home after working a night shift, everyone else is just starting to wake up, so that means that it can be really noisy. The neighbors play the radio, and bang doors and shout to wake their children up. So even though I'm really tired, it's just really hard to get to sleep.

**Interviewer** How many hours do you usually sleep?

**Marc** Before I became a police officer, I used to sleep about eight or nine hours a night, but I think now I probably don't sleep more than six hours.

**3 Steph**

**Interviewer** Why do you have problems sleeping?

**Steph** I have a lot of problems sleeping because of jet lag. I have to travel a lot in my job and I take a lot of long-haul flights. I fly to New York quite often and I arrive maybe at 6:00 in the evening my time, but when it's only 1:00 in the afternoon in New York. So at 5:00 in the afternoon New York time, I'll be feeling tired and ready for bed because it's my bed time. But I can't go to sleep because I'm probably still working or having dinner with my American colleagues. Then when I do finally get to bed at say midnight, I find that I wake up in the middle of the night because my body thinks that it's morning because it's still working on UK time.

**Interviewer** And can you get back to sleep when you wake up?

**Steph** No, that's the problem. I can't get back to sleep. And then the next day when I have meetings I feel really sleepy. It's very hard to stay awake all day. And just when I'm finally used to being on New York time, then it's time to fly back to the UK. And flying west to east is even worse.

**Interviewer** Oh! Why's that?

**Steph** Because when I get off the plane it's early morning in the UK. But for me, on New York time, it's the middle of the night. It takes me four or five days to recover from one of those trips.

**Interviewer** Wow! That must be really difficult for you.

**Steph** Yeah, it is.

🔊 6.9

I know a lot about sleep. I've been involved in sleep research for over 36 years. I call myself a sleep expert, and I think that if you are going to give advice about sleep, you should follow your own rules. So here are some things you should know about my sleep habits.

1 I sleep in a different bedroom from my partner. Everyone should sleep alone. It's much better, if you can, to have your own room. You can wake refreshed, rather than be angry because your partner snored all night. My partner wasn't offended when I suggested we had separate rooms. In fact, she found she slept much better. Apparently, I make funny noises in my sleep.

2 I sleep under natural materials. I wouldn't dream of getting into a bed made with hot, sweaty, manmade fibers. If you're really hot, it's hard to fall asleep or stay asleep. This is why we turn over at night – not just to relieve pressure, but to find a cool spot. To sleep well, we need to lose one degree of body temperature, and cotton is excellent at keeping us cool.

3 I'm obsessive about pillows. Pillows are really necessary for good sleep. It's essential that your body is in the right position, and a pillow should fill the gap between your shoulder and neck, to keep the neck and spine aligned when you lie on your side. I have two pillows because I'm tall and that works for me, but if one pillow holds you in the correct position, that's fine too. I wash my pillows every six months and dry them outside.

4 I sleep with the window open. Fresh air is good for sleep, and a build-up of carbon dioxide disturbs it. It's the warmth under the comforter that's important, not the warmth of the room. So keep your bedroom door open and open the window at least a centimeter every night, all year round. Even if it's minus 5 degrees, I keep the window open, and curl up with a hot water bottle.

5 I don't have dinner late. I prefer to eat before 7:00 p.m. If you have a large meal too close to bedtime, your body will still be working to digest it, and not resting. Eating your main meal three or four hours before bed is ideal.

6 I drink coffee in the evenings. After dinner in a restaurant I will happily order an espresso. Many people are insensitive to caffeine. Unless you know that you're sensitive to caffeine, it's actually the worrying that you've drunk caffeine that keeps you awake, not the caffeine itself.

7 I need nine and a half hours of sleep. It's a myth that you need an average of eight hours of sleep. Sleep need is genetic – some people might need four hours, others eleven. The right amount of sleep for you is something you can figure out based on how many hours you need to feel alert during the day. That figure stays the same for you throughout your life. I always wake up at the same time early every morning, so to get the amount of sleep I need, I know I need to be in bed by 9:30 p.m.

8 I read a book before going to sleep. Everyone should have a way to relax before going to sleep. I read a non-thrilling book, often short stories, or a book with short chapters. You don't want something where every chapter ends on a cliffhanger, because that makes you want to read on.

🔊 6.10

**Part 1**

I think it's very interesting that human beings are the only animals which listen to music for pleasure. A lot of research has been done to find out why we listen to music, and there seem to be three main reasons. Firstly, we listen to music to make us remember important moments in the past, for example, when we met someone for the first time. Think of Humphrey Bogart in the film *Casablanca*, saying, "Darling, they're playing our song." When we hear a certain piece of music, we remember hearing it for the first time in some very special circumstances. Obviously, this music varies from person to person.

Secondly, we listen to music to help us change activities. If we want to go from one activity to another, we often use music to help us make the change. For example, we might play a certain kind of music to prepare us to go out in the evening, or we might play another kind of music to relax us when we get home from work. That's mainly why people listen to music in cars, and they often listen to one kind of music when they're going to work and another kind when they're coming home. The same is true of people on buses and trains.

The third reason why we listen to music is to intensify the emotion that we're feeling. For example, if we're feeling sad, sometimes we want to get even sadder, so we play sad music. Or we're feeling angry and we want to intensify the anger then we play angry music. Or when we're planning a romantic dinner, we lay the table, we light candles, and then we think, "What music would make this even more romantic?"

🔊 6.12

**Part 2**

Let's take three important human emotions: happiness, sadness, and anger. When people are happy, they speak faster and their voice is higher. When they are sad, they speak more slowly and their voice is lower, and when people are angry, they raise their voices or shout. Babies can tell whether their mother is happy or not simply by the sound of her voice, not by her words. What music does is, it copies this, and it produces the same emotions. So, faster, higher-pitched music will sound happy. Slow music with lots of falling pitches will sound sad. Loud music with irregular rhythms will sound angry. It doesn't matter how good or bad the music is, if it has these characteristics, it will make you experience this emotion.

Let me give you some examples. For happy, for example, the first movement of Beethoven's *Seventh Symphony*. For angry, say, *Mars*, from *The Planets*, by Holst. And for sad, something like Albinoni's *Adagio for Strings*.

Of course, the people who exploit this most are the people who write film soundtracks. They can take a scene which visually has no emotion and they can make the scene either scary or calm or happy, just by the music they write to go with it. Think of the music in the shower scene in Hitchcock's film *Psycho*. All you can see is a woman having a shower, but the music makes it absolutely terrifying.

🔊 7.1

*F1 = female student 1, M1 = male student 1, F2 = female student 2, F3 = female student 3, M2 = male student 2*

**F1** Where's my milk? It's not here.

**M1** I haven't seen it. You must have finished it.

**F1** I definitely didn't finish it. I was keeping some for my cereal this morning. One of you must have used it.

**F2** It can't have been me. I only drink my oat milk. Could you have finished it last night and then forgotten? Did you have something before going to bed?

**F1** No I didn't. I just drank a glass of water.

**M1** Someone might have given it to the cat.

**F1** Oh come on. We all know she drinks water, not milk. I'm telling you, last night I know there was some milk in the refrigerator. MY milk.

**M1** Well, I don't know what's happened to it. In any case, you should have put your name on it.

**F1** I did put my name on it! In capital letters!

**F3** And it wasn't me, because I stayed at my Mom's last night, and I had breakfast there before getting back here.

**F1** What are you drinking Jack?

**M2** Just coffee.

**F1** Yes, white coffee. That's where my milk went. You didn't have any milk of your own in the refrigerator.

**F2** Ooh, Jack, you bad boy!

**F1** Well, you can go to the supermarket and get me some more.

**M2** OK, OK, calm down. I'll go and get you some milk…

🔊 7.7

In life, we sometimes have disagreements with people. It could be with your partner, with your boss, with your parents, or with a friend. When this happens, the important thing is to try not to let a difference of opinion turn into a heated argument. But, of course, it's easier said than done.

The first thing I would say is that the way you begin the conversation is very important. Imagine you live with your partner, and you're feeling annoyed because you feel that you always do most of the housework. If you say, "Look, you're not doing your share of the housework," you're beginning the conversation in a very negative way, and the discussion will very soon turn into an argument. It's much more constructive to say something like, "I think we should take another look at how we divide up the housework. Maybe there's a better way of doing it."

My second piece of advice is simple. If you're the person who's in the wrong, just admit it! This is the easiest and best way to avoid an argument. Just apologize – say to your roommate, your parents, or your husband, "Sorry, it was my fault," and move on. The other person will have much more respect for you if you do that.

The next tip is, don't exaggerate. Try not to say things like, "You always forget our wedding anniversary," when maybe this has only happened once before, or, "You never ever remember to turn off the lights." This will just make the other person get very defensive because what you're saying about them just isn't true.

If you follow these tips, you may often be able to avoid an argument. But if an argument does start, it's important to keep things under control and there are ways to do this.

The most important thing is not to raise your voice. Raising your voice will just make the other person lose their temper, too. If you find yourself raising your voice, stop for a minute and take a deep breath. Say, "I didn't mean to shout. I'd rather not argue with you, but this is very important to me," and continue calmly. If you can talk calmly and quietly, you'll find the other person will be more ready to think about what you're saying.

It's also very important to stick to the point. Try to keep to the topic you're talking about. Don't bring up old arguments, or try to bring in other issues. Just concentrate on solving the one problem you're having, and leave the other things for another time. So, for example, if you're arguing about the housework, don't suddenly say, "And another thing, I was really disappointed with my birthday present – you didn't make any effort at all."

And my final tip is that, if necessary, call "Time out" like in a sporting event. If you think that an argument is getting out of control, then you can say to the other person, "Listen, I'd rather talk about this tomorrow when we've both calmed down." You can then continue talking about it the next day when maybe both of you are feeling less tense and angry. That way, there's a better chance that you'll be able to reach an agreement. You'll also probably find that the problem is much easier to solve when you've both had a good night of sleep.

But I want to say one last thing that I think is very important. Some people think that arguing is always bad, but that isn't true. Conflict is a normal part of life, and dealing with conflict is an important part of any relationship, whether it's three people sharing an apartment, a married couple, or just two good friends. If you don't learn to argue properly, then when a real problem comes along, you won't be prepared to face it together. Think of all the smaller arguments as training sessions. Learn how to argue cleanly and fairly. It will help your relationships become stronger and last longer.

🔊 7.10

This still is from the movie *Atonement*, a period drama set in the 1930s. It shows Keira Knightley, who plays Cecilia Tallis, the elder daughter of a wealthy family, and James McAvoy who plays Robbie, the son of the family's housekeeper. Cecilia is studying at Cambridge University, and, unusually, Robbie is too, his studies being paid for by Cecilia's father. Despite moving in very different circles in school, they have always been close and they are now back at the family home for the holidays. This evening, there's going to be a dinner party, to which Robbie has been invited. In this shot, he is following her in to dinner. She is feeling anxious and indecisive, because she has just realized that she is in love with him, but she knows that their relationship would be frowned upon given their difference in status. Despite this, soon after they declare their love for each other. The movie was one of Knightley's first big starring roles. It won several awards and was nominated for several others, including costume design. This green dress is one of the stunning outfits she appears in.

🔊 7.12

A Meryl Streep was nominated for an Oscar for her performance as Katherine Graham in *The Post*. The movie is about how Graham, the first female publisher of a major American newspaper—*The Washington Post*—and her staff published classified government documents about the US's involvement in the Vietnam War. The movie, set in 1971, focuses on Katherine as she tries to balance the deaths of her husband and father with managing the newspaper and a busy social life. Katherine feels nervous about running the newspaper because she has little business or journalistic experience. In this still, Katherine is talking to the paper's executive editor about possibly getting and publishing US government secrets about the war. Her expression shows a mixture of feelings: concern for publishing the material and risk facing legal action from the US government, perhaps some disappointment that the US government had these secret files, and perhaps some worry as she weighs making the right decision for herself, her paper, and the United States.

B This is a scene from the fantasy movie *Fantastic Beasts and Where to Find Them*, which is a prequel to the Harry Potter movies. Set in 1926, the movie stars Eddie Redmayne as the wizard Newt Scamander, who comes to New York with a suitcase containing several magical creatures. When he's at the bank, one of the creatures escapes from the suitcase. In this scene, he's desperately trying to recapture it, and is watching, horrified, as it starts stealing things from people in the bank. J.K. Rowling herself both wrote the script and co-produced the movie, and it was the first movie set in Harry Potter's wizarding world to win an Oscar.

C Frances McDormand, who won an Oscar for best actress in *Three Billboards Outside Ebbing, Missouri*, is without doubt one of the most versatile actresses of her generation. This still is from the Coen brothers' black comedy *Burn after Reading*, which also starred George Clooney and Brad Pitt. McDormand plays the role of Linda Litzke, a personal trainer, who, with her co-worker Chad, tries to steal money from a retired CIA worker. Linda is in desperate need of money, mainly because she's obsessed with expensive cosmetic surgery. In this scene, she's discussing with the doctor the work she wants done. During the discussion, the doctor has suggested that she have an operation to get rid of her crow's feet – the lines and wrinkles around the eyes. Linda protests that they're baby, tiny crow's feet, and as the doctor explains the procedure, she feels more and more unsure and indecisive about what to do. The genius of McDormand's acting is that although the character of Linda is self-centered, superficial and not very bright, McDormand manages to portray her as a true American heroine.

D This still shows Daniel Kaluuya in the 2017 horror movie *Get Out*. Daniel plays the role of Chris, a young black photographer, who goes to meet the parents of his white girlfriend Rose, who live in a large house in the country. Although the parents try to make it clear that they're not at all racist, Chris quickly realizes that there is something very strange about them, and about the black servants they employ. In this scene, Rose's mother, a psychiatrist who practices hypnotherapy, is hypnotizing him. Although in theory it is to help him to stop smoking, here she gets him to relive the horror and the shock of the evening when he was six years old and his mother was killed in a car accident. Kaluuya was nominated for an Oscar for his performance, and the movie won the Oscar for best screenplay.

🔊 7.14

Exercise 2 is called: Stroking an animal.

This exercise is often used in drama classes for beginners, to help them to develop their body language. It should be done in a group.

Each person must think of an animal they really like. It can be a wild or tame animal, big or small. Then imagine stroking it. Think about where it is, in your hand, in your arms, standing or sitting next to you. Now, one by one, mime the action for the rest of the group. They have to guess which animal it is.

OK, now exercise 3 is called: What were they wearing?

The exercise is aimed at developing attention. Attention is very important for an actor because you have to be able to observe every detail of other people.

This exercise is done in a group, with one person acting as the host. In a group, sit in a circle and, for three minutes, try to focus on what everyone is wearing. It's important to remember as many details as you can: clothes, accessories, etc. After three minutes, close your eyes unless you're the host of the game, and the host asks questions, for example, "Anna, tell me, please, what's Helen wearing?" "John, what color are Anna's shoes?" etc. At the end, everyone opens their eyes and checks the answers.

The last exercise we're going to do today is exercise 4: The "magic" image.

Showing emotions on stage or on camera can be very hard for some beginners. One trick, which this exercise helps with, is to develop a way of recalling the desired emotion.

The exercise can be done individually or in groups. Choose one emotion, for example, "anger," and then on a piece of paper, write down some situations that make you angry, for example, noisy neighbors, or bad drivers. If you're doing this in a group, show each other what you've written down – you may want to choose some ideas from another person's list to add to your own list. Choose no more than five situations in total. When you have your final list, think of an image for each situation, for example, for noisy neighbors, it could be a dog, for bad drivers, a car, and so on. Now the important part – you need to create one new image on the sheet of paper that combines your separate anger images, for example, a car with a dog in the back, etc. This is your "magic image" of anger. Recalling this image will help you to show anger when you're acting. You can do the same thing with other emotions, such as happiness, sorrow, and so on. So now let's actually do these exercises. We'll start with number two, stroking an animal. So, if you can get into groups of five or six, we'll get going.

🔊 8.1

### Stay safe

Street crime is often unplanned, so making yourself less of a target, moving with purpose, and being aware of your surroundings will go a long way to keeping you safe when you're out and about. Here are eight important pieces of advice.

1 Be prepared. Always plan your route in advance. Carry a fully charged cell phone and some cash, and tell someone where you're going.

2 Be assertive. From the moment you step out onto the street in the morning, you need to look assertive, and act and walk with confidence. This will always make you appear in control and you will seem much less vulnerable.

3 Be aware. Using a cell phone, whether you're calling, messaging, or looking up information, reduces your awareness of your surroundings. So does listening to loud music on headphones, or wearing a hooded jacket or sweatshirt.

4 Hide it. Keep your valuables hidden either in a bag or under your clothes. This includes your phone, other devices such as cameras or tablets, and jewelry. Remember – out of sight, out of mind.

5 Go against the flow. When you're walking on the sidewalk, always face towards the oncoming traffic. This will make it more difficult for thieves on two-wheels to ride up from behind and snatch your bag. But, don't forget to still be aware of anyone approaching from ahead of you.

6 Trust your instincts. At night, try to avoid walking alone in places such as parks and quiet side streets, or in fact, in any area you don't know. If you do have to walk, keep to busy places where there is a lot of activity, good lighting, and security cameras. And if you're on public transportation, it's much better to travel with people you know or stick to routes that other people are using.

7 Make a plan. Discuss with friends what to do if something were to go wrong on your night out together, for example, if you were to get separated. Agree on a backup plan and keep an eye on each other during the evening. And stick to what you've agreed.

8 Look out for trouble. If a stranger offers you a ride, don't accept it, even if you're tired, or running late for an appointment. Be careful whose car you get into, especially at airports or train stations. Illegal drivers often don't have a valid driver's license and they overcharge passengers. Don't accept a ride from someone you don't know especially when you can a call a trustworthy ride-sharing service. Stay safe!

🔊 8.7

**Newsreader** Police in Stockport are looking for a man who is said to be the most polite armed robber. The robber always says please and thank you when he orders store workers to give him money from the cash register. It is believed that he is a tall man in his early forties and that he wears a mask and rubber gloves during the robberies. It is thought that he has robbed at least four stores in Stockport in recent weeks. DI Anderson from Greater Manchester Police has given a warning to the public.

**Police Officer** He is reported to be polite to his victims, but there's nothing polite about armed robbery. Last week, this man used a knife to threaten store workers and they were terrified. Saying please and thank you doesn't change that.

🔊 8.11

**Story 1**

And now, news from around the country. In Fayetteville, Georgia, a truck filled with instant ramen noodles worth approximately $98,000 was stolen from a Chevron gas station near Georgia Interstate Highway 85 North. According to a report filed by the victim with local authorities, the truck disappeared sometime last week. The victim persuaded the gas station's owner to give him permission to park the tractor-trailer there. When the truck driver went back to the gas station to get his truck, it was gone, along with all the instant noodles. Lt. Allen Stevens, who works for the Fayette County Sheriff's Office was reported as saying that this is the first "ramen noodle theft that has ever occurred here in Fayette County." What does $98,000 worth of instant ramen noodles translate into? Well, on average, one package costs about 29 cents. That means that there were more than 300,000 packages of instant ramen in the stolen truck. While most nutritionists probably would not recommend eating instant ramen more than once or twice a month, there is enough for one person to eat three times a day for the next 300 years!

**Story 2**

And now for our last story today – a zoo in Egypt has denied painting a donkey with black stripes in order to make it look like a zebra. Egyptian student Mahmoud Sarhan, 18, was visiting the zoo in Cairo, when he noticed the animal, which had strange looking black stripes. Mr. Sarhan was suspicious, and took a photo of the animal, which appeared to have strange black marks on its face, and posted it online. He later told the media, "I knew it was a donkey as soon as I saw it. I'm an artist. I know the different shape of a donkey and a zebra, so it was easy to tell the difference." After the image was was shared on social media, it went viral. Egyptian news site Extranews.tv approached a local vet, who agreed to examine the photo. He pointed out that zebras usually have a black nose and mouth, whereas the animal in Mr. Sarhan's photo appears to be pale in this area. The vet added that authentic zebra stripes are usually straighter and clearer than those on the animal in Mr. Sarhan's photo. The local radio station contacted the zoo's director, Mohamed Sultan. However, he refused to admit that the animal was a donkey.

🔊 9.1

The first point to bear in mind is that nothing, nothing, is ever free. How often have you seen ads saying things like, "Get a free Bluetooth speaker when you subscribe to our magazine for six months"? There's something about the word "free" that immediately attracts us – I want it! It makes us feel clever, as if we're going to get something for nothing. But, of course, that Bluetooth speaker (which, incidentally, will probably break the second time you use it) wasn't free at all. In spite of what the ad said, its price was really included in the magazine subscription. So, don't trust any ad that offers something for free.

A second trick that advertisers use is when they tell us, "There are only a few left! Buy now while supplies last!" What happens to us when we read or hear these words? Even though we don't really need the products, and maybe don't even like them, we immediately want to be among the lucky few who have them. But – let's be clear about this – companies just don't run out of products. Do you really think the manufacturers couldn't produce a few more, if they thought they could sell them? Of course they could.

When it comes to new products, we, the consumers, are like sheep and we follow each other. So, another way advertisers have of getting us to use something is to tell us, "Everybody's using it." And of course, we think everybody can't be wrong, so the product must be fantastic. So as to make us believe it, they use expressions like, "It's a must-have" or "It's the *in* thing," and they combine this with a photograph of a large group of people, so that we can't fail to get the message. But don't be fooled. Even if everybody is using it (and they may not be), everybody can be wrong.

Another favorite message is "You too can look like this," accompanied by a photo of a fabulous-looking man or woman. But the problem is, you can't look like this because actually the woman or man in the photo is a model and also because he or she doesn't really look like that, either. The photo has been airbrushed in order to make the model look even slimmer, with perfect skin, and even more attractive than they are in real life.

Ads also often mention a particular organization that recommends their product – for example things like, "Our dog treats are recommended by the International Association of Dog Nutritionists" – well, that's probably an organization that the company set up themselves. Or, "A recent independent study found that our toothpaste cleans your teeth better than any other brand." What study was it? Who commissioned the study? It was probably produced for the company itself, and paid for by them, too.

Finally, what annoys me the most is, "Trust me, I'm a doctor" or "Trust me, I'm a celebrity." The idea is that if a celebrity is using the product, it must be fantastic, or if a doctor recommends it, it must really work. But be careful. Although the actress is holding the product in the photo, do you really think she colors her hair with it at home? And the doctor in the ad, is he really a doctor or just an actor wearing a white coat?

🔊 9.11

1 I think I'd have to say Venice in Italy. In spite of all the tourists, all the clichés, I still think it's the most beautiful city I know. I always remember the first time I went – I arrived by train – and we stepped out of the train station and suddenly it was all there, the canals, the wonderful old buildings. What makes it beautiful for me is the light, the combination of the reflections of the churches and palaces in the water, the wonderful winding streets alongside canals, which are all different but also all similar – it's an incredibly easy city to get lost in. And of course, the fact that there are no cars, no traffic. I fell totally in love with it that first time, and I've been back since then and loved it just as much. It's difficult to think of just one thing to see, I mean, Piazza San Marco is beautiful, the Rialto bridge, but I wouldn't say they were the things I remember the most. I would actually say just wander, without a map or a goal and get lost. Everything is beautiful. The one thing I'd say to do is go on a *vaporetto* – a water bus – down the Grand Canal. I don't think gondolas are worth it – they're ridiculously expensive – and you can enjoy everything just as much on a *vaporetto*.

2 The most beautiful city I've been to recently is probably Curitiba, which is in southern Brazil. I think one of the things I liked about it most was, it's described as the greenest city on earth, and they've really focused on creating a quality public transportation system, there's a huge number of parks in Curitiba, in fact, there's so much grass that the local authority use sheep to cut the grass, not lawnmowers. And I just think that what I like about it is their commitment to trying to make the city, uh, an environmentally-friendly place to live. One place you need to see there is the Wire Opera House which, it's built in the middle of an artificial lake in the middle of a park, and it's built out of steel tubes, it's really extraordinary, and beautiful I think. And if I had to recommend one thing to do I'd say go for a walk in the Bosque Alemão, it's one of the wonderful parks in Curitiba, and visit the free environmental university that is built up in the trees just nearby. Its mission is to educate people about the environment, and I just think that's a wonderful goal to have.

3 The most beautiful city I've ever been to is Banff in Alberta, Canada – well it's not really a city—it's really more like a town, but anyway it's one of my all-time favorite places to visit. What makes it beautiful for me is that it looks like it came out of an old, western movie, it's, uh, there are old, rugged buildings that aren't too tall, and it has a rustic feel, kind of like you might see a cowboy riding a horse along the main street at any given moment, and the whole place is like that. There aren't any modern skyscrapers in Banff, but what does catch your eye is that the town is surrounded by gorgeous, snow-topped mountains. There are lots of things to do – there's a great museum, The Whyte Museum, and there's good shopping, but I think that the town is just amazing to look at and also there are very few cars, so you can just walk around. I'd suggest walking along the Bow River, or if you're more adventurous, you can rent a canoe and paddle in the river. Something everyone who visits

**Go online** to listen to the audio and see all the Listening scripts

Banff needs to do is take the gondola up Sulphur Mountain, find a comfortable chair on the deck of the visitor's center at the top, order something to eat and drink, and take in the view of the town below nestled in the mountains. It's amazing.

4 I know lots of beautiful cities and, uh, I wouldn't choose one above all the others, but one I always love going back to is Edinburgh in Scotland, and something I really love about Edinburgh is that because it's kind of compact, more or less wherever you are in the city you can see outside the city, so you can see the ocean, you can see the hills around, so you always have a sense of the city and the landscape and I really like that. And one place, one thing I would recommend people to see in Edinburgh is something called the Scotsman's Steps which is a staircase that goes from the wall that joins the old town to the new town and it's actually an art work, it's called work number 1059 by an artist named Martin Creed and it's basically a staircase made of marble steps, each one is a different color marble, so you really have a feel of going somewhere, you're going from one color to the next, and I love that place. And something I would do in Edinburgh would be to walk along the river Leith either way, either from the port of Leith up into the city or the other way, because it's like a secret part of Edinburgh and you see Edinburgh from a different perspective.

5 The most beautiful city I've been to is Kyoto in Japan. It's a really wonderful place because it's a mix of, well, like many Japanese cities, very, very modern buildings and a lot of traditional, uh, temple areas as well and you can walk down any Japanese shopping street and find a big supermarket or a modern office building next to a little temple where you step back in time many centuries. The one place that I would recommend that you see is the Kinkaku-ji temple, that is a very, very famous tourist site, it has a golden pavilion in the middle and it's the most wonderful place. It gets very, very busy but I was lucky enough to visit it when I lived in Japan and I was able to stay with a friend and go there very early in the morning to avoid the crowds. One thing you need to do if you go to Kyoto is to try to stay not in a modern hotel but in a ryokan which is a traditional Japanese guest house where you can sleep on tatami matting and have, uh, Japanese breakfast which is rice, eggs, fish, and seaweed.

🔊 10.1

1
**Child** Why is the sky blue?
**Scientist** To understand why the sky is blue, we first need to understand a little about light. Although light from the Sun looks white, it's really made up of many different colors, as we see when they are spread out in a rainbow. Light is like a wave of energy, and each color has a different wavelength. Red is the longest, and blue and violet are the shortest. When the Sun's light reaches the Earth's atmosphere, it's scattered by tiny molecules of gas in the air. Shorter wavelengths (violet and blue) are scattered the most widely, and our eyes are much more sensitive to blue than violet, so we see more of the blue light than the other colors. So that's why we see the sky as blue.

2
**Child** Why is the sea salty?
**Scientist** Most of our planet's surface is covered in salt water. But where does the salt come from? Well, some of it comes from rocks on the bottom of the ocean, but most of it actually comes from the land around us. Every time it rains, tiny amounts of mineral salts dissolve into rivers, and these eventually get to the ocean. Rivers aren't very salty, because they flow continually, but the Sun's heat causes the ocean water to evaporate, so the salt in the ocean becomes more concentrated.

3
**Child** Why can we sometimes see the moon during the day?
**Scientist** We all know that the Sun produces a lot of strong light. So, when it's in the sky, we can't see the stars, or the other planets. The moon doesn't produce light – it reflects the light of the Sun. The moon is visible for about 12 out of every 24 hours because of the way it rotates around the Earth. This means it's visible for some time during daylight nearly every day.

4
**Child** Why do we have a leap year?
**Scientist** A year is the amount of time it takes the Earth to go around the Sun, and we've divided our calendar year into 365 days. However, it actually takes the Earth 365 days, 5 hours, 48 minutes and 45 seconds to go around the Sun. To deal with this difference, we add one day (24 hours) to our calendar every four years. This adjustment is not exactly correct, because it effectively adds 6 hours per year rather than the exact amount of the difference.

5
**Child** Why do we blink?
**Scientist** A "blink of an eye" lasts only a tenth of a second. Every time you blink, your eyelids spread fluid across the surface of your eyes, to keep them moist, and also to stop them from getting dirty. Blinking also keeps eyes safe from things that might damage them, such as bright light and sometimes, bigger objects coming into our eyes like a small insect. Blinking stops the activity in your brain that detects changes, so you never notice that you actually stop seeing for a very short time when you blink.

6
**Child** Why does cutting onions make us cry?
**Scientist** For a vegetable, onions have very complicated chemistry. When you cut them, a chemical reaction changes molecules in the onion into a gas. When this gas reaches the cornea, the transparent layer that covers and protects the outer part of your eye, the cornea senses it as an irritant. It acts to protect your eyes by making you cry, and the tears clean your eyes.

7
**Child** What is a cloud?
**Scientist** We all enjoy looking at clouds and seeing their different shapes, but what's the science behind them? Well, the sky is full of drops of water. But most of the time you can't see them because they are too small; the drops have turned into water vapor. As the water vapor goes higher in the sky, the air gets cooler. The cooler air causes the drops to start to stick to things, like pieces of dust, ice, or sea salt, which make them visible. So that's what we see when we see clouds.

8
**Child** What is a black hole?
**Scientist** This is another physics question. A black hole is caused by gravity. There are places in space where gravity pulls so hard that even light cannot get out. The reason that gravity is so strong in a black hole is that a lot of matter – that's physical "stuff"– has been compressed into a tiny space. A lot of matter has a high mass and this creates a strong gravitational pull. Inside a black hole, space is falling faster than light, which is why light can't escape.

🔊 10.11

**Host** When Neil Armstrong became the first man to walk on the Moon on July 20th, 1969, a global audience of 500 million people were watching and listening. As he climbed down the steps from the spacecraft and stepped onto the moon they heard him say, "That's one small step for man, one giant leap for mankind." It seemed like the perfect quote for such a momentous occasion. But from the moment he said it, people have argued about whether Armstrong got his lines wrong and made a mistake. James, tell us about it.

**James** Well, Armstrong always said that he wrote those words himself, which became some of the most famous and memorable words in history, during the time between landing on the moon and actually stepping out of the capsule onto the moon. That was almost seven hours.

**Host** And so what is the controversy about what Armstrong said when he stepped down the ladder onto the moon?

**James** The question is, did he say, "one small step for man" or "one small step for a man". That's to say did he use the indefinite article or not? It's just a little word, but there's a big difference in meaning. Armstrong always insisted that he wrote "one small step for a man, one giant leap for mankind". Of course, this would have been a meaningful sentence. If you say "a man" then it clearly means that this was one small step for an individual man, i.e. himself, but one giant leap for mankind, that's to say, men and women in general. But what everybody actually heard was, "One small step for man, one giant leap for mankind", with no indefinite article, and that sentence means, "One small step for people in general, one giant leap for people in general." And that doesn't really make sense.

**Host** So, did he just get the line wrong when he said it?

**James** Well, Armstrong himself was never sure if he actually said what he wrote. In his biography *First Man*, he told the author James Hansen, "I must admit that it doesn't sound like the word 'a' is there. On the other hand, certainly the 'a' was intended, because that's the only way it makes sense." He always regretted that there'd been so much confusion about it. But, almost four decades later, Armstrong was proved to be right. Peter Shann Ford, an Australian computer expert, used very hi-tech sound techniques to analyze his sentence and he discovered that the "a" was said by Armstrong. It's just that he said it so quickly that you couldn't hear it on the recording that was broadcast to the world on July 20th, 1969.

**Host** Was Armstrong relieved to hear this?

**James** Yes, he was. I think it meant a lot to him to know that he didn't make a mistake.

🔊 10.15

**Elizabeth I A** I know I have the body of a weak and feeble woman, but I have the heart and stomach of a king, and a king of England, too.

**Abraham Lincoln B** It is rather for us to be here dedicated to the great task remaining before us - that from these honored dead we take increased devotion to that cause for which they gave the last full measure of devotion – that we here highly resolve that these dead shall not have died in vain – that this nation, under God, shall have a new birth of freedom – and that government of the people, by the people, for the people, shall not perish from the earth.

**Emmeline Pankhurst C** The title of my speech today is "The laws that men have made." Men politicians are in the habit of talking to women as if there were no laws that affect women. "The fact is," they say, "the home is the place for women. Their interests are the rearing and training of children. These are the things that interest women. Politics have nothing to do with these things, and therefore politics do not concern women."

**Winston Churchill D** We shall fight on the beaches, we shall fight on the landing grounds, we shall fight in the fields and in the streets, we shall fight in the hills; we shall never surrender.

**John F. Kennedy E** And so, my fellow Americans, ask not what your country can do for you; ask what you can do for your country. My fellow citizens of the world, ask not what America will do for you, but what together we can do for the freedom of man.

**Martin Luther King, Jr. F** I have a dream that my four little children will one day live in a nation where they will not be judged by the color of their skin but by the content of their character. I have a dream today!

**Nelson Mandela G** I have cherished the ideal of a democratic and free society in which all persons live together in harmony, and with equal opportunities. It is an ideal which I hope to live for and to achieve. But, if needs be, it is an ideal for which I am prepared to die.

**Barack Obama H** For when we have faced down impossible odds, when we've been told we're not ready, or that we shouldn't try, or that we can't, generations of Americans have responded with a simple creed that sums up the spirit of a people. Yes, we can! Yes, we can! Yes, we can!

🔊 **10.16**

**Host** Welcome to today's program. Our topic today is public speaking. Public speaking is right up there at the top of what most people say they're most afraid of. There is even a name for it – *glossophobia*. But hopefully after this program you will feel a lot more confident if you do have to make a speech or give a presentation.
First, we have Lynne Parker, an expert in the art of public speaking, who's going to tell us some of her do's and don'ts. Then after that, we're going to talk to Anya Edwards from Chile. Anya was a finalist in last year's English Speaking Union International public speaking competition. Lynne, I believe you have six key tips for us, is that right?

**Lynne** Yes, that's right. My first tip, and maybe the most important one, is be yourself. This applies both to how you speak, and to what you actually do on the stage, whether that's standing up, sitting down, or moving about. Do what you feel comfortable with. The only don't regarding how you are on stage I'd say is, try not to continually walk up and down, because this tends to distract people from what you're saying.

**Host** Yes, I find that distracting, actually.

**Lynne** Second, if you're using PowerPoint, don't just type out your talk. You want people to listen to what you're saying, not to read ahead. Slides are best for illustrating your talk or for drawing attention to a point. Pictures are often better than words, but if you use words, do keep it short. And do remember the 10-20-30 rule. Do you know what that is?

**Host** Uh, no, do tell us.

**Lynne** The 10-20-30 rule is that the ideal presentation should have 10 slides, last 20 minutes, and never have a font size on the slides that's less than 30 points.

**Host** Ah, great, that's an easy one to remember. And tip number 3?

**Lynne** Maintain eye contact with your audience, whether it's to 500 people in a room or 20 people in a classroom or around a table. Don't spend the whole talk looking at your notes or slides.

**Host** How can you maintain eye contact with 500 people?

**Lynne** Well, you can't with all of them, of course, but a good technique is to scan the audience occasionally from side to side and front to back, to give the impression you're talking to everyone.

**Host** Number 4?

**Lynne** Rehearse, rehearse, rehearse. In front of a mirror, or even better – video yourself. It'll make you aware of how you use your hands and body, and even what clothes look right.

**Host** Number 5?

**Lynne** Include a couple of good sound bites. Whenever you hear something good, write it down because you might be able to use it later.

**Host** So sound bites, rather than stories or examples?

**Lynne** Well, no, not instead of – a good story or example can also help to illustrate a situation or help people to remember the point you were making. Just don't make it too long, and if you're telling a little story, remember, good stories have a beginning, a middle and an end.

**Host** And your last point?

**Lynne** Listen to other speakers. There are lots of good resources online, such as TED talks and The Moth, which is a great storytelling website. Also, listen to people talking when you're out and about, for example traveling on public transportation or in line at the supermarket. You never know what witty remarks or good stories you might pick up along the way.

**Host** Thank you very much, Lynne.

🔊 **10.17**

**Host** And now we have Anya on the line, from Chile.

**Anya** Hello.

**Host** Anya, you took part in the competition last year, is that right?

**Anya** Yes.

**Host** Can you tell us a little about it?

**Anya** Well, it's open to people from any country between the ages of 16 and 18. First, you compete at home, so for me, in Chile, and then the international finals take place in London.

**Host** What exactly did you have to do there?

**Anya** So you have to give two speeches. The first one is a prepared speech that is a maximum of five minutes on a subject that they give you – that year for me it was on the role of education. And then after your speech, you have to answer questions for three to four minutes. And then the second speech, and this was definitely the scariest, was the impromptu speech. You are given three subjects to choose from which you've never seen before, and then 15 minutes to choose one and prepare a speech of 3 minutes.

**Host** What did you choose?

**Anya** I chose the title "to be grown up is a state of mind."

**Host** Were you nervous?

**Anya** I was nervous, very nervous. But then I've never not been nervous before speaking in front of an audience. I've done a lot of drama, of acting, and that's taught me that nerves are good because you can learn to channel them into a better performance.

**Host** How is public speaking different from acting?

**Anya** Well in many ways they're similar because you need many of the same qualities: to be able to stand in front of an audience confidently and speak clearly, to be convincing. But I'd say that public speaking is harder because you can't rely on anyone else. If you miss a line, there won't be someone next to you to give you your cue, and you're the main focus of attention 100% of the time.

**Host** And what did you learn from the experience?

**Anya** I think it was one of the most useful skills I've ever learned, and that any person can have, because if you've learned to do it well, and practiced, it means that you'll never ever have to worry about standing up and speaking in front of other people.

**Host** What tips would you give to someone about writing a speech?

**Anya** Well for writing a speech, I'd say, to start by talking about the topic out loud and record whatever comes into your head on your phone. Then listen back to it and start by ordering your ideas on paper. And if you think the subject you have to talk about is a little dry, try to come up with some anecdotes to illustrate it. Also, use plain simple language. Vocabulary that's too complicated puts people off.

**Host** And to deliver it?

**Anya** I agree entirely with Lynne about being authentic, about being yourself. If you want your speech to be effective, people need to believe what you say, and in order to convince them, you need to be convinced yourself.

## question formation

**1** How long **have you** been waiting? How many children 🔊1.3 **does your sister** have? **Should we** buy her a present?

**2** Why **didn't you** like the movie? **Isn't this** a beautiful place? **Don't you** have to be at school today?

**3** **What** are you talking **about**? **Who** does this bag belong **to**?

**4** **Who lives** in that house? **How many people follow** you on Twitter?

**1** We make questions with tenses where there is an auxiliary verb (*be, have*, etc.) and with modal verbs (*should, must*, etc.) by inverting the subject and the auxiliary / modal verb. With the simple present and past, we add the auxiliary verb *do / does* or *did* before the subject.

**2** We often use negative questions to show surprise when we expect somebody to agree with us, or to check whether something is true.

**3** If a verb is usually followed by a preposition, e.g., *talk about something*, the preposition comes at the end of the question, not at the beginning. **NOT** ~~About what are you talking?~~

• We often just use the question word and the preposition, e.g., **A** *I'm thinking.* **B** *What about?*

**4** When *who / what / which*, etc., is the **subject** of questions in the simple present or past, we <u>don't</u> use *do / did*, e.g., *Who wrote this?* **NOT** ~~Who did write this?~~

### indirect questions

Could you tell me **what time the store next door opens?** 🔊1.4
Do you know **if (whether) Mark's coming to the meeting**?

• We use indirect questions when we want to ask a question in a more polite way. We begin with a phrase such as *Can / Could you tell me…? Do you know…? Do you think…? Do you remember…? Would you mind telling me…? Do you have any idea…?*

• Compare:
*What time does the post office open?* (direct question) and *Could you tell me what time the post office opens?* (indirect question)

• In indirect questions, the order is subject + verb. *Can you tell me where it is?* **NOT** ~~Can you tell me where is it?~~

• We don't use *do / did* in the second part of the question. *Do you know where he lives?* **NOT** ~~…where does he live?~~

• You can use *if* or *whether* in questions <u>without</u> a question word and after: *Can you tell me, Do you know*, etc.

> 🔍 **Other expressions followed by the word order of indirect questions**
>
> The word order of indirect questions is used after:
> *I wonder…*, e.g., **I wonder** *why they didn't come.*
> *I'm not sure…*, e.g., **I'm not sure** *what time it starts.*
> *I can't remember…*, e.g., **I can't remember** *where I left my phone.*
> *I'd like to know…*, e.g., **I'd like to know** *what time you're coming home.*

**a** Order the words to make questions.

tomorrow can't Why come you ?
*Why can't you come tomorrow?*

1 I Should her tell I feel how ?
2 friend known long best have How you your ?
3 tell when you train next leaves the Could me ?
4 are What about you thinking ?
5 on do weekend you What doing the like ?
6 music to does What Junko kind like listening of ?
7 you time movie know finishes Do what the ?
8 class students yesterday to many came How ?
9 you remember is where Do the restaurant ?
10 housework family in Who your the does ?

**b** Complete the questions with the words in parentheses.

Where <u>did you go</u> on vacation last year? (you / go)

1 How often _____ ? (you / usually exercise)
2 Who _____ *The Great Gatsby*? (write)
3 Could you tell me how much _____? (this book / cost)
4 I can't remember where _____ my car this morning. (I / park)
5 _____ your trip to Paris last weekend? (you / enjoy)
6 What kind of work _____? (your sister / do)
7 Who _____ the last cookie? (eat)
8 Do you know what time _____ on Saturdays? (the swimming pool / open)
9 Why _____ the present you gave her? (your sister / not like)
10 _____ play your music so loud? I can't concentrate. (you / have to)

🔶 p.7

## auxiliary verbs

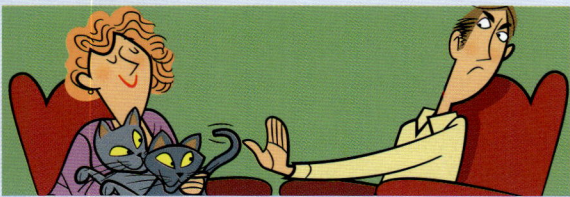

1 I like cats, but my husband **doesn't**. 🔊 1.14
  Sally's coming tonight, but Angela **isn't**.

2 **A** I loved his latest movie.
  **B** **So did I.**
  **A** I haven't finished the book yet.
  **B** **Neither have I.**
  Andrew's a doctor and **so is his wife**.

3 **A** I don't like shopping online.
  **B** I **do**. I buy a lot of my clothes online.

4 **A** I went to a psychic yesterday.
  **B** **You did?**
  **A** I'll make dinner tonight.
  **B** **You will?** That's great!

5 **A** You didn't lock the door!
  **B** I **did** lock it; I know I **did**.
  **A** Silvia isn't coming.
  **B** She **is** coming. I just spoke to her.

6 You won't forget, **will** you?
  She can speak Italian, **can't** she?

- We use auxiliary verbs (*do*, *have*, etc.) or modal verbs (*can*, *must*, etc.):

1 to avoid repeating the main verb / verb phrase, e.g., **NOT** ~~I like cats,
  but my husband doesn't~~ **like cats**.

2 with *so* and *neither* to say that someone or something is the same. Use
  *so* + auxiliary + subject to respond to a statement with an affirmative
  verb, and *neither* + auxiliary + subject to respond to a statement with a
  negative verb.

- We use an affirmative auxiliary verb after *neither*, e.g., *Neither did I.*
  **NOT** ~~Neither didn't I.~~

3 to respond to a statement and say that you (or someone or something)
  are different.

4 to make "reply questions." These often show interest or surprise.

5 to show emphasis in an affirmative sentence, often when you want
  to contradict what somebody says. With the simple present and
  simple past, we add *do / does / did* before the main verb. With other
  auxiliaries, e.g., *be*, *have*, *will*, the auxiliary verb is stressed and
  not contracted.

6 to make tag questions, we use an affirmative auxiliary with a negative
  verb, and a negative auxiliary with an affirmative verb.

- Tag questions are often used simply to ask another person to agree
  with you, e.g., *It's a nice day, isn't it?* In this case, the tag question is said
  with falling intonation, i.e., the voice goes down.

- Tag questions can also be used to check something you think is true,
  e.g., *She's a painter, isn't she?* In this case, the tag question is said with
  rising intonation, as in a normal *yes / no* question.

---

**a** Complete the mini-dialogues with an auxiliary or modal verb.

  **A** You didn't remember to buy coffee.
  **B** I *did* remember. It's in the cabinet.

1 **A** He's booked the flights, _____ he?
  **B** Yes, I think so.

2 **A** It's hot today, _____ it?
  **B** Yes, it's boiling.

3 **A** Why don't you like classical music?
  **B** I _____ like it, but it isn't my favorite.

4 **A** I wouldn't like to be a celebrity.
  **B** Neither _____ I.

5 **A** Mike's arriving tomorrow!
  **B** He _____? I thought he was arriving today.

6 **A** What did you think of the movie?
  **B** Tom liked it, but I _____. I thought it
    was awful.

7 **A** Emma doesn't like me.
  **B** She _____ like you. She just doesn't want to
    go out with you.

8 **A** Are you a vegetarian?
  **B** Yes, I am, and so _____ my boyfriend.

9 **A** You'll remember to call me, _____ you?
  **B** Yes, of course!

10 I really want to go to Thailand, but my
   wife _____. She hates the heat.

**b** Complete the conversation with a suitable
auxiliary verb.

  **A** You're Tom's sister,
    *aren't* you?
  **B** Yes, I'm Carla.
  **A** It's a great club,
    [1]_____ it?
  **B** Well, it's OK. But
    I don't like the music
    much.
  **A** You [2]_____?
    I love it! I've never
    been here before.

  **B** Neither [3]_____ I. I don't go clubbing very often.
  **A** Oh, you [4]_____? I [5]_____. In fact, I usually
    go most weekends.
  **B** You [6]_____? I can't afford to go out every
    weekend.
  **A** I didn't see you at Tom's birthday party last Saturday.
    Why [7]_____ you go?
  **B** I [8]_____ go, but I got there really late because
    my car broke down.
  **A** Oh, that's why I didn't see you. I left early.
  **B** I'd like something to drink. I'm really thirsty after all
    that dancing.
  **A** So [9]_____ I.  p.11

---

🔵 **Go online** to review the grammar for each lesson

## present perfect simple and continuous

**present perfect simple:** *have / has* + past participle

> 1 **Have** you ever **broken** a bone?  🔊 2.12
>    I**'ve** never **seen** him before.
> 2 I**'ve called** for an ambulance, but it **hasn't arrived** yet.
>    I**'ve** already **told** you three times.
> 3 It's the best book I**'ve** ever **read**.
> 4 I**'ve known** Keiko since I was a child.
>    My sister **has been** sick for ten days now.
> 5 How many Patricia Cornwell novels **have** you **read**?
>    They**'ve seen** each other twice this week.

- We use the present perfect simple:
1 to talk about past experiences when you don't say when something happened, often with *ever* or *never*.
2 with *yet* and *already*.
3 with superlatives and *the first, second, last time*, etc.
4 with nonaction verbs (= verbs not usually used in the continuous form, e.g., *be, need, know, like*, etc.) to say that something started in the past and is still true now.
- This use is common with time expressions like *How long...?, for* or *since, all day / evening*, etc.
- Don't use the simple present in this situation. **NOT** *I know Keiko since I was a child.*
5 when we say or ask *how much / many* we have done or *how often* we have done something up to now.

**present perfect continuous:** *have / has* + *been* + verb + *-ing*

> 1 How long **have** you **been waiting** to see the doctor?  🔊 2.13
>    He**'s been messaging** his girlfriend all evening.
> 2 I **haven't been sleeping** well recently.
>    It**'s been raining** all day.
> 3 I**'ve been shopping** all morning. I'm exhausted.
>    My shoes are filthy. I**'ve been working** in the yard.

- We use the present perfect continuous:
1 with action verbs (e.g., *run, listen, study, cook*) to say that an action started in the past and is still happening now (unfinished actions).
- This use is common with time expressions like *How long...?, for* or *since, all day / evening*, etc.
- Don't use the present continuous in this situation. **NOT** *I'm living here for the last three years.*
2 for repeated actions, especially with a time expression, e.g., *all day, recently*.
3 for continuous actions that have just finished (but that have present results).

**present perfect simple or continuous?**

> 1 I**'ve been feeling terrible** for days.  🔊 2.14
>    He**'s liked** classical music since he was a teenager.
> 2 She**'s been having** a good time at school.
>    They**'ve had** that car for at least ten years.
> 3 We**'ve lived** in this town since 2010.
>    We**'ve been living** in a rented house for the last two months.
> 4 I**'ve painted** the kitchen. I**'ve been painting** the kitchen.

1 To talk about an unfinished action, we usually use the present perfect continuous with action verbs (e.g., *run, listen, study, cook*) and the present perfect simple with nonaction verbs (e.g., *be, need, know, like*, etc.).
2 Some verbs can be action or nonaction, depending on their meaning, e.g., *have a good time* = action, *have a car* = nonaction.
3 With the verbs *live* or *work*, you can often use the present perfect simple or continuous. However, we usually use the present perfect continuous for more temporary actions.
4 The present perfect simple emphasizes the completion of an action (= the kitchen has been painted). The present perfect continuous emphasizes the duration of an action (= the painting of the kitchen may not be finished yet).

---

**a** Circle the correct form. Check (✓) if both are possible.

   Have you ever *tried / been trying* caviar?

1 She's *worked / been working* here since July.
2 Your mother has *called / been calling* three times this morning!
3 The kids are exhausted because they've *run / been running* around all day.
4 Tim and Lucy haven't *seen / been seeing* our new house yet.
5 I've never *met / been meeting* her boyfriend. Have you?
6 It's *snowed / been snowing* all morning.
7 My brother has *lived / been living* alone since his divorce.
8 I've *read / been reading* all morning. I've now *read / been reading* 100 pages.

**b** Complete the sentence with the present perfect simple or continuous of the verb in parentheses.

   *I've bought* a new car. Do you like it? (buy)

1 We _____ Jack and Ann for years. (know)
2 You look really sweaty. _____ at the gym? (you / work out)
3 Emily _____ her homework yet, so I'm afraid she can't go out. (not do)
4 They don't live in Toronto. They _____. (move)
5 I hope they're getting along OK. They _____ a lot recently. (argue)
6 We _____ for hours. Is this the right way? (walk)
7 Why is my laptop on? _____ it? (you / use)
8 Oh, no! I _____ my finger on this knife. (cut)

➜ p.18

## using adjectives as nouns, adjective order

### adjectives as nouns

1 In most African countries, **the young** still look up to 🔊 2.15
**the old**.
**The poor** are getting poorer, and **the rich** are getting richer.
**The government** needs to create more jobs for **the unemployed**.
2 **The English** are famous for drinking tea.
**The Chinese** invented paper.
**The Dutch** make wonderful cheeses.

- You can use *the* + some adjectives to talk about groups of people, e.g.,
1 specific groups in society, such as *the young*, *the old* (or *the elderly*), *the sick* (= people who are ill), *the blind*, *the deaf*, *the homeless*, *the dead*.
2 some nationalities that end in *-ch*, *-sh*, *-ese*, and *-ss*, such as *the French*, *the Spanish*, *the British*, *the Japanese*, *the Irish*, *the Swiss*, etc. (most other nationality words are nouns and are used in the plural, e.g., *the Brazilians*, *the Peruvians*, *the Turks*, *the South Koreans*, *the Argentinians*, etc.).
- You can also use adjective + *people* to talk about a group of people, e.g., *poor people*, *homeless people*, *old people*, *Thai people*.
- To talk about one person, use, e.g., *a Japanese woman*, *a rich man*, etc., **NOT** ~~a Japanese, a rich~~.

### adjective order

We have a **charming old** house near the lake. 🔊 2.16
She has **long brown** hair.
I bought a **beautiful Italian leather** belt.

- You can put more than one adjective before a noun (often two and occasionally three). These adjectives go in a particular order, e.g., **NOT** ~~an old charming house~~.
- Opinion adjectives, e.g., *beautiful*, *nice*, *charming*, always go <u>before</u> descriptive adjectives, e.g., *big*, *old*, *round*.
- If there is more than one descriptive adjective, they go in this order:

| OPINION | SIZE | AGE | SHAPE | COLOR | PATTERN | ORIGIN / PLACE | MATERIAL | NOUN |
|---------|------|-----|-------|-------|---------|----------------|----------|------|
| expensive | little | brand new | long | purple | striped | French | silk | scarf |
| beautiful | | | | | | Japanese | | car |

**a** Rewrite the <u>underlined</u> phrase using *the* + an adjective.

<u>People from Vietnam</u> enjoy spicy food.
*The Vietnamese*

1 <u>People from the Netherlands</u> tend to be good at languages.
2 Clara Barton took care of <u>the people who weren't well</u> during the American Civil War.
3 The system of reading for <u>people who can't see</u> is called Braille.
4 <u>People from China</u> have a fascinating history.
5 Ambulances arrived to take <u>the people who had been injured</u> to the hospital.
6 <u>People from Switzerland</u> are usually very punctual.
7 The worst season for <u>people without a home</u> is winter.
8 There is a discount for <u>people without a job</u>.
9 The World War II monument was erected to honor <u>the people who died</u>.
10 There are special TV shows for <u>people who can't hear</u>, that use sign language.

**b** Write the adjectives in parentheses in the correct place. Change *a* to *an* where necessary.

a big parking lot (empty)   *a big empty parking lot*
1 a man (young / attractive)
2 shoes (old / dirty)
3 a velvet jacket (black / beautiful)
4 a girl (teenage / tall / American)
5 a beach (sandy / long)
6 a log cabin (charming / old)
7 a leather bag (Italian / stylish)
8 eyes (huge / dark)
9 a dog (black / friendly / old)
10 a T-shirt (striped / cotton)

➜ p.21

## narrative tenses: simple past, past continuous, past perfect, past perfect continuous

### narrative tenses

> 1 We **arrived** at the airport and **checked in**.  🔊 3.10
> 2 We **were having** dinner when the plane hit some turbulence. At nine o'clock most people on the plane **were reading** or **were trying** to sleep.
> 3 When we arrived at the airport, we suddenly realized that we**'d left** one of the suitcases in the taxi.
> 4 We**'d been flying** for about two hours when suddenly the captain told us to fasten our seat belts because we were flying into some very bad weather.

1 We use the **simple past** to talk about consecutive actions or situations in the past, i.e., for the main events in a story.

2 We use the **past continuous** (was / were + verb + -ing) to describe a longer continuous past action or situation that was in progress when another action happened, or to describe an action or situation that was not complete at a past time.

3 We use the **past perfect** (had + past participle) to talk about the "earlier past," i.e., things that happened <u>before</u> the main event(s).

4 We use the **past perfect continuous** (had been + verb + -ing) with action verbs (go, play, watch, etc.) to talk about longer continuous actions or situations that started before the main events happened and continued up to that point. Nonaction verbs (e.g., be, have, know, like, etc.) are not usually used in the past continuous or past perfect continuous.

### past perfect simple or continuous?

> Lina was crying because she**'d been reading** a very sad book.  🔊 3.11
> Lina didn't want to see the movie, because she**'d** already **read** the book.

- The past perfect continuous emphasizes the <u>continuation</u> of an activity. The past perfect simple emphasizes the <u>completion</u> of an activity.

**a** (Circle) the correct verb form.

Ava and Ryan Miller (got)/ were getting a nasty surprise when they ¹had checked in / were checking in at Calgary International Airport yesterday with their baby, Alec. They ²had won / won three free plane tickets to Mexico in a competition, and they ³were looking forward to / had been looking forward to their trip for months. But, unfortunately, they ⁴had been forgetting / had forgotten to get a passport for their son, so Alec couldn't fly. Luckily, they ⁵had arrived / were arriving very early for their flight, so they still had time to do something about it. They ⁶had run / ran to the police station in the airport to apply for an emergency passport. Ava ⁷was going / went with Alec to the photo booth, while Ryan ⁸had filled out / was filling out the forms. The passport was ready in an hour, so they ⁹hurried / were hurrying to the gate and ¹⁰got / had got on the plane just in time.

**b** Put the verb in parentheses in the past perfect simple (had done) or continuous (had been doing). If you think both are possible, use the continuous form.

His English was very good. He*'d been learning* it for five years. (learn)

1 I was really fed up because we _____ for hours. (wait)
2 She went to the police to report that someone _____ her bag. (steal)
3 It _____ all morning. The streets were wet, and there were puddles everywhere. (rain)
4 She got to work late because she _____ her phone at home and _____ go back and get it. (leave, have to)
5 I almost didn't recognize Tony at the party. He _____ a lot since I last saw him. (change)
6 The tourists' faces were very red. They _____ in the sun all morning and they _____ any sunscreen. (sit, not put on)
7 I could see from their expressions that my parents _____. (argue)
8 Jamilla had a bandage on her arm because she _____ off her bike that morning. (fall)
9 I was amazed because I _____ such an enormous plane before. (never see)
10 How long _____ you _____ before you realized that you were lost? (walk)

⬅ p.28

# 3B

## the position of adverbs and adverbial phrases

1 He walks very **slowly**. 🔊 **3.14**
  I speak five languages **fluently**.
  The driver was **seriously** injured in the accident.
2 I **hardly ever** have time for breakfast.
  Liam's **always** late for work.
  I would **never** have thought you were 40.
3 It rained **all day yesterday**.
  My parents will be **here in half an hour**.

4 I'm **nearly** finished.
  We're **incredibly** tired.
  My husband works **a lot**, but he doesn't earn **much**.
5 **Unfortunately**, the package never arrived.
  **Ideally**, we should leave here at 10:00.

- Adverbs can describe an action (e.g., *he walks **slowly***) or modify adjectives or other adverbs (e.g., *it's **incredibly** expensive, he works **very** hard*). They can either be one word (e.g., *often*) or a phrase (e.g., *once a week*).

1 **Adverbs of manner** describe how somebody does something. They usually go after the verb or verb phrase, however, with passive verbs they usually go in mid-position (before the main verb but after an auxiliary verb).

2 **Adverbs of frequency** go before the main verb but after the verb *to be*.

- *sometimes*, *usually*, and *normally* can also be put at the beginning of the phrase or sentence for emphasis, e.g., *Sometimes the weather can be very wet, but not today.*
- If there are two auxiliary verbs, the adverb goes after the first one.

3 **Adverbs of time and place** usually go at the end of a sentence or clause. Place adverbs usually go before time adverbs. **NOT** *My parents will be in half an hour here.*

- Adverbs of time can also go at the beginning for emphasis, e.g., ***Soon** it will be my birthday!* **OR** *It will be my birthday **soon**!*

4 **Adverbs of degree** describe how much something is done, or modify an adjective.

- *nearly* and *almost* are used before a verb or verb phrase.
- *extremely*, *incredibly*, *very*, etc., are used with adjectives and adverbs, and go before them.
- *a lot* and *much* are often used with verbs and go after the verb or verb phrase.
- *a little / a little bit (of)* can be used with adjectives or verbs, e.g., *I'm a little tired. We rested a little bit after the flight.*

5 **Comment adverbs** (which give the speaker's opinion) usually go at the beginning of a sentence or clause. Other common comment adverbs are: *luckily, basically, clearly, obviously, apparently, eventually,* etc.

> 🔍 **Other adverbs**
> Most other adverbs go in mid-position, e.g., *I **just** need ten more minutes. I didn't speak to Kelly at the party – I didn't **even** see her. She'll **probably** come in the end.*

---

**a** Underline the adverbs or adverbial phrases in each sentence. Correct the word order if it's wrong.

> We're going to be <u>unfortunately</u> late. ✗
> *Unfortunately, we're going to be late.*
> He can speak Turkish <u>fluently</u>. ✓

1 She liked a lot the present.
2 Mark came last night very late home.
3 The ambulance arrived at the scene of the accident after a few minutes.
4 A young man was hurt badly and was taken to the hospital.
5 I was incredibly tired last night.
6 She's lazy a little bit about doing her homework.
7 I forgot your birthday almost, but my sister fortunately reminded me.
8 We luckily had taken an umbrella, because it started to rain right away.
9 Mary doesn't always eat healthily – she often has snacks between meals.
10 Yadier has been apparently fired.

**b** Put the adverbs in parentheses in the normal position in these sentences.

> *seriously*
> I'm ⟨considering resigning from my job. (seriously)

1 Their house was damaged in the fire. (badly, last week)
2 Ben is at his friend's house. (often, in the evening)
3 My father takes a nap. (usually, in the afternoon)
4 Julia left and she didn't say goodbye. (early, even)
5 Martin eats quickly. (always, incredibly)
6 His brother died in a skiing accident. (apparently, nearly)
7 We're going to the movies. (probably, tonight)
8 I send emails. (rarely, nowadays)
9 I bought a beautiful new coat. (just, really)
10 Maya realized that she was going to learn to drive. (eventually, never)

 p.31

 **Go online** to review the grammar for each lesson

## future perfect and future continuous

### future perfect: *will have* + past participle

> The rain **will have stopped** by this afternoon. 🔊 4.1
> Some people think that sea levels **will have risen** by as much as 3 feet in 50 years.
> Laura **won't have arrived** before dinner, so I'll leave some food on the stove for her.
> When **will they have learned** enough English to be able to communicate fluently?

- We use the future perfect (*will have* + past participle) to say something will be finished before a certain time in the future.
- This tense is frequently used with the time expressions **by** *Saturday / March / 2030*, etc., or **in** *two weeks / months*, etc.
- *by* + a time expression = at the latest. With *in*, you can say *in six months*.
- We form the negative with *won't have* + past participle, and make questions by inverting the subject and *will / won't*.

### future continuous: *will be* + verb + *-ing*

> 1 Don't call between 7:00 and 8:30 because we**'ll be having** dinner then. 🔊 4.2
> Good luck with your test tomorrow. I**'ll be thinking** of you.
> **Will** you **be waiting** for me when I get off the train?
> This time tomorrow, I**'ll be sitting** on the beach **watching** the sunset.
> 2 You don't need to get up early. We **won't be leaving** until about 9:30.
> I**'ll be going** to the supermarket later. Do you want anything?

1 We use the future continuous (*will be* + verb + *-ing*) to say that an action will be in progress at a certain time in the future.

Compare:
*Come at around 7:30.* **We'll have** *dinner at 8:00.* (= we will start dinner at 8:00)
and
*Don't call between 7:00 and 8:30 because* **we'll be having** *dinner.* (= at 8:00 we will already have started having dinner)

- We form the negative with *won't be* + verb + *-ing* and make questions by inverting the subject and *will / won't*.

2 We sometimes use the future continuous, like the present continuous, to talk about things that are already planned or decided.

---

**a** Complete the sentence using the future perfect or future continuous.

> The movie starts at 7:00, but I won't arrive until 7:15. When I arrive at the movie theater, the movie *will have started*. (start)

1 The flight to Miami takes off at 9:00 and lands at 10:30. At 10:00 they _____ to Miami. (fly)

2 I usually save $200 a month. By the end of the year, I _____ $2,400. (save)

3 Rebecca leaves at 6:30. It takes her an hour to get to work. At 7:00 tomorrow, she _____ to work. (drive)

4 The meeting starts at 2:00 and finishes at 3:30. Don't call me at 2:30, because we _____ a meeting. (have)

5 Sam is paying for his car. The last payment is in May. By June, he _____ for his car. (pay)

6 Their last test is on May 31st. By the end of May, they _____ their tests. (finish)

7 She writes a chapter of her novel a week. This week she's on chapter five. By the end of this week, she _____ five chapters. (write)

8 Sonia is usually at the gym between 6:30 and 7:30. There's no point calling Sonia now. It's 7:00 and she _____ at the gym. (work out)

**b** Complete the conversation with the verbs in parentheses in the future perfect or continuous.

A Well, it looks like we*'ll be having* very different weather in the future if climate change continues. (have)

B What do you mean?

A Well, they say *we'll be having* much higher temperatures here in New York, as high as 96°. And remember, we
1 _____ on the beach – we (not lie)
2 _____ in 96°, which is very (work)
different. And islands like Puerto Rico
3 _____ by 2100 because (disappear)
of the rise in sea levels. They say the number of storms and tsunamis
4 _____ by the middle of (double)
the century, too, so even more people
5 _____ to the cities by (move)
then, looking for work. Big cities
6 _____ even bigger by (grow)
then. Can you imagine the traffic?

B I don't think there will be a problem with the traffic. Gas 7_____ (run out)
completely by then anyway, so nobody will have a car. Someone
8 _____ a new method of (invent)
transportation, so we 9_____ (get)
around in flying taxis or something.

← p.37

## zero and first conditionals, future time clauses (with all present and future forms)

### zero conditional

> **If** you **want** to be in shape, you **need to** exercise every day.  🔊 4.9
>
> **If** people **are wearing** headphones while walking, they often **don't notice** other people.
>
> **If** you **haven't been** to New York, you **haven't lived**.

- We use zero conditionals to talk about something that is always true or always happens as a result of something else. We use *if* + simple present, and the simple present in the other clause.
- You can also use the present continuous or present perfect in either clause.

### first conditional

> **If** the photos **are** good, **I'll send** them to you.  🔊 4.10
>
> **If** you**'re not going** to Jason's party, **I'm not going to go** either.
>
> **If** I **haven't come back** by 9:00, **start** dinner without me.
>
> **I'll have finished** in an hour **if** you **don't** disturb me.

- We use first conditionals to talk about something that will probably happen in the future as a result of something else. We use *if* + a present tense, and a future tense in the other clause.
- You can use any present form in the *if*-clause (simple present, continuous, or perfect) and any future form (*will, going to,* future perfect, future continuous) or an imperative in the other clause.

### future time clauses

> I'll be ready **as soon as** I**'ve had** a cup of coffee.  🔊 4.11
>
> Text me **when** your train**'s coming into** the station.
>
> I'm not going to buy the new model **until** the price **has gone down** a little.
>
> I'm not going to work overtime this weekend **unless** I **get** paid for it.
>
> Take your umbrella **in case** it**'s raining** when you leave work.

- Future time clauses are similar to the *if*-clause in first conditional sentences, but instead of *if*, we use expressions like: *as soon as, when, until, unless, before, after,* and *in case* followed by a present (not a future) tense. This can be any present form, e.g., simple present, present continuous, present perfect. We can use any future form or imperative in the other clause.
- We use *in case* when we do something in order to be ready for future situations / problems. Compare the use of *if* and *in case*:
- *I'll take an umbrella if it's raining.* = I'll only take an umbrella if it's raining.
- *I'll take an umbrella in case it rains.* = I'll take an umbrella anyway because it might rain.

**a** Circle the correct form.

> If Rob *has studied* / *had studied* enough, he'll easily pass the exam.

1. If you *aren't feeling* / *won't be feeling* better tomorrow, you should go to the doctor.
2. If we're lucky, we *have sold* / *'ll have sold* our house by New Year's.
3. I'll pay for dinner – if I *have* / *'ll have* enough money!
4. If we continue playing like this, we *'ll have scored* / *have scored* ten goals by halftime.
5. Don't call Sophie now. If it's eight o'clock, she *'ll bath* / *'ll be bathing* the baby.
6. If you don't hurry up, you *don't get* / *won't get* to school on time.
7. You can be fined if you *aren't wearing* / *won't be wearing* a seat belt in your car.
8. If you go out with wet hair, you *'ll catch* / *'ll be catching* a cold.
9. My suitcase *always gets* / *will always get* lost if I have a connecting flight.
10. I *won't go* / *don't go* to work on Monday if my daughter is still sick.

**b** Complete the sentence with a time expression from the box.

---

after   as soon as (x2)   before   if   in case (x2)
unless (x2)   until   when

---

> I'll call you <u>as soon as</u> my plane lands.

1. I'm going to pack my suitcase _____ I go to bed.
2. Take your phone with you _____ you get lost.
3. I'll be leaving work early tomorrow _____ there's a last-minute crisis.
4. Let's meet _____ I'm in Toronto next week.
5. There's a crisis! Please call me _____ you possibly can.
6. _____ I'm late tomorrow, start the meeting without me.
7. Mei Ting will have packed some sandwiches _____ we get hungry.
8. Dan will be playing soccer in the park _____ it gets dark. Then he'll go home.
9. Lunch is ready now. Then, _____ we've eaten, we could go for a walk.
10. Don't call 911 _____ it's a real emergency.

🔄 p.41

## unreal conditionals

### second conditional sentences: *if* + simple past, *would / wouldn't* + base form

1 If there **was** a fire in this hotel, it **would be** very difficult to escape.  **5.14**
I **wouldn't have** a car if I **didn't live** in the suburbs.
2 If it **wasn't raining** so hard, we **could get** to the top of the mountain.
3 If I **were** you, **I'd make** Jimmy wear a helmet when he's riding a bike.

1 We use second conditional sentences to talk about a hypothetical or imaginary situation in the present or future and its consequences.
2 In the *if*-clause you can also use the past continuous. In the other clause you can use *could* or *might* instead of *would*.
3 With the verb *be* you can use *was* or *were* for *I*, *he*, and *she* in the *if*-clause, e.g., *If Dan was / were here, he would know what to do.* However, in conditionals beginning *If I were you…* to give advice, we always use *were*.

### third conditional sentences: *if* + past perfect, *would / wouldn't have* + past participle

1 If they **had found** the river sooner, they **would** all **have survived**. **5.15**
I **wouldn't have gotten** lost if I **hadn't taken** the wrong path.
2 He **would have died** if he **hadn't been wearing** a helmet.
If the weather **had been** better, I **might have arrived** earlier.

1 We use third conditional sentences to talk about a hypothetical past situation and its consequences.
2 You can also use the past perfect continuous in the *if*-clause. You can also use *could have* or *might have* instead of *would have* in the other clause.
• In the past perfect simple and continuous, *had* can be contracted to *'d*, e.g., *If they'd found the river sooner…*

### second or third conditional?

1 If you **came** to class more often, you **would** probably **5.16** **pass** the exam.
2 If you **had come** to class more often, you **would** probably **have passed** the exam.

• Compare the two conditionals:
1 = You don't come to class enough. You need to come more often if you want to pass the exam.
2 = You didn't come to class enough, so you failed.

> 🔍 **Mixed conditionals**
> We sometimes mix second and third conditionals if a hypothetical situation in the past has a present / future consequence, e.g., *You wouldn't be so tired if you had gone to bed earlier last night.*
> *If he really loved you, he would have asked you to marry him.*

---

**a** Complete the sentence with the correct form of the verb in parentheses, using a second or third conditional.

If Tim *hadn't gotten injured,* he would have played in the championship game. (not get injured)

1 I _____ so much food if you'd told me you weren't hungry. (not make)
2 If I were you, I _____ money to members of your family. (not lend)
3 If Jack were here, I _____ him to help me. (ask)
4 Joe _____ an accident if he hadn't been driving so fast. (not have)
5 I'd run a half-marathon if I _____ in better shape. (be)
6 If you _____ where you were going, you wouldn't have fallen. (look)
7 I'm sure you _____ dancing if you came to the classes with me. (enjoy)
8 We'd go to the local restaurant more often if they _____ the menu from time to time. (change)
9 Nina wouldn't have gone abroad if she _____ to find a job here. (be able)
10 If you _____ for a discount in the store, they might have given you one. (ask)

**b** Complete the sentence using a second or third conditional.

You didn't wait ten minutes. You didn't see Jim.
If *you'd waited ten minutes, you would have seen Jim.*

1 Luke missed the train. He was late for the interview.
If Luke _____ the train, he _____ late for the interview.
2 Maxie didn't buy the top. She didn't have enough money.
Maxie _____ the top if she _____ enough money.
3 It started snowing. We didn't reach the top.
If it _____ snowing, we _____ the top.
4 Rebecca drinks too much coffee. She sleeps badly.
If Rebecca _____ so much coffee, she _____ badly.
5 I don't drive to work. There's so much traffic.
I _____ to work if _____ so much traffic.
6 Matt doesn't work very hard. He won't get promoted.
If Matt _____ harder, he _____ promoted.
7 We ran for the bus. We caught it.
If we _____ for the bus, we _____ it.

↩ p.49

# 5B

 **GRAMMAR BANK**

## *wish* for present / future

### *wish* + simple past

> I wish I **was** ten years younger!  🔊 **5.17**
> I wish I **could** understand what they're saying.
> I wish we **didn't live** so far from my parents.

- We use *wish* + person / thing + simple past to talk about things we would like to be different in the present / future (but that are impossible or unlikely).
- After *wish*, you can use *was* or *were* with *I, he, she,* and *it,* e.g., *I wish I was / were taller.*

### *wish* + *would* / *wouldn't*

> I wish the bus **would come**. I'm freezing.  🔊 **5.18**
> I wish you**'d spend** more time with the children.
> I wish you **wouldn't leave** your shoes there. I almost tripped over them.
> I wish bike riders **wouldn't ride** on the sidewalk!

- We use *wish* + person / thing + *would* / *wouldn't* to talk about things we want to happen, or stop happening, because they annoy us.
- You can't use *wish* + *would* for a wish about yourself, i.e., **NOT** ~~I wish I would…~~, ~~I wish we would…~~.

## *wish* for past regrets

### *wish* + past perfect

> I wish I**'d worked** harder in school.  🔊 **5.21**
> I wish I **hadn't spoken** to him like that!
> I wish she**'d told** me her true feelings.

- We use *wish* + past perfect to talk about things that happened or didn't happen in the past and that we now regret.

> 🔍 **if only…**
> *if only* is sometimes used instead of *I wish* in certain situations, to express deep regret, e.g., *If only I had worked harder in school (I wouldn't have such a boring job now).*

---

**a** Write sentences with *I wish* + simple past for 1–5, and *I wish…would / wouldn't* for 6–10.

> I'd like to be taller.    *I wish I was taller.*
> It annoys me that you don't put away your clothes.
> *I wish you'd put away your clothes!*

**I'd like these things to be different**

1  I'd like to be in better shape.

_____

2  I'd like my sister not to share a room with me.

_____

3  I'd like to be able to dance.

_____

4  I'd like my grandmother not to be dead.

_____

5  I'd like to live in a country with a better climate.

_____

**It annoys me that…**

6  salespeople aren't more polite.

_____

7  you turn the heat up all the time.

_____

8  my brother doesn't clean our room.

_____

9  the neighbor's dog barks at night.

_____

10  it doesn't stop raining.

_____

⬅ p.51

**b** Rewrite the sentence beginning with *I wish* + past perfect.

> I regret having written that email.
> I wish *I hadn't written that email.*

1  I regret not seeing Prince live.
   I wish _____.

2  He regrets not learning to cook at school.
   He wishes _____.

3  Do you regret buying a used car?
   Do you wish _____?

4  Jenny regrets marrying her first husband.
   Jenny wishes _____.

5  My parents regret moving to the city.
   My parents wish _____.

6  Does Tom regret not studying law?
   Does Tom wish _____?

7  I regret having my hair cut so short.
   I wish _____.

8  They regret not going to the wedding.
   They wish _____.

⬅ p.53

---

**Go online** to review the grammar for each lesson

## used to, be used to, get used to

### used to / didn't use to + base form

1. I **used to sleep** for eight hours every night, but now I only sleep for six. 🔊 6.3
   I didn't recognize him. He **didn't use to have** a beard.
2. When I lived in Mexico as a child, we **used to have** pan dulce for breakfast. We **would buy** them every morning from the local baker.

1. We use *used to / didn't use to* + base form to talk about past habits or repeated actions or situations / states that have changed.

- *used to* doesn't exist in the present tense. For present habits, use *usually* + the simple present, e.g., *I usually walk to work.* **NOT** ~~I use to walk to work.~~

2. We can also use *would* (instead of *used to*) to refer to repeated actions in the past with action verbs (e.g., *run, listen, study, cook*, etc.). However, we can only use *used to*, not *would*, for nonaction verbs (e.g., *be, need, know, like*, etc.). *Alan didn't use to be so thin.* **NOT** ~~Alan wouldn't be so thin.~~

- With *would*, you must use a past time expression, or it must be already clear that you are talking about the past.

- We can use the simple past, often with an adverb of frequency, in the same way as *used to* and *would* to talk about repeated past actions, e.g., *I often got up / used to get up / would get up early when I lived in Africa, to watch the sun rise.*

### be used to / get used to + gerund

1. I'm **used to sleeping** with the curtains open. I've never slept with them closed. 🔊 6.4
   Carlos has just moved to Hong Kong. He **isn't used to driving** on the left.
2. A I can't **get used to working** at night. I feel tired all the time.
   B Don't worry, you'll **get used to it** fast.

1. Use *be used to* + gerund to talk about things you are accustomed to doing, or a new situation that is **now** familiar or less strange.

2. Use *get used to* + gerund to talk about a new situation that is **becoming** familiar or less strange.

The difference between *be used to* and *get used to* is exactly the same as the difference between *be* and *get* + adjective, e.g., *It's dark* and *It's getting dark.*

---

**a** Right (✓) or wrong (✗)? Correct the mistakes in the highlighted phrases.

> I can't get used to getting up so early. ✓
> She isn't used to have a big dinner in the evening. ✗
> *She isn't used to having*

1. When we were children, we used to playing soccer on the street.
2. The first time we visited China, we couldn't get used to eat with chopsticks.
3. Have you gotten used to living in the suburbs, or do you still miss the city?
4. I'm really sleepy this morning. I'm not used to going to bed so late.
5. There used to be a movie theater in our town, but it closed down three years ago.
6. Paul would have very long hair when he was younger.
7. I don't start work until 9:30, so I use to get up at about 8:00.
8. Did you use to wear a uniform to school?
9. It's taking me a long time to be used to living on my own.
10. When I had tests in college, I would stay up all night studying.

**b** Complete the sentence with *used to*, *be used to*, or *get used to* (positive or negative) and the verb in parentheses.

> My boyfriend is Japanese, so he *isn't used to driving* on the right. (drive)

1. When Luis started his first job, he couldn't _____ at 6:00 a.m. (get up)
2. I didn't recognize you! You _____ long hair, didn't you? (have)
3. Isabelle _____ an apartment when she was in college, but now she has a house of her own. (rent)
4. When we were children, we _____ all day playing soccer in the park. (spend)
5. Jasmine has been a nurse all her life, so she _____ nights. (work)
6. I've never worn glasses before, but now I'll have to _____ them. (wear)
7. Reiko is an only child. She _____ her things. (share)
8. Although I've lived in Brazil for years, I've never _____ dinner at nine or ten o'clock at night. (have)
9. I _____ spinach, but now I love it. (like)
10. If you want to lose weight, then you'll have to _____ less. (eat)

➜ p.56

## gerunds and infinitives

### verbs followed by the gerund, the infinitive, or the base form

1 I **enjoy listening** to music.   We **couldn't help laughing**. 🔊 6.14
2 I'm really **looking forward to seeing** you.
   I think you should **give up drinking** coffee after dinner.
3 I **want to speak** to you.   They **can't afford to buy** a new car.
4 I'd **rather eat in** than go out tonight.   She **let** him **borrow** her car.
5 It **started to rain**.   It **started raining**.

- When one verb follows another, the first verb determines the form of the second. This can be the gerund (verb + -ing) or the infinitive (with to), or the base form (without to).
1 Use the **gerund** after certain verbs and expressions, e.g., *enjoy, can't help, feel like*.
2 When a phrasal verb is followed by another verb, the second verb is in the **gerund**.
3 Use the **infinitive** (**with to**) after certain verbs, e.g., *want, afford*.
4 Use the **base form** (**without to**) after modal verbs and some expressions, e.g., *might, would rather*, and after the verbs *make* and *let*.
5 Some verbs, e.g., *start, begin* and *continue* can be followed by the gerund or infinitive (with to) **with no difference in meaning**.

➡ p.164 **Appendix** Verb patterns: verbs followed by the gerund or the infinitive

🔍 *like, love, hate*, and *prefer*
   *like, love, hate*, and *prefer* are usually used with the gerund in English, but they can also be used with the infinitive.
   We tend to use the gerund when we talk generally and the infinitive when we talk specifically, e.g.,
   *I like swimming.* (general)   *I like to swim first thing in the morning.* (specific)
   When *like, love, hate*, and *prefer* are used with *would*, they are always followed by *to* + infinitive, e.g., *I'd prefer to stay at home tonight.*

### verbs that can be followed by the gerund or infinitive with a change in meaning

1 **Remember to lock** the door. 🔊 6.15
   I **remember going** to Lima as a child.
2 Sorry, I **forgot to do** it.
   I'll never **forget seeing** the Taj Mahal.
3 I **tried to open** the window.
   **Try calling** Yi Yi on her cell phone.
4 You **need to clean** the car.
   The car **needs cleaning**.

1 *remember* + **infinitive** = not forget to do something, to do what you have to do
   *remember* + **gerund** = (remember doing something) have or keep an image in your memory of something you did or that happened in the past
2 *forget* + **infinitive** = not remember to do something that you have to do
   *forget* + **gerund** = be unable to remember something that you did or that happened in the past
3 *try* + **infinitive** = make an attempt or effort to do something difficult
   *try* + **gerund** = use, do, or test something in order to see if it is good, suitable, etc.
4 *need* + **gerund** is a passive construction, e.g., *the car needs cleaning* = needs to be cleaned  **NOT** ~~needs to clean~~

---

**a** Complete the sentence with a gerund, an infinitive (with *to*), or a base form (without *to*) from the box.

call  carry  clean  come  do  drive  eat out  ~~go out~~
take  wait  work

   I'm exhausted! I don't feel like _going out_ tonight.
1 I suggest _____ a taxi to the airport tomorrow.
2 Even though the snow was really deep, we managed _____ to the local store and back.
3 We'd better _____ some shopping – there isn't much food for the weekend.
4 I'm very impatient. I can't stand _____ in lines.
5 I was exhausted, and a young man offered _____ my bags.
6 My parents used to make me _____ my room.
7 We threatened _____ the police if the boys didn't stop throwing stones.
8 Do you feel like _____ to the gym with me?
9 I'd prefer _____ instead of getting takeout.
10 I don't mind _____ late tonight if you want me to.

**b** Circle the correct form.

   Your hair needs *cutting* / *to cut*. It's really long!
1 I'll never forget *to see* / *seeing* the Grand Canyon for the first time.
2 I need *to call* / *calling* the helpline. My computer has crashed.
3 Have you tried *to take* / *taking* a pill to help you sleep?
4 I'm sure my keys are somewhere. I can remember *to lock* / *locking* the door this morning.
5 I had to run home because I had forgotten *to turn* / *turning* the oven off.
6 Our house needs *to paint* / *painting*. Do you know any good house painters?
7 Did you remember *to send* / *sending* your sister a card? It's her birthday today.
8 We tried *to reach* / *reaching* the top of the mountain, but we had to turn back because of the bad weather.

⬅ p.61

## past modals

**must, may / might / could, can't / couldn't + have + past participle**

1 I **must have left** my phone at Anna's. I definitely remember having it there.
🔊 7.3

  You **must have seen** something. You were there when the accident happened.

2 Somebody **might have stolen** your wallet when you were getting off the train.

  I wonder why she's not here. I suppose she **could have forgotten** about the meeting.

  He still hasn't arrived. I **may not have given** him the right directions.

3 She **can't have gone** to work. Her car's still there.

  You **couldn't have seen** their faces very clearly. It was too dark.

• We use *must, may / might / could*, or *can't / couldn't + have + past participle* to make deductions or speculate about past actions.

1 We use *must have* when we are almost sure that something happened or was true.

  The opposite of *must have* is *can't have* **NOT** ~~mustn't have~~ – see 3.

2 We use *might / may / could + have* when we think it's possible that something happened or was true.

• We can also use *may / might not have* (but **NOT** ~~couldn't have~~) to talk about the possibility that something didn't happen. **NOT** ~~I couldn't have given him the right directions.~~

3 We use *can't have* and *couldn't have* when we are almost sure something didn't happen or that it is impossible. We only use *couldn't have* when the speculation is about the distant past, e.g., *They couldn't have been married. They both died young.*

### should have + past participle

We're going the wrong way. We **should have turned** left at the traffic light.
🔊 7.4

• We use *should / shouldn't + have + past participle* to say that somebody didn't do the right thing, or to express regret or criticism.

• We can use *ought / oughtn't to have* as an alternative to *should / shouldn't have*, e.g., *I ought to have told you earlier.* However, *should have* is more common, especially in speaking.

• *must have* and *should have* have completely different meanings. Compare:
*She should have called me.* = I told her to call me but she didn't.
and
*She must have called me.* = I'm sure she called me. I think that missed call was her number.

---

**a** Rewrite the **bold** sentences using *must / might (not) / can't + have + verb.*

  **I'm certain I left my umbrella at home.**
  *I must have left my umbrella at home.*

1 Holly's crying. **Maybe she had an argument with her boyfriend.** *She…*

2 **I'm sure Ben got my email.** I sent it first thing this morning. *Ben…*

3 **I'm sure Sam and Ginny didn't get lost.** They have Google maps on their phone. *They…*

4 **You saw Ellie yesterday? That's impossible.** She was in bed with the flu. *You…*

5 **Maybe John didn't see you.** That's why he didn't say hello. *John…*

6 **I'm sure Lucy bought a new car.** I saw her driving a blue Honda Civic. *Lucy…*

7 **I'm sure Alex wasn't very sick.** He was only out of work for one day. *Alex…*

8 They didn't go to Tom's wedding. **Maybe they weren't invited.** *They…*

9 This tastes very sweet. **I'm sure you used too much sugar.** *You…*

10 **It definitely wasn't my phone** that rang in the movie theater. Mine was turned off. *It…*

**b** Respond to the first sentence using *should / shouldn't have* + a verb from the box.

buy   drive   go   invite   ~~learn~~   sit   take   write

  **A** We couldn't understand anybody in Mexico City.
  **B** You *should have learned* some Spanish before going.

1 **A** Tom told me the date of his party, but I can't remember it.
  **B** You _____ it down.

2 **A** Sorry I'm late! The traffic was terrible.
  **B** You _____ here. The subway is faster.

3 **A** Amanda was rude to everyone at my party.
  **B** You _____ her. You know what she's like.

4 **A** I don't have any money left after going shopping.
  **B** You _____ so many shoes.

5 **A** You look really tired.
  **B** I know. I _____ to bed earlier last night.

6 **A** The chicken's still frozen solid.
  **B** I know. You _____ it out of the freezer earlier.

7 **A** I think I got a sunburn on my face.
  **B** I'm not surprised. You _____ in the sun all afternoon without any sunscreen.
  ⟵ p.66

## verbs of the senses

*look / feel / smell / sound / taste*

**1** You **look tired**.        🔊 **7.11**
That cake **smells good**!
These jeans don't **feel comfortable**.

**2** Tim **looks like his father**.
Are you sure this is coffee? It **tastes like tea**.
This material **feels like silk** – is it?

**3** She **looks as if she's been crying**.
It **smells as if something's burning**.
It **sounds as if it's raining**.

**4** I saw Jane this morning. She **looked** sad.
I spoke to Jane this morning. She **seemed** sad.

**1** We use *look*, *feel*, etc. + adjective.

**2** We use *look*, *feel*, etc. + *like* + noun (phrase).

**3** We use *look*, *feel*, etc. + *as if* + clause.

- You can use *…like* or *…as though* instead of *…as if*, e.g., *It sounds like / as though it's raining.*

**4** We use *look* to describe the specific impression we get from someone's appearance. We use *seem* to describe a general impression we get (not necessarily appearance).

- *seem* can be followed by the same structures as *look*, e.g., *Mark seems like a nice man.*

---

🔍 **feel like**

*feel like* can also be used as a verb meaning *want / would like*. It is followed by a noun or a verb in the gerund, e.g., *I **feel like pasta** for lunch today.* (= I'd like pasta for lunch today). *I **don't feel like going** to bed.* (= I don't want to go to bed).

**as**

*as* is often used before *if* to talk about how something appears, sounds, feels, etc.: *It looks as if it's going to snow.* However, it is also used:

- to describe somebody or something's job or function: *She works as a nurse. You can use that box as a chair.*
- to compare people or things: *She's as tall as me now.*
- to give a reason: *As it was raining, we didn't go out.* (*as = because*)
- to say that something happened while something was happening: *As they were leaving, the mail carrier arrived.* (*as = when / at the same time*)
- after *such* to give an example, e.g., *I like berries, such as strawberries and raspberries.*

---

**a** Match the sentence halves.

| | | |
|---|---|---|
| 1 | That group sounds like | F |
| 2 | That boy looks | |
| 3 | Nora looks like | |
| 4 | That guitar sounds | |
| 5 | Tom looks as if | |
| 6 | Our car sounds as if | |
| 7 | Your new cashmere sweater feels | |
| 8 | This apple tastes | |
| 9 | It smells as if | |
| 10 | Your perfume smells like | |
| 11 | This cake tastes as if | |
| 12 | The restaurant seems like | |

A   her mother.
B   a really nice place.
C   very soft.
D   someone has been smoking in here.
E   really sweet.
F   ~~Coldplay.~~
G   too young to be driving a car.
H   it's got coffee in it.
I   roses.
J   it's going to break down any moment.
K   he just ran a marathon.
L   awful! You need to tune it.

**b** Circle the correct form.

Your boyfriend *looks / **looks like*** a basketball player. He's huge!

1 You're so pale! You *look / look as if* you've seen a ghost!
2 What's for dinner? It *smells / smells like* delicious!
3 I think John and Megan have arrived. That *sounds / sounds like* their car.
4 Have you ever tried frogs' legs? I've heard, they *taste like / taste as if* chicken.
5 Are you OK? You *sound / sound as if* you have a cold.
6 Can you turn the heat on? It *feels / feels like* really cold in here.
7 You *seem / seem like* really happy. Does that mean you got the job?
8 Your new bag *feels / feels like* real leather. Is it?
9 Let's throw this milk away. It *tastes / tastes like* a little strange.
10 Can you close the window? It *smells / smells as if* someone is having a barbecue.

← p.70

 **Go online** to review the grammar for each lesson    145

## the passive (all forms); *have something done; it is said that…, he is thought to…,* etc.

### the passive (all forms)

> **1** The trial **is being held** this week. ◉ 8.8
> Jim **was arrested** last month.
> We saw that one of the windows **had been broken**.
> People used **to be imprisoned** for stealing bread.
> He paid a fine to avoid **being sent** to jail.
> **2** People think he **was blackmailed by** his ex-wife.
> The purse **was discovered by** a dog-walker.

**1** We use the passive when we talk about an action but are not so interested in who or what does / did the action.
- To make the tense or form, we use the verb *be* + past participle, e.g., *Murderers are usually sentenced to life in prison. The prisoner will be released next month.* The tense changes are shown by the verb *be*, e.g., *are, will be,* etc.

**2** To mention the person or thing that did the action (the agent), we use *by*. However, in the majority of passive sentences, the agent is not mentioned.

### have something done (causative *have*)

> **1** I just **had** my bank account **hacked**. ◉ 8.9
> We **had** our passports **stolen** from our hotel room.
> **Have** you ever **had** your car **vandalized**?
> **2** We just **had** a burglar alarm **installed**.
> You ought to **have** your locks **changed**.
> We need to **have** the broken window **repaired**.

**1** We can use *have something done* to refer to something (usually bad) that is done to us.
- Remember, *have* is the main verb, so it changes according to the tense. We use auxiliary verbs (*do, did,* etc.) to make questions and negatives.

**2** This structure is also used to talk about something that we arrange (and usually pay) for someone to do for us, because we can't or don't want to do it ourselves.

### is said that…, he is thought to…, etc.

| active | passive ◉ 8.10 |
|---|---|
| **1** They say that the fire was started deliberately. | **It is said that** the fire was started deliberately. |
| People think that the mayor will resign. | **It is thought that** the mayor will resign. |
| **2** People say the man is in his 40s. | **The man is said to be** in his 40s. |
| The police believe he has left the country. | **He is believed to have left** the country. |

- This formal structure is used especially in news reports with the verbs *know, tell, understand, report, expect, say, believe,* and *think.* It makes the information sound more impersonal.

**1** We use *It is said, believed,* etc. + *that* + clause.

**2** We use *He, The man,* etc. (i.e., the subject of the clause) + *is said, believed,* etc. + infinitive (e.g., *to be*) or perfect infinitive (e.g., *to have been*) when talking about the past.

---

**a** Rewrite the sentence in the passive.

> The police caught the burglar immediately.
> *The burglar was caught immediately.*

1 Somebody has stolen my phone.
   My phone…
2 They are painting my house.
   My house…
3 They'll hold a meeting to discuss the problem.
   A meeting…
4 If they hadn't found the burglar in time, he would have left the country.
   If the burglar…
5 Miranda thinks someone was following her last night.
   Miranda thinks she…
6 I hate somebody waking me up when I'm fast asleep.
   I hate…
7 They're going to close the local police station.
   The local police station…

**b** Complete the second sentence using *have something done.*

> I was mugged and my iPhone was stolen.
> *I was mugged and I had my iPhone stolen.*

1 Tim's social media account was hacked.
   Tim…

2 Has someone ever snatched your bag?
   Have you ever…
3 They need to get someone to check the security camera to make sure that it's working.
   They…
4 Someone took our photo in front of the Colosseum.
   We…
5 As a result of the burglary, they're going to pay someone to put in a safe.
   As a result of the burglary, they…

**c** Rephrase the sentence to make it more formal.

> People think the murderer is a woman.
> It *is thought that the murderer is a woman.*
> The murderer *is thought to be a woman.*

1 Police believe the burglar is a local man.
   The burglar…
2 People say the muggers are very dangerous.
   It…
3 Police think the robbers entered through an open window.
   The robbers…
4 Police say the murderer has disappeared.
   It…
5 Lawyers expect that the trial will last three weeks.
   The trial…
   ← p.78

## reporting verbs

### structures after reporting verbs

1 Jack **offered to drive** me to the airport. 🔊 8.12
  I **promise not to tell** anybody.
2 The doctor **advised me to rest**.
  I **persuaded my sister not to go out** with Max.
3 I **apologized for being** so late.
  The police **accused Karl of stealing** the car.

- To report what other people have said, we can use *say* or a specific verb, e.g.,
  *"I'll drive you to the airport."*
  Jack **said** he would drive me to the airport. **OR**
  Jack **offered** to drive me to the airport.
- After specific reporting verbs, there are three different grammatical patterns (1–3 in the chart).
- In negative sentences, we use the negative infinitive (*not to do*) or the negative gerund (*not doing*), e.g., *He reminded me not to be late. She regretted not going to the party.*
- In group 3, we can use a perfect gerund with very little difference in meaning, e.g., *He admitted stealing the money. He admitted having stolen the money.*

### Grammatical patterns after reporting verbs

| | | | |
|---|---|---|---|
| 1 | + infinitive | agree offer refuse promise threaten | (not) to do something |
| 2 | + person + infinitive | advise persuade ask remind convince tell encourage warn invite | somebody (not) to do something |
| 3 | + -*ing* form | apologize (to somebody) for insist on accuse somebody of recommend admit regret blame somebody for suggest deny | (not) doing something |

🔍 **Verbs that use a *that* clause**
With *agree, admit, deny, promise,* and *regret,* you can also use *that* + clause.
*Leo admitted stealing the watch.*
*Leo admitted that he had stolen the watch.*

---

**a** Complete the sentence with the gerund or infinitive of the verb in parentheses.

The auto mechanic advised me *to buy* a new car. (buy)

1 Jamie insisted on _____ for the meal. (pay)
2 Lauren has agreed _____ late next week. (work)
3 I warned Suki _____ through the park at night. (not walk)
4 The man admitted _____ the woman's bag. (steal)
5 The doctor advised Luisa _____ drinking coffee. (give up)
6 The boss persuaded Ji-Su _____ the company. (not leave)
7 Freya accused me of _____ to steal her phone. (try)
8 I apologized to Sofia for _____ her birthday. (not remember)
9 Were you able to convince your parents _____ tonight instead of tomorrow? (come)
10 My neighbor denies _____ my car, but I'm sure it was him. (damage)

**b** Complete the sentence using a reporting verb from the box and the correct form of the verb in parentheses. Use an object where necessary.

accuse   invite   offer   promise   recommend
refuse   remind   suggest   threaten

Diana said to me, "I'll take you to the train station."
Diana *offered to take* me to the train station. (take)

1 Ryan said, "Let's go for a walk. It's a beautiful day."
  Ryan _____ for a walk. (go)
2 "You copied Anna's exam!" the teacher said to Ken.
  The teacher _____ Anna's exam. (copy)
3 Sam's neighbor told him, "I'll call the police if you have another party."
  Sam's neighbor _____ the police if he had another party. (call)
4 The children said, "We aren't going to bed. It's much too early."
  The children _____ to bed. (go)
5 Ramon said to me, "Would you like to have dinner with me?"
  Ramon _____ dinner with him. (have)
6 Molly said to Jack, "Don't forget to call the electrician."
  Molly _____ the electrician. (call)
7 Ricky said, "I'll never do it again."
  Ricky _____ it again. (do)
8 Sarah said, "You really have to try Giacobazzi's. It's a fantastic restaurant."
  Sarah _____ Giacobazzi's. She said it was fantastic. (try)

↩ p.81

 **Go online** to review the grammar for each lesson

## clauses of contrast and purpose

### clauses of contrast

> **1  Although / Though** the ad said it would last 🔊 9.3
> for years, my dishwasher stopped working after two months.
> My dishwasher stopped working after two months,
> **although / though** the ad said it would last for years.
> My dishwasher stopped working again **even though** I'd had
> it repaired the week before.
> My dishwasher has never stopped working. I hardly ever use
> it, **though**.
>
> **2  In spite of / Despite…**
> her age, my mother is still very active.
> being 85, my mother is still very active.
> the fact that she's 85, my mother is still very active.

- We use *although*, *though*, *even though*, and *in spite of* or *despite* to express a contrast.
- **1** *although*, *though* and *even though* are usually used at the beginning or in the middle of a sentence.
- *though* is more informal than *although*.
- *even though* is stronger than *although / though* and is used to express a big or surprising contrast.
- *though* can also be used as an adverb, usually at the end of a sentence, after a comma. In this case, it means *however*.
- **2** After *in spite of* or *despite*, we can use a noun, a verb in the *-ing* form, or *the fact that* + subject + verb.
- Remember <u>not</u> to use *of* after *despite*. **NOT** ~~Despite of the rain,…~~

### clauses of purpose

> | | to | 🔊 9.4 |
> |---|---|---|
> | **1** I went to the bank | **in order to** | talk to the bank manager. |
> | | **so as to** | |
> | **2** I went to the bank **for** a meeting with the bank manager. | | |
> | **3** I went to the bank **so that** I could talk to the manager in person. | | |
> | **4** I wrote down what he said | **so as not to** | forget it. |
> | | **in order not to** | |

- Use *to*, *in order to*, *so as to*, *for*, and *so that* to express purpose.
- **1** After *to*, *in order to*, and *so as to*, use a base form.
- *in order to* and *so as to* are more formal than *to*.
- **2** Use *for* + a noun, e.g., *for a meeting*.
- You can also use *for* + gerund to describe the exact purpose of a thing, e.g., *This liquid is for cleaning metal*.
- **3** After *so that*, use a subject + modal verb (*can, could, would,* etc.).
- When there is a change of subject in a clause of purpose, we use *so that*, e.g., *We bought a new car so that the children would have more space*. **NOT** ~~to / in order to / so as to the children…~~ This is the only way of expressing purpose when there is a change of subject.
- **4** To express a negative purpose, use *so as not to* or *in order not to*, e.g., *I wrote down what he said in order not to forget it*. **NOT** ~~…to not forget it.~~

---

**a**  Complete the sentences with **one** word.

We're very happy in our new house, *though* there's a lot to do.

1. We loved the movie _____ the fact that it was nearly three hours long!
2. Carl doesn't like spending money _____ though he's very rich.
3. They went down to the harbor _____ see if they had fresh fish.
4. I'll make a list so _____ not to forget anything.
5. My mother called the doctor in _____ to make an appointment.
6. The cake tasted good in _____ of not looking like the photo in the recipe book.
7. I turned the heat on high so _____ the house will warm up quickly.
8. I must say that _____ the service was poor, the meal was delicious.
9. I stopped at a roadside diner _____ a quick meal before continuing on my trip.
10. He really isn't very fashionable. He sometimes tries to wear a fun tie to work, _____.

**b**  Rewrite the sentences.

Despite not getting very good reviews, the book sold really well.
Even though *the book didn't get very good reviews, it sold really well.*

1. We took a taxi so as not to arrive late.
   We took a taxi so that…
2. Despite earning a fortune, she drives a very old car.
   Although…
3. Everyone enjoyed the movie even though the ending was sad.
   Everyone enjoyed the movie in spite of…
4. The plane managed to land despite the terrible weather conditions.
   The plane managed to land, even though…
5. I told her I enjoyed the meal she had made me so that I wouldn't offend her.
   I told her I enjoyed the meal she had made me so as…
6. The police closed the roads so as to allow the president's car through safely.
   The police closed the roads in order…

← p.87

## uncountable and plural nouns

### uncountable nouns

> 1 The **weather** is fantastic there, and there's ◀)) 9.12
> very little **traffic**, so you can walk everywhere.
> The **scenery** is beautiful here, but it's spoiled by all the **trash**
> people leave.
> 2 Could you give me **some advice** about where to stay?
> One useful **piece of advice** is to get a metro card.
> 3 The new opera house is made mainly of **glass**.
> Can I have **a glass** of tap water, please?

1 The following nouns are always uncountable: *behavior, health, politics* (and other words ending in *-ics*, e.g., *gymnastics, economics*), *progress, trash, scenery, traffic, weather, work.*

- Uncountable nouns don't have a plural form, and they use a singular verb. **NOT** ~~The sceneries are beautiful here.~~

- Don't use *a / an* with uncountable nouns. **NOT** ~~There's a terrible traffic this evening.~~

2 These nouns are also uncountable: *advice, bread, equipment, furniture, homework, information, luck, luggage, news, research, toast.* With these, you can use *a piece of* to talk about an individual item.

3 Some nouns can be either countable (C) or uncountable (U), but the meaning changes, e.g., *a glass* (C) = the thing you drink out of; *glass* (U) = the material used to make windows. Other examples: *business, iron, light, paper, space, time.*

### plural and collective nouns

> 1 One of the best museums is on **the outskirts** of ◀)) 9.13
> the city.
> My **clothes are** filthy. I'll put on **some clean pants** / I'll put on
> **a pair of clean pants**.
> 2 The hotel **staff is** very efficient.
> The **cabin crew is coming around** with the snack cart in just
> a few minutes.

1 *arms* (= guns, etc.), *belongings, clothes, manners, outskirts, scissors,* and *pants / shorts* are plural nouns with no singular. They need a plural verb, and they can't be used with *a / an*.

- If the word refers to something with two parts, e.g., *scissors, shorts, pants,* etc., it can be used with *a pair of* or *some*.

2 *crew, family, government, staff, team,* etc. are collective singular nouns and refer to a group of people. They need a singular verb.

- *police* is always used with a plural verb.

---

**a** Circle the correct form. Check (✓) if both are correct.

The traffic *is* / *are* awful during rush hour.
1 Gymnastics *is* / *are* my favorite sport.
2 I bought *a pair of* / *some* new jeans.
3 Harvey's clothes *look* / *looks* really expensive.
4 The flight crew *work* / *works* hard to make passengers comfortable.
5 I found out *some* / *a piece of* interesting information at the meeting.
6 Could I have *a paper* / *a piece of paper* to write down the new words?
7 I think I'll have *a* / *some* time after lunch to help you with that report.
8 I have *a* / *some* good news for you about your job application.
9 We've made a lot of *progress* / *progresses* this semester.
10 Hello, Reception? Do you have *an* / *some* iron I could use?

**b** Right (✓) or wrong (✗)? Correct the mistakes in the highlighted phrases.

In our language lab, the equipment is all new. ✓
The news are good. ✗ *The news is*
1 We had a beautiful weather when we were on vacation.
2 They have some comfortable furnitures in their house.
3 My brother gave me a useful piece of advice.
4 Do you have a scissors? I need to wrap this present.
5 My team has won every game this season.
6 I need to buy a new pants for my interview tomorrow.
7 Your glasses are really dirty. Can you see anything?
8 The homeworks were very difficult last night.
9 There isn't any space in my suitcase. Can I put this jacket in yours?
10 The police is sure that they know who was responsible for the vandalism.

← p.91

 **Go online** to review the grammar for each lesson

## quantifiers: *all, every, both*, etc.

### *all, every, most*

> 1 **All** animals need food.  🔊 10.6
> **All** fruit contains sugar.
> **All (of) the** scientists at the conference agree with the theory.
> The animals **all** look sad.   The animals are **all** healthy.
> 2 **Everybody** is here.   **Everything** is very expensive.
> 3 **Most people** live in cities.
> **Most of the people** in this class are women.
> 4 **All of us** work hard and **most of us** come to class every week.
> 5 **Every** room has a bathroom.
> I work **every** Saturday.

1 We use *all* or *all (of) the* + a plural or uncountable noun.
- *all* = in general, *all (of) the* = specific
- *all* can be used before a main verb (and after *be*).

2 We use *everybody / everything* (= all people, all things) + singular verb, e.g., *Everything is very expensive.* **NOT** ~~All is very expensive.~~
- We sometimes use *not* before *everybody / everything*, etc., e.g., *Not everybody likes sunbathing.*

3 We use *most* to say *the majority*; *most* = general, *most of* = more specific.

4 We often use *all / most of* + an object pronoun, e.g., *all of us, most of them, all of you, most of it.*

5 Use *every* + singular countable noun to mean "all of a group."

> 🔍 **every and all + time expressions**
> Note the difference between *every* and *all* + time expressions.
> *every day* = Monday to Sunday
> *all day* = from morning to night

### *no, none, any*

> 1 Is there **any** milk?  Sorry, there's **no** milk. There **isn't any** (milk).  🔊 10.7
> 2 A  Is there **any** food?
> B  No, **none**. / There's **none**. But **none of us** are hungry.
> 3 Come **any** weekend! **Anyone** can come.

1 We use *no* + a noun after a ⊞ verb, or *any* + noun after a ⊟ verb, to refer to zero quantity.

2 We use *none* in short answers, or with a ⊞ verb to refer to zero quantity. We can also use *none + of* + pronoun / noun.

3 We use *any* (and *anything, anyone*, etc.) and a ⊞ verb to mean it doesn't matter what, who, etc.

### *both, neither, either*

> 1 **Both** Pierre **and** Marie Curie were scientists. **Neither** Pierre  🔊 10.8
> **nor** Marie Curie was (were) aware of the dangers of radiation.
> Marie Curie wanted to study **either** physics **or** mathematics.
> In the end, she studied the two subjects.
> 2 She and her husband **both** won Nobel Prizes.
> Pierre and Marie were **both** interested in radium.
> 3 **Both of them** won the Nobel Prize.
> **Neither of them** realized how dangerous radium was.

1 We can use *both...and..., neither...nor...,* and *either...or...* to join two nouns, verbs, or other kinds of expressions.
- Use *both...and...* + nouns to talk about two people / things, etc., when they are the same. The verb is always plural.
- Use *neither...nor* + nouns to refer to two people / things, etc., when you mean not the one and not the other. You can use either a singular or plural verb. *Neither John nor his brother live / lives at home.*
- Use *either...or...* to talk about a choice between two alternatives.

2 When *both* refers to the subject of a clause, it can also be used before a main verb but after *be*.

3 We often use *both / either / neither + of* + object pronoun, e.g., *us, them,* etc., or *+ of the* + noun.

**a** Ⓒircle the correct word or phrase.

We've eaten (all the)/ all cake.
1 *Most of / Most* my family lives near me.
2 *All / Everything* is ready for the party. We're just waiting for the guests to arrive.
3 *Most / Most of* people enjoy the summer here, but for some it's too hot.
4 Gina goes dancing *all / every* Friday night.
5 We don't have *any / no* onions for the soup.
6 *Any / None* of us want to go out tonight. We're all exhausted.
7 *Nobody / Anybody* can go to the festival. It's free.
8 I have two very close friends, but unfortunately *either / neither* of them lives near me.
9 I'd like to have a bigger table, but there's *no / none* room in my kitchen.

**b** Right (✓) or wrong (✗)? Correct the wrong sentences.

Both Mike and Alan passed the exam. ✓
He neither watches the news or reads a newspaper. ✗
*He neither watches the news nor reads a newspaper.*
1 Both the kitchen and the bathroom needs cleaning.
2 The food wasn't cheap nor tasty.
3 I have two children, but neither of them look like me.
4 My sister and I both were late for school.
5 It's or Jane's or Karen's birthday today.
6 Neither the food nor the service in this restaurant is good enough for what they charge.
7 Neither my best friends called to see how I was.
8 We can walk either or take the bus.
9 My parents love horses, and both of them ride every day.
10 We can go on vacation either in July or in August.

↩ p.99

# 10B

## articles

### basic rules: *a / an / the*, no article

1 My neighbor just got **a** dog and **a** cat.  ◀)) 10.12
   **The** dog is **an** Alsatian and **the** cat is **a** Siamese.
   Jack got into **the** car and drove to **the** courthouse.
2 **Children** are often better than **adults** at new technology.
   I don't like **sports** or **classical music**.
3 **Last night** I **came home** late and went straight **to bed**.

1 Use *a* or *an* when you mention somebody or something for the first time or say who or what somebody or something is. Use *the* when it's clear who or what somebody or something is (e.g., it has been mentioned before, or it's unique, i.e., the only one that exists or that you own).
2 Don't use an article to speak in general with plural and uncountable nouns.
3 Don't use an article in phrases like *at home / work, go / come home / to bed, next / last (week)*, etc.

### institutions

My son is in **high school**.  ◀)) 10.13
They're building **a new high school** in my town.
He was sent **to prison** for two years.
My grandmother used to work in **the prison** as a nurse.

- With words like *prison / jail, church, school,* and *college / university*, don't use an article when you are thinking about the institution and the usual purpose it is used for. If you are just thinking about the building, use *a* or *the*.

### more rules: geographical names

1 **South Korea** is in **East Asia**.  ◀)) 10.14
2 **Macy's** is one of the most famous department stores in the **US**.
3 **Lake Maracaibo** and **Lake Titicaca** are both in South America.
4 **The Danube River** flows into **the Black Sea**.
5 **The Metropolitan Museum** is located on **Fifth Avenue** in New York.

- We **don't usually use** *the* with the names of:
1 most countries, continents, and regions ending with the name of a country / continent (e.g., *North America, Southeast Asia*), individual islands, states, provinces, towns, and cities (exceptions: *the US / United States, the UK / United Kingdom, the Netherlands, the Czech Republic*).
2 roads, streets, parks, bridges, stores, and restaurants (exceptions: highways and numbered roads: *the Trans-Canada Highway, the 405*).
3 individual mountains and lakes.
- We **usually use** *the* with the names of:
4 mountain ranges, rivers, oceans, seas, canals, deserts, and island groups.
5 the names of theaters, hotels, galleries, museums, buildings, and monuments.

---

**a** Circle the correct article.

James bought (a) / *the* / (–) new suit last weekend.
1 The weather was awful, so we stayed at *a* / *the* / (–) home.
2 *A* / *The* / (–) washing machine we bought last week has stopped working already.
3 I love reading *a* / *the* / (–) historical novels.
4 Sarah had had an exhausting day, so she went to *a* / *the* / (–) bed early.
5 I saw a man walking with a woman in the park. *A* / *The* / (–) woman was crying.
6 The teachers are on strike, so the children aren't going to *a* / *the* / (–) school.
7 Turn left immediately after *a* / *the* / (–) gas station and go up the hill.
8 My neighbor's in *a* / *the* / (–) prison because he didn't pay his taxes.
9 People are complaining because the town council has refused to build *a* / *the* / (–) new fire station.
10 Visitors are not allowed to enter *a* / *the* / (–) church after 7 p.m.

**b** Complete the sentence with *the* or (–).

They're going to *the* US to visit family.
1 _____ Sicily is the largest island in _____ Mediterranean.
2 Cairo is on _____ Nile River.
3 We didn't have time to visit _____ National Gallery when we were in Washington, D.C.
4 _____ American southwest is famous for its beautiful deserts and canyons.
5 _____ Mount Everest is in _____ Himalayas.
6 The largest inland lake is _____ Caspian Sea.
7 We stayed at _____ Peninsula Hotel while we were in Hong Kong.
8 *Romeo and Juliet* is playing at _____ Globe Theatre.
9 Manila is the capital of _____ Philippines.
10 I've always wanted to visit _____ Argentina.

 p.100

 **Go online** to review the grammar for each lesson

# Illnesses and injuries

## 1 MINOR ILLNESSES AND CONDITIONS

**a** Match the sentences with the pictures.

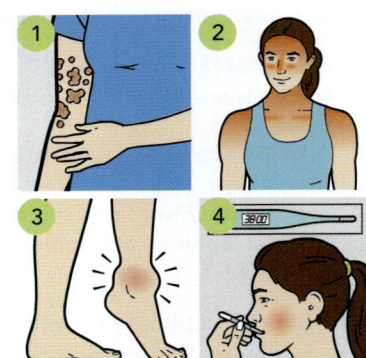

She has / She's got…

☐ a **cough** /kɔf/

☐ a **headache** /ˈhɛdeɪk/ (<u>back</u>ache, <u>ear</u>ache, <u>stom</u>achache, <u>tooth</u>ache)

☐ **1** a **rash** /ræʃ/

☐ a **temperature** /ˈtɛmprətʃər/

☐ **sunburn** /ˈsʌnbərn/

☐ She's **sick**. / She's **vomiting**. /ˈvɑmətɪŋ/.

☐ She's **sneezing**. /ˈsnizɪŋ/

☐ Her **ankle's swollen**. /ˈswoʊlən/

☐ Her back **hurts**. /hɜrts/ / Her back **aches**. /eɪks/

☐ Her **finger's bleeding**. /ˈblidɪŋ/

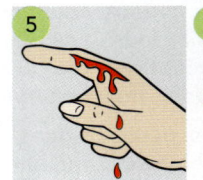

**b** 🔊 **2.1** Listen and check.

**c** Match the illnesses and conditions with their cause or symptoms.

1  **B**  He has **a sore throat**. /sɔr θroʊt/
2  ☐  He has **diarrhea**. /daɪəˈriə/
3  ☐  He **feels sick**. /ˈfilz sɪk/
4  ☐  He's **fainted**. /ˈfeɪntəd/
5  ☐  He has a **blister** on his foot. /ˈblɪstər/
6  ☐  He has **a cold**. /ə ˈkoʊld/
7  ☐  He has **the flu**. /flu/
8  ☐  He feels **dizzy**. /ˈdɪzi/
9  ☐  He's **cut himself**. /ˈkʌt hɪmˈsɛlf/

A  He has a temperature and he aches all over.
B  ~~It hurts when he talks or swallows food.~~
C  It's so hot in the room that he's lost consciousness.
D  He's been to the bathroom five times this morning.
E  He feels like he's going to vomit.
F  He's sneezing a lot and he has a cough.
G  He feels like everything is spinning around.
H  He's been walking in uncomfortable shoes.
I  He's bleeding.

**d** 🔊 **2.2** Listen and check.

## 2 INJURIES AND MORE SERIOUS CONDITIONS

**a** Match the injuries with their causes or symptoms.

1  **C**  He's **unconscious**. /ʌnˈkɑnʃəs/
2  ☐  He's had an **allergic reaction**. /əˈlɜrdʒɪk riˈækʃn/
3  ☐  He's **sprained** his ankle. /spreɪnd/
4  ☐  He has **high** (low) **blood pressure**. /ˈblʌd prɛʃər/
5  ☐  He has **food poisoning**. /ˈfud pɔɪzənɪŋ/
6  ☐  He's **choking**. /ˈtʃoʊkɪŋ/
7  ☐  He's **burned** his hand. /bɜrnd/

A  He spilled some boiling water on himself.
B  He fell badly and now it's swollen.
C  ~~He's breathing, but his eyes are closed and he can't hear or feel anything.~~
D  It's 180 over 140.
E  He ate some chicken that wasn't fully cooked.
F  He was eating a steak and a piece got stuck in his throat.
G  He was stung by a wasp and now he has a rash and has difficulty breathing.

> 🔍 **Common treatments for…**
> **a cut** minor: put a bandage on it and antibiotic ointment, major: get stitches
> **headaches** take <u>pain</u>killers
> **an infection** take anti<u>bio</u>tics
> **a sprained ankle** put ice on it and <u>ban</u>dage it
> **an allergic reaction** take anti<u>his</u>tamine <u>tab</u>lets / pills or apply cream

**b** 🔊 **2.3** Listen and check.

**ACTIVATION** Cover the illnesses, injuries, and conditions in **1a / c** (1–9) and **2a** (1–7). Look at the pictures, or causes and symptoms, and say the sentences.

## 3 PHRASAL VERBS CONNECTED WITH ILLNESS

**a** Match the **bold** phrasal verbs to their meanings.

Please **lie down** on the table. I'm going to examine you.
I'd been standing for such a long time that I **passed out**, and when I **came around** I was lying on the floor.
It often takes a long time to **get over** the flu.
A few minutes after drinking the liquid I had to run to the bathroom to **throw up**.

1  _____ faint
2  _____ put your body in a horizontal position
3  _____ vomit, be sick
4  _____ get better / recover from something
5  _____ become conscious again

**b** 🔊 **2.4** Listen and check.  🔙 p.16

# Clothes and fashion

## 1 DESCRIBING CLOTHES

**a** Match the adjectives and pictures.

**Fit**
- [ ] loose /lus/
- [1] tight /taɪt/

**Style**
- [ ] hooded /ˈhʊdəd/
- [ ] long-sleeved /lɔŋ slivd/ (*also* short-sleeved)
- [ ] sleeveless /ˈslivləs/
- [ ] turtleneck /ˈtərtlˌnɛk/
- [ ] V-neck /ˈvi nɛk/

**Pattern**
- [ ] dotted /ˈdɑtəd/
- [ ] patterned /ˈpætərnd/
- [ ] plaid /plæd/
- [ ] plain /pleɪn/
- [ ] striped /straɪpt/

**b** 🔊 2.17 Listen and check.

**c** Match the phrases and pictures.

**Materials**
- [ ] a cotton undershirt /ˈkɑtn ˈʌndərˌʃərt/
- [ ] a denim vest /ˈdɛnəm vɛst/
- [ ] a fur collar /fər ˈkɑlər/
- [ ] a lace top /leɪs tɑp/
- [1] a linen suit /ˈlɪnən sut/
- [ ] a Lycra swimsuit /ˈlaɪkrə ˈswɪmsut/
- [ ] a silk scarf /sɪlk skɑrf/
- [ ] a velvet bow tie /ˈvɛlvət boʊ taɪ/
- [ ] a wool cardigan /wʊl ˈkɑrdɪgən/
- [ ] leather sandals /ˈlɛðər ˈsændlz/
- [ ] suede boots /sweɪd buts/

**d** 🔊 2.18 Listen and check.

**ACTIVATION** Cover the words and phrases. Look at the photos and describe the items.

## 2 ADJECTIVES TO DESCRIBE CLOTHES AND THE WAY PEOPLE DRESS

**a** Complete the sentences with an adjective.

casual /ˈkæʒuəl/   classic /ˈklæsɪk/
fashionable /ˈfæʃənəbl/   old-fashioned /oʊld ˈfæʃnd/
scruffy /ˈskrʌfi/

1 She always wears _____ clothes to work – she hates dressing formally.
2 He looks really _____. His clothes are old and dirty.
3 Jane looked very _____ in her new suit. She wanted to make a good impression.
4 That tie's a little _____! Is it your dad's?
5 I like wearing _____ clothes that don't go out of fashion.

**b** 🔊 2.19 Listen and check.

**ACTIVATION** Say one item you own for each adjective in the box.

## 3 VERBS AND VERB PHRASES

**a** Match the sentences.
1 [C] I'm going to **dress up** tonight.
2 [ ] Please **hang up** your coat.
3 [ ] These jeans don't **fit** me.
4 [ ] That skirt really **suits** you.
5 [ ] Your bag **matches** your shoes.
6 [ ] I need to **get changed**.
7 [ ] Hurry up and **get undressed**.
8 [ ] Get up and **get dressed**.
9 [ ] That tie doesn't really **go with** your shirt.

A Don't leave it on the chair.
B I just spilled coffee on my shirt.
C I'm going to a party.
D They don't look good together.
E It's bath time.
F They're too small.
G They're almost the same color.
H You look great in it.
I Breakfast is on the table.

**b** 🔊 2.20 Listen and check.

**ACTIVATION** Cover 1–9. Look at A–I and remember the matching sentences.

↩ p.22

 **Go online** to review the vocabulary for each lesson

# Air travel

## 1 AT THE AIRPORT

**a** Match the words and definitions.

| | |
|---|---|
| 1 [A] Airport terminal | 6 ☐ Departures board |
| 2 ☐ Bag(gage) drop | 7 ☐ Gate |
| 3 ☐ Baggage claim | 8 ☐ Runway |
| 4 ☐ Check-in desk | 9 ☐ Security |
| 5 ☐ Customs | 10 ☐ (airline) Lounge |

A a building at an airport divided into Arrivals and Departures

B an electronic display showing **flight times** and if the flight is **on time**, **boarding**, **closed**, or **delayed**

C where you hand in any checked **baggage** (bags, suitcases, etc.) and are given a **boarding pass if you don't already have one**

D where you take your luggage to check it in if you already have your boarding pass

E where they check that you are not trying to take prohibited items (e.g., **liquids** or **sharp objects**) onto the plane, by **scanning** your **carry-on luggage** and making you walk through a metal detector

F where passengers who are traveling **business** or **first class** can wait for their flight

G where you show your boarding pass and ID and **board** your flight

H where planes **take off** and **land**

I where you **collect** your luggage on arrival, and where there are usually **carts** for carrying heavy suitcases

J where your luggage may be **checked** to see if you are bringing **illegal goods** into the country

**b** 🔊 **3.5** Listen and check.

**ACTIVATION** Cover the words and look at the definitions. Say the words.

## 2 ON BOARD

**a** Complete the text with the words in the box.

aisle /aɪl/    cabin crew /ˈkæbən kru/    connecting flight /kəˈnɛktɪŋ flaɪt/
direct flights /dəˈrɛkt flaɪts/    jet lag /ˈdʒɛt læg/
long-haul flights /lɔŋ hɔl ˈflaɪts/    row /roʊ/    seat belts /ˈsit bɛlts/
turbulence /ˈtərbyələns/

I often fly to Chile on business. I always choose an ¹aisle seat, so that I can get up and walk around more easily. My favorite place to sit is the emergency exit ²_____ so I have more legroom. Sometimes there's ³_____ when the plane flies over the Andes, which I don't enjoy, and the ⁴_____ tells the passengers to put their ⁵_____ on.
There aren't any ⁶_____ to Santiago from Calgary, so I usually have to get a ⁷_____ in Toronto. Whenever I take ⁸_____, I always suffer from ⁹_____ because of the time difference and I feel tired for several days.

**b** 🔊 **3.6** Listen and check.

**ACTIVATION** Cover the words in the box. Read the text aloud with the correct words in the blanks.

## 3 *TRAVEL, TRIP, OR JOURNEY?*

**a** Complete the sentences with *travel, trip,* or *journey.*

1 Have a good *trip*! Hope the weather's great!

2 **A** How long was your _____ across China?
   **B** It was about two months long, and it was amazing.

3 Do you have to _____ much for your job?

4 Have a good _____! See you when you get back.

**b** 🔊 **3.7** Listen and check. Which word…?

1 is usually used as a verb

2 just refers to going from one place to another

3 covers going somewhere, staying there, and coming back.

## 4 PHRASAL VERBS RELATED TO AIR TRAVEL

**a** Complete the sentences with a phrasal verb from the box in the past tense.

check in    drop off    fill out    get off
get on    pick up (x2)    take off

1 My husband *dropped* me *off* at the airport two hours before the flight.

2 I _____ _____ online the day before I was going to fly.

3 As soon as I _____ _____ the plane, I put my bag in the overhead compartment.

4 The plane _____ _____ late because of the bad weather.

5 When I _____ _____ my luggage at the baggage claim, I bumped into an old friend who had been on the same flight.

6 I _____ _____ the immigration form for the US, which the cabin crew gave me shortly before landing.

7 When I _____ _____ the plane, I felt exhausted after the long flight.

8 My flight arrived really late at night, but luckily, a friend _____ me _____ at the airport.

**b** 🔊 **3.8** Listen and check.

← p.26

# Adverbs and adverbial phrases

## 1 CONFUSING ADVERBS AND ADVERBIAL PHRASES

**a** Match each pair of adverbs with a pair of sentences. Then decide which adverb goes where and write it in the **Adverbs** column.

- right now / <u>actually</u>
- <u>especially</u> / <u>specially</u>
- ever / <u>even</u>
- **1** hard / <u>hardly</u>
- in the end / at the end
- late / <u>lately</u>
- near / <u>nearly</u>
- still / yet

1 He trains very ▢ – at least three hours a day.
  It's incredibly foggy. I can ▢ see anything.
2 I hate it when people arrive ▢ for meetings.
  I haven't heard from Mike ▢. He must be very busy.
3 ▢ of a movie, I always stay and watch the credits roll.
  I didn't want to go, but ▢ they persuaded me.
4 I love most kinds of music, but ▢ jazz.
  My wedding dress was ▢ made for me by a dressmaker.
5 She looks younger than me, but ▢ she's two years older.
  ▢ they're renting a house, but they're hoping to buy one soon.
6 I'm ▢ finished with my book. I'm on the last chapter.
  Excuse me, is there a bank ▢ here?
7 Have you found a job ▢?
  He's 35, but he ▢ lives with his parents.
8 Have you ▢ been to the US?
  I've been all over the US – I've ▢ been to Alaska!

**Adverbs**

*hard* _____
*hardly* _____
_____
_____
_____
_____
_____
_____
_____
_____
_____
_____
_____
_____
_____
_____

**b** 🔊 **3.16** Listen and check.

**ACTIVATION** Cover the **Adverbs** column and look at sentences 1–8. Say the adverbs.

## 2 COMMENT ADVERBS

**a** Read the sentences. Then match the **bold** adverbs with definitions 1–8.

I thought the job was going to be difficult, but **in fact** it's very easy. /ɪn ˈfækt/

It took us over five hours to get there, but **eventually** we were able to relax. /ɪˈvɛntʃəli/

**Ideally**, we'd go to Australia if we could afford it. /aɪˈdiəli/

**Basically**, it's a pretty simple idea. /ˈbeɪsɪkli/

I thought they'd broken up, but **apparently**, they're back together again. /əˈpɛrəntli/

…so you can tell it was a really awful weekend. **Anyway**, let's forget about it and talk about something else. /ˈɛniˌweɪ/

He's only 14, so **obviously** he can't stay at home on his own. /ˈɑbviəsli/

She's been sick for weeks, but **gradually** she's beginning to feel better. /ˈɡrædʒuəli/

1 _____ in a perfect world
2 *in fact* the truth is; actually (used to emphasize something, especially the opposite of what was previously said)
3 _____ in the main and most important way
4 _____ clearly (used to give information you expect other people to know or agree with)
5 _____ little by little
6 _____ according to what you have heard or read
7 _____ in any case (used to change or finish a conversation)
8 _____ in the end; after a series of events or difficulties

**b** 🔊 **3.17** Listen and check.

**ACTIVATION** Cover the definitions and look at the sentences. Say what the adverbs mean.

 **p.31**

# Weather

## 1 WHAT'S THE WEATHER LIKE?

**a** Put the words or phrases in the correct place in the chart.

below zero /bɪˈloʊ ˈzɪroʊ/   boiling /ˈbɔɪlɪŋ/   breeze /briz/   chilly /ˈtʃɪli/   cool /kul/   damp /dæmp/   drizzling /ˈdrɪzlɪŋ/
freezing /ˈfrizɪŋ/   humid /ˈhyuməd/   mild /maɪld/   pouring /ˈpɔrɪŋ/   (rain)   showers /ˈʃaʊərz/   warm /wɔrm/

|  | 5 It's _____. (pleasant and not cold) | 8 It's _____. (warm and wet but not raining) |  |
|---|---|---|---|
| 1 It's _cool_. (a little cold) | 6 It's _____. (a pleasantly high temperature) | 9 It's _____. (cold and slightly wet) | |
| 2 It's _____. (unpleasantly cold) | | 10 It's _____. (raining lightly) | 13 There's a _____. (a light wind) |
| **It's cold.** ❄ | **It's hot.** ☀ | **It's raining / wet.** 💧 | **It's windy.** 💨 |
| 3 It's _____. (very cold) | 7 It's _____ / It's scorching. (unpleasantly hot) | 11 There are _____. (raining intermittently) | |
| 4 It's _____. (−10°) | | 12 It's _____. (raining a lot) | |

**b** Complete the sentences with *fog*, *mist*, and *smog*.

When the weather's foggy or misty, or there's _smog_, it is difficult to see.
1 _____ isn't usually very thick, and often occurs in the mountains or near the ocean.
2 _____ is thicker, and can be found in towns and in the country.
3 _____ is caused by pollution and usually occurs in big cities.

**c** ◑ 4.3 Listen and check **a** and **b**.

## 2 EXTREME WEATHER

**a** Match the words and definitions.

blizzard /ˈblɪzərd/   drought /draʊt/   flood /flʌd/
hail /heɪl/   heat wave /ˈhit weɪv/   hurricane /ˈhərəkeɪn/
lightning /ˈlaɪtnɪŋ/   monsoon /mɑnˈsun/   thunder /ˈθʌndər/

1 _heat wave_ (*noun*) a period of unusually hot weather
2 _____ (*noun*) a long, usually hot, dry period when there is little or no rain
3 _____ (*noun and verb*) small balls of ice that fall like rain
4 _____ (*noun*) a flash of very bright light in the sky caused by electricity
5 _____ (*noun and verb*) the loud noise that you hear during a storm
6 _____ (*noun*) a snow storm with very strong winds
7 _____ (*verb and noun*) when everything becomes covered with water
8 _____ (*noun*) a violent storm with very strong winds (also *cyclone*, *tornado*, *typhoon*)
9 _____ (*noun*) the season when it rains a lot in southern Asia

**b** ◑ 4.4 Listen and check.

**ACTIVATION** Cover the weather words and look at the definitions. Say the weather words.

## 3 ADJECTIVES TO DESCRIBE WEATHER

**a** Complete the weather forecast with these adjectives.

bright /braɪt/   changeable /ˈtʃeɪndʒəbl/   clear /klɪr/
heavy /ˈhevi/   icy /ˈaɪsi/
settled /ˈsetld/ (= not likely to change)
strong /strɔŋ/   sunny /ˈsʌni/   thick /θɪk/

In the western part of New York it will be very cold, with ¹_strong_ winds and ²_____ rain. There will also be ³_____ fog in the hills and valleys, though it should clear by midday. Driving will be dangerous because the roads will be ⁴_____. However, the Hudson Valley and the Tri-state area will have ⁵_____ skies and it will be ⁶_____ and sunny, though the temperature will still be low. Over the next few days the weather will be ⁷_____, with some showers, but occasional ⁸_____ periods. It should become more ⁹_____ over the weekend.

**b** ◑ 4.5 Listen and check.

**ACTIVATION** What kind of weather do you associate with the different seasons where you live?

← p.38

# Feelings

## 1 ADJECTIVES

**a** Match the feelings and the situations.

1 *B* "I feel really **miserable**." /ˈmɪzrəbl/
2 *F* "I feel a little **homesick**." /ˈhoʊmsɪk/
3 ☐ "I'm a little **disappointed**." /dɪsəˈpɔɪntəd/
4 ☐ "I'm very **lonely**." /ˈloʊnli/

5 ☐ "I'm incredibly **proud**." /praʊd/
6 ☐ "I'm really **fed up**." /fɛd ˈʌp/
7 ☐ "I'm very **grateful**." /ˈɡreɪtfl/
8 ☐ "I'm very **upset**." /ʌpˈsɛt/
9 ☐ "I'm so **relieved**." /rɪˈlivd/
10 ☐ "I'm very **offended**." /əˈfɛndəd/

A You discover that your beloved dog has disappeared.
B ~~You've been stuck at home all weekend and it's been raining.~~
C A stranger gives you a lot of help with a problem.
D You are abroad and you think someone has stolen your passport, but then you find it.
E You don't get a job you were hoping to get.
F ~~You go to study abroad and you're missing your family and friends.~~
G You move to a new town and don't have any friends.
H You've been doing the same job for a long time and it's really boring.
I Someone in your family wins an important prize.
J A friend doesn't invite you to his wedding.

**b** 🔊 **5.4** Listen and check.

## 2 STRONG ADJECTIVES

**a** Match the strong adjectives describing feelings with their definitions.

| | | |
|---|---|---|
| astonished /əˈstɑnɪʃt/ | bewildered /bɪˈwɪldrd/ | delighted /dɪˈlaɪtəd/ |
| desperate /ˈdɛspərət/ | devastated /ˈdɛvəsteɪtəd/ | horrified /ˈhɔrəfaɪd/ |
| overwhelmed /oʊvərˈwɛlmd/ | stunned /stʌnd/ | thrilled /θrɪld/ |

1 *stunned* — very surprised and unable to move or react
2 _____ extremely upset
3 _____ very happy and excited
4 _____ incredibly happy
5 _____ (SYN *amazed*) very surprised
6 _____ with little hope, and ready to do anything to improve the situation
7 _____ feeling such strong emotions that you don't know how to react
8 _____ extremely confused
9 _____ extremely shocked or disgusted

**b** 🔊 **5.5** Listen and check.

**ACTIVATION** Make true sentences for five of the adjectives in **1a** and **2a**.

## 3 INFORMAL OR SLANG WORDS AND EXPRESSIONS

**a** Look at the <mark>highlighted</mark> words and phrases and try to figure out their meaning.

1 *B* I was <mark>scared stiff</mark> when I heard the bedroom door opening. /skɛrd ˈstɪf/
2 ☐ You look a little <mark>down</mark>. What's the problem? /daʊn/
3 ☐ I'm absolutely <mark>worn out</mark>. I want to relax and put my feet up. /wɔrn aʊt/
4 ☐ When I saw her, <mark>I couldn't believe my eyes</mark>. She looked ten years younger.
5 ☐ I'm <mark>sick and tired of</mark> listening to you complain about your job.
6 ☐ He finally passed his driver's test. He's <mark>jumping for joy</mark>!

**b** Match the words and phrases in **a** to the feelings.

A sad or depressed
B ~~terrified~~
C extremely happy
D exhausted
E fed up or irritated
F astonished

**c** 🔊 **5.6** Listen and check.

**ACTIVATION** Cover the sentences in **a**. Look at the feelings in **b**. Remember the informal words and expressions.

🔙 p.47

🔄 **Go online** to review the vocabulary for each lesson

# Verbs often confused

**a** Complete the **verbs** column with the correct verb in the right form.

| | verbs |
|---|---|
| **argue / discuss** | |
| 1 I need to ___ the problem with my boss. | _____ (= talk about something) |
| 2 I often ___ with my parents about doing housework. | _____ (= speak angrily to somebody) |
| **notice / realize** | |
| 3 I didn't ___ you were so unhappy. | _____ (= understand fully, become aware of something) |
| 4 I didn't ___ that Karen had changed her hair color. | _____ (= see, observe) |
| **avoid / prevent** | |
| 5 Jack always tries to ___ arguing with me. | _____ (= try not to do something) |
| 6 My dad can't ___ me from seeing my friends. | _____ (= stop) |
| **lend / borrow** | |
| 7 When are you going to pay me back the $50 that I ___ you? | _____ (= give something to somebody that you want them to give back) |
| 8 Could I ___ your car tonight? I know you're not using it. | _____ (= ask for something that you intend to give back) |
| **mind / matter** | |
| 9 My parents don't ___ if I stay out late. | _____ (= have a problem / feel strongly) |
| 10 It doesn't ___ if we're five minutes late. | _____ (= be a problem) |
| **remember / remind** | |
| 11 Can you ___ me to call my mom later? | _____ (= help somebody to remember) |
| 12 ___ to turn off the lights before you go. | _____ (= not forget) |
| **expect / wait** | |
| 13 I ___ that Daniel will forget our anniversary. He always does. | _____ (= think that something will happen) |
| 14 We'll have to ___ half an hour for the next train. | _____ (= stay where you are until something happens) |
| **wish / hope** | |
| 15 I ___ I was a little taller! | _____ (= want something to be true, even if it is unlikely or impossible) |
| 16 I ___ that you can come. I haven't seen you in a long time. | _____ (= want something to happen) |
| **beat / win** | |
| 17 The Dallas Cowboys ___ the game 28-10. | _____ (= be successful in a competition) |
| 18 The Dallas Cowboys ___ the New York Jets 28-10. | _____ (= defeat somebody) |
| **refuse / deny** | |
| 19 Tom always ___ to discuss the problem. | _____ (= say you don't want to do something) |
| 20 Tom always ___ that he has a problem. | _____ (= say that something isn't true) |
| **raise / rise** | |
| 21 The cost of living is going to ___ again this month. | _____ (= go up) |
| 22 It's hard not to ___ your voice when you're arguing. | _____ (= make something go up) |
| **lay** (past *laid*) / **lie** (past *lay*) | |
| 23 Go and ___ on the bed if you're tired. | _____ (= put your body in a horizontal position) |
| 24 I usually ___ my baby on the bed to change his diaper. | _____ (= put something or somebody in a horizontal position) |
| **steal / rob** | |
| 25 The men had been planning to ___ the bank. | _____ (= take something from a person or place by threat or force) |
| 26 If you leave your bike unlocked, somebody might ___ it. | _____ (= take money or property that isn't yours) |
| **advise / warn** | |
| 27 I think I should ___ you that Liam doesn't always tell the truth. | _____ (= tell somebody that something unpleasant is likely to happen) |
| 28 My teachers are going to ___ me on what to study next year. | _____ (= tell somebody what you think they should do) |

**b** 🔊 **7.9** Listen and check.     **ACTIVATION** Cover the verbs column. Say the sentences with the correct verbs.

⟵ p.68

# The body

## 1 PARTS OF THE BODY AND ORGANS

**a** Match the words and pictures.

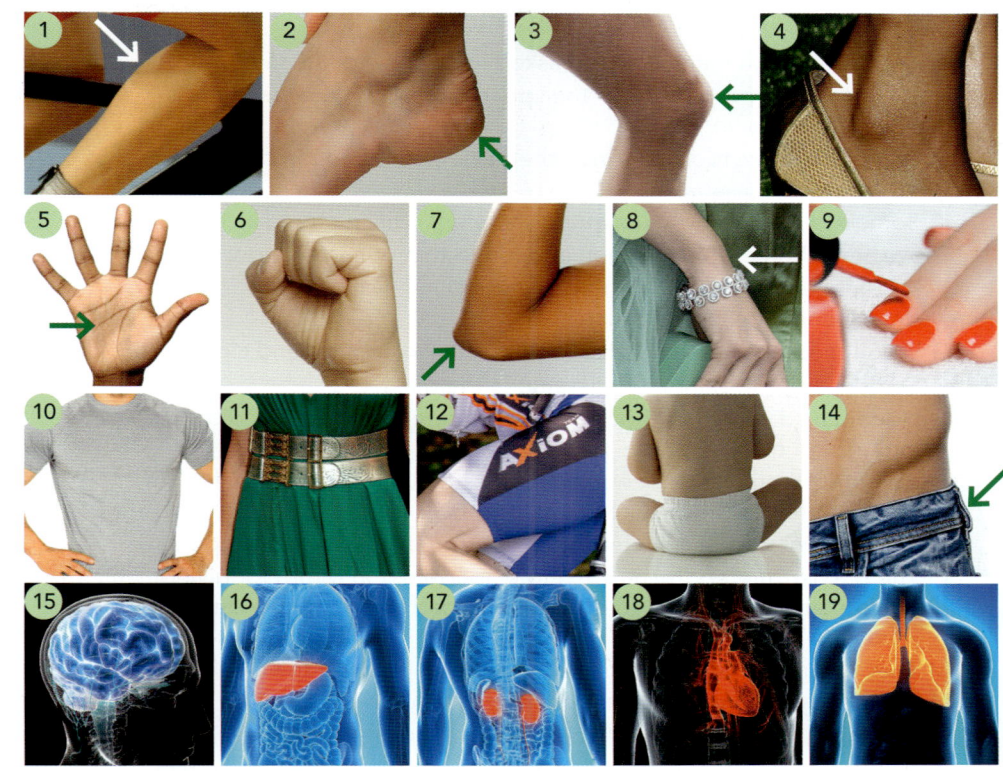

- ankle /'æŋkl/
- *1* calf /kæf/ (pl calves)
- heel /hil/
- knee /ni/

- elbow /'ɛlboʊ/
- fist /fɪst/
- nails /neɪlz/
- palm /pɑm/
- wrist /rɪst/

- bottom /'bɑtəm/
- chest /tʃɛst/
- hip /hɪp/
- thigh /θaɪ/
- waist /weɪst/

- brain /breɪn/
- heart /hɑrt/
- kidneys /'kɪdniz/
- liver /'lɪvər/
- lungs /lʌŋz/

**b** ◉ **7.16** Listen and check.

**ACTIVATION** Cover the words. Look at the pictures and say the words.

## 2 VERBS AND VERB PHRASES

**a** Complete the verb phrases with the parts of the body.

arms   eyebrows   hair (x2)   hand   hands
head   nails   nose   shoulders   teeth
thumb   toes

1. **bite** your *nails* /baɪt/
2. **blow** your _____ /bloʊ/
3. **brush** your _____ / **brush** your _____ /brʌʃ/
4. **comb** your _____ /koʊm/
5. **fold** your _____ /foʊld/
6. **hold** somebody's _____ /hoʊld/
7. **touch** your _____ /tʌtʃ/
8. **suck** your _____ /sʌk/
9. **shake** _____ / **shake** your _____ /ʃeɪk/
10. **shrug** your _____ /ʃrʌg/
11. **raise** your _____ /reɪz/

**b** ◉ **7.17** Listen and check.

**c** Read the sentences. Write the part of the body related to the **bold** verb.

1. He **winked** /wɪŋkt/ at me to show that he was only joking. *eye*
2. The steak was tough and difficult to **chew** /tʃu/. _____
3. When we met, we were so happy, we **hugged** /hʌgd/ each other. _____
4. Don't **scratch** /skrætʃ/ the mosquito bite. You'll only make it worse. _____
5. He **waved** /weɪvd/ goodbye sadly to his girlfriend as the train left the station. _____
6. Some women think a man should **kneel** /nil/ down when he proposes marriage. _____
7. The teacher **frowned** /fraʊnd/ when she saw all the mistakes I had made. _____
8. The painting was so strange, I **stared** /stɛrd/ at it for a long time. _____
9. She got out of bed, and **yawned** /yɔnd/ and **stretched** /strɛtʃt/. _____ / _____
10. If you don't know the word for something, just **point** /pɔɪnt/ at what you want. _____

**d** ◉ **7.18** Listen and check.

**ACTIVATION** In pairs, **A** say a verb phrase to **B**. **B** do the action.

 p.72

Ⓖ **Go online** to review the vocabulary for each lesson

159

# Crime and punishment

## 1 CRIMES AND CRIMINALS

a Match the examples to the crimes in the chart.

A ~~They took a rich man's son and asked for money for his safe return.~~
B He deliberately drove above the speed limit and caused a fatal accident.
C Two passengers took control of the plane and made the pilot land in the desert.
D Someone copied my handwriting and signed my name to a check.
E We came home from vacation and found that our TV was gone.
F A teenager got into the Pentagon's computer system and downloaded some secret data.
G When the police searched his car, it was full of contraband cigarettes.
H Someone threw paint on the statue in the park.
I He said he'd send the photos to a newspaper if the actress didn't pay him a lot of money.
J An armed man in a mask walked into a store and shouted, "Give me all the money in the cash register!"
K The accountant was transferring money into his own bank account.
L The builder offered the mayor a free apartment in return for giving his company permission to build a new apartment building on some wetlands.
M They committed a violent crime to cause fear among the civilians.
N Somebody stole my car last night from outside my house.
O A man held out a knife and made me give him my wallet.
P A woman followed a pop singer everywhere he went, watching him and sending him constant messages on the internet.

| | | Crime | Criminal | Verb |
|---|---|---|---|---|
| 1 | | blackmail /'blækmeɪl/ | blackmailer | blackmail |
| 2 | | bribery /'braɪbəri/ | – | bribe |
| 3 | | burglary /'bərgləri/ | burglar | break in / burglarize |
| 4 | | forgery /'fɔrdʒəri/ | forger | forge |
| 5 | | fraud /frɔd/ | fraudster | commit fraud |
| 6 | | hacking /'hækɪŋ/ | hacker | hack (into) |
| 7 | | hijacking /'haɪdʒækɪŋ/ | hijacker | hijack |
| 8 | A | kidnapping /'kɪdnæpɪŋ/ | kidnapper | kidnap |
| 9 | | mugging /'mʌgɪŋ/ | mugger | mug |
| 10 | | murder /'mərdər/ | murderer | murder |
| 11 | | robbery /'rɑbəri/ | robber | rob |
| 12 | | smuggling /'smʌglɪŋ/ | smuggler | smuggle |
| 13 | | stalking /'stɔkɪŋ/ | stalker | stalk |
| 14 | | terrorism /'tɛrərɪzəm/ | terrorist | use violent actions, etc. |
| 15 | | theft /θɛft/ | thief | steal |
| 16 | | vandalism /'vændlɪzəm/ | vandal | vandalize |

b ◆ 8.3 Listen and check.

**ACTIVATION** Cover the chart and look at situations A–P. Say the crimes.

## 2 WHAT HAPPENS TO A CRIMINAL

a Complete the sentences with the words in the box.

**The crime**

arrested /ə'rɛstɪd/   caught /kɔt/
charged /tʃɑrdʒd/   ~~committed~~ /kə'mɪtɪd/
investigated /ɪn'vɛstəgeɪtɪd/
questioned /'kwɛstʃənd/

1 Carl and Adam *committed* a crime. They robbed a large supermarket.
2 The police _____ the crime.
3 Carl and Adam were _____ driving to the airport in a stolen car.
4 They were _____ and taken to a police station.
5 The police _____ them for ten hours.
6 Finally, they were _____ with (= officially accused of) armed robbery.

**The trial**

accused /ə'kyuzd/   acquitted /ə'kwɪtɪd/
court /kɔt/   evidence /'ɛvədəns/
guilty (opposite innocent) /'gɪlti/
judge /dʒʌdʒ/   jury /'dʒʊri/
proof /pruf/   punishment /'pʌnɪʃmənt/
sentenced /'sɛntənst/   verdict /'vərdɪkt/
witnesses /'wɪtnəsɪz/

7 Two months later, Carl and Adam appeared in _____.
8 They were _____ of **armed robbery** and car theft.
9 _____ told the court what they had seen or knew.
10 The _____ (of 12 people) looked at and heard all the _____.
11 After two days, the jury reached their _____.
12 There was no _____ that Adam had committed the crime.
13 He was _____ and allowed to go free.
14 Carl was found _____. His **fingerprints** were on the gun used in the robbery.
15 The _____ decided what Carl's _____ should be.
16 He _____ him to ten years in **prison (jail)**.

b ◆ 8.4 Listen and check. ◔ p.77

# The media

## 1 THE LANGUAGE OF HEADLINES

> 🔍 **The language of headlines**
> Newspaper headlines, especially in tabloids*, often use short snappy words. These words use up less space and are more emotive, which helps to sell newspapers.
>
> *newspapers with smaller pages that print short articles with lots of photos, often about famous people*

**a** Match the highlighted "headline verbs" with their meaning.

| 1 | **President backs senator in latest scandal** |
| 2 | **Thousands of jobs axed by US companies** |
| 3 | **Stock market hit by oil fears** |
| 4 | **Astronaut bids to be first man on Mars** |
| 5 | **POLITICIANS CLASH OVER NEW CAR TAX PROPOSAL** |
| 6 | **Tennis star vows to avenge defeat** |
| 7 | **Police quiz witness in murder trial** |
| 8 | **Famous actress in restaurant bill spat** |

A  have been cut
B  question, interrogate
C  is going to attempt
D  supports
E  disagree
F  has been badly affected
G  argument
H  promises

**b** ▶ 8.16 Listen and check.

**ACTIVATION** Cover A–H. Look at 1–8 and say the meanings.

## 2 JOURNALISTS AND PEOPLE IN THE MEDIA

**a** Match the words and definitions.

advice columnist /əd'vaɪs 'kɑləmnɪst/   critic /'krɪtɪk/   editor /'ɛdətər/
freelance journalist /'friːlæns 'dʒɜrnəlɪst/   host /hoʊst/
newscaster /'nuzkæstər/   paparazzi (pl) /pɑpə'rɑtsi/
reporter /rɪ'pɔrtər/   sports commentator /spɔrts 'kɑmənteɪtər/

1  *critic*_____ a person who writes (a review) about the good / bad qualities of books, concerts, theater, movies, etc.
2  _____ a person who describes a sports event while it's happening on TV or radio
3  _____ a person who collects and reports news for newspapers, radio, or TV
4  _____ a person who is in charge of a newspaper or magazine, or part of one, and who decides what should be in it
5  _____ a person who introduces a television or radio show, and talks to guests
6  _____ a person who writes articles for different papers and is not employed by any one paper
7  _____ a person who reads the news on TV or radio
8  _____ photographers who follow famous people around to get photos of them to sell to newspapers and magazines
9  _____ a person who writes in a newspaper or magazine giving advice to people in reply to their letters

**b** ▶ 8.17 Listen and check.

**ACTIVATION** Are there any people in the media in your country that you really like or really dislike?

## 3 ADJECTIVES TO DESCRIBE THE MEDIA

**a** Match the sentences.
1  The reporting in the paper was very **sensational**. /sɛn'seɪʃənl/
2  The news on Channel 12 is really **biased**. /'baɪəst/
3  I think *The New York Times* is the most **objective** of the Sunday papers. /əb'dʒɛktɪv/
4  The movie review was very **accurate**. /'ækyərət/
5  I think the report was **censored**. /'sɛnsərd/

A  It said the plot was poor but the acting good, which was true.
B  It bases its stories just on facts, not on feelings or beliefs.
C  The newspaper wasn't allowed to publish all the details.
D  It made the story seem more shocking than it really was.
E  You can't believe anything you hear on it. It's obvious what political party they support!

**b** ▶ 8.18 Listen and check.

**ACTIVATION** Name publications you know that are sensational, biased, or objective.

← p.82

🔄 **Go online** to review the vocabulary for each lesson

# Business

## 1 VERBS AND EXPRESSIONS

**a** Complete the sentences with a verb from the box in the correct form (simple present, simple past, or past participle).

become   close down   drop   grow   expand   export   import
launch   manufacture   market   merge   produce   set up   take over

1 Apple products are easy to _market_ because people are immediately attracted to the stylish designs.
2 In 1989, Pepsi-Cola _____ **a new product** called *Pepsi A.M.*, which was aimed at the "breakfast cola drinker." It was an immediate **flop**.
3 The Spanish airline Iberia _____ with British Airways in 2011 and became one of the world's biggest airline groups.
4 Although GAP stands for Genuine American Product, most of its clothes are _____ in Asia.
5 Prosciutto is a kind of Italian ham. Two of the best-known kinds are San Daniele and Parma, which are _____ in the Friuli and Emilia regions of Italy, and are _____ all over the world.
6 When General Mills _____ Blue Buffalo (a gourmet pet food maker), the smaller company became part of the larger organization.
7 The supermarket chain Tesco _____ **the market leader** in 1995, and is still the UK's biggest-selling **chain**.
8 The first Zara store was opened in La Coruña in Spain in 1975, where its **head office** still is today. The company started to _____ into new markets in 1988, and it now has **branches** in 96 countries.
9 Many banks are now offering loans to people who want to _____ a new **small business**.
10 The cost of living in Iceland is so high because so many food products have to be _____.
11 During **a boom** period, the economy _____ quickly and living standards improve.
12 During **a recession**, many companies _____ and living standards _____.

**b** 🔊 **9.5** Listen and check. What do the bold words mean?

**c** *Do* or *make*? Put the phrases in the correct column.

business (with)   a deal (= business agreement)   a decision
an investment   a job   a loss (opposite *profit*)
market research   money   well / badly

| do | make |
|---|---|
| business (with) | |
| | |
| | |

**d** 🔊 **9.6** Listen and check.

**ACTIVATION** Cover the columns in **c**. Say the phrases in the box with *do* or *make*.

## 2 IDIOMS WITH *BUSINESS*

> 🔍 **business**
> *business* is an uncountable noun when it means trade, work, etc., e.g., *do business* **NOT** ~~do a business~~. It is only countable when it means a company, store, or factory, e.g., *I'm going to set up a business.*

**a** Match the idioms with *business* to their meanings A–H.

1 ☐ I think we've been through everything on today's agenda. Now, is there any other business?
2 ☐ Now that so many people book their vacations and travel online, many travel agencies have gone out of business.
3 ☐ Let's get down to business right away – we'll take a break in an hour or so.
4 ☐ She looks very determined – like a woman who means business.
5 ☐ **A** What are you doing?
   **B** I'm sorry, but it's none of your business.
6 ☐ **A** Is he your new boyfriend?'
   **B** Mind your own business!
7 ☐ He arranged to meet his ex-business partner because they had some unfinished business.
8 ☐ Why are you taking your tennis racket on a work trip? It's never a good idea to mix business with pleasure.

A important things that still need to be discussed or dealt with
B (informal) it's not something that concerns you
C start dealing with the matter that needs to be dealt with, or doing the work that needs to be done
D closed down because there is no more money or work
E (informal) have serious intentions
F things that are discussed at the end of an official meeting
G try to do something enjoyable when you also need to work
H (informal) think about your own affairs and don't get involved in other people's lives

**b** 🔊 **9.7** Listen and check.

**ACTIVATION** Cover the idioms and look at the definitions. Say the idioms. ➔ p.89

# Word building

## 1 PREFIXES AND SUFFIXES THAT ADD MEANING

**a** Match the **bold** prefixes in sentences 1–11 to their meanings A–K.

1  G  Mumbai is a very **over**crowded city.
2  ☐  Tokyo was one of the first **mega**cities.
3  ☐  This part of the city is very poor and **under**developed.
4  ☐  London is a very **multi**cultural city, with many different races and religions.
5  ☐  The quickest way to get around New York is on the **sub**way.
6  ☐  Many people in Montreal are **bi**lingual – they speak English and French.
7  ☐  If you want to avoid the traffic jams in Bangkok, take the **mono**rail.
8  ☐  The **auto**pilot was turned on after the plane had taken off.
9  ☐  Vandalism, especially breaking public property, is very **anti**social behavior.
10 ☐  I **mis**understood the directions and now I'm completely lost.
11 ☐  He's earning a **post**graduate degree in aeronautical engineering.

A  against
B  many
C  big
D  not enough
E  one
F  by (it)self
G  ~~too much~~
H  two
I  after
J  under
K  wrongly

**b**  🔊 **9.14**  Listen and check.

**c**  Match the **bold** suffixes to their meaning.

1  ☐  There are a lot of home**less** people in this city. / The situation is hope**less**.
2  ☐  Be care**ful** how you drive! / The instructions were very use**ful**.
3  ☐  The police usually wear bullet**proof** vests. / My watch is water**proof**.
4  ☐  Their new laptops are completely unbreak**able**. / I don't think the tap water here is drink**able**.

A  with
B  can be done
C  resistant to
D  without

**d**  🔊 **9.15**  Listen and check.

**ACTIVATION** Cover sentences 1–11 in **a**. Look at meanings A–K and say the prefixes.

## 2 NOUNS FORMED WITH SUFFIXES

> 🔍 **Common noun suffixes**
> **For nouns made from verbs:**
> **-ion / -(a)tion**  po<u>ll</u>ute – po<u>ll</u>ution; ex<u>p</u>ect – ex<u>pect</u>ation
> **-ment**  de<u>v</u>elop – de<u>v</u>elopment
> **For nouns made from adjectives:**
> **-ness**  cold – <u>cold</u>ness
> **-ence / -ance**  conven<u>i</u>ent – co<u>n</u>venience; a<u>b</u>undant – a<u>b</u>undance
> **For abstract nouns made from nouns or adjectives:**
> **-hood**  <u>neigh</u>bor – <u>neigh</u>borhood
> **-ism**  <u>modern</u> – <u>modern</u>ism

**a** Complete the chart with nouns from the words in the box.

| absent | brother | child | distant | employ | entertain | excite |
| friendly | govern | ignorant | improve | intend | lonely | race |
| reduce | ugly | vandal | violent | weak |

| -ion / -(a)tion | -ment | -ness | -ence / -ance | -ism | -hood |
|---|---|---|---|---|---|
|  |  |  |  |  |  |

**b**  🔊 **9.16**  Listen and check.

**ACTIVATION** Cover the chart and look at the words in the box. Say them with the correct suffix.

## 3 NOUNS THAT ARE DIFFERENT WORDS

> 🔍 **Noun formation with spelling or word change**
> Some nouns made from verbs or adjectives are completely different words, e.g., *choose – choice, poor – <u>poverty</u>*.

**a** Write the verb or adjective for the following **nouns**.

| | | Noun |
|---|---|---|
| 1 | _____ (verb) | loss /lɔs/ |
| 2 | _____ (verb) | death /dɛθ/ |
| 3 | _____ (verb) | su<u>cc</u>ess /sək'sɛs/ |
| 4 | _____ (verb) | thought /θɔt/ |
| 5 | _____ (verb) | belie<u>f</u> /bɪ'lif/ |
| 6 | _____ (adj.) | heat /hit/ |
| 7 | _____ (adj.) | strength /strɛŋkθ/ |
| 8 | _____ (adj.) | <u>hunger</u> /'hʌŋɡər/ |
| 9 | _____ (adj.) | height /haɪt/ |
| 10 | _____ (adj.) | width /wɪdθ/ |

**b**  🔊 **9.17**  Listen and check.

**ACTIVATION** Cover the **noun** column. Look at the verbs and adjectives and say the nouns.

🔶 p.93

 **Go online** to review the vocabulary for each lesson

163

# Appendix

## VERB PATTERNS: verbs followed by the gerund, infinitive, or base form

### Gerund

| | |
|---|---|
| admit | In court the accused admitted (to) stealing the documents. |
| avoid | I always try to avoid driving during rush hour. |
| be worth | It isn't worth going to the exhibition. It's really boring. |
| can't help | We can't help laughing when my dad tries to speak French. His accent is awful! |
| can't stand | I can't stand talking to people who only talk about themselves. |
| deny | Miriam denied killing her husband, but the jury didn't believe her. |
| enjoy | I used to enjoy flying, but now I don't. |
| feel like | I don't feel like going out tonight. |
| finish | Have you finished writing the report yet? |
| give up* | Karen has given up eating meat, but she still eats fish. |
| imagine | I can't imagine living in the country. I think I would get bored after a week. |
| involve | My girlfriend's job involves traveling at least once a month. |
| keep (on) | I keep (on) telling my husband to lose some weight, but he just won't listen. |
| look forward to | We are really looking forward to seeing you again. |
| mind | I don't mind doing housework. I find it very relaxing. |
| miss | Does your mother miss working now that she has retired? |
| postpone | We'll have to postpone going to the beach until the weather warms up. |
| practice | The more you practice speaking English the more fluent you'll get. |
| recommend | I recommend taking a bus tour because it's the best way to see Manhattan. |
| regret | I regret not traveling more before I got my first job. |
| risk | If I were you, I wouldn't risk walking through the park at night. |
| spend | I spent a half an hour looking for my glasses this morning. |
| stop | Once I open a bag of chips, I can't stop eating them. |
| suggest | A friend of mine suggested visiting Washington, D.C. in the spring. |

\* All phrasal verbs which are followed by another verb, e.g., *give up*, etc., are followed by the gerund.

### Infinitive

| | |
|---|---|
| afford | I can't afford to go on vacation this summer. |
| agree | I agreed to pay David back the money he lent me by next week. |
| appear | The results appear to support the scientist's theory. |
| arrange | I arranged to meet Sofia outside the restaurant. |
| be able | I won't be able to work for two weeks after the operation. |
| can't wait | We can't wait to see your new house – it sounds great. |
| choose | I chose to study abroad for a year, and it's the best thing I've ever done. |
| decide | They've decided to call off the wedding. |
| deserve | Kim deserves to get the job. She's a very strong candidate. |
| expect | We're expecting to get our test scores on Friday. |
| happen | Tom happened to be at Alan's when I called, so I invited him to our party, too. |
| help* | The organization I work for helps young people to find work abroad. |
| hesitate | Don't hesitate to ask a staff member if you need anything. |
| hope | I'm hoping to set up my own company if I can get a bank loan. |
| learn | I wish I had learned to play the guitar when I was younger. |
| make | This car was made to perform well on wet roads. |
| manage | Did you manage to get to the airport in time? |
| offer | Lucy has offered to give me a ride to the train station. |
| plan | We're planning to have a big party to celebrate. |
| pretend | I pretended to be enthusiastic, but really I didn't like the idea at all. |
| promise | Sarah always promises to help me in the kitchen, but she never does. |
| refuse | My neighbor refused to turn down the music, and I had to call the police. |
| seem | Something seems to be wrong with the washing machine. |
| teach | Jack's father taught him to drive when he was 17. |
| tend | My boss tends to lose her temper when she's feeling stressed. |
| threaten | The teacher threatened to call my parents and tell them what I had done. |
| want | The police want to interview anyone who witnessed the crime. |
| would like | Would you like to try the dress on? The changing rooms are over there. |

\* *help* can be followed by the infinitive or the base form.
The organization I work for helps young people (to) find work abroad.

### Base form

| | |
|---|---|
| can | Can you help me carry these suitcases? |
| had better | You'd better leave now if you want to catch that train. |
| let | Let me pay for coffee – it's my turn. |
| make | Monica makes her two teenagers do the dishes every evening after dinner. |
| may | There's a lot of traffic today, so we may be a little late. |
| might | It might rain tomorrow, so please bring an umbrella or a raincoat. |
| must | I must remember to set the burglar alarm before I leave work. |
| should | Should we book a table for tomorrow night? It's a very popular restaurant. |
| would rather | You look tired. Would you rather stay home tonight and watch TV? |

p.143

# Irregular verbs

| Infinitive | Past simple | Past participle |
| --- | --- | --- |
| be /bi/ | was/were /wʌz/ /wər/ | been /bin/ |
| beat /bit/ | beat | beaten /'bitn/ |
| become /bɪ'kʌm/ | became /bɪ'keɪm/ | become |
| begin /bɪ'gɪn/ | began /bɪ'gæn/ | begun /bɪ'gʌn/ |
| bite /baɪt/ | bit /bɪt/ | bitten /'bɪtn/ |
| break /breɪk/ | broke /broʊk/ | broken /'broʊkən/ |
| bring /brɪŋ/ | brought /brɔt/ | brought |
| build /bɪld/ | built /bɪlt/ | built |
| burn /bərn/ | burned /bərnd/ (burnt) /bərnt/ | burned (burnt) |
| buy /baɪ/ | bought /bɔt/ | bought |
| can /kæn/ | could /kʊd/ | – |
| catch /kætʃ/ | caught /kɔt/ | caught |
| choose /tʃuz/ | chose /tʃoʊz/ | chosen /'tʃoʊzn/ |
| come /kʌm/ | came /keɪm/ | come |
| cost /kɔst/ | cost | cost |
| cut /kʌt/ | cut | cut |
| deal /dil/ | dealt /dɛlt/ | dealt |
| do /du/ | did /dɪd/ | done /dʌn/ |
| draw /drɔ/ | drew /dru/ | drawn /drɔn/ |
| dream /drim/ | dreamed /drimd/ (dreamt) /drɛmt/ | dreamed (dreamt) |
| drink /drɪŋk/ | drank /dræŋk/ | drunk /drʌŋk/ |
| drive /draɪv/ | drove /droʊv/ | driven /'drɪvn/ |
| eat /it/ | ate /eɪt/ | eaten /'itn/ |
| fall /fɔl/ | fell /fɛl/ | fallen /'fɔlən/ |
| feel /fil/ | felt /fɛlt/ | felt |
| find /faɪnd/ | found /faʊnd/ | found |
| fly /flaɪ/ | flew /flu/ | flown /floʊn/ |
| forget /fər'gɛt/ | forgot /fər'gɑt/ | forgotten /fər'gɑtn/ |
| get /gɛt/ | got /gɑt/ | gotten /'gɑtn/ |
| give /gɪv/ | gave /geɪv/ | given /'gɪvn/ |
| go /goʊ/ | went /wɛnt/ | gone /gɔn/ |
| grow /groʊ/ | grew /gru/ | grown /groʊn/ |
| hang /hæŋ/ | hung /hʌŋ/ | hung |
| have /hæv/ | had /hæd/ | had |
| hear /hɪr/ | heard /hərd/ | heard |
| hit /hɪt/ | hit | hit |
| hurt /hərt/ | hurt | hurt |
| keep /kip/ | kept /kɛpt/ | kept |
| kneel /nil/ | knelt /nɛlt/ | knelt |
| know /noʊ/ | knew /nu/ | known /noʊn/ |
| lay /leɪ/ | laid /leɪd/ | laid |
| learn /lərn/ | learned /lərnd/ | learned |

| Infinitive | Past simple | Past participle |
| --- | --- | --- |
| leave /liv/ | left /lɛft/ | left |
| lend /lɛnd/ | lent /lɛnt/ | lent |
| let /lɛt/ | let | let |
| lie /laɪ/ | lay /leɪ/ | lain /leɪn/ |
| lose /luz/ | lost /lɔst/ | lost |
| make /meɪk/ | made /meɪd/ | made |
| mean /min/ | meant /mɛnt/ | meant |
| meet /mit/ | met /mɛt/ | met |
| pay /peɪ/ | paid /peɪd/ | paid |
| put /pʊt/ | put | put |
| read /rid/ | read /rɛd/ | read /rɛd/ |
| ride /raɪd/ | rode /roʊd/ | ridden /'rɪdn/ |
| ring /rɪŋ/ | rang /ræŋ/ | rung /rʌŋ/ |
| rise /raɪz/ | rose /roʊz/ | risen /'rɪzn/ |
| run /rʌn/ | ran /ræn/ | run |
| say /seɪ/ | said /sɛd/ | said |
| see /si/ | saw /sɔ/ | seen /sin/ |
| sell /sɛl/ | sold /soʊld/ | sold |
| send /sɛnd/ | sent /sɛnt/ | sent |
| set /sɛt/ | set | set |
| shake /ʃeɪk/ | shook /ʃʊk/ | shaken /'ʃeɪkən/ |
| shine /ʃaɪn/ | shone /ʃoʊn/ | shone |
| shut /ʃʌt/ | shut | shut |
| sing /sɪŋ/ | sang /sæŋ/ | sung /sʌŋ/ |
| sit /sɪt/ | sat /sæt/ | sat |
| sleep /slip/ | slept /slɛpt/ | slept |
| speak /spik/ | spoke /spoʊk/ | spoken /'spoʊkən/ |
| spend /spɛnd/ | spent /spɛnt/ | spent |
| stand /stænd/ | stood /stʊd/ | stood |
| steal /stil/ | stole /stoʊl/ | stolen /'stoʊlən/ |
| swell /swɛl/ | swelled /swɛld/ | swelled swollen /'swoʊlen/ |
| swim /swɪm/ | swam /swæm/ | swum /swʌm/ |
| take /teɪk/ | took /tʊk/ | taken /'teɪkən/ |
| teach /titʃ/ | taught /tɔt/ | taught |
| tell /tɛl/ | told /toʊld/ | told |
| think /θɪŋk/ | thought /θɔt/ | thought |
| throw /θroʊ/ | threw /θru/ | thrown /θroʊn/ |
| understand /ʌndər'stænd/ | understood /ʌndər'stʊd/ | understood |
| wake /weɪk/ | woke /woʊk/ | woken /'woʊkən/ |
| wear /wɛr/ | wore /wɔr/ | worn /wɔrn/ |
| win /wɪn/ | won /wʌn/ | won |
| write /raɪt/ | wrote /roʊt/ | written /'rɪtn/ |

# Vowel sounds

| | | usual spelling | | ! but also |
|---|---|---|---|---|
| | tree | ee | bleed sneeze | people thief |
| | | ea | beat steal | key relieved |
| | | e | even medium | receipt |
| | fish | i | linen silk | pretty women |
| | | | trip fit | guilty decided |
| | | | fill pick | village physics |
| | ear | eer | career | seriously zero |
| | | | volunteer | weird |
| | | ere | here we're | |
| | | ear | nearly clear | |
| | cat | a | pack campus | |
| | | | active cash | |
| | | | balance stand | |
| | egg | e | denim dress | friendly leather |
| | | | trendy belt | deaf threaten |
| | | | ever yet | anybody said |
| | chair | air | airport stairs | their there |
| | | | fair hair | wear |
| | | are | scared stare | area |
| | clock | o | cotton top | watch want |
| | | | drop shot | calm |
| | | | cottage off | |
| | saw | a | bald wall | thought caught |
| | | aw | yawn draw | exhausted |
| | | al | stalker talk | launch |
| | horse | (o)or | sore floor | warm course |
| | | | outdoor | board |
| | | ore | bore score | |
| | boot | oo | loose cool | suit recruit |
| | | u* | argue refuse | shoe prove |
| | | ew | chew news | through |

* especially before consonant + e

| | | usual spelling | | ! but also |
|---|---|---|---|---|
| | bull | u | full put | could should |
| | | oo | hooded | would woman |
| | | | woolen | |
| | | | stood good | |
| | tourist | | A very unusual sound. | |
| | | | jury sure plural | |
| | up | u | cut scruffy | money someone |
| | | | lungs | enough touch |
| | | | stunned | flood blood |
| | | | upset discuss | |
| | computer | | Many different spellings. /ə/ is always | |
| | | | unstressed. | |
| | | | collar patterned advise complain | |
| | | | information sandals | |
| | bird | er | verdict prefer | research worker |
| | | ir | dirty skirt | worth worse |
| | | ur | hurt burn | journey |
| | owl | ou | hour mouth | drought |
| | | | proud around | |
| | | ow | showers frown | |
| | phone | o* | choke chose | throw elbow |
| | | | froze fold | below although |
| | | oa | toast | shoulders |
| | | | approach | |
| | car | ar | scarf smart | heart |
| | | | sharp hardly | |
| | train | a* | ache lace | break steak |
| | | ai | faint plain | great weight |
| | | ay | may lay | suede obey |
| | boy | oi | boiling avoid | |
| | | | point noise | |
| | | oy | enjoy | |
| | | | employer | |
| | bike | i* | striped ice | buy eyes |
| | | y | Lycra stylish | height aisle |
| | | igh | tight flight | |

☐ vowels   ☐ vowels followed by /r/   ☐ diphthongs

# Consonant sounds

| | | usual spelling | ! but also |
|---|---|---|---|
| parrot | p<br>pp | postpone polluted<br>hope damp<br>disappointed<br>kidnapping | |
| bag | b<br>bb | brain bribe<br>objective biased<br>robbery hobby | |
| key | c<br>k<br>ck | court critic<br>kidneys shake<br>shocked homesick | choir orchestra<br>stomachache<br>question<br>expect accuse |
| girl | g<br>gg | regret grateful<br>colleague forget<br>hugged mugging | |
| flower | f<br>ph<br>ff | fist theft<br>physicist symphony<br>offended staff | enough laugh<br>tough |
| vase | v | velvet vandalism<br>nervous prevent<br>evidence review | of |
| tie | t<br>tt | taste tend<br>stand chest<br>matter bottom | produced<br>passed |
| dog | d<br>dd | deny murder<br>editor confident<br>addictive suddenly | failed bored |
| snake | s<br>ss<br>ce/ci | stops sick<br>witness loss<br>notice censored | science<br>scenery<br>fancy |
| zebra | z<br>zz<br>s | breeze freezing<br>dizzy blizzard<br>nose raise spends<br>agrees | |
| shower | sh<br>ti (+ vowel)<br>ci (+ vowel) | shrug brush wish<br>clash<br>ambitious<br>sensational<br>special<br>sociable | sugar sure<br>chic |
| television | An unusual sound.<br>decision conclusion usually genre | | |

| | | usual spelling | ! but also |
|---|---|---|---|
| thumb | th | thunder thick<br>healthy thigh<br>death teeth | |
| mother | th | the that with<br>further rather | |
| chess | ch<br>tch<br>t (+ure) | change chilly<br>scratch stretch<br>departure<br>temperature | |
| jazz | j<br>g<br>dge | jet-lag hijack<br>generous<br>manager<br>knowledge judge | |
| leg | l<br>ll | lie liver<br>heel lonely<br>colleague pillow | |
| right | r<br>rr | rise ride<br>risky pretend<br>terrorism<br>arrested | written<br>wrong |
| witch | w<br>wh | win waste<br>waist wave<br>while wherever | one once |
| yacht | y<br>before u | yet year<br>youth yourself<br>university argue | |
| monkey | m<br>mm | mild remind<br>seem remember<br>commit<br>commentator | comb |
| nose | n<br>nn | nails honest<br>announce<br>beginning | kneel<br>knew |
| singer | ng<br>before g/k | length<br>belongings<br>hang bring<br>wink sink | |
| house | h | humid hail<br>behavior inhabit<br>inherit perhaps | who<br>whose<br>whole |

☐ voiced ☐ unvoiced

Go online to watch the Sound Bank videos

# OXFORD
## UNIVERSITY PRESS

198 Madison Avenue
New York, NY 10016 USA

Great Clarendon Street, Oxford, ox2 6dp,
United Kingdom

Oxford University Press is a department of the
University of Oxford. It furthers the University's
objective of excellence in research, scholarship,
and education by publishing worldwide. Oxford is a
registered trade mark of Oxford University Press in the
UK and in certain other countries

© Oxford University Press 2021

The moral rights of the author have been asserted

First published in 2021

2025  2024  2023

10 9 8 7 6

| isbn: 978 0 19 490685 2 | Student Book with Online Practice Pack |
| isbn: 978 0 19 490686 9 | Student Book Component |
| isbn: 978 0 19 490684 5 | Student Online Practice |

Printed in China

This book is printed on paper from certified and
well-managed sources

### ACKNOWLEDGMENTS

*The authors would like to thank all the teachers and students around the world whose feedback has helped us to shape American English File.*

*The authors would also like to thank:* all those at Oxford University Press (both in Oxford and around the world) and the design team who have contributed their skills and ideas to producing this course.

*Finally very special thanks from Clive to Maria Angeles, Lucia, and Eric, and from Christina to Cristina, for all their support and encouragement. Christina would also like to thank her children Joaquin, Marco, and Krysia for their constant inspiration.*

*The publisher and authors would also like to thank the following for their invaluable feedback on the materials:* Zahra Bilides, Paz Alonso, Vanessa Ferroni, Dagmara Lata, Sandy Millin, Sarah Giles, Jane Hudson, Yolana Calpe, Rosa María Iglesias Traviesas, Michale Jarvis, Pedro Irazabel Brian Brennan, Robert Anderson, Magdalena Muszyńska, Gyula Kiss, Juliana Stucker, Elif Barbaros, Kenny McDonnell

*The publisher and authors are very grateful to the following who have provided information, personal stories, and/or photographs:* Alex, Ali, Dominic, Ghislaine, Heidi, Jane, Jeanie, Jo, Krysia, Peter, Tom, Richard Hall p.28, Mike Bench p.39, Sophie Rees p.43, Ali Brookes pp.46–47, Brennan Wenck-Reilly p.57, John Sloboda p.60, Thomas Ormerod p.73, Anya Edwards p.102, Jeff Neil pp.14–15, Marion Pomeranc pp.34–35, Candida Brady pp.54–55, Simon Callow pp.74–75, George Tannenbaum pp.94–95, and The Conversation participants: Debbie Bird, Sarah Baetens, Alice Dillon, Ida Berglöw Kenneway, David Poole, Emma Forward, Simon Warren, Joanne Bowlt, Syinat Tagaeva, Mark Boulle, John Bowlt and Devika Pandit

*The authors and publisher are grateful to those who have given permission to reproduce the following extracts and adaptations of copyright material including Noé Colle's teacher who challenged him to write his short story.*
p.6 Adapted from "The Q&A interview: Simone Biles" by Rosanna Greenstreet which first appeared in the "Weekend Guardian". Reproduced by permission. p.7 Adapted from "The Q&A interview: Dan Stevens" by Rosanna Greenstreet which first appeared in the "Weekend Guardian". Reproduced by permission. p.8 Adapted from "Would YOU get the job? The 20 toughest interview questions…" by Stephanie Linning, MailOnline. Reproduced by permission of Solo Syndication. p.9 Adapted from "Top 10 weird job interview questions" by Aimee Picchi, CBS News. Reproduced by permission. p.10 Adapted from "Victorian ghost buster is vindicated at last" by Ben Mcintyre, The Times, 1 January 2016. Reproduced by permission. p.10 Adapted from "7 Ships That Disappeared Without a Trace" by Claire Cock-Starkey, 5 August 2016, www.metalfloss.com. Reproduced by permission. TBC p.16 Adapted from "Sorting Fact from Fiction: 15 Common First Aid Myths", KG Safety Services. Reproduced by permission. p.19 Adapted from "Confessions of a cyberchondriac" by Anita Chaudhuri, The Sunday

Times, 26 April 2009, © News UK/News Licensing. Reproduced by permission. p.20 Adapted from "'She feels like family to me': when age is no barrier to friendship" by Deborah Linton, www.theguardian.com, 9 June 2018. Copyright Guardian News & Media Ltd 2019. Reproduced by permission. p.22 Adapted words from "How to make one piece of clothing work for all ages" by Emily Cronin, Stella, 4th September 2016. © Telegraph Media Group Limited 2016. Reproduced by permission. p.25 Adapted from "Nasa astronaut returns from space younger than him" by Oliver Moody, The Times, 3 February 2017. © News UK/News Licensing. Reproduced by permission. p.26 Adapted from "Revealed: The secret to securing the perfect plane" by Gavin Haines, 6 November 2017, © Telegraph Media Group Limited 2017. Reproduced by permission. p.28 Adapted from "Passengers alarmed after bat flies through Spirit Airlines plane: 'I'll never fly Spirit again'" by Mahira Dayal, 6 August 2019, www.yahoo.com/lifestyle/. Reproduced by permission. p.30 50 words from "Departed" by Connell Wayne Regner, © Connell Wayne Regner. Reproduced by permission. p.30 Adapted from "Alone" by Verity Park from https://fiftywordstories.com. Reproduced by permission of the author. p.30 Adapted from "Paper Tiger" by Katya Duft, https://fiftywordstories.com. Reproduced by permission. p.31 Adapted from "Fond of Hard Rock" by Noe Colle from https://fiftywordstories.com. Reproduced by permission. p.36 Adapted from "Are you as environmentally friendly as you think? Personality quiz" by Ben Ambridge, www.guardian.com, 14 May 2017. Copyright Guardian News & Media Ltd 2019. Reproduced by permission. p.38 Adapted from "Climate Stories Project" http://www.climatestoriesproject.org, copyright Climate Stories Project 2019. Reproduced by permission. p.42 Adapted from "Why are deadly extreme sports more popular than ever?" by Leo Benedictus, www.guardian.com, 20 August 2016. Copyright Guardian News & Media Ltd 2019. Reproduced by permission. p.45 Adapted from "Travels' biggest bang: 10 incredible volcanoes that are great to climb" by Amy Horsfield, www.wanderlust.co.uk, 17 February 2017. Reproduced by permission. p.52 Adapted from "What is your biggest regret? Here are people's devastatingly honest answers" by Emma Freud, www.theguardian.com, 31 October 2017. Copyright Guardian News & Media Ltd 2019. Reproduced by permission. p.57 Adapted text and photo from "Segmented Sleep" by Brennan Wenck-Reilly, www.brennanwenck.com. Reproduced by permission of the author. p.59 Adapted from "The expert's rules for a great night's sleep" by Anna Maxted, The Times 21 July 2018, © News UK/News Licensing. Reproduced by permission. p.62 Adapted from "Why you should listen to music while you work" by Mike Wright, 7th September 2017. © Telegraph Media Group Limited 2017. Reproduced by permission. p.62 Adapted from "The surgeon's cut: what do doctors listen to in the operating theatre?" by Homa Khaleeli, www.guardian.com, 5 August 2015. Copyright Guardian News & Media Ltd 2019. Reproduced by permission. p.65 Adapted from "The Power of Music for Sleep and Performance" by Dr. Michael Breus, www.thesleepdoctor.com. Reproduced by permission. p.69 Adapted from "How to win any argument using science" by Victoria Woollaston, MailOnline. Reproduced by permission of Solo Syndication. p.73 Adapted from "The best way to spot a liar… or is it?" by Professor Thomas Ormerod, © Thomas Ormerod. Reproduced by permission of the author. p.76 Extract from "Stay Safe" from www.met.police.uk. Reproduced by Courtesy of the Mayor's Office of Policing and Crime. p.78 Adapted from "The 15 Unluckiest Dumb Criminals Ever" by Andy Simmons and Priscilla Torres, originally published in Readers Digest, www.rd.com. Copyright © 2018 by Trusted Media Brands, Inc. Used by permission. All rights reserved. p.79 Adapted from "Man shocked to learn his identity has been stolen to con women" by Rosie Hopegood, www.themirror.co.uk, 1 April 2018. Reproduced by permission of Mirrorpix. p.83 Adapted from "10 tips on how to spot fake news" by Rob Waugh, The Telegraph, 7 May 2019. Reproduced by permission of the author. p.86 Adapted from "18 false advertising scandals that cost some brands millions" by Julien Rath. Copyrighted 2017. Business Insider. 2105571:0719p. Reproduced by permission of Wrights Media acting on behalf of Business Insider Magazine. p.88 Adapted text and cover image from *Fifty Things that Made the Modern Economy* by Tim Harford, Copyright © 2017 Tim Harford, Little, Brown Book Company Limited. Reproduced by permission. p.90 Adapted from "What makes a city attractive?" by Francesca Perry, www.guardian.com, 10 February 2015. Copyright Francesca Perry/Guardian News & Media Ltd 2019. Reproduced by permission. p.92 Adapted text and photos "Sleepy in Songdo, Korea's smartest city" by Linda Poon, 22 June 2018, © 2018 CityLab, a division of The Atlantic Media Group LLC. All rights reserved. Distributed by Tribune Content Agency. p.96 Adapted from "Quiz: Can you answer the simple science questions parents struggle to answer" by Mark Molloy, 3rd May 2016. © Telegraph Media Group Limited 2016. Reproduced by permission. p.98 Adapted from "Science Fact or Fiction? The Plausibility of 10 Sci-fi Concepts" by Adam Hadhazy, www.livescience.com, 20 September 2013. Reproduced by permission. p.101 Adapted from "From Martin Luther King to Churchill and Obama: the 10 best speeches - ever", Philip Collins, The Times, 25 September 2017, © News UK/News Licensing. Reproduced by permission. p.105 Adapted from "The Voice of Reason" by John Shammas, www.thesun.co.uk, 14 March 2018 © The Sun/News Licensing. Reproduced by permission. p.107 Adapted from "Air France passengers describe mid-air terror as engine disintegrates over Atlantic" by David Chazan, 30 September 2017 © Telegraph Media Group Limited 2017. Reproduced by permission.
*Sources:* www.businessinsider.com; XX. *The Necklace* by Guy de Maupassant.

*Although every effort has been made to trace and contact copyright holders before publication, this has not been possible in some cases. We apologize for any apparent infringement of copyright and if notified, the publisher will be pleased to rectify any errors or omissions at the earliest opportunity.*

*Illustrations by* Peter Bull pp 26, 38, 107, 112; Petros Bouloubasis/ Advocate Art p 96; Canary Pete p 8; Stephen Collins p 116; Sam Dedel/Lemonade Illustration p 76; DILBERT © 2000 Scott Adams. Used By permission of Andrews McMeel Syndication. All rights reserved p102; Isla Fletcher p 66 (handwriting); John Haslam pp 132, 133, 135, 136, 137, 141, 142, 144, 155, 157; Matthew Hollings/ Illustrationweb pp 118, 153; Peter Hudspith pp 30, 31; Joe McLaren pp 68–69; Willie Ryan/Illustrationweb pp 16, 152; Garry Walton/ Meiklejohn Illustration pp 32–33, 46–47

*Commissioned photography by* Gareth Boden p 153 (suit, waistcoat, swimsuit); MM Studios pp 19 (mug), 22 (cardigan), 88 (Playstation, Nespresso, HP printer, Gillette razor), 89 (razors); Oxford University Press video stills pp 15, 23 (Huit jeans), 25 (headshots), 35 (the Conversation), 43 (Grace Doyle), 45 (headshots), 54 (Candida Brady), 55 (the Conversation), 63 (Isata Kanneh-Mason), 65 (headshots), 74 (Simon Callow), 75 (the Conversation), 83, 85 (headshots), 94 (George Tannenbaum), 105 (headshots).

*Pronunciation chart artwork by* Ellis Nadler

*We would also like to thank the following for permission to reproduce the following photographs:* Cover: Hobbit/Shutterstock. 123RF pp 19 (woman/ocusfocus), 66 (Cathy Yeulet); Advertising Archives pp 86

(Red Bull), 87 (Olay); Alamy pp 6 (Simone Biles/Aflo Co. Ltd.), (Biles/Erich Schlegel), 7 (Downton Abbey/PictureLux/The Hollywood Archive), 10 (Flannan Island/Ian Cowe), 21 (family portrait/Ashok Tholpady), 25 (astronauts/NASA), 28 (pilot/Hero Images Inc.) (Spirit airlines/Markus Mainka), 34 (Black Beauty/CBW), (Nancy Drew/AztecBlue), (Twilight/CBW), 42 (paragliding/Hemis), (wingsuit flying/Oliver Furrer), 45 (Mount Misti/Pep Roig), (Mount Ngauruhoe/robertharding), 48 (jaguar/Avalon/Bruce Coleman Inc), 49 (footprint/Mode Images), (paddling canoe/Jacques Jangoux), 54 (Trashed/Everett Collection Inc), 70 (Keira Knightley/AF archive), (Meryl Streep/Landmark Media), (Eddie Redmayne/Allstar Picture Library/Warner Bros/AF archive), (Frances McDormand/Focus Features/PictureLux / The Hollywood Archive), (Daniel Kaluuya/Warner Bros/Moviestore collection Ltd), 86 (Activia/Keith Homan), 91 (1/Matthias Scholz), (2/Pulsar Imagens), (3/Ceri Breeze), (5/J Marshall - Tribaleye Images), 94 (Boss/jeremy sutton-hibbert), 98 (speed of light/Quality Stock), (invisibility Harry Potter/ITAR-TASS News Agency), (invisibility cloisters/Francisco Martinez), 99 (Neptune/Irina Dmitrienko), 100 (Neil Armstrong/NASA Archive), 101 (Elizabeth I/IanDagnall Computing), (Emmeline Pankhurst/Granger Historical Picture Archive), (Winston Churchill/David Cole), (John F Kennedy/Pictorial Press Ltd), 117 (Eddie Gerald), 121 (NY Diner/Randy Duchaine), 153 (scarf/Valery Voennyy), 159 (calf/Simon Balson), (knee/Fitness People by Vision); British Newspaper Archive p 10 (newspaper Northants Evening Telegraph, 27/12/1900); Courtesy of Steve Bustin p 79; Captainbijou.com p 94 (MOM Brands/Farina cereal), 159 (thigh/Paul Doyle); Sarah Bench p.39 (Mike Bench); Stewart Cohen/stewartcohen.com p 73 (security officer); Courtesy of Anya Edwards p 102; Corbis p 159 (bottom/Markus Moellenberg); Getty Images pp 7 (portrait/Matthias Clamer), 29 (birth on plane/Anadolu Agency), (baggage claim/Peter Cade), 40–41 (AFP), 42 (bungee jumping/Image taken by Mayte Torres), 49 (plane Amazon aerial/Photodisc), 50 (woman/Klubovy), 53 (man/Tetra Images), (woman/Klaus Vedfelt), 72 (upsidedowndog), 74 (rehearsal/Digital Vision), 80 (ramen noodles/George), 82 (Chris Graythen), 86 (VW car/Ramin Talaie), 95 (Nike/Prashanth Vishwanathan/Bloomberg via Getty Images), (Apple/Gilles Mingasson/Liaison), 101 (Abraham Lincoln/Archive Photos), (Martin Luther King/Francis Miller/The LIFE Picture Collection), (Nelson Mandela/Pool Bouvet/De Keerle/Gamma-Rapho), (Barack Obama/Alfredo Estrella), 105 (Stephen Hawking/Bruno Vincent), 113 (jasmine/Vincenzo Lombardo), 119 (family at home/Hans Neleman), (cinema/PhotoAlto Agency RF Collections), 120 (baseball player/Yeatts), 121 (NYC gastropub/Lonely Planet), 153 (sandals/Trish Gant), 159 (ankle/FilmMagic), (fist/JazzIRT), (wrist/George Pimentel/WireImage), (waist/MJ Kim); The Guardian/ Eyevine pp 20 (Dilys and Sian/Thomas Butler), 21 (Dave and John/ Thomas Butler), 91 (4/Martin Creed), 107 (Thomas Butler), 111 (Thomas Butler); iStockphoto pp 48 (raft/TheSilverFox), 58 (yawning/icon river), 98 (intelligent machines/Abidal), 121 (NYC pizza/wdstock), 153 (bow tie/Maddrat), 159 (hip/John Sommer); Little, Brown Book Group Limited p 88 *Fifty Things that made the Modern Economy*, by Tim Harford, 2017; Mary Evans Picture Library p 10 (map from *The Sphere*, 19th January 1901); Courtesy Barack Obama Presidential Library p 103; Courtesy of Professor Thomas Ormerod p 73; Reproduced by permission of Oxford University Press p 48 green texture behind Jungle text; p 60 cover image of *Handbook of Music and Emotion*, Edited by Patrik N. Juslin and John Sloboda, 2011; Oxford University Press pp 14, (Jeff Neil), 34 (Marion Pomeranc), (The Hand-Me-Down Horse), 35 (e-book reader), 113 (kitten and vinegar); OUP\Shutterstock p 60 (guitar neck/AlexMaster), (cello bow/Yuriyfx), 61 (guitar/AlexMaster), (saxophone/AGCuesta), (cello/Yuriyfx), (flute/cowardlion); Courtesy of Lynne Parker p 102; Courtesy of Sophie Rees p 43; Mahmud Sahran p 80 ('zebra'); By kind permission of San Antonio Aquarium & Austin Aquarium p 80 (shark theft); Cover image of *Northern Lights* Text Copyright © Philip Pullman 1995, Cover Design by Crush Design, 2011 Reproduced by permission of Scholastic Ltd. All rights reserved; Science Photo Library p 159 (brain/ heart/ kidneys/ liver/ lungs/all Sciepro); Shutterstock Editorial 74 (Old Vic/Alisdair Macdonalds), (Amadeus/Graham Wiltshire), (Four Weddings and a Funeral/Zophrus/Channel 4/Working Title/Kobal), 75 (Daniel Day Lewis/Miramax/Dimension Films/Kobal), (Laurence Olivier/Romulus Films/Park Circus); Shutterstock pp 10 (sky/SeaSandSun), 12 (dugdax), 14 (holding pen/leolintag), (oak tree/S Mercer), (cactus/JoMo333), (apple tree/Mazzzur), 18 (Suteren), 22 (slippers/cretolamna), (mini-skirt/Tarzhanova), (shorts/inchic), (T-shirt/Artem Avetisyan), (jeans/Eyes wide), (blazer and chinos/everytime), 23 (shirt/East), 26 (Khairil Azhar Junos), 29 (car lost/Yalcin Sonat), (broken window/Adalet Semsovic), 34 (If I Ran the Circus/Julie Clopper) 36 (namtipStudio), 37 (fossil fuel/Macrovector), (recycling symbol/picoStudio), (tap/Arcady), (temperature/AVIcon), 38 (thunderstorm/Pictureguy), (hurricane/FotoKina), (rainbow/muratart), (blue sky/irin-k), 39 (man/Luis Molinero), 42 (skydiving/Germanskydiver), 43 (wave background/EpicStockMedia), 45 (Mount Teide/eldeiv), 48 (leaf texture/GoodStudio), 49 (Amazon River/Nowaczyk), 50 (hearts/Markus Gann), (secret tunnels/gracioustiger), (biscuits/The FirstFotoLab), (mountain landscape/Iakiv Pekarskyi), (dog/Csanad Kiss), (Whatsapp background/topform), 53 (Speaker 2/Natali12389), 56 (Rawpixel.com), 57 (candle-stick/S-Belov), 58 (drill/Pavel K), (bed/babsy17), (mites/lantapix), (fly/Potapov Alexander), 60 (violin/AGCuesta), (keyboard/Smileus), 61 (drums/grekoff), (conductor/LifetimeStock), 63 (surgeons/Gorodenkoff), (Dmitriy Samorodinov), 67 (head and speech bubble/olga kryukova), 71 (pathdoc), 78 (handcuffs/DenisProduction.com), 80 (fever/ArtOfPhotos), 90 (night scene/mart), 92 (Songdo/PKphotograph), 97 (Natykach Nataliia), 98 (aliens/Albert Ziganshin), (teleportation/Sergey Nivens), (invisibility cloak outline/Leo Stock Pix), (instant learning/Gorodenkoff), 99 (Pluto/Dotted Yeti), 108 (namtipStudio), 109 (cabbage/matin), (mango/matin), (rose/satitsrihin), (ice lolly/Lucie Lang), (fur coat/lynnette), (fever/ArtOfPhotos), 113 (camembert/picturepartners), (chilli pepper/mexrix), 153 (vest/Quality Master), (fur collar/Karkas), (lace top/Karkas), (cardigan/NYS), (boots/Karkas), 156 (icons/RedKoala), (dock in fog/frankie's), 158 (emoji/flower travelin' man), 159 (heel/ShotPrime Studio), (elbow/ Steven Frame), (nails/Tamara83), (palm/alexandre zveiger), (chest/Daniel_Dash), 160 (handcuffs/grmarc), 162 (walking in city/Rawpixel.com); Courtesy of Dr Neil Stanley p 59; Reproduced by kind permission of Summersdale Publishers, photo from *Lost in the Jungle* by Yossi Ghinsberg p 48 (*from left to right* Kevin Gale, Tico Tudela and Yossi Ghinsberg) © Kevin Gale); Brennan Wenck-Reilly/www.brennanwenck.com p 57 (night view of San Francisco, *From Angel Island*); From John A. Love, *A Natural History of Lighthouses*, Whittles Publishing, 2015, ISBN 978-184995-154-8 Photo © Steven Gibbons p 10 (three lighthouse Keepers *from left to right* Thomas Marshall, Donald Macarthur and James Ducat).